Authors & Artists for Young Adults

ISSN 1040-5682

Authors & Artists for Young Adults

VOLUME 5

**Agnes Garrett and Helga P. McCue,
Editors**

 *Gale Research Inc.* · *DETROIT* · *NEW YORK* · *LONDON*

Managing Editor: Anne Commire

Editors: Agnes Garrett, Helga P. McCue

Associate Editors: Elisa Ann Ferraro, Eunice L. Petrini

Assistant Editors: Marc Caplan, Marja Hiltunen, Linda Shedd

Sketchwriters: Catherine Coray,
Johanna Cypis, Marguerite Feitlowitz, Mimi H. Hutson,
Deborah Klezmer, Dieter Miller, Beatrice Smedley

Researcher: Catherine Ruello

Editorial Assistants: Joanne J. Ferraro, June Lee,
Susan Pfanner

Production Manager: Mary Beth Trimper
External Production Assistant: Marilyn Jackman

Art Director: Arthur Chartow
Keyliner: C. J. Jonik

Production Supervisor: Laura Bryant
Internal Production Associate: Louise Gagné

The paper used in this publication meets the minimum requirements
of American National Standard for Information Sciences—Permanence
Paper for Printed Library Materials, ANSI Z39.48-1984. ∞™

Copyright © 1990
Gale Research Inc.
835 Penobscot Bldg.
Detroit, MI 48226-4094
All rights reserved.

Library of Congress Catalog Card Number
ISBN 0-8103-5054-8
ISSN 1040-5682

Printed in the United States of America

Published simultaneously in the United Kingdom
by Gale Research International Limited
(An affiliated company of Gale Research Inc.)

Contents

Introduction

"[Today's youth] is a generation whose grade-school years were informed and enlivened by Betsy Byars, who teaches the basic lesson to the next generation of book buyers: that a novel must entertain first before it can do anything else. But I don't get these readers until they hit puberty. They haven't even budded, and already the Blume is off. I don't get them till puberty, and it's the darkest moment of life. For while puberty is the death of childhood, it isn't the birth of reason.

"Puberty is the same gulag we all once did time in, robbed of the certainties of grade school and still years away from a driver's license. Puberty is waking up every morning wondering which sex you are, if any. Puberty is the practice of strict sexual segregation with all the girls on one side of an invisible line and all the boys on the other: big women, little men. Like a Shaker meeting but without the hope of eternal life. Puberty is no fun, and changing the name of the junior high to the middle school has fooled nobody. In America puberty is deciding at the age of twelve or so to divorce your own parents, charging irreconcilable differences. The children of the underclass hit the streets then and are thereafter out of reach of home and school and books. The children of the middle class recede to their rooms and lock themselves into elaborate sound systems, paid for by parents, that eliminate the possibility of a parental voice. They are free of us at twelve.

"I write for these people whose own parents haven't seen them for days. In our impotence we've reasoned that children must be given freedoms in order to learn how to handle them. But it doesn't work that way. The prematurely emancipated young transfer all their need for a dominating, problem-solving authority from weak adults at home and school to the peer group. The only government they recognize is the vengeful law-giving of each other.

"That's what I write: counterculture literature of individuality to a conformist readership. I write books for the knapsacks of young soldiers of both sexes going forth every school day hoping to survive the 'Chocolate War.' I write for the inmates of schools where you cannot win a letter sweater for literacy. You can win a letter sweater only for mindless conformity, for listening to language from the coach that would get the librarian into big trouble. I write for a generation of young people who don't have to drop by the library, even on the way to the Gifted Program. They don't have to drop by anywhere except, perhaps, the shopping mall."

—Richard Peck

"The time of adolescence is in itself a wonderful age to write about. It combines an idealism and honesty and a wily sophistication that no other time of life enjoys. The teenager has vitality and enjoys life although he sees the ugliness and absurdities as well as the joys.

"Adolescents are also engaged in some of the most important 'work' they will ever do. It is the time when one establishes one's identity and comes of age in a number of critical areas—social, political, cultural, sexual. Conflict prevails during these years with one's parents, teachers, peers and, most painfully, with oneself."

—Hila Colman

Authors and Artists for Young Adults is a new reference series designed to bridge the gap between Gale's *Something about the Author*, designed for children, and *Contemporary Authors*, intended for adults. This new series is aimed entirely at the needs and interests of the often overlooked young adults. We share the concerns of librarians who must send young readers to the adult reference shelves for which they may not be ready. *Authors and Artists for Young Adults* will give high school and junior high school students information about the life and work of their favorite creative artists—the people behind the books, movies, television programs, plays, lyrics, cartoon and animated features that they most enjoy. Although most of these will be present-day artists, the series is open to people of all time periods and all countries whose work has a special appeal to young adults today. Some of these artists may also be profiled in *Something about the Author* or *Contemporary Authors*, but their entries in *Authors and Artists for Young Adults* are completely updated and tailored to the information needs of the young adult user.

Entry Format

Authors and Artists for Young Adults will be published in two volumes each year. Each volume in the series will furnish in-depth coverage of about twenty authors and artists. The typical entry consists of:

—A personal section that includes date and place of birth, marriage, children, and education.

—A comprehensive bibliography or film-ography including publishers, producers, and years.

—Adaptations into other media forms.

—Works in progress.

—A distinctive sidelights section where secondary sources and exclusive interviews concentrate on an artist's craft, artistic intentions, career, world views, thematic discussions, and controversies.

—A "For More Information See" section arranged in chronological order to increase the scope of this reference work.

While the textual information in *Authors and Artists for Young Adults* is its primary reason for existing, entries are complemented by illustrations, photographs, movie stills, manuscript samples, dust jackets, book covers, and other relevant visual material.

A cumulative Author/Artist Index appears at the back of this volume.

Highlights of This Volume

A sampling of the variety of creative artists featured in this volume includes:

POUL ANDERSON......was ill in bed mining through a pile of magazines sent by a friend, when the teenager struck gold. Devouring *Thrilling Wonder Stories, Startling Stories, Amazing Stories,* and *Astounding Science Fiction,* Anderson was hooked. "I spent much of my tiny allowance on subscriptions. These didn't give me enough science fiction, so I started writing my own, in longhand." An aspiring physicist, he attended the University of Minnesota, where his focus soon shifted to astronomy. Thanks to his strong background in science, Anderson, now a full-time author, is one of the comparatively few 'hard' science fiction writers. When creating an imaginary planet, he calculates specifics such as the planet's orbit, irradiation, axial tilt, and rate of rotation before eventually getting down to the planet's geography, place names, flora, and fauna. The winner of seven Hugo Awards, with works translated into eighteen languages, Anderson acknowledges a basic attitude which underlies his writing, namely, that "this is a wonderful universe in which to live, that it's great to be alive, and that all it takes is the willingness to give ourselves a chance to experience what it has to offer."

STAN LEE......was one of the principal founders of Marvel Comics and the creator of such favorite superheroes as "The Fantastic Four," "Spiderman," and the "Incredible Hulk." "Let us savor the sound of those heart-warming words . Let us bask in the glow of the pleasure of promise. Marvel Comics. Not so much a name as a special state of mind. Not so much a group of magazines as a mood, a movement, a mild and momentary madness." Beginning with "The Fantastic Four," Lee began changing the face of comics by creating multi-faceted characters like the "Moleman," a villain with whom the reader is asked to sympathize. "It was a first. It was an attempt to portray a three-dimensional character in a world that had been composed of stereotypes. To comic bookdom, it was tantamount to the invention of the wheel." Often hailed as the savior of comic books, Lee has spent decades working to elevate comics to a level of respectability deserving of popular, modern mythology. "I think there's something in the human condition that makes us love stories that are imaginative and fanciful, stories about people who are bigger and stronger and more capable than we are. We are always looking for heroes."

LOIS LOWRY......has no memory "of the process of becoming literate," though she was able to read and write by the age of three. "It just happened, I think, as I became aware that letters had sounds and if you put them together they made words, and if you put the words together they made stories." And stories made up one of Lowry's favorite places—the public library. "The librarian—a woman—sat behind a high counter and looked down at me when I stood on tiptoe and handed her my chosen books. She did something magic to the books. Thump, thump, with her special, magical tool—pressing it definitively onto the books in a gesture only librarians are allowed to make. One book I chose when I was ten was called *A Tree Grows in Brooklyn*....It became one of my favorite books, it and *The Yearling*. Combining both books, I had two not-exactly-compatible dreams. I yearned to live in teeming slums, and to forge a life for myself among poverty-stricken streets. If that wasn't possible—and it seemed likely that it wasn't—my second choice was to live in a swamp and have mostly animals for friends, and one poor little crippled boy, who would die young so that I could weep at his graveside."

HARRY MAZER......didn't begin writing until he was in his mid-thirties, finding that it had taken him that long to "develop the *sitzfleisch* I needed just to keep me down in a chair long enough even to begin to think about writing. I naively believed that if I sat in front of that blank paper long enough I'd sure write something....And finally it happened. I wrote a line, and then another....I wrote: 'Isabel, you'll never know what you did to me. How could you? I never spoke to you' ...Isabel was a girl in my sixth-grade class in PS 96 in the Bronx, a tall, skinny girl with long hair. I followed her slavishly around for weeks. My sixth-grade picture shows me a big fat kid, in need of a haircut, the only one wearing a dark shirt in a field of white shirts and blouses. I never spoke to Isabel. She noticed me only once. I was across the street one day. She was with a girl friend. When they saw me they threw their arms around each other and started laughing and jeering at me. That was the story I started writing when I finally sat down to write, more than twenty years after the event. 'Isabel, you'll never know what you did to me.' How I loved that line."

NORMA FOX MAZER......developed a reputation for being "a famous crybaby. In the family they called me the faucet. They said, 'You only have to look at Norma cross-eyed and she cries.' I cried if the boys teased me. I cried if someone hit me. I cried if I did something wrong. I cried if I was scared. Or sad. Or happy....The sense of myself as different became something I lived with, almost unnoticed, yet I was never free of its effects. I felt an outsider, someone poised on this earth, but not solidly planted." At fifteen, she met Harry Mazer for the first time, but it wasn't until their second meeting two years later that Norma decided "that I would let Harry Mazer fall in love with me...." They married in 1950, and although Mazer is now a mother of four, she still works to stay in touch with her own childhood, with "that adolescent me, that girl who was, as I remember her, insecure, unsure, dreaming, yearning, longing, that girl who was hard on herself, who was cowardly and brave, who was confused and determined—that girl who was me....I call on her when I write....I believe in the reality of the past."

Forthcoming Volumes

Among the artists planned for future volumes are:

Judy Angell
Maya Angelou
Jean Auel
Avi
Richard Bach
Bianca Bradbury
Robin Brancato
Sue Ellen Bridgers
Bruce Brooks
Claude Brown
Edgar Rice Burroughs
Tracy Chapman
Agatha Christie
Christopher Collier
Wes Craven
Cameron Crowe
Jim Davis
Annie Dillard

Thomas J. Dygard
Bob Dylan
Amy Ehrlich
Louise Erdrich
William Faulkner
Judith S. George
Rumer Godden
Eileen Goudge
Chester Gould
Bette Greene
Judith Guest
Deborah Hautzig
Ann Head
Hermann Hesse
Jamake Highwater
Marjorie Holmes
John Hughes
Victor Hugo

Barry Lopez
Ann M. Martin
Milton Meltzer
Gloria Naylor
Joan Lowry Nixon
Janet Quin-Harkin
Ntozake Shange
Stephen Sondheim
Steven Spielberg
Mary Stolz
Mildred D. Taylor
Julian Thompson
J. R. R. Tolkien
Garry Trudeau
Bill Watterson
Tab Williams
Meg Wolitzer
Feenie Ziner

The editors of *Authors and Artists for Young Adults* welcome any suggestions for additional biographees to be included in this series. Please write and give us your opinions and suggestions for making our series more helpful to you.

Acknowledgments

Grateful acknowledgment is made to the following publishers,
authors, and artists for their kind permission to reproduce copyrighted material.

ACE BOOKS. Cover illustration by Royo from *Conan the Rebel* by Poul Anderson. Copyright © 1980 by Conan Properties, Inc. Reprinted by permission of Ace Books.

ATHENEUM PUBLISHERS. Jacket illustration by Ed Martinez from *The Nargun and the Stars* by Patricia Wrightson. Text copyright © 1970 by Patricia Wrightson. Jacket illustration copyright © 1986 by Ed Martinez./ Jacket illustration by Ed Martinez from *A Little Fear* by Patricia Wrightson. Text copyright © 1983 by Patricia Wrightson. Jacket illustration copyright © 1983 by Ed Martinez./ Jacket illustration by Ronald Himler from *Balyet* by Patricia Wrightson. Text copyright © 1989 by Patricia Wrightson. Jacket illustration copyright © 1989 by Ronald Himler./ Jacket illustration by Beth Peck from *Night Outside* by Patricia Wrightson. Text copyright © 1979 by Patricia Wrightson. Illustrations copyright © 1985 by Beth Peck. All reprinted by permission of Atheneum Publishers.

AVON BOOKS. Cover illustration by Vaughn Bode and Besil Gogos from *Earthman's Burden* by Poul Anderson and Gordon R. Dickson. Copyright © 1957 by Poul Anderson and Gordon R. Dickson. Reprinted by permission of Avon Books.

BAEN BOOKS. Cover illustration by Stephen Hickman from *The Devil's Game* by Poul Anderson./ Cover illustration by David Cherry from *The Broken Sword* by Poul Anderson. Copyright © 1971 by Poul Anderson./ Cover illustration by Michael Whelan from *The Enemy Stars* by Poul Anderson. Copyright © 1958, 1979 by Poul Anderson. All reprinted by permission of Baen Books.

BALLANTINE/DEL REY/FAWCETT BOOKS. Cover illustration from *Hot Money* by Dick Francis. Copyright © 1987 by Dick Francis./ Cover illustration from *Banker* by Dick Francis. Copyright © 1982 by Dick Francis./ Cover illustration from *Whip Hand* by Dick Francis. Copyright © 1979 by Dick Francis./ Cover illustration from *The Edge* by Dick Francis. Copyright © 1988 by Dick Francis./ Cover illustration by Michael Whelan from *The Ice Is Coming* by Patricia Wrightson. Copyright © 1977 by Patricia Wrightson. All reprinted by permission of Ballantine/Del Rey/Fawcett Books.

BANTAM BOOKS. Cover illustration by Frank Morris from *The Girl Who Invented Romance* by Caroline B. Cooney. Text copyright © 1988 by Caroline B. Cooney. Cover illustration copyright © 1988 by Frank Morris./ Cover photographs by Nancy Ney from *Family Reunion* by Caroline B. Cooney. Text copyright © 1989 by Caroline B. Cooney. Cover photographs copyright © 1989 by Nancy Ney./ Cover illustration by Steve Assel from *Among Friends* by Caroline B. Cooney. Text copyright © 1987 by Caroline B. Cooney. Cover illustration copyright © 1987 by Steve Assel./ Cover illustration by Kolada from *A Summer to Die* by Lois Lowry. Copyright © 1977 by Lois Lowry./ Cover illustration from *Anastasia Krupnik* by Lois Lowry. Text copyright © 1979 by Lois Lowry. Cover illustration copyright © 1981 by Bantam Books, Inc./ Cover illustration from *In Summer Light* by Zibby Oneal. Text copyright © 1985 by Zibby Oneal. Cover illustration copyright © 1986 by Bantam Books, Inc./ Cover illustration by Allen Welkes from *Fingers* by William Sleator. Text copyright © 1983 by William Sleator. Cover illustration copyright © 1985 by Allen Welkes. All reprinted by permission of Bantam Books.

BERKLEY PUBLISHING CORP. Jacket illustration by Tony Roberts from *The Earth Book of Stormgate* by Poul Anderson. Copyright © 1978 by Poul Anderson./ Cover illustration from *Someone Is Hiding on Alcatraz Island* by Eve Bunting. Copyright © 1984 by Eve Bunting. Both reprinted by permission of Berkley Publishing Corp.

THE CONTINUUM PUBLISHING CORP. Sidelight excerpts from an article "Toni Cade Bambara," by Claudia Tate, in *Black Women Writers at Work*. Copyright © 1983 by Claudia Tate. Reprinted by permission of The Continuum Publishing Corp.

T. Y. CROWELL, INC. Jacket illustration by Eric Jon Nones from *The Girl of His Dreams* by Harry Mazer. Text copyright © 1987 by Harry Mazer. Jacket illustration copyright © 1987 by Eric Jon Nones. Jacket copyright © 1987 by Harper & Row, Publishers, Inc. Reprinted by permission of T. Y. Crowell, Inc.

DELACORTE PRESS. Sidelight excerpts from an article "Up in Seth's Room," by Norma Mazer, Winter/1979-Spring/1980 in *Notes from Delacorte Press Books for Young Readers*./ Sidelight excerpts from an article "The War on Villa Street," by Harry Mazer, Winter/1978-Spring/1979 in *Notes from Delacorte Press Books for Young Readers*./ Sidelight excerpts from an article "Island within andwithout: Thoughts about Writing 'The Island Keeper,' " by Harry Mazer, Winter/1980-Spring/1981 in *Notes from Delacorte Press Books for Young Readers*./ Sidelight excerpts from an article "Writing for the Young," by Harry Mazer, Summer/Fall, 1975 in *Notes from Delacorte Press for Young Readers*./ Jacket illustration by Gary Watson from *Dear Bill, Remember Me? and Other Stories* by Fox Mazer. Copyright © 1976 by Norma Fox Mazer. All reprinted by permission of Delacorte Press.

DELL PUBLISHING CO. Cover illustration from *Taking Care of Terrific* by Lois Lowry. Copyright © 1983 by Lois Lowry./ Cover illustration from *Anastasia Has the Answers* by Lois Lowry. Copyright © 1986 by Lois Lowry. Cover illustration by Chuck Pyle from *Switcharound* by Lois Lowry. Copyright © 1985 by Lois Lowry./ Cover illustration from *The Dollar Man* by Harry Mazer. Copyright © 1974 by Harry Mazer./ Cover illustration from *The War on Villa Street* by Harry Mazer. Copyright © 1978 by Harry Mazer./ Cover illustration by Tom Freeman from *The Last Mission* by Harry Mazer. Copyright © 1979 by Harry Mazer./ Cover illustration from *A Figure of Speech* by Norma Fox Mazer. Copyright © 1973 by Norma Fox Mazer. All reprinted by permission of Dell Publishing Co.

DODD, MEAD & CO. Jacket illustration from *Seventeenth Summer* by Maureen Daly. Copyright 1942 by Dodd, Mead & Co. Reprinted by permission of Dodd, Mead & Co.

DOUBLEDAY & CO. Sidelight excerpts from an article "Commitment: Toni Cade Bambara Speaks," by Beverly Guy-Sheftall and others in *Sturdy Black Bridges: Visions of Black Women in Literature./* Sidelight excerpts from an article "Salvation Is the Issue," by Toni Cade Bambara in *Black Women Writers (1950-1980): A Critical Evaluation,* edited by Mari Evans. Both reprinted by permission of Doubleday & Co.

E. P. DUTTON. Jacket illustration by James Nazz from *Interstellar Pig* by William Sleator. Copyright © 1984 by William Sleator./ Jacket illustration by Richard Cuffari from *House of Stairs* by William Sleator. Copyright © 1974 by William Sleator./ Jacket illustration by Paul Van Munching from *The Duplicate* by William Sleator. Copyright © 1988 by William Sleator./ Jacket illustration by Michael Hays from *Singularity* by William Sleator. Copyright © 1985 by William Sleator./ Jacket illustration by John Jude Palencar from *The Boy Who Reversed Himself* by William Sleator. Copyright © 1986 by William Sleator. All reprinted by permission of E. P. Dutton.

FABER & FABER. Sidelight excerpts from *William Golding: The Man and His Books* by John Carey. Reprinted by permission of Faber & Faber.

FARRAR, STRAUS & GIROUX, INC. Jacket illustration by Fred Marcellino and Sidelight excerpts from *Upon the Head of the Goat: A Childhood in Hungary, 1939-1944* by Aranka Siegal. Text copyright © 1981 by Aranka Siegal. Illustrations copyright © 1981 by Fred Marcellino./ Jacket illustration by Laurie Dolphin and Sidelight excerpts from *Grace in the Wilderness: After the Liberation, 1945-1948* by Aranka Siegal. Copyright © 1985 by Aranka Siegal. Illustrations copyright © 1985 by Laurie Dolphin./ All reprinted by permission of Farrar, Straus & Giroux, Inc.

HARCOURT BRACE JOVANOVICH, INC. Jacket illustration by Lambert Davis and jacket design by Michael Farmer from *A Sudden Silence* by Eve Bunting. Copyright © 1988 by Eve Bunting./ Jacket illustration by Noela Young from *The Feather Star* by Patricia Wrightson. Text copyright © 1962 by Patricia Wrightson. Illustrations copyright © 1962 by Hutchinson & Co. Ltd./ Jacket illustration by Denise Hilton-Putnam and jacket design by Nancy J. Ponichtera from *Will You Be My POSSLQ?* by Eve Bunting. Copyright © 1987 by Eve Bunting./ Jacket illustration by Robert Steele and jacket design by Michael Farmer from *Sixth-Grade Sleepover* by Eve Bunting. Copyright © 1986 by Eve Bunting./ Jacket design by Paul Bacon Studio from *The Spire* by William Golding. Copyright © 1964 by William Golding./ Cover illustration by Terrence M. Fehr from *Free Fall* by William Golding. Copyright © 1959 by William Golding./ Cover illustration by Terrence M. Fehr from *Pincher Martin [The Two Deaths of Christopher Martin]* by William Golding. Copyright © 1956 by William Golding. All reprinted by permission of Harcourt Brace Jovanovich, Inc.

HARPER & ROW, PUBLISHERS, INC. Cover illustration by Richard Williams from *If I Asked You, Would You Stay?* by Eve Bunting. Copyright © 1984 by Eve Bunting. Cover illustration copyright © 1987 by Richard Williams and Harper & Row, Publishers, Inc./ Frontispiece illustration and Sidelight excerpts from *The Sport of Queens: The Autobiography of Dick Francis.* Copyright © 1957, 1968, 1969 by Dick Francis./ Jacket illustration by Matt Mahurin from *In Country* by Bobbie Ann Mason. Text copyright © 1985 by Bobbie Ann Mason. Jacket illustration copyright © by Matt Mahurin./ Jacket illustration by William Low and jacket design by Suzanne Noli from *Love Life* by Bobbie Ann Mason. Text copyright © 1989 by Bobbie Ann Mason. Jacket illustration copyright © 1989 by William Low./ Cover illustration by William Low from *Shiloh and Other Stories* by Bobbie Ann Mason. Text copyright © 1982 by Bobbie Ann Mason. Cover illustration copyright © by William Low./ Jacket illustration by LaNelle Mason from *Spence & Lila* by Bobbie Ann Mason. Text copyright © 1988 by Bobbie Ann Mason. Jacket illustration copyright © by LaNelle Mason./ Jacket illustration from *Native Son* by Richard Wright. Copyright 1940 by Richard Wright. Copyright renewed © 1968 by Ellen Wright./ Cover illustration by One & One Studio and Sidelight excerpts from *Black Boy: A Record of Childhood and Youth* by Richard Wright. Copyright 1937, 1942, 1944, 1945 by Richard Wright./ Sidelight excerpts from *American Hunger* by Richard Wright. Copyright 1944 by Richard Wright. Copyright renewed © 1977 by Ellen Wright./ Sidelight excerpts from *Richard Wright Reader,* edited by Ellen Wright and Michael Fabre. Copyright © 1978 by Ellen Wright and Michael Fabre./ Jacket illustration by Irving Miller from *The Outsider* by Richard Wright. Copyright 1953 by Richard NormaWright./ Jacket illustration by Ronald Himler from *Dragonwings* by Laurence Yep. Copyright © 1975 by Laurence Yep./ Jacket illustration by David Wiesner from *The Serpent's Children* by Laurence Yep. Text copyright © 1984 by Laurence Yep. Jacket illustration copyright © 1984 by David Wiesner and Harper & Row, Publishers, Inc./ Cover illustration by David Wiesner from *Dragon of the Lost Sea* by Laurence Yep. Copyright © 1982 by Laurence Yep. Cover illustration © 1982 by David Wiesner. Cover copyright © 1988 by Harper & Row, Publishers, Inc./ Jacket illustration by Allen Say and Sidelight excerpts from *Child of the Owl* by Laurence Yep. Copyright © 1977 by Laurence Yep./ Jacket illustration by David Wiesner from *Mountain Light* by Laurence Yep. Text copyright© 1985 by Laurence Yep. Jacket illustration copyright © 1985 by David Wiesner and Harper & Row, Publishers, Inc. All reprinted by permission of Harper & Row, Publishers, Inc.

THE HORN BOOK, INC. Sidelight excerpts from an article *"The Geranium Leaf,"* by Patricia Wrightson./ Sidelight excerpts from an article "Ever Since My Accident: Aboriginal Folklore and Australian Fantasy," by Patricia Wrightson./ Sidelight excerpts from an article "In Summer Light," by Zibby Oneal, January/February, 1987 in *Horn Book Magazine*./ Sidelight excerpts from an article "The Green Cord," by Laurence Yep, May/June, 1989 in *Horn Book Magazine*. All reprinted by permission of The Horn Book, Inc.

HOUGHTON MIFFLIN CO. Jacket illustration by Ted Lewin from *Rabble Starkey* by Lois Lowry. Text copyright © 1987 by Lois Lowry. Jacket illustration © 1987 by Ted Lewin. Reprinted by permission of Houghton Mifflin Co.

J. B. LIPPINCOTT CO. Jacket illustration by Stephen Harrington from *The Haunting of Safekeep* by Eve Bunting. Text copyright © 1985 by Eve Bunting. Jacket illustration copyright © 1985 by Stephen Harrington and Harper & Row, Publishers, Inc. Reprinted by permission of J. B. Lippincott Co.

LITTLE, BROWN & CO., INC. Illustration by Berke Breathed from *'Toons for Our Times, A Bloom County Book of Heavy Meadow Rump 'n Roll* by Berke Breathed. Copyright © 1984 by The Washington Post Co./ Illustration by Berke Breathed from *Bloom County, "Loose Tails"* by Berke Breathed. Copyright © 1983 by The Washington Post Co. Both reprinted by permission of Little, Brown & Co., Inc.

LUNA PUBLICATIONS. Sidelight excerpts from an article "Speaking of Science Fiction: The Paul Waimer Interviews" by Paul Waimer. Reprinted by permission of Luna Publications.

MARVEL ENTERTAINMENT GROUP, INC. Sidelight excerpts from *Origins of Marvel Comics* by Stan Lee. Copyright © 1974 by Marvel Entertainment Group, Inc./ Illustrations from *Marvel Masterworks, Volume I* by Stan Lee and Steve Ditko. Copyright © 1962, 1963, 1964, 1987 by Marvel Entertainment Group, Inc./ Illustration from *The Incredible Hulk #1* by Stan Lee./ Illustration from *Captain America* by Stan Lee. All reprinted by permission of Marvel Entertainment Group, Inc.

WILLIAM MORROW & CO., INC. Jacket illustration by Fredericka Ribes from *After the Rain* by Norma Fox Mazer. Text copyright © 1987 by Norma Fox Mazer. Jacket illustration copyright © 1987 by Fredericka Ribes./ Jacket illustration by Michael Deas from *Taking Terri Mueller* by Norma Fox Mazer. Copyright © 1981 by Norma Fox Mazer./ Jacket illustration by Michael Deas from *Downtown* by Norma Fox Mazer. Copyright © 1984 by Norma Fox Mazer. All reprinted by permission of William Morrow & Co., Inc.

NEW AMERICAN LIBRARY. Cover illustration from *A Circus of Hells* by Poul Anderson. Copyright © 1970 by Poul Anderson./ Cover illustration from *Grace in the Wilderness: After the Liberation 1945-1948* by Aranka Siegal. Copyright © 1985 by Aranka Siegal. Both reprinted by permission of New American Library.

W. W. NORTON & CO., INC. Sidelight excerpts from an article *"What It Is I Think I'm Doing Anyhow,"* by Toni Cade Bambara in *The Writer on Her Works,* edited by Janet Sternburg. Copyright © 1980 by Janet Sternburg. Reprinted by permission of W. W. Norton & Co., Inc.

NOSTALGIA, INC. Illustrations from *Marvel Comics Postcard Book.* Copyright © 1978 by Marvel Comics Group. All reprinted by permission of Nostalgia, Inc.

POCKET BOOKS. Cover illustration from *Seventeenth Summer* by Maureen Daly. Copyright © 1968 by Pocket Books. Reprinted by permission of Pocket Books.

THE PUTNAM PUBLISHING GROUP, INC. Jacket photograph by Caroline Greyshock from *Don't Blame the Music* by Caroline B. Cooney. Copyright © 1986 by Caroline B. Cooney./ Jacket design by Richards, Sullivan, Brock & Associates from *Twice Shy* by Dick Francis. Copyright © 1982 by Dick Francis./ Jacket design by Richards, Brock, Miller, Mitchell & Associates from *Straight* by Dick Francis. Copyright © 1989 by Dick Francis. Jacket design copyright © 1989 by Richards, Brock, Miller, Mitchell & Associates./ Cover illustration from *Lord of the Flies* by William Golding. Copyright 1954 by William Golding. All reprinted by permission of The Putnam Publishing Group, Inc.

RANDOM HOUSE, INC. Cover illustration by Montiel from *The Salt Eaters* by Toni Cade Bambara. Copyright © 1980 by Toni Cade Bambara. Reprinted by permission of Random House, Inc.

SCHOLASTIC, INC. Cover illustration from *New Year's Eve* by Caroline B. Cooney. Copyright © 1988 by Caroline B. Cooney./ Cover illustration from *Saturday Night* by Caroline B. Cooney. Copyright © 1986 by Caroline B. Cooney./ Jacket illustration by Deborah Chabrian from *Acts of Love* by Maureen Daly. Text copyright © 1986 by Maureen Daly. Jacket illustration copyright © 1986 by Deborah Chabrian./ Jacket illustration by Michael Deas from *City Light* by Harry Mazer. Copyright © 1988 by Harry Mazer. Jacket illustration copyright © 1988 by Michael Deas. All reprinted by permission of Scholastic, Inc.

THE SCRIBNER BOOK COMPANIES, INC. Sidelight excerpts from *All the Strange Hours: The Excavation of a Life* by Loren Eiseley. Copyright © 1975 by Loren Eiseley./ Sidelight excerpts from *The Night Country* by Loren Eiseley. Copyright © 1971 by Loren Eiseley. Both reprinted by permission of The Scribner Book Companies, Inc.

"Bloom County's" farewell strip, by Berke Breathed, August 6, 1989 in *New York Daily News*. Reprinted by permission of The Washington Post Writers Group./ Berke Breathed's July 29, 1989 strip in *The Burlington Free Press*. Reprinted by permission of The Washington Post Writers Group./ First strip of Berke Breathed's new comic,"Outland," September 10, 1989 in *Sunday Daily News*. Copyright © 1989 by The Washington Post Writer's Group. Reprinted by permission of The Washington Post Writer's Group./ Sidelight excerpts from an article "Hans Christian Andersen Award Acceptance Speech," by Patricia Wrightson, March/April, 1986 in *Horn Book*. Reprinted by permission of Patricia Wrightson./ Sidelight excerpts from an article "New Trends in Children's Books," by Eve Bunting, April, 1979 in *The Writer*. Reprinted by permission of The Writer, Inc./ Sidelight excerpts from an article "Think Picture Book," by Eve Bunting, September, 1988 in *The Writer*. Copyright © 1988 by The Writer, Inc. Reprinted by permission of The Writer, Inc./ Sidelight excerpts from an article "What's New in Children's Books?," by Eve Bunting, April, 1984 in *The Writer*. Copyright © 1984 by The Writer, Inc. Reprinted by permission of The Writer, Inc./ Sidelight excerpts from an article "Writing Dragonwings," by Laurence Yep, January, 1977 in *The Reading Teacher*. Reprinted by permission of Laurence Yep.

Photo Credits

Toni Cade Bambara: Copyright © by Nikky Finney; Berke Breathed: Copyright © by Jody Boyman; Caroline B. Cooney: Saybrook Studio; Loren Eiseley: Frank Ross; Lois Lowry: Amanda Smith; Bobbie Ann Mason: Thomas Victor; Zibby Oneal: Julie Steedman; Aranka Siegal: Copyright © by Richard Olson; Laurence Yep: Kathleen Yep.

Authors
& Artists
for Young
Adults

Poul Anderson

G iven name pronounced "pohwl"; born November 25, 1926, in Bristol, Pa.; son of Anton William (an engineer) and Astrid (a secretary; maiden name, Hertz) Anderson; married Karen J. M. Kruse (an editorial and research assistant), December 12, 1953; children: Astrid May (Mrs. Greg Bear). *Education:* University of Minnesota, B.S. (with distinction), 1948. *Home:* 3 Las Palomas, Orinda, Calif. 94563. *Agent:* Scott Meredith Literary Agency, 845 Third Ave., New York, N.Y. 10022.

■ Career

Free-lance writer, except for occasional temporary jobs, 1948—. *Member:* Institute for Twenty-First Century Studies, Science Fiction Writers of America (president, 1972-73), American Association for the Advancement of Science, Mystery Writers of America (northern California regional vice-chairman, 1959), Society for Creative Anachronism, Scowrers (secretary, 1957-62), Elves, Gnomes, and Little Men's Science Fiction Chowder and Marching Society.

■ Awards, Honors

Morley-Montgomery Prize for Scholarship in Sherlock Holmes, 1955; First Annual Cock Robin Mystery Award, 1959, for *Perish by the Sword*; Guest of Honor, World Science Fiction Convention, 1959; Hugo Award from the World Science Fiction Convention, 1961, for short fiction "The Longest Voyage," 1964, for short fiction "No Truce with Kings," 1969, for novelette "The Sharing of Flesh," 1972, for novella "The Queen of Air and Darkness," 1973, for novelette "Goat Song," 1979, for novelette "Hunter's Moon," and 1982, for novella "The Saturn Game"; Forry Award from the Los Angeles Science Fantasy Society, 1968, for achievement; Nebula Award for Novellettes from the Science Fiction Writers of America, 1971, for "The Queen of Air and Darkness," and 1972, for "Goat Song"; Hugo Award runner-up from the World Science Fiction Convention, 1973, for *There Will Be Time*; August Derleth Award from the British Fantasy Society, 1974, for *Hrolf Kraki's Saga*, Gandalf Award, Grand Master of Fantasy from the World Science Fiction Convention, 1978.

■ Writings

Science-Fiction Novels:

Vault of the Ages (juvenile), Winston, 1952, reissued, G. K. Hall, 1979.
Brain Wave, Ballantine, 1954, reissued, Walker, 1969.
The Broken Sword, Abelard, 1954, revised edition, Ballantine, 1971.

No World of Their Own (bound with *The 1,000 Year Plan* by Isaac Asimov), Ace, 1955, published separately as *The Long Way Home*, Gregg, 1978.

Star Ways, Avalon, 1956, published as *The Peregrine*, Ace, 1978.

Planet of No Return (bound with *Star Guard* by Andre Norton), Ace, 1957, published as *Question and Answer*, 1978.

War of the Wing-Men, Ace, 1958, published as *The Man Who Counts*, 1978.

The Snows of Ganymede, Ace, 1958.

Virgin Planet, Avalon, 1959.

The Enemy Stars, Lippincott, 1959.

The War of Two Worlds (bound with *Threshold of Eternity* by John Brunner), Ace, 1959.

We Claim These Stars! (bound with *The Planet Killers* by Robert Silverberg), Ace, 1959.

The High Crusade, Doubleday, 1960, reissued, Manor Publishing, 1975.

Earthman, Go Home! (bound with *To the Tombaugh Station* by Wilson Tucker), Ace, 1961.

Twilight World, Torquil, 1961.

Mayday Orbit (bound with *No Man's World* by Kenneth Bulmer), Ace, 1961.

Three Hearts and Three Lions, Doubleday, 1961, reissued, Berkley, 1978.

Orbit Unlimited, Pyramid, 1961, reissued, Panther, 1976.

The Makeshift Rocket (bound with *Un-Man and Other Novellas*), Ace, 1962.

After Doomsday, Ballantine, 1962.

Shield, Berkley, 1963.

Let the Spacemen Beware! (bound with *The Wizard of Starship Poseidon* by K. Bulmer), Ace, 1963, published separately as *The Night Face*, 1978.

Three Worlds to Conquer, Pyramid, 1964.

The Star Fox, Doubleday, 1965.

The Corridors of Time, Doubleday, 1965.

Ensign Flandry, Chilton, 1966, new edition, G. K. Hall, 1979.

World without Stars, Ace, 1966.

Satan's World, Doubleday, 1969.

The Rebel Worlds, Signet, 1969 (published in England as *Commander Flandry*, Severn House, 1978).

A Circus of Hells, Signet, 1970.

Tau Zero, Doubleday, 1970.

The Byworlder, Signet, 1971.

Operation Chaos, Doubleday, 1971.

The Dancer from Atlantis, Doubleday, 1971.

There Will Be Time, Doubleday, 1972.

Hrolf Kraki's Saga, Ballantine, 1973.

The People of the Wind, Signet, 1973, new edition, Gregg, 1977.

The Day of Their Return, Doubleday, 1974.

Fire Time, Doubleday, 1974.

A Midsummer Tempest, Doubleday, 1974.

(With Gordon Ecklund) *Inheritors of Earth*, Chilton, 1974.

The Worlds of Poul Anderson (contains *Planet of No Return*, *The War of Two Worlds*, and *World without Stars*), Ace, 1974.

A Knight of Ghosts and Shadows, Doubleday, 1975 (published in England as *Knight Flandry*, Severn House, 1980).

(With Gordon R. Dickson) *Star Prince Charlie* (juvenile), Putnam, 1975.

The Winter of the World, Doubleday, 1976.

Mirkheim, Berkley, 1977.

The Avatar, Putnam, 1978.

Two Worlds (contains *Question and Answer* and *World without Stars*), Gregg, 1978.

The Merman's Children, Putnam, 1979.

A Stone in Heaven, Ace, 1979.

The Last Viking, three volumes, Zebra, 1980.

The Devil's Game, Pocket Books, 1980.

The Road of the Sea Horse, Zebra Books, 1980.

Conan the Rebel #6, Bantam, 1980.

(With Mildred D. Broxon) *The Demon of Scattery*, Ace, 1980.

The Golden Horn, Zebra Books, 1980.

The Sign of the Raven, Zebra Books, 1980.

The Long Night, Pinnacle Books, 1983.

Orion Shall Rise, Pocket Books, 1983.

Agent of Vega, Ace, 1983.

Bat-Twenty-One, Bantam, 1983.

The Game of Empire, Baen Books, 1985.

Time Wars, Tor Books, 1986.

(With wife, Karen Anderson) *Roma Mater*, Baen Books, 1986.

Conan the Rebel #17, Ace.

Space Wars, Tor Books, 1988.

The Year of the Ransom (juvenile; illustrated by Paul Rivoche), Walker, 1988.

(With K. Anderson) *Dahut*, Baen Books, 1988.

(With K. Anderson) *The Dog and the Wolf*, Baen Books, 1988.

(With K. Anderson) *Gallicenae*, Baen Books, 1988.

Space Folk, Baen Books, 1989.

No Truce with Kings (bound with *Ship of Shadows* by Fritz Leiber), Tor Books, 1989.

The Boat of a Million Years, Tor Books, 1989.

The Shield of Time, Tor Books, 1990.

Short Story Collections:

(With G. R. Dickson) *Earthman's Burden,*
 Gnome Press, 1957.
Guardians of Time, Ballantine, 1960, revised
 edition, Pinnacle Books, 1981.
*Strangers from Earth: Eight Tales of Vaulting
 Imagination,* Ballantine, 1961.
Un-Man and Other Novellas (bound with *The
 Makeshift Rocket*), Ace, 1962.
Trader to the Stars, Doubleday, 1964.
Time and Stars, Doubleday, 1964.
Agent of the Terran Empire (includes *We Claim
 These Stars!*), Chilton, 1965.
Flandry of Terra (includes *Earthman, Go Home!*
 and *Mayday Orbit*), Chilton, 1965.
The Trouble Twisters, Doubleday, 1966.
The Horn of Time, Signet, 1968.
Beyond the Beyond, New American Library,
 1969.
*Seven Conquests: An Adventure in Science
 Fiction,* Macmillan, 1969.
Tales of the Flying Mountains, Macmillan, 1970.
*The Queen of Air and Darkness and Other
 Stories,* Signet, 1973.
The Many Worlds of Poul Anderson, edited by
 Roger Elwood, Chilton, 1974, published as
 The Book of Poul Anderson, DAW Books,
 1975.
Homeward and Beyond, Doubleday, 1975.
Homebrew, National Education Field Service
 Association Press, 1976.
The Best of Poul Anderson, Pocket Books, 1976.
The Earth Book of Stormgate, Putnam, 1978.
The Night Face and Other Stories, Gregg, 1978.
The Dark between the Stars, Berkley
 Publications, 1980.
Explorations, Pinnacle Books, 1981.
Fantasy, Pinnacle Books, 1981.
Winners, Pinnacle Books, 1981.
Cold Victory, Pinnacle Books, 1981.
The Psychotechnic League, Tor Books, 1981.
The Gods Laughed, Pinnacle Books, 1982.
Maurai and Kith, Tor Books, 1982.
Starship, Pinnacle Books, 1982.
New America, Pinnacle Books, 1982.
Conflict, Pinnacle Books, 1983.
Time Patrolman, Pinnacle Books, 1983.
(With G. R. Dickson) *Hoka!,* Simon & Schuster,
 1983.
Annals of the Time Patrol (contains *Time
 Patrolman* and *Guardians of Time*),
 Doubleday, 1984.
(With K. Anderson) *The Unicorn Trade,* Tor
 Books, 1984.

Paperback edition of the 1957 collection of short
stories.

Past Times, Tor Books, 1984.
Dialogue with Darkness, Tor Books, 1985.
(With others) *Berserker Base,* Tor Books, 1985.

Other Novels:

Perish by the Sword, Macmillan, 1959.
Murder in Black Letter, Macmillan, 1960.
The Golden Slave, Avon, 1960.
Rogue Sword, Avon, 1960.
Murder Bound, Macmillan, 1962.

Nonfiction:

Is There Life on Other Worlds?, Crowell, 1963.
Thermonuclear Warfare, Monarch, 1963.
The Infinite Voyage: Man's Future in Space
 (young adult), Macmillan, 1969.

Contributor:

Martin Greenberg, editor, *All about the Future,* Gnome Press, 1955.

The Day the Sun Stood Still: Three Original Novellas of Science Fiction (contains *A Chapter of Revelation* by P. Anderson, *Thomas the Proclaimer* by Robert Silverberg, and *Things Which Are Caesar's* by Gordon Dickson), T. Nelson, 1972.

Reginald Bretnor, editor, *Science Fiction: Today and Tomorrow,* Harper, 1974.

R. Bretnor, editor, *The Craft of Science Fiction,* Harper, 1976.

Damon Knight, editor, *Turning Points: Essays on the Art of Science Fiction,* Harper, 1977.

Andrew J. Offutt, editor, *Swords against Darkness,* Zebra Books, Volume I, 1977, Volume III, 1978, Volume IV, 1979.

Paperback cover of the 1954 reprint.

L. Sprague de Camp, editor, *The Blade of Conan,* Ace, 1979.

Other:

(Adapter) Christian Molbech, *The Fox, the Dog, and the Griffin: A Folktale* (juvenile), Doubleday, 1966.

(Author of introduction) *The Best of L. Sprague de Camp,* Ballantine, 1978.

Contributor to Anthologies:

Groff Conklin, editor, *Possible Worlds of Science Fiction,* Vanguard, 1951.

Anthony Boucher, editor, *A Treasury of Great Science Fiction,* Doubleday, 1959.

I. Asimov, editor, *The Hugo Winners,* Doubleday, 1962.

Miriam Allen de Ford, editor, *Space, Time, and Crime,* Paperback Library, 1964.

Masters of Science Fiction, Belmont Books, 1964.

I. Asimov, editor, *The Hugo Winners,* Doubleday, 1971.

I. Asimov, editor, *The Hugo Winners,* Doubleday, 1972.

Ben Bova, editor, *The Science Fiction Hall of Fame,* Doubleday, 1973.

R. Bretnor, editor, *The Future at War,* Ace, 1979.

Writer of television documentary on the space program for the United States Information Agency, 1963-64. Anderson's books have been translated into eighteen foreign languages, including German, Italian, French, Japanese, Danish, Swedish, Spanish, and Dutch. Contributor of short stories, some under pseudonyms A. A. Craig and Winston P. Sanders, to periodicals, including *Astounding Science Fiction, Magazine of Fantasy and Science Fiction, Galaxy, Analog Science Fiction/Science Fact, Isaac Asimov's Science Fiction Magazine, Boys' Life, Foundation: The Review of Science Fiction,* and *National Review.*

■ Adaptations

Computer game (based on *The High Crusade*), IRS Hobbies, 1983.

"Award-Winning Science Fiction by Poul Anderson" (cassette; includes "The Longest Voyage," "The Queen of Air and Darkness," "No Truce with Kings," and "The Man Who Came Early"), Listening Library.

"Yonder—Seven Tales of the Space Age" (cassette), Caedmon, 1986.

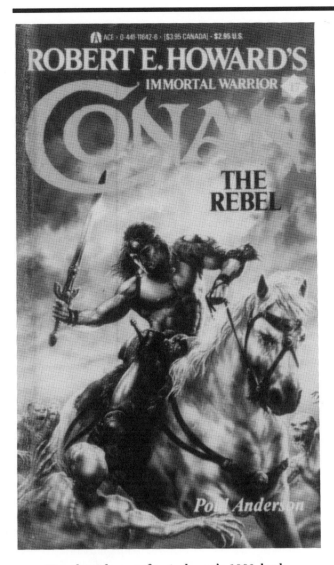

Paperbound cover for Anderson's 1980 book.

Cover art by Michael Whelan for the Baen paperback.

■ Sidelights

"Although I was born in the USA, my parents were from Scandinavia, and named me for a grandfather; hence the spelling. This was in 1926."

"In grade school the teachers kept telling me I wasn't spelling my own name right, and I got my back up about it. The proper pronunciation is not an Anglo-Saxon noise—about midway between 'powl' and 'pole.' I'll answer to anything.

"My father, Anton William Andersen, was born over here but educated in Denmark. He was the son of a sea captain and no relation to the great Hans Christian. He disliked his first name and never used it, being Will or Willy to his friends. During World War One he came back to join the United States Army. There he grew tired of explaining the spelling of his surname and Anglicized it to Anderson.

"A literary tradition exists on the other side; my mother, Astrid Hertz, was descended from both Carsten Hauch and Henrik Hertz. Her own father was a physician in Copenhagen, where she was born. After a series of jobs and experiences more varied than was usual for a respectable young lady in those days, she crossed the Atlantic to work as a secretary in what was then the Danish legation in Washington. By a most unlikely chance, she met Will Anderson again. They had gone to the same school in the old country but afterward lost touch with each other. Since his discharge from the Army he had stayed on in America, working as a civil engineer. Now they started dating, and early in 1926 they were married.

"I was less than a year old when a change of job for my father took the family to Port Arthur, Texas. There he advanced to chief estimator at the Texaco plant, and there, in 1930, my brother [John] was born.

"The suburb was a wonderland for boys, full of trees to climb and vacant lots to romp in. Once a pile of bricks lay for weeks next door; we made castles out of it and burrows in it, at considerable risk to our necks. Clay soil could be molded into figures which the sun baked dry. My parents had a good-sized boat, which Dad had built himself, and we were often out on the water, sometimes for a weekend across the state line. The Yacht Club was a fine site for crabbing or for holding a barbecue. On vacations we'd get as far afield as Carlsbad Caverns or the Ozarks—or Europe....

"John and I were not entirely assimilated to the culture around us. Our parents took care to keep the family bilingual, another deed for which we remain ever grateful. We celebrated Christmas in the Danish style, emphasis on the eve rather than the day. With the selflessness typical of American husbands in that era of male chauvinist piggery, Dad gave his wife several trips back to the old country to visit her folks there, and she took us children along. So we came to address and think of her as Mor, Danish for 'Mother.'

"I sometimes wonder what our lives would have become if they had continued like this. Surely Dad would have gone far, as his associates did. But one fall day in 1937 turned chilly. He started back home to get his overcoat. On the way, his car collided with another. Both drivers were instantly killed.

"[My parents] had always considered it a sacred obligation to see their children through college, and had been putting money aside for this. Dad's attitude toward his wife was equally old-fashioned; he carried plenty of insurance. Taxes and inflation had not yet made thrift impossible, so the savings account was in good shape too. Mor was not left rich, but she wasn't badly off.

"For several months she tried to carry on in Port Arthur. It was hopeless. The place was too haunted. She longed to go back to Denmark, where she had many friends and relatives, some of them in influential positions. Why not settle there? In the spring of 1938 she put the three of us on a train to upstate New York, where a friend of hers had an artist husband and a son about my age. We spent a while with them before crossing the Atlantic.

"Denmark, to which we proceeded by rail, was like another planet. If I am not being sentimental, it was still more charming then than now. Everybody was so cheerful and *decent*–including an aunt of mine who had been a Communist since 1917 and her current lover. Grandfather was dead but Grandmother remained very much alive, a tall and imposing lady with a mane of white hair. Mor's cousin Jens was a fabulous Dionysian figure. Cousins of about my own age were a lot more fun than any kids in Texas. All of these persons would later be active in resisting the Nazi occupation, but that was for the future; this was the last golden summer.

"But...it was becoming too obvious that war was on the way. Mor was long since a naturalized American. What concerned her more, though, was that her sons were Americans born. In fall we returned.

"We three drove back to Minnesota. There Mor bought her farm, forty acres of plowland, pasture, and second-growth woods. It had no buildings, so while the house and barn and the rest were under construction we spent several months, 1939-40, in Northfield.

"Those years are pretty bad in my memory. I was a total social misfit. It didn't help that the war came along, gasoline was rationed, and I couldn't get into town on my own even if time had permitted after my farm chores or if, for that matter, I had wanted to. My grades were excellent and my deportment got me a name for prissiness among the other boys. They hadn't heard me out on the farm, swearing at a horse or cow or balky piece of machinery; there I earned a certain admiration from hardened men. As for school, except for the occasional fire-kindling teacher, it was something to be outlived.

"Anyway, I had my private world to retreat to, the world of books and, specifically, science fiction.

"Shortly after my arrival in Minnesota, [a friend] sent me a bundle of magazines. They seemed to be terrible pulp trash, and I didn't intend to read them, but fell sick abed for a few days and had nothing else. Immediately I was hooked. *Thrilling Wonder Stories; Startling Stories; Amazing Stories;* above all, the cerebral *Astounding Science Fiction.*

"I spent much of my tiny allowance on subscriptions. These didn't give me enough science fiction, so I started writing my own, in longhand.

"I didn't intend to make a career of this, but I did daydream about moonlighting at it and perhaps, someday, seeing words of mine in print, right up there with the words of Robert Heinlein, Isaac Asimov, or A. E. van Vogt.

Cover for Anderson's 1970 paperback.

"After high school graduation in 1944 I tried to enlist in the army—were we not in a glorious crusade which our leaders assured us would bring peace forever after?—but was turned down because of my scarred eardrums. A routine draft call later that year had the same result.

"Carleton College had offered me a small scholarship, on the basis of my high school grades, but I chose to enroll at the University of Minnesota. This was because its Institute of Technology offered an almost 100 percent scientific program. . . .My aim was to become a physicist.

"The war ended, for the nonce, at Hiroshima and Nagasaki. As a reader of science fiction, perhaps I understood a little better than most folk what this meant. But I don't claim any prophetic insights, and in fact the world has gone down ways that nobody predicted. I suspect it always will.

"Abruptly campus was flooded with veterans enrolling on GI benefits. They were generally fine guys, for whom I felt a certain wistful admiration, though they hardly ever boasted of their combat doings. They did, however, overcrowd my classes. It seemed as if everybody wanted to be a nuclear physicist. This was one reason why I moved over more toward astronomy. Another was a growing realization that not only was I awkward in the laboratory, I lacked any mathematical gift. It was easy to learn theorems that somebody else had proven, but where it came to creating a demonstration for myself, I wasn't much."[1]

A discussion about the atomic bomb led to the idea for a story, which Anderson submitted to *Astounding* magazine. "Months passed. I went off to a summer job in the north woods. I was back at school that fall before a letter came. John Camp-

Cover illustration by Stephen Hickman for the Baen paperbound edition.

bell, the editor, had *read* 'Tomorrow's Children.' He wanted to *buy* and *print* it. That kind of experience comes one to a lifetime.

"This first effort of mine appeared in the spring of 1947. In the following year or so I wrote and sold a couple more, for what was then fairly good money. This may have been a factor causing me to run out of academic steam. More and more, my attention went to other things than studies. I did graduate in 1948 'with distinction,' my college's equivalent of 'cum laude,' but my heart was no longer entirely in it.

"This was when I settled into a writing career in earnest. Graduating into a recession, with no money left for further studies, but being a bachelor who had never had a chance to develop expensive tastes, I thought I'd support myself by my stories while I looked around for steady employment. The search was half-hearted, and eventually petered out. I liked too much being my own boss, precarious though the living often was. Only slowly did it dawn on me that writing had, all along, been what nature cut me out to do.

"Mostly I was selling to the magazines, especially *Astounding,* as it was then called (nowadays *Analog*). My early pieces there tended to be rather cold and abstract. However, for a brief span I became a mainstay of *Planet Stories,* which featured blood-and-thunder adventure yarns—along with experimental work by such people as Ray Bradbury, which nobody else would touch. And the first novel I wrote which saw print, *The Broken Sword,* is a rather passionate love story among other things. It took years to find a publisher, and meanwhile I did a juvenile book on commission, which was therefore my premier appearance at that length.

"In 1952...I encountered a young lady by the name of Karen Kruse."[1] They were married in December, 1953. "For the next several years we lived in Berkeley. In those days the town was civilized, stimulating, amiably wacky. Its climate was better than that of San Francisco, which was only a short drive away anyhow. Here our daughter Astrid was born, in 1954. She tied us down somewhat; doubtless we could have traveled more with her than we did, but in the event decided not to. She was worth it. She still is.

"With a background in both physics and writing, I was offered a good post as a tech writer at the Lawrence Radiation Laboratory. This required a clearance for top secret material. I told the FBI men about my Communist aunt and the rest. If that was disqualifying, I said, they should so inform me and I'd withdraw my application with no hard feelings. They said it wasn't necessarily, and later called me in for another interview. That was obviously just a fishing expedition, full of questions about people I knew scarcely or not at all. I must say the agents were courteous, and it was perhaps not nice of me to start using sesquipedalian words in order that the man with the stenotype must ask me how to spell them.

"Time passed. There was no word. Karen and I got broker and broker. Finally I gave up and took another offer. I am told that this was a favorite trick of the government's. If officialdom had no sound reason not to clear somebody, but didn't want to, it stalled him till he could wait no longer and went away. I don't think this exactly expedited defense work.

"My job was at a local Department of Agriculture laboratory, as a very junior-grade chemist. Boss and co-workers were likeable, but it was intensely boring, and perhaps this is a reason why, after the nine months of probation usual in civil service, I was gently told that they couldn't use me.

"By then, however, that was a deliverance. My paychecks had kept us going. Evenings and weekends I wrote. The earnings from that paid off our debts and gave us a stake. When my mild bondage ended, in 1957, we celebrated by taking Astrid and Mor on a camping trip up the north coast. Ever since, I have been a full-time free-lance writer, and have done pretty well financially."[1]

"Obviously only a very small part of literature can properly be called science fiction, and for that matter science fiction is by no means the only sort of writing I have done. Still, I have written quite a lot of it, and am proud to have done so, because science fiction *is,* and always has been part of literature. Its long isolation, strictly a twentieth-century phenomenon, is ending; its special concepts and techniques are becoming common property, employed not only by the mass media but by some of our most respected writers; in turn, it is shedding artistic parochialism and thus starting to communicate beyond a small circle of enthusiasts. This is good, because the particular concerns of science fiction never have been parochial; they have included, or tried to include, all of space, time, and fate. Not that I wish to make exaggerated claims. I merely set forth that science fiction is one human accomplishment, among countless others, which has something to offer the world. Lest even this sound too pompous, let me say that at the very least it is often a lot of fun."[2]

"I'm one of the comparatively few people in the field who writes what is called 'hard' science fiction.

"A knowledge of science has given me a great deal to write about. Of course, this need not be true, and is not true, of everybody else who has a background in the sciences.

"Nowadays, what's usually meant by ['hard' science fiction] is writing which is more or less based on 'real' science—actual physics, chemistry, biology, astronomy, etc.—and to a considerable extent extrapolates from this, with a minimum of imaginary laws of nature."[3]

"For example, if there's going to be an imaginary planet, I'll start with the type of star, and that already conditions a number of things. Then the planet has a certain orbit around the star. One figures that out. This gives you what irradiation it gets, etc. The axial tilt comes in there also, rate of rotation, and of course you can't be quite arbitrary about the rotation rate, because there are reasons to think it doesn't just happen arbitrarily. Earth and Mars have the rotation period they do which is very nearly the same, not just by accident but because this is how it works. So you figure in elements like that. Of course you have to do a lot of guessing. There's an awful lot we don't know. Eventually you try to get it down to the planet's geography, place names, flora, fauna, etc. Plus if it's got inhabitants you've got a whole world to create—beings with their own evolution and history."[4]

Anderson's inspiration has come from a wide variety of sources. "Influences upon a writer are often hard to identify, but I think I know what some of the more important ones have been for me. There were editors John Campbell and Tony Boucher, who provided all sorts of inspiration and opportunity while scarcely ever trying to dictate. Besides H. G. Wells and Olaf Stapledon in science fiction, there were the giants of the Campbell Golden Age. Towering elsewhere have been the classical Greeks, the Icelandic Eddas and sagas, the King James Bible, Shakespeare, Mark Twain, Rudyard Kipling, Robinson Jeffers, and a Dane by the name of Johannes V. Jensen. I don't mean that my stuff measures up to any of this, only that I've tried. Science, technology, history, the whole world around us and the whole universe around it, provide endlessly fascinating subject matter."[1]

Paperback cover for Anderson's 1981 book.

"My basic notion about writing is that there is no reason for it unless it's either a reference work or gives the reader something new, something the reader could not have predicted. Else why should the reader bother?

"The 'something' may be, let's say, a recipe in a cookbook; or a line of poetry, a way of making a statement that we would never have thought of for ourselves; or a fact we didn't know before; or an event in a story; or a psychological insight into a character—anything, just so it's new and interesting. When we re-read something, it's presumably either because it has enough depth that we will find something new; or imperfect memory, being refreshed, creates that illusion; or, at least, we nostalgically try to capture a little of the thrill that newness once gave us.

"Surprise need not be identical with suspense. We know Hornblower won't get killed in any story; but we want to know what actually will happen, as well as get further glimpses of a different age. And, of course, the great psychological writers can take the drabbest-looking little person and show us depth after depth in him, with no more overt action than a walk to the corner grocery.

"There is another element the reader wants: fairness. Even in the most hairy-chested adventure story, what happens should look plausible in terms of what went before; that is, ideally the reader should think, 'My God, how *is* Joe Hero going to get out of that bear trap?' and then afterward, 'Oh, yes, sure.' This is even more true of the hero who solves his problems by his wits. The clues need not be explicitly in the text. I remember one of the old Alexander Botts yarns in which at the end he got out of a quandry by constructing a Mobius strip. Surely the average Satevepost reader had never heard of a Mobius strip; but he might have, and that was enough to satisfy....Even on the most elevated level, when a Huck Finn or a Dmitri Karamazov does or says something, no matter how surprising, we want to feel that this is right, that it is believable of the character as we have come to know him.

"These aren't hard-and-fast rules, of course. In all kinds of human endeavor, geniuses keep breaking the rules, but they'll apply pretty well to the vast majority of competent writing. Surprise, newness, if you prefer; fairness, logic, if you prefer."[5]

"I don't confine myself to a specific area or approach. I try to be as varied as possible, and not to say the same things over and over again. It would be boring for me as well as my readers. However, there is a basic attitude, I suppose, which underlies my writing—namely, that this is a wonderful universe in which to live, that it's great to be alive, and that all it takes is the willingness to give ourselves a chance to experience what it has to offer. If I preach at all, it's probably in the direction of individual liberty, which is a theme that looms large in my work."[3]

Anderson begins his writing processes when circumstances are right for doing so. "Once or twice I had obligations to meet when I wasn't feeling good, and I think that showed. I did the best I could, but nonetheless I don't think it was up to the usual standard, even though it was saleable. But I feel good most of the time anyway. I'm a fairly happy person.

"I do, however, get emotionally involved while writing a story. Say you've developed a character, spent a lot of time doing his biography, and start

him off in the story...and very frequently the character takes over.

"This is a very common experience for a writer; you'll think you have the whole scene planned, but then the characters come on and they know what they're doing and suddenly it's going quite differently from the way you'd planned but the right way. They're on the stage, not you, and they know what they're doing. So you've lived with somebody like this for a hundred or two hundred typewritten pages, which means a good many days of concentrated work. Then the guy gets killed off, or something awful happens to him. ...This is going to affect you for sure.

"I'm in the class of writers who pretty much want to know everything there is to know about the background and characters, etc. before starting to write."[4]

"For me, a story may be a long while gestating; in the meantime I'll putter around the house, go for miles-long walks, garden, go boating, take a trip, or whatever. As the basic concept takes shape, I begin to see what is required, and start doing backgrounding work. This may involve library research, interviews with knowledgeable people in a given field, visits to sites, etc. But for a science fiction yarn, it's mostly a matter of sitting down and developing things.

"For a novel, I write a biography of each important character. For a shorter story, this may not be necessary, though even here it's best that the characters be more than mere names. Always there's a lot which doesn't get into the manuscript for sheer lack of space."[5]

"As a rule, dialogue comes easily to me. I don't claim that mine is the most convincing in science fiction. (That's the province of Avram Davidson, with L. Sprague de Camp or G. C. Edmondson probably second.) Still, various people, including a TV producer whose business it is to know, have told me my dialogue is all right. No surprise; the characters supply it.

"For me, the hard part of a story is generally the descriptive. Sometimes I'm lucky and hit the mother lode and everything is gold and gravy. But oftenest I'll spend many minutes searching for an exact right word or phrase....Suffice it to say here that this is still largely happening in Dream Time. I know when I've found the right word because that's how it *feels*.

"Or I'll believe I know. Disillusionment frequently follows. Toward the end of a day I'll have done my chapter, or whatever the unit is. (The length depends on how well or badly things went, but 3000 words is a pretty fair guess at the average.) Next comes the conscious part. I read it over and think, 'Judas priest, this is awful. How could I ever spew out such garbage?' So I trudge across it word by word, making pencilled changes, and changing these changes because something further on demands that, and at last decide it isn't too terrible. . . .After all that scribbling, nobody but me can read the manuscript. Having taken a break, I'll go back for a third time, and the stuff looks better yet, though corrections are needed here and there. By then the hour is likely to be rather late.

"This study and rewriting are (I think) almost totally conscious. At most, I'll let my inner ear decide if a given sentence is euphonious and has the appropriate rhythm. Otherwise it's a matter of taking what came out during Dream Time and trying to refine it according to well-established rules: which are not mechanical rules, but a distillation from the experience of centuries."[6]

The creation of language is an important and enjoyable part of science-fiction writing for Anderson. "For a science-fiction writer, Greek and Latin are especially valuable as a source of readily understood neologisms. My wife, who is a bit of a classical scholar, coined the words 'Polesotechnic' and 'sophont' for me; I introduced them, and the latter word, meaning 'intelligent being,' seems to be catching on, to my great delight. On my own, I came up with plant names like 'glycophyllon' (sweetbranch), animal names like 'spathodont' (swordtooth) and geographical names like 'Oronesia' (Mountain Islands), whose meanings are self-evident to a reasonably well-read person and should not unduly confuse the rest. To be sure, English-derived names convey an image more readily—e.g., 'copperbark,' 'braidwood,' 'crownbuck,' 'flittery,' 'twyhorn,' 'Mount Lorn,' 'Mistwood,' 'Stormgate.'

"The word in its context should sound right. Sometimes, for instance, because of meter or whatever, it is better to write 'crepuscular' than 'twilit' or 'dusky,' even though Anglo-Saxon is more often preferable for a piece of physical or emotional description. Such judgments are usually subjective, unconscious or semi-conscious, though the conscious mind should always review them afterward.

"Another thing to bear in mind is that we have more than one sense. In fact, we have much more than five; hunger, equilibrium, and temperature are a few of them. Following Flaubert, I try to invoke at least three in every scene. It doesn't take many words.

"While a writer does necessarily draw on his own experience of life, that experience includes people entirely different from himself, as well as reading, conversation, drama, introspection, dreams, and endlessly much else. None of his characters, their psychotypes, habits, beliefs, morals, need have anything to do directly with him. Indeed, most fiction writers make an effort to avoid self-portrayal, or the portrayal of any living person, even under a changed name. Characters are normally syntheses. To give a personal example, I am not a woman like Donya of Hervar, a Catholic like Nicholas van Rijn, a warrior like Skafloc, a royalist like Prince Rupert, a Communist like Arne Torvald, a bisexual like Iason Philippou, a puritan like Joshua Coffin, a drifter like Skip Wayburn. . .etc., etc., confining the list to those whom I have treated sympathetically.

"In the second place, for the sake of a story writers often set forth an idea which they do not believe in. As an elementary example within science fiction, Isaac Asimov has used faster-than-light travel and L. Sprague de Camp has used time travel, though they are on record as considering these to be utter impossibilities. More significant may be concepts of human relationships. For instance, in 'No Truce with Kings' I suggested that feudalism is the highest form of social organization of which man is capable for any length of time, and we ought to accept this and make the best of it. In real life, I don't maintain that. It may or may not be true; we do not have any evidence which is scientifically meaningful, and perhaps we never will. It was just a thought which intrigued me and which I saw as the basis for a narrative.

"A writer may even depict a society or a relationship between individuals of which he disapproves as one which nevertheless works and whose participants feel reasonably well off; *vide* various stories by Jerry Pournelle. (I mention him because he has said this in print.) For that matter, interested though I am in 'heroic' eras like the Homeric and the Viking, I'd be the last person who'd want to see them revived."[6]

Anderson loves to write, for various reasons. "In many ways, writing is a compensation for loneliness. It certainly was when I was in my teens. Besides being stuck out on a farm, I was a very asocial kid, as many writers were. Subsequently, though, I've developed many close friendships and, if anything, my wife and I have more of a social life today than we can readily handle. As for writing itself, I don't feel any sense of loneliness when I'm writing. In fact, I hate it when somebody opens that study door. There's also this camaraderie among science-fiction writers and readers. We meet at conventions, we talk to each other, we form close friendships. Sometimes marriages even result from such meetings; this is how I met my wife. If there's any problem at all, it's how to keep from getting too involved in the social side of it to find time to think, to read, to write."[3]

"I've...confessed that I myself write not for the sake of writing, but to have written, in order to be free to go traveling or sailing or whatever else I really want to do. Yet I have also admitted to a sense of workmanship, a desire to do my best. How? To what end? What is the writer as a writer actually trying to accomplish? This is not irrelevant to his finished product, because he'll tend to employ that set of techniques—that style, if you wish, though there's more to technique than style and more to style than technique—which best suits his purpose.

"Basically, then, in my fiction I seek to entertain by telling stories. Both these predicates require a little expansion.

"'Entertainment' need not be mindless time-killing. On the contrary, I take the word to mean, 'That which engages attention and arouses interest, including emotion.' In this sense, the most lofty tragedies of Euripides and the most rarefied thought of Einstein are entertaining...to some of us, who may find the TV sitcoms a crashing bore. My hope is to entertain people who enjoy thinking.

"The point is, I give to my work everything that is mine at the time to give....I simply don't consider myself any kind of priest. I'd give up writing long before I gave up...numerous other pleasures.

"It would be improper, because unauthorized, to name people who've made the same admission to me when it got drunk enough out, but believe me, they include quite a few top-rankers. For that matter, Shakespeare quit when he'd made his pile, and appears to have been a frustrated actor anyway. Dostoyevsky churned out much of his fiction as newspaper serials; sometimes the editor had to snatch copy right off his desk in order to get it to press in time. Robert Graves regarded his brilliant historical novels as potboilers, which supported him so he could compose poems that I, at least, find stodgy. One can multiply examples, also in other

arts; for instance, most of Bach's music was done to order.

"The moral is that we should never judge a work by its creator's personality, nor by what he says about it, but strictly on its own merits. This looks childishly obvious. Nevertheless, I keep being amazed at how many people, in and out of academe, can't imagine it."[6]

Anderson has received a label from critics to which he takes exception. "What is interesting these days is an image that I am told I have acquired: the ultimate Male Chauvinist Pig. Strange. Of that slender percentage of readers from whom any writer gets continuing feedback, a startling proportion of mine are women: and a couple of these have said that the typical Anderson heroine is so competent that she gives them an inferiority complex. This female type of mine is nothing new, either. You can find her in books copyrighted in the 1950s. She's there because I have, in real life, known several like her and immensely admired them.

"Then why am I labeled MCP? Is it because I usually write from a masculine viewpoint? No, probably not. So do most male writers, and some female ones, such as Leigh Brackett. In my own case, I do this largely because I understand the masculine psyche a little better than the feminine. (For similar reasons, I seldom have a viewpoint character who is ethnically very different from me—unless the story is far enough in the future that one can assume that cultures have changed in unpredictable ways.)

"The likeliest reason I can think of for my having gotten this name is twofold. First, I have not leaped to embrace the feminist ideology, any more than any other ideology which becomes fashionable. But that's probably minor. A writer is still allowed to remain neutral, at least in his pay copy. My debates with various ladies have generally been private and always civilized. Moreover, they have opened my eyes to things I had not been aware of before, inequities which are perfectly real, and I have told them so.

"Second, however: Once upon a time Joanna Russ published an essay in the now defunct magazine *Vertex*, deploring the MCPism in science fiction. I ventured to publish a mild reply in the same place, arguing that science fiction had, if anything, long been in the forefront of egalitarianism, and that the relative dearth of women characters in it prior to about 1960 was due not to prejudice but to the requirements of the kind of story that was mostly being written in those days. Never mind whether Ms. Russ or I was right, or in what degree. My guess is that the simple fact that I dared to disagree with her in print was enough."[6]

Indeed, Anderson holds his readers in high esteem. "Most of the people who read science fiction tend to be individualists in one way or another. They have individualistic personalities, even though they might describe themselves as 'liberals' or 'conservatives.' They tend to be very self-directed people—people who desire to determine the direction of their own lives."[3]

The social and political climate has had an effect on Anderson's artistic liberty. "As a writer, I, for example, have a number of freedoms now I did not have ten or twenty years ago. I can use sex now more, in my work, get a little explicit when I see fit. But on the other hand that's fairly trivial. Any writer worth his salt ought to be able to work his way around such restrictions. . .and they used to.

"I myself have had an extraordinarily fortunate life, am still doing so, and plan to continue thus for long years. It might have been more satisfying to be an astrophysicist or an oceanographer, but maybe it wouldn't have, and in any event, there is ample satisfaction in writing, plus ample leisure in which to do other things. At seventh and last, as they say in Danish, I owe my thanks for this to the readers. To you."[6]

Footnote Sources:

[1] *Contemporary Authors Autobiography Series,* Volume 2, Gale, 1985.
[2] *Contemporary Authors New Revision Series,* Volume 2, Gale, 1981.
[3] Jeffrey Elliot, "Interview: Poul Anderson," *Galileo,* number 11/12, 1979.
[4] Elton E. Elliott, "An Interview with Poul Anderson," *Science Fiction Review,* May, 1978.
[5] Paul Walker, *Speaking of Science Fiction: The Paul Walker Interviews,* Luna, 1978.
[6] Poul Anderson, "Poul Anderson: Talar Om Science Fiction," *Algol,* summer-fall, 1978.

■ For More Information See

Periodicals:

Library Journal, June 15, 1954 (p. 1169).

National Review, January 12, 1964 (p. 1074ff).
Esquire, January, 1966 (p. 58).
Magazine of Fantasy and Science Fiction, March, 1971 (p. 14ff), December, 1971 (p. 25), April, 1972.
Luna Monthly, June, 1972 (p. 1ff).
Books and Bookmen, August, 1972 (p. xii).
Foundation, March, 1973 (p. 81ff), January, 1974 (p. 44).
Publishers Weekly, May 28, 1973, October 22, 1973, January 14, 1983, March 11, 1988.
Algol, May, 1974 (p. 11ff).
Galileo, July, 1979 (p. 19ff).
New York Times Book Review, October 28, 1979 (p. 15ff).
Starship, winter, 1979-80 (p. 8ff).
Washington Post Book World, February 24, 1980 (p. 7), May 29, 1983.
Future Life, May, 1981 (p. 26ff).
Science Fiction and Fantasy Book Review, April, 1982.
Analog, September, 1983 (p. 53ff).

Books:

Roger C. Peyton, *A Checklist of Poul Anderson,* privately printed, 1965.
Reginald Bretnor, editor, *Science Fiction: Today and Tomorrow,* Harper, 1974.
Donald H. Tuck, compiler, *The Encyclopedia of Science Fiction and Fantasy,* Volume 1, Advent Publishers, 1974.
David Stever and Andrew Adams Whyte, *The Collector's Poul Anderson,* privately printed, 1976.
R. Bretnor, editor, *The Craft of Science Fiction,* Harper, 1976.
Sandra Miesel, *Against Time's Arrow: The High Crusade of Poul Anderson,* Borgo, 1978.
Jeffrey M. Elliot, *Science Fiction Voices #2,* Borgo, 1979.
Contemporary Literary Criticism, Volume 15, Gale, 1980.
Dictionary of Literary Biography, Volume 8: *Twentieth-Century American Science-Fiction Writers,* Gale, 1981.
Charles Platt, *Dream Makers, Volume II: The Uncommon Men and Women Who Write Science Fiction,* Berkley, 1983.

Cassette:

"An Interview with Poul Anderson," Center for Cassette Studies.

Collections:

De Grummond Collection at the University of Southern Mississippi.

Toni Cade Bambara

Born in 1939, in New York, N.Y. *Education:* Queens College (now Queens College of the City University of New York), B.A., 1959; City College of the City University of New York, M.A., 1964; *Office:* Scribe Film/Video Center, 1520 Kater St., Philadelphia, Pa. 19135.

■ Career

Free-lance lecturer, writer, programmer in independent films and American literature. City College of the City University of New York, New York City, English instructor in SEEK Program, 1965-69; New Careers Program, Newark, N.J., English instructor in SEEK Program, 1969; Livingston College, Rutgers University, New Brunswick, N.J., assistant professor, 1969-71, associate professor, 1971-74; Duke University, Durham, N.C., visiting professor of African American studies, 1974; Stephens College, Columbia, Mo., visiting professor of African American studies, 1975; Neighborhood Arts Center, Atlanta, Ga., artist-in-residence, 1975-79; Atlanta University, visiting professor, 1977, research mentor and instructor, School of Social Work, 1977, 1979; Spelman College, Atlanta, Ga., writer-in-residence, 1978-1979.

Founder and director of Pamoja Writers Guild, 1976-85. Conducted numerous workshops on writing, self-publishing, and community organizing for community centers, museums, prisons, libraries, and universities. Lectured and conducted literary readings at many institutions, including the Library of Congress, Smithsonian Institution, Afro-American Museum of History and Culture, and for numerous other organizations and universities. Member of advisory board, Sojourner Productions, *Black Film Review, Essence*, Black International Cinema (Berlin/Bedford-Stuyvesant), Sisters in Support of South African Sisterhood. *Member:* National Association of Third World Writers, Screen Writers Guild of America, African American Film Society, Southern Collective of African-American Writers (founding member).

■ Awards, Honors

Peter Pauper Press Journalism Award from the *Long Island Star*, 1958; John Golden Award for Fiction from Queens College (now Queens College of the City University of New York), 1959; Theatre of Black Experience Award, 1969, for service; Rutgers University Research Fellowship, 1972, for curriculum work; *Tales and Stories for Black Folks* was selected an Outstanding Book of the Year by the *New York Times*, 1972; Black Child Development Institute Service Award, 1973, for service to Black children; Black Rose Award from *Encore*, 1973, for short story "Gorilla, My Love;" Black Community Award from Livingston College, Rutgers University, 1974, for service to students.

Award from the National Association of Negro Business and Professional Women's Club League, for service to Black women; George Washington Carver Distinguished African American Lecturer Award from Simpson College; *Ebony*'s Achievement in the Arts Award; Black Arts Award from the University of Missouri; National Endowment for the Arts Individual Literature Grant, 1981; American Book Award, 1981, for *The Salt Eaters*; Best Documentary Award from the Pennsylvania Association of Broadcasters, and Documentary Award from the National Black Programming Consortium, both 1986, both for "The Bombing of Osage"; Langston Hughes Medallion from the Langston Hughes Society of City College of New York, 1986; Zora Hurston Award from Morgan State College, 1986.

■ Writings

Gorilla, My Love: Short Stories, Random House, 1972.
The Sea Birds Are Still Alive: Collected Stories, Random House, 1977.
The Salt Eaters (novel), Random House, 1980.
(Author of foreword) Cherrie Moraga and Gloria Anzaldua, editors, *This Bridge Called My Back: Radical Women of Color*, Persephone Press, 1981.
(Author of foreword) *The Sanctified Church: Collected Essays by Zora Neale Hurston*, Turtle Island, 1982.

Screenplays:

"Zora," WGBH-TV, 1971.
"The Johnson Girls," National Educational Television, 1972.
"Transactions," School of Social Work, Atlanta University, 1979.
"The Long Night," American Broadcasting Company, 1981.
"Epitaph for Willie," K. Heran Productions, 1982.
"Tar Baby" (based on Toni Morrison's novel), Sanger/Brooks Film Productions, 1984.
"Raymond's Run," Public Broadcasting System, 1985.
"The Bombing of Osage," WHYY-TV, 1986.
"Cecil B. Moore: Master Tactician of Direct Action," WHYY-TV, 1987.

Editor:

(And contributor, under name Toni Cade) *The Black Woman*, 18th edition, New American Library, 1970.

(And contributor) *Tales and Stories for Black Folks*, Doubleday, 1971.
(With Leah Wise) *Southern Black Utterances Today*, Institute for Southern Studies, 1975.

Contributor:

Addison Gayle, Jr., editor, *Black Expression: Essays by and about Black Americans in the Creative Arts*, Weybright, 1969.
Jules Chametsky, editor, *Black and White in American Culture*, University of Massachusetts Press, 1970.
Ruth Miller, *Backgrounds to Blackamerican Literature*, Chandler Publishing, 1971.
Janet Sternburg, editor, *The Writer on Her Work*, Norton, 1980.
Paul H. Connolly, *On Essays: A Reader for Writers*, Harper, 1981.
Howe, editor, *Women Working*, Feminist Press, 1982.
Mari Evans, editor, *Black Women Writers (1950-1980): A Critical Evaluation*, Doubleday, 1984.
Baraka and Baraka, editors, *Confirmations*, Morrow, 1984.
Claudia Tate, editor, *The Black Writer at Work*, Howard University Press, 1984.

Bambara's works have been translated into six languages. Contributor to *What's Happnin, Somethin Else*, and *Another Eye*, all readers published by Scott, Foresman, 1969-70. Contributor of articles and book and film reviews to periodicals, including *Massachusetts Review, Negro Digest, Liberator, Prairie Schooner, Redbook, New York Times, Ms., Callaloo, First World, Audience, Black Works, Umbra*, and *Onyx*. Guest editor *Southern Exposure 3*, spring/summer, 1976.

■ Work in Progress

Ground Cover, a novel based on the Atlanta Missing and Murdered Children's case; co-author with Louis Massiah "Come as You Are," a feature film script about homeless movement insurgency.

■ Sidelights

Toni Cade Bambara is a well known and respected activist, professor of English and African American studies, editor of anthologies of Black literature, and author of short stories and a novel. "All writers, musicians, artists, choreographers/dancers, etc., work with the stuff of their experiences. It's the translation of it, the conversion of it, the shaping of it that makes for the drama. I've never been convinced that experience is linear, circular, or even random. It just is. I try to put it in some kind of order to extract meaning from it, to bring meaning to it."[1]

Born March 25, 1939 in New York City, Bambara grew up in Harlem, Bedford-Stuyvesant, and Queens, as well as Jersey City, New Jersey. Educated in both public and private schools, Bambara credits her mother for much of her success. "She did the *New York Times* and the *London Times* crossword puzzles. She read books. She built bookcases. She'd wanted to be a journalist. She gave me permission to wonder, to dawdle, to daydream. My most indelible memory of 1948 is my mother coming upon me in the middle of the kitchen floor with my head in the clouds and my pencil on the paper and her mopping around me. My mama had been in Harlem during the renaissance. She used to hang out at the Dark Tower, at the Renny, go to hear Countee Cullen, see Langston Hughes over near Mt. Morris Park. She thought it was wonderful that I could write things that almost made some kind of sense. She used to walk me over to Seventh Avenue and 125th Street and point out the shop where J. A. Rogers, the historian, was knocking out books. She used to walk me over to the Speaker's Corner to listen to the folks. Of course, if they were talking 'religious stuff,' she'd keep on going to wherever we were going; but if they were talking union or talking race, we'd hang tough on the corner.

"I wasn't raised in the church. I learned the power of the word from the speakers on Speaker's Corner—trade unionists, Temple People as we called Muslims then, Father Divinists, Pan-Africanists, Abyssinians as we called Rastas then, Communists, Ida B. Wells folks. We used to listen to 'Wings over Jordan' on the radio; and I did go to this or that Sunday school over the years, moving from borough to country to city, but the sermons I heard on Speaker's Corner as a kid hanging on my mama's arm or as a kid on my own and then as an adult had tremendous impact on me. It was those marvelously gifted, extravagantly verbal speakers that prepared me later for the likes of Charlie Cobb, Sr., Harold Thurman, Revun Doughtery, and the mighty, mighty voice of Bernice Reagon.

"My daddy used to take me to the Apollo Theater, which had the best audience in the world with the possible exception of folks who gather at Henry Street for Woodie King's New Federal theater plays. There, in the Apollo, I learned that if you are going to call yourself some kind of communicator, you'd better be good because the standards of our community are high. I used to hang out a bit with my brother and my father at the Peace Barber Shop up in Divine territory [an area in Harlem around Father Divine's church] just north of where we lived, and there I learned what it meant to be a good storyteller. Of course, the joints I used to hang around when I was supposed to be walking a neighbor's dog or going to the library taught me more about the oral tradition and our high standards governing the rap, than books.

"The musicians of the forties and fifties, I suspect, determined my voice and pace and pitch. I grew up around boys who carried horn cases and girls who couldn't wait for their legs to grow and reach the piano pedals. I grew up in New York City, bebop heaven—and it's still music that keeps that place afloat. I learned more from Bud Powell, Dizzy, Y'Bird, Miss Sassy Vaughn about what can be communicated, can be taught through structure, tone, metronomic sense, and just sheer holy boldness than from any teacher of language arts, or from any book for that matter. For the most part, the voice of my work is bop."[1]

There wasn't much sexual stereotyping in Bambara's family. "I think within my household not a great deal of distinction was made between pink and blue. We were expected to be self-sufficient, to be competent, and to be rather nonchalant about expertise in a number of areas. Within the various neighborhoods I've lived in, there was such a variety of expectations regarding womanhood or manhood that it was rather wide-open. In every neighborhood I've lived in, for example, there were always big-mouthed women, there were always competent women, there were always beautiful women, independent women as well as dependent women, so that there was a large repertoire from which to select. And it wasn't until I got older, I would say maybe in college, that I began to collide with the concepts and dynamics of 'role-appropriate behavior' and so forth. I had no particular notion about being groomed along one particular route as opposed to another as a girl-child. My self-definitions were strongly internal and improvisational."[2]

Bambara began writing early and remembers her first story. "I was really little. I'm talking about kindergarten. Sometimes even now, a line will come out that will take me back to some utterance made in a story or poem I wrote or tried to write when I was in pink pajamas and bunny slippers. It's weird. I've been in training, you might say, for quite a while. Still am."[2]

"It's been a long apprenticeship. I began scribbling tales on strips from my daddy's *Daily News.* Then, I'd wait by the bedroom door, chewing on a number two pencil, for those white sturdy squares my mama's stockings came wrapped around. I'd fashion two-part, six-block-long sagas to get my classmates to and from P.S. 186.

"Would linger recklessly in doorways, hallways, basements, soaking up overheards to convert into radio scripts I'd one day send out. In the various elementary schools, I scripted skits for Negro History Week. In junior high, I overwhelmed English teachers with three-for-one assignments. In high school, I hogged the lit journal."[3]

"I can't remember a time when I was not writing. The original motive was to try to do things that we were not encouraged to do in the language arts programs in the schools, namely, to use writing as a tool to get in touch with the self. In the schools, for example, writing, one of the few crafts we're taught, seems to be for the purpose of teaching people how to plagiarize from the dictionary or the encyclopedia and how to create as much distance from your own voice as possible. That was called education. I'd call it alienation. You had to sift out a lot, distort a lot, and lie a lot in order to jam the stuff of your emotional, linguistic, cultural experience into that form called the English composition.

"The original motive for writing at home was to give a play to those notions that wouldn't fit the English composition mold, to try and do justice to a point of view, to a sense of self. Later on, I discovered that there was a certain amount of applause that could be gotten if you turned up with the Frederick Douglass play for Negro History Week or the George Washington Carver play for the assembly program. That talent for bailing the English teachers out created stardom, and that became another motive.

"As I got older, I began to appreciate the kinds of things you could tap and release and learn about self if you had a chance to get cozy with pencil and paper. And I discovered too that paper is very patient. It will wait on you to come up with whatever it is, as opposed to sitting in class and having to raise your hand immediately in response to someone else's questions, someone else's concerns."[2]

Bambara's writing was influenced by common, every day events rather than from books by other authors. "I have no clear ideas about literary influence. I would say that my mother was a great influence, since mother is usually the first map maker in life. She encouraged me to explore and express. And, too, the fact that people of my household were big on privacy helped. And I would say that people that I ran into helped, and I ran into a great many people because we moved a lot and I was always a nosey kid running up and down the street, getting into everything.

"Particular kinds of women influenced the work. For example, in every neighborhood I lived in there were always two types of women that somehow pulled me and sort of got their wagons in a circle around me. I call them Miss Naomi and Miss Gladys, although I'm sure they came under various names. The Miss Naomi types were usually barmaids or life-women, nighttime people with lots of clothes in the closet and a very particular philosophy of life, who would give me advice like, 'When you meet a man, have a birthday, demand a present that's hockable, and be careful.' Stuff like that. Had no idea what they were talking about. Just as well. The Miss Naomis usually gave me a great deal of advice about beautification, how to take care of your health and not get too fat. The Miss Gladyses were usually the type that hung out the window in Apartment 1-A leaning on the pillow giving single-action advice on numbers or giving you advice about how to get your homework done or telling you to stay away from those cruising cars that moved through the neighborhood patrolling little girls. I would say that those two types of women, as well as the women who hung out in the beauty parlors (and the beauty parlors in those days were perhaps the only womanhood institutes we had—it was there in the beauty parlors that young girls came of age and developed some sense of sexual standards and some sense of what it means to be a woman growing up)—it was those women who had the most influence on the writing.

"I think that most of my work tends to come off the street rather than from other books. Which is not to say I haven't learned a lot as an avid reader. I devour pulp and print. And of course I'm part of the tradition. That is to say, it is quite apparent to the reader that I appreciate Langston Hughes, Zora Hurston, and am a product of the sixties spirit. But I'd be hard pressed to discuss literary influences in any kind of intelligent way."[2]

January, 1959. Earned her B.A. in Theatre Arts and English. "In Queens College, the theatre club lured me away from the bio-chem labs. And encouraged by two writing courses, I wrote novels, stories, plays, film scripts, unnameables, operas, you-name-its, none of which were ever finished, though a group of nearly finished pieces copped the John Golden Award the year I graduated....For the next fifteen years or so, while students were definitely the center of my days and nights, writing was the featured attraction of the predawn in-betweens."[3]

In the same year, she won the Pauper Press Journalism Award from the *Long Island Star.*

1959-1961. While taking graduate courses in modern American fiction at City College in New York City, she worked as a social investigator for the New York State Department of Welfare and published her first short story, "Sweet Town," under the name Toni Cade.

1961-1963. Went to the University of Florence, studied commedia del arte in Milan and mime at Ecole de Mime Etienne Decrous in Paris. Returned to New York to work as recreation director at Metropolitan Hospital and program director at Colony House Community Center in Brooklyn.

1964. Earned her M.A. at City College of City University of New York.

1965-1969. Worked as an English instructor in the SEEK program of City College, and as director and advisor for the Theater of the Black Experience. Continued to write in her spare time. "I began writing in a serious way—though I can't recall a time when I wasn't jotting stuff down and trying to dramatize lessons learned—when I got into teaching. It was a way to keep track of myself, to monitor myself. I'm a very seductive teacher, persuasive, infectious, overwhelming, irresistible. I worked hard in the classroom to teach students to critique me constantly, to protect themselves from my nonsense; but let's face it, the teacher-student relationship we've been trained in is very colonial in nature. It's fraught with dangers. The power given teachers over students' minds, students' spirits, students' development—my God! To rise above that, to insist of myself and of them that we refashion that relationship along progressive lines demanded a great deal of courage, imagination, energy and will.

"Writing was a way to 'hear' myself, check myself. Writing was/is an act of discovery. I frequently discovered that I was dangerous, a menace, virtually unfit to move the students and myself into certain waters. I would have to go into the classroom and beat them up for not taking me to the wall, for succumbing to mere charm and flash, when they should have been challenging me, 'kicking my ass.' I will be eternally grateful to all

Cover of the 1981 Vintage edition.

those students at City College and Livingston/Rutgers for the caring and courageous way they helped to develop me as a teacher, a person, a writer."[1]

1969. Became an assistant professor at Livingston State College of Rutgers University in New Jersey.

About 1970 daughter, Karma, was born. "Even after she is grown, and even if I never teach again, I will still use writing as a way to stay on center, for I'll still be somebody's neighbor, somebody's friend, and I'll still be a member of our community under siege or in power. I'll still need to have the discipline writing affords, demands. I do not wish to be useless or dangerous, so I'll write. And too, hell, I'm a writer. I am compelled to write."[1]

Adopted the surname Bambara when she discovered a signature on a sketchbook in her great-grandmother's trunk. Using the name Bambara, she published her first book, *The Black Woman,* an anthology of poetry, short stories and essays by black women. "Addison Gayle. . .a friend and colleague back in the early sixties, urged me to assemble a book on the black woman rather than run off at the mouth about it. It was Addison who got me the contract to do the second book, *Tales and Short Stories for Black Folks.* I can't remember who clubbed me over the head to start doing reviews for Dan Watts's *Liberator,* but that experience certainly impacted on what and how and why I write; and the support I get now from my editor and friend, Toni Morrison—well, I just can't say what that does for me. She'll feed me back some passage I've written and say, 'Hmm, that's good, girl.' That gives me a bead on where I am and keeps me going."[1]

1971. Published a second anthology, *Tales and Stories for Black Folks.* "The first half of the book consists of stories I wished I had read growing up, stories by Alice Walker, Pearl Crayton, and particularly Langston Hughes. The stories in the second half of the book were documents that came out of a course that I was teaching (a freshman composition course, which has always been my favorite). The students had begun working with kids in an independent community school and I asked them to produce term paper projects that were usable to someone. So a great many of them took traditional European tales and changed them so as to promote critical thinking, critical reading for the young people they were working with outside of the class. And out of that group of term papers came a number of really remarkable, thoughtful pieces, such as 'The True Story of Chicken Licken,' which raises questions about the nature of truth or the nature of responsible journalism. The story pivoted on the idea that perhaps it was not a piece of sky that fell on Chicken Licken's head after all but maybe she got caught up in a community action and got hit on the head by the cops and then they put out a press release that she had been attacked by a piece of cloud. All of the stories in the second half of the book came out of the materials that had been submitted to me by students that year."[2]

1972. Published her own collection of short stories, *Gorilla, My Love.* "When I originally drafted the title story of my first story collection, *Gorilla, My Love,* the tone was severe, grim. The confrontations between the kid and the adults who so nonchalantly lie to and de-spirit little kids were raging red. Writing in a rage can produce some interesting pyrotechnics, but there are other ways to keep a fire ablaze, it seems to me. Besides, I

know that everything will be O.K. for that little girl, so tough, so compassionate, so brave. Her encounter with the movie manager who put a come-on title on the marquee and then screened another movie altogether, and her encounter with her uncle who promised to marry her when she grew up and then turned right around and married some full-grown woman—those are rehearsals that will hold her in good stead in later encounters with more menacing and insidious people."[4]

"There are certain kinds of spirits that I'm *very* appreciate of, people who are very tough, but very compassionate. You put me in any neighborhood, in any city, and I will tend to gravitate toward that type. The kid in 'Gorilla' is a kind of person who will survive, and she's triumphant in her survival. Mainly because she's so very human, she cries, her caring is not careless. She certainly is not autobiographical except that there are naturally aspects of my own personality that I very much like that are similar to hers. She's very much like people I like. However, I would be hard pressed to point out her source in real life."[2]

During the seventies, Bambara was primarily concerned with writing short stories, which was ". . .deliberate, coincidental, accidental, and regretful! Regretful, commercially. That is to say, it is financially stupid to be a short story writer and to spend two years putting together eight or ten stories and receiving maybe half the amount of money you would had you taken one of those short stories and produced a novel. The publishing companies, reviewers, critics, are all geared to promoting and pushing the novel rather than any other form.

"I prefer the short story genre because it's quick, it makes a modest appeal for attention, it can creep up on you on your blind side. The reader comes to the short story with a mind-set different than that with which he approaches the big book, and a different set of controls operating, which is why I think the short story is far more effective in terms of teaching us lessons.

"Temperamentally, I move toward the short story because I'm a sprinter rather than a long-distance runner. I cannot sustain characters over a long period of time. Walking around, frying eggs, being a mother, shopping—I cannot have those characters living in my house with me for more than a couple of weeks. In terms of craft, I don't have the kinds of skills *yet* that it takes to stay with a large panorama of folks and issues and landscapes and moods. That requires a set of skills that I don't know anything about yet, but I'm learning.

"I prefer the short story as a reader, as well, because it does what it does in a hurry. For the writer and the reader make instructive demands in terms of language precision. It deals with economy, gets it said, and gets out of the way. As a teacher, I also prefer the short story for all the reasons given. And yes, I consider myself primarily a short story writer."[2]

1973. "I was in Cuba. . .and had the occasion not only to meet with the Federation of Cuban women but sisters in the factories, on the land, in the street, in the parks, in lines, or whatever, and the fact that they were able to resolve a great many class conflicts as well as color conflicts and organize a mass organization says a great deal about the possibilities here."[2]

"Though writing, editing, and scripting for years, I did not acknowledge to myself that I was a writer, that writing was my way of doing my work in the world, till I returned from Cuba in the summer of 1973. There I learned what Langston Hughes and others, most especially my colleagues in the Neo-Black Arts Movement, had been teaching for years—that writing is a legitimate way, an important way, to participate in the empowerment of the community that names me.

"I returned home to a stack of mail from readers raising questions, picking bones, offering amens and right-ons—critical feedback and accreditation from *the* authenticating audience. I was a writer. Somehow 'writer' in my head was a vigorous, typewriting obsessive who worked at a huge desk, wore suede elbow patches on cashmere sleeves, smoked a pipe, and had a wife and a secretary who kept the house quiet and the pages in order. 'Serious writer' was a fearless-looking warrior in bullet belt and feathered cloak, with the ritual knife in the teeth ready to cut through nonsense. My image of myself, on the other hand, despite my breakthrough from my bourgeois training that promoted 'literaphilia' as a surrogate for political action and 'sensibility' as a substitute for social consciousness, was that of a somnambulent oyster in whose tissues an irritating gritty somethin-or-other was making sleep and daydreaming a lumpy affair."[3]

1974. Served as humanities consultant to the New Jersey Department of Corrections and art consultant to the New York State Arts Council. Moved with Karma to Atlanta.

1975. Was visiting professor of Afro-American studies at Stephens College in Columbia, Missouri. Also did some travelling. "I was in Vietnam in the summer of 1975 as a guest of the Women's Union and again was very much struck by the women's ability to break through traditional roles, traditional expectations, reactionary agenda for women, and come together again in a mass organization that is programmatic and takes on a great deal of responsibility for the running of the nation."[3]

1976. Artist-in-residence at Stephens College and a consultant to the Georgia Arts Council. Founded and directed Pamoja Writer's Guild and was a founder of the Southern Collective of Afro-American Writers.

1977. Became a visiting professor at Atlanta University and research mentor and instructor in the School of Social Work. Published a second collection of her short stories, *The Sea Birds Are Still*

Paperback edition of Bambara's first book.

Alive. "'Broken-Field Running,' in the 1977 collection *The Sea Birds Are Still Alive*, was. . .a challenge. It wasn't so much a problem in pitch as a problem in balancing the elements of mood. I'd been observing architectural changes in my community since the street rebellions. Schools, public housing, parks were being designed in such a way as to wreck community sovereignty, to render it impossible for neighbors to maintain surveillance and security of turf. I was enraged. I wrote a blazing essay on the subject, snarling, shooting from both hips. Hadn't a clue as to how to finish it or to whom to send it. Wrote a story instead. The first problem then was balancing the essay voice and the story voice; the second to keep the two dominant emotions of the narrator stabilized, in tension. The story is an odd sort of moody piece about a combatant, a teacher whose faith is slipping, whose belief in the capacity for transformation is splintering. I was trying to get at how difficult it is to maintain the fervent spirit at a time when the Movement is mute, when only a few enclaves exist. The teacher's work, her friend, her training, and most of all her responsibility to the children help to keep her centered, help to keep her in touch with the best of herself. But her task is rough.

"Time out to say this—I often read in reviews that my stories are set in the sixties and are nostalgic and reminiscent of days when revolution was believed in. News to me. With the exception of 'The Long Night,' all the stories in *Sea Birds* are in the 'right now' time they were drafted. I suppose for too many people the idea that struggle is neither new nor over is hard to grasp, that there is a radical tradition as old as the *H.M.S. Jesus* or whatever that ship was that hauled over the first boatload.

"Back to 'Broken-Field Running.' It was spring 1974 and I'd just returned from a rally at which I heard that genocide was a fact in the Colored World, that the struggle was all over 'cause nobody cared anymore and blah, blah, blah, blah, accompanied by statistics and all the evangelical zeal of the brimstone tent belters. So in that woe-is-us mood, I began work on the story. And before I knew it, my character Lacy had picked it up and run off with it. Even while she was slipping in the snow and so in need of all kinds of support now that the thousands of combatants of a few years ago were/are no longer very visible, she managed to horse around enough to keep the story from getting depressing—depression being, to my mind, a form of collaboration. The kids in her orbit after all, are

proof, mandate, motive to keep on keeping on. I guess then, that the message is—and I am a brazenly 'message' writer, which seems to unsettle many reviewers—that in periods of high consciousness, one has to build the network and the foundation to sustain one through periods of high conflict and low consciousness. What goes around, comes around, as folks say.

"Of course it is difficult to maintain the faith and keep working toward the new time if you've had no *experience* of it, not *seen* ordinary people actually transform selves and societies. That is the back-and-forth of the story 'The Apprentice' in *Sea Birds.* The younger sister who narrates the story underestimates her own ability to fashion a revolutionary outlook, for she's not seen what my other character, the organizer Naomi, has seen. We, however, know that she will grow. She's got fine spirit for all her caterwauling. And we suspect too, I imagine, that whatever moved her into the circle of community workers and made her an apprentice in the first place will continue to operate, to inform her choices. And too, Naomi is kinda fun to hang out with. And that is the way many join ranks, after all, through an attraction to a given person. It's like the gospel song instructs, 'You never know who's watching you,' who's taking you as a model, I seem to recall that I invited Naomi onto the scene as a way of answering the grim reapers at that 1974 rally. If you're trying to recruit people to a particular kind of work, the recruiter has to stand for something attractive. I'd be willing to follow Naomi anywhere. She has heart to spare.

"I got a lot of mixed reactions about the story 'The Organizer's Wife' in *Sea Birds.* Feminist types didn't like the title; some said they refused to read the story because the title was such a putdown. Others like the fact that Virginia, the lead character, kicked the preacher's ass for more reasons than for turning her husband in but, nonetheless, would have been happier had she left town or died in childbirth, by way of my protesting the system. Some letters and calls said I should have had Graham, the organizer, die some gruesome death in that southern jail to protest, etc. Kill Graham off and have Virginia go batty, or leave, or die in childbirth? What kind of message would that have been? How would I have explained that to my daughter? She's looking forward to growing up as a responsible change agent. I'm well aware that we are under siege, that the system kills, that the terms of race and class war have not altered very much. But death is not a truth that inspires, that pumps up the heart, that mobilizes. It's defeatist to dwell always on the consequences of risks. It's proracist to assume we can't take a chance. I am not interested in collaborating with the program of the forces that systematically underdevelop. So Graham lives and Virginia wakes up.

"'The Organizer's Wife,' written in 1975 and set in 1975, is a love story, layer after layer. Lovers and combatants are not defeated. That is the message of that story, the theme of the entire collection, the wisdom that gets me up in the morning, honored to be here. It is a usable truth."[4]

1978-1979. Became artist-in-residence at Spelman College in Atlanta, where she began working on her first novel. "I began the novel *The Salt Eaters* the way a great many of my writings begin, as a journal entry. I frequently sit down and give myself an assignment—to find out what I know about this or that, to find out what I think about this or that when I am cozy with myself and not holding forth to a group or responding to someone's position. Several of us had been engaged in trying to organize various sectors of the community—students, writers, psychic adepts, etc.—and I was struck by the fact that our activists or warriors and our adepts or medicine people don't even talk to each other. Those two camps have yet to learn—not since the days of Toussaint [Toussaint L'Ouverture was the black liberator of Haiti] anyway, not since the days of the maroon communities, [escaped slaves in the Americas] I suspect—to appreciate each other's visions, each other's potential, each other's language. The novel, then, came out of a problem-solving impulse—what would it take to bridge the gap, to merge those frames of reference, to fuse those camps? I thought I was just making notes for organizing; I thought I was just exploring my feelings, insights. Next thing I knew, the thing took off and I no longer felt inclined to invest time and energy on the streets. I had to sort a few things out. For all my speed-freak Aries impulsiveness, I am a plodder; actually, my Mercury conjunct with Saturn is in Aries, too, so I like to get things sorted before I leap. I do not like to waste other people's time and energy. I will not waste mine.

"The writing of *The Salt Eaters* was bizarre. I'll spare you the saga of the starts and fits and stutterings for the length of a year. I began with such a simple story line—to investigate possible ways to bring our technicians of the sacred and our guerillas together. A Mardi Gras society elects to reenact an old slave insurrection in a town torn by wildcat strikes, social service cutbacks, etc. All hell breaks loose. I'm sliding along the paper, writing

Softcover for the 1982 collection of short stories.

about some old Willie Bobo on the box and, next thing I know, my characters are talking in tongues; the street signs are changing on me. The terrain shifts, and I'm in Brazil somewhere speaking Portuguese. I should mention that I've not been to Brazil yet, and I do not speak Portuguese. I didn't panic. It was no news to me that stuff comes from out there somewhere. I dashed off about thirty pages of this stuff, then hit the library to check it out. I had to put the novel aside twice; but finally, one day I'm walking out in the woods that some folks here call a front yard, and I slumped down next to my favorite tree and just said, 'Okay, I'm stepping aside, y'all. I'm getting out of the way. What is the story I'm supposed to be telling? Tell me.' Then I wrote *The Salt Eaters*. It was a trip to find the narrator's stance. I didn't want merely a witness or a camera eye. Omniscient author never has attracted me; he or she presumes too much. First person was out because I'm interested in a group of people. Narrator as part-time participant was rejected, too. Finally, I found a place to sit, to stand, and a way to be—the narrator as medium through whom the people unfold the stories, and the town telling as much of its story as can be told in the space of one book."[1]

1980. Consultant for the National Endowment for the Arts. The novel *The Salt Eaters* was published and dedicated to "my first friend, teacher, map maker, landscape aide—Mama Helen Brent Henderson Cade Brehon—who in 1948, having come upon me daydreaming in the middle of the kitchen floor, mopped around me.

"Bless the workers and beam on me if you please."[5]

Bambara described the sources for her work. "Different stories have different sources. Poets, for example, frequently hear a line—just a hip line—and they may play with it; chew on it all day, or for a week. And they just build the whole poem around it just to give it a setting or have an occasion for getting that line off.

"Some stories have for me very clear memories in terms of source. For example, the title story from the collection, *The Sea Birds Are Still Alive* came out of anecdotes, tales, and stories that people in Vietnam and Laos shared with me in the summer of '75 when I was visiting southeast Asia. There's a line of the narrator in a section where the little girl resists torture and interrogation because she remembers what the old folks taught her about revolution—you can amend past crimes and be human again. What you do and don't do matters very much for the ancestors and for the contemporary people and for the yet unborn children. That line actually came from an old revolutionary that I interviewed in Vietnam.

"The title story of the first collection *Gorilla, My Love* is about betrayal. It's about the careless way in which grownups violate the contract between grownups and children. In the case of this story, an uncle promised a little girl that he would marry her when he grew up. He was just teasing, but she was quite serious. That story had its source in an event that occurred in New York and Brooklyn, in about 1950 something. I had gone to a puppet show that the children were putting on. The children were all ready with their puppets and seated in the front row. They were ready to begin, but the adult coordinator of the program kept looking at her watch and said, 'We'll wait a few more minutes for the people to get here.' This bewildered the children who thought they were people, and

thought they were important enough to start their own program. That started me thinking how often we do that. That kind of nonchalant little murder we commit. Simply because kids are kids and they're little and can't take us to court."[6]

Bambara's ideal audience "is really the people. The audience that gives me the most feedback tends to be folks I run across in the wash house or on the bus or on a train or just sort of traveling around. People who write letters usually on the back of something. And I think it's because their response is straight. It's not a review; it's not a critique; it's not professional. It's just a straight or gut response. I've had people stop me in the street and say, 'Look, I just read something and I want to pick a bone with you because I don't think that's how it happens and I doubt this and what about so and so.' Or people who stop me and just sort of grab me by the shoulders, kiss me on the cheek, and say, 'I really like the way you did justice to that farmer or that beauty parlor lady because nobody does justice to those people and I'm glad you did that.' That kind of feedback; that kind of audience is my very best audience. The community that calls me sister or daughter or Mama can make or break me because it's only that group that I'm serving. If that audience is not reached there's almost no point in doing it."[6]

1981. While working as a consultant for the Georgia State Arts Council and the Black Arts South Conference, she won the American Book Award for *The Salt Eaters*.

Combining her background in performance with her writing, Bambara began to work on screenplays and plays, producing several documentaries. "What is noticeable to me about my current writing is the stretch out toward the future. I'm not interested in reworking memories and playing with flashbacks. I'm trying to press the English language, particularly verb tenses and modes, to accommodate flash-forwards and potential happenings. I get more and more impatient, though, with verbal language, print conventions, literary protocol and the like; I'm much more interested in filmmaking. Quite frankly, I've always considered myself a film person. I am a fanatic movie watcher, and my favorite place to be these days is in a screening room, or better yet, in the editing room with those little Mickey Mouse gloves on. There's not too much more I want to experiment with in terms of writing. It gives me pleasure, insight, keeps me centered, sane. But, oh, to get my hands on some movie equipment.

"An awful lot of my stories, particularly the first-person riffs and bebop pieces, were written, I suspect, with performance in mind. I still recall the old days, back in the fifties, looking for some damn thing to use in auditions. There's just so much you can do with Sojourners' 'Ain't I a Woman' and trying to recast Medea as a New Orleans swamp hag. It does my heart good to have Ruby Dee swoop down on me—which she manages to do somehow, that Amazon of small proportions—for writing things like 'Witchbird,' an eminently performable story about a mature woman—as they say in the fashion ads—tired of being cast as mammy or earthmother of us all. I've started a lot of plays, mainly because I can't bear the idea of sisters like Rosalind Cash, Gloria Foster, Barbara O. Jones—the list goes on—saddled with crap or given no scripts at all. But finally, I think I will be moving into film production because I want to do it right; I want to script *Marie Laveau* for Barbara O. Jones and do *Harper's Ferry* with the correct cast of characters—Harriet Tubman, Mary Ellen or Mammy Pleasants, Frederick Douglass, the Virginia brothers and sisters waiting to be armed. Now can't you just see Verta Mae and Maya Angelou and William Marshall and Al Freeman, Jr., in a movie such as that?

"My interests have evolved, but my typing hasn't gotten any better. I no longer have the patience to sit it out in the solitude of my backroom, all by my lonesome self, knocking out books. I'm much more at home with a crew swapping insights, brilliances, pooling resources, information. My main interest of the moment, then, is to make films."[1]

1986. Won the Documentary Award from the Pennsylvania Association of Broadcasters and the Documentary Award from the National Black Programming Consortium, both for "The Bombing of Osage," produced by WHYY-TV. But Bambara remains a writer, and describes her working method: "There's no particular routine to my writing, nor have any two stories come to me the same way. I'm usually working on five or six things at a time; that is, I scribble a lot in bits and pieces and generally pin them together with a working title. The actual sit-down work is still weird to me. I babble along, heading I think in one direction, only to discover myself tugged in another, or sometimes I'm absolutely snatched into an alley. I write in longhand or what kin and friends call deranged hieroglyphics. I begin on long, yellow paper with a juicy ballpoint if it's one of those 6/8 bop pieces. For slow, steady, watch-the-voice-kid, don't-let-the-mask-slip-type pieces, I prefer short, fat-lined white paper and an ink pen. I usually work it over and beat it up and sling it around the room a lot before I get to the typing stage. I hate to type—hate, hate—so things get cut mercilessly at that stage. I stick the thing in a drawer or pin it on a board for a while, maybe read it to someone or a group, get some feedback, mull it over, and put it aside. Then, when an editor calls me to say, 'Got anything?' or I find the desk cluttered, or some reader sends a letter asking, 'You still breathing?' or 'I need some dough,' I'll very studiously sit down, edit, type, and send the damn thing out before it drives me crazy.

"I lose a lot of stuff; that is, there are gobs of scripts and stories that have gotten dumped in the garbage when I've moved, and I move a lot. My friend, Jan, was narrating a story I did years ago and someone asked, 'Where can I find it?' Damned if I know. It was typed beautifully, too, but it was twenty-four pages long. Who can afford to print it? It'll either turn up or not. Nothing is ever lost, it seems to me. Besides, I can't keep up with half the stuff in my head. That's why I love to be in workshops. There are frequently writers who get stumped, who dry up and haven't a clue. Then, here I come talking about this idea and that scenario—so things aren't really lost."[1]

Bambara's advice to other writers includes what she often says at her writing workshops: "Experiment with new material, I've often encouraged at workshops. Let rice paper and a bamboo drawing stick seduce you into a haiku. Get cozy with some brown wrapping paper. Try out a felt-point italic pen. Compose with a brush. Write on the back of posters. Visit the paper mills, ransack the art-supply shops. I recall from years of teaching freshman English, particularly at Rutgers/Livingston, that students did remarkably better work once they found materials that suited them. Spiral notebooks felt like braces on the teeth to some. Legal pads reminded one too much of a probation officer. Soft black zippered loose-leafs the welfare investigator's badge. Steno pads too confining. Red margins a straitjacket. Blue exam books, even for rough drafts, caused tremors. I'd accept assignments on the back of somebody else's stationery, on newsprint, on whatever. The issue was not economics—though all of us were broke—but affinity. The issue in workshops with poets and prosers who've lost their voice writing term papers or dissertations was—newness. If the usual tools were notebooks and ball-points, try sketch pads and pens, index cards and felt-points."[3]

And, in another interview, she offered this advice: "I have no shrewd advice to offer developing writers about this business of snatching time and space to work. I do not have anything profound to offer mother-writers or worker-writers except to say that it will cost you something. Anything of value is going to cost you something. I'm not much of a caretaker, for example, in relationships. I am not consistent about giving vibrancy and other kinds of input to a relationship. I don't always remember the birthdays, the anniversaries. There are periods when I am the most attentive and thoughtful lover in the world, and periods, too, when I am just unavailable. I have never learned, not yet anyway, to apologize for or continually give reassurance about what I'm doing. I'm not terribly accountable or very sensitive to other people's sense of being beat back, cut out, blocked, shunted off. I will have to learn because the experience of *The Salt Eaters* tells me that I will be getting into that long-haul writing again, soon and often.

"I've had occasion, as you can well imagine, to talk about just this thing with sister writers. How do the children handle your 'absence'—standing at the stove flipping them buckwheats but being totally elsewhere? How does your man deal with the fact that you are just not there and it's nothing personal? Atrocity tales, honey, and sad. I've known playwrights, artists, filmmakers—brothers I'm talking about—who just do not understand, or maybe pretend not to understand, that mad fit that gets hold of me and makes me prefer working all night and morning at the typewriter to playing poker or going dancing. It's a trip. But some years ago, I promised myself a period of five years to tackle this writing business in a serious manner. It's a priority item now—to master the craft, to produce, to stick to it no matter how many committee meetings get missed.

"My situation isn't nearly as chary as others I know. I'm not a wife, and my daughter couldn't care less what the house looks like as long as the hamper isn't overflowing. I'm not a husband; I do not have the responsibility of trying to live up to 'provider.' I'm not committed to any notion of 'career.' Also, I'm not addicted to anything—furniture, cars, wardrobe, etc.—so there's no sense of sacrifice or foolishness about how I spend my time in non-money-making pursuits. Furthermore, I don't feel obliged to structure my life in respectably routine ways; that is to say, I do not mind being perceived as a 'weirdo' or whatever. My situation is, perhaps, not very characteristic; I don't know. But to answer the question—I just flat out announce I'm working, leave me alone and get out of my face. When I 'surface' again, I try to apply the poultices and patch up the holes I've left in relationships around me. That's as much as I know how to do. . .so far."[1]

When asked why she writes, Bambara answered: "I'm compelled to write. It's my meditation. Some people have mantras; others go to therapists. Different people have different ways to maintain a balance of sanity. I write because I must. If I didn't I'd probably be homicidal in two weeks. I write because I've got hold of something. If I write I may save somebody else some time—might lift someone's spirits. I don't write because it's a career. If there were no more presses, no more publishing houses, I'd still be writing."[6]

Footnote Sources:

[1] Claudia Tate, "Toni Cade Bambara," *Black Women Writers at Work*, Continuum, 1983.
[2] Beverly Guy-Sheftall and others, "Commitment: Toni Cade Bambara Speaks," *Sturdy Black Bridges: Visions of Black Women in Literature*, Anchor Books, 1979.
[3] Toni Cade Bambara, "Salvation Is the Issue," *Black Women Writers (1950-1980): A Critical Evaluation*, edited by Mari Evans, Anchor Books, 1984.
[4] T. C. Bambara, "What It Is I Think I'm Doing Anyhow," *The Writer on Her Work*, edited by Janet Sternburg, Norton, 1980.
[5] T. C. Bambara, *The Salt Eaters*, Random House, 1980.
[6] Kay Bonetti, "The Organizer's Wife: A Reading by and Interview with Toni Cade Bambara," American Audio Prose Library, February 2, 1982.

■ For More Information See

Addison Gayle, Jr., editor, *Black Expression: Essays by and about Black Americans in the Creative Arts*, Weybright, 1969.
New York Times Book Review, February 21, 1971, May 2, 1971, November 7, 1971, October 15, 1972, December 3, 1972, March 27, 1977 (p. 7), June 1, 1980 (p. 14), November 1, 1981.
New York Times, October 11, 1972, October 15, 1972, April 4, 1980.
Saturday Review, November 18, 1972, December 2, 1972 (p. 97ff), April 12, 1980 (p. 40ff).
Sewanee Review, November 18, 1972, December 2, 1972.
Village Voice, April 12, 1973 (p. 39ff).
Black World, July, 1973.
Redbook, September, 1973 (p. 73ff).
Washington Post Book World, November 18, 1973, March 30, 1980 (p. 1ff).
Newsweek, May 2, 1977.
National Observer, May 9, 1977 (p. 23).
Ms., July, 1977 (p. 36ff), July, 1980 (p. 28ff).
Chicago Tribune Book World, March 23, 1980.
Los Angeles Times Book Review, May 4, 1980.
New Yorker, May 5, 1980 (p. 169ff).

Encore, June, 1980.
First World, fall, 1980 (p. 48ff).
Paul Connolly, *On Essays: A Reader for Writers,* Harper, 1981.
Drum, spring, 1982.
Times Literary Supplement, June 18, 1982, September 27, 1985.
Ebony, November, 1984 (p. 59ff).

Contemporary Literary Criticism, Volume 29, Gale, 1984.
Peggy Whitman Prenshaw, editor, *Women Writers of the Contemporary South,* University Press of Mississippi, 1984.
Dictionary of Literary Biography, Volume 38: *Afro-American Writers after 1955: Dramatists and Prose Writers,* Gale, 1985.

Berke Breathed

S urname rhymes with "method"; born June 21, 1957, in Encino, Calif.; son of John W. (an oil equipment executive) and Jane (a housewife; maiden name, Martin) Breathed; married Jody Boyman (a photographer), May 10, 1986. *Education:* University of Texas at Austin, B.A., 1979. *Politics:* "Middle-winger." *Religion:* Agnostic. *Agent:* Esther Newberg, International Creative Management, 40 West 57th St., New York, N.Y. 10019. *Office:* c/o Washington Post Writer's Group, 1150 15th St., NW, Washington, D.C. 20071.

■ Career

University of Texas at Austin, photographer and columnist for *Daily Texan* (university newspaper), 1976-78; cartoonist and writer, 1978—.

■ Awards, Honors

Harry A. Schweikert, Jr. Disability Awareness Award from the Paralyzed Veterans of America, 1982, and Pulitzer Prize for Editorial Cartooning, 1987, both for comic strip "Bloom County"; Fund for Animals Genisis Award, 1990, for "outstanding cartoonist focusing on animal welfare issues."

■ Writings

Comics:

Bloom County: "Loose Tails," Little, Brown, 1983.
Toons for Our Times: A Bloom County Book, Little, Brown, 1984.
Penguin Dreams: And Stranger Things, Little, Brown, 1985.
Bloom County Babylon: Five Years of Basic Naughtiness, Little, Brown, 1986.
Billy and the Boingers Bootleg, Little, Brown, 1987.
Tales Too Ticklish to Tell, Little, Brown, 1988.
The Night of the Mary Kay Commandos: Featuring Smell-O-Toons, Little, Brown, 1989.
Happy Trails, Little, Brown, 1990.

Author and artist of "Bloom County," a comic strip syndicated by Washington Post Writer's Group, 1980-89, and "Outland," 1989—. Author and artist of "Opus Goes Home," *Life,* May, 1987.

■ Work in Progress

Various film and book projects.

■ Sidelights

The comic strip "Bloom County" first appeared in 1980, earning its creator, Berke Breathed, a Pulitzer Prize for Editorial Cartooning. Just a year out of college when he approached major newspaper syndicates with two anthologies of his work, Breathed was roundly rejected. Then a call from the *Washington Post* reached the *Daily Texan*

From *'Toons for Our Times, A Bloom County Book of Heavy Meadow Rump 'n' Roll* by Berke Breathed.

offices; sales manager Al Leeds was looking for someone to create a new strip. He commissioned Breathed. "[Leeds] had confidence I'd come up with something and hadn't the faintest idea what would work. They took what I gave them. No one at the *Post*, except Al Leeds, had anything nice to say about the future of the strip.

"I did not want to draw a very easily defined strip—which made it very difficult to sell. 'Bloom County' could not be summarized in one sentence, like 'Garfield: A cat who hates the world.' The only thing I was sure I wanted to do was write about current events and topicality. Those were not things the salesman at the syndicate wanted to hear."[1]

"I got 100 dollars a month for a while, did other things to make a living, and considered drawing a comic strip just as natural as waking up and brushing my teeth. I did the strip that day, and I'm through, and I go on. I had no larger visions of what I wanted, I certainly never thought it would make me any money. Money and the comic strips never was an association before. It didn't even occur to me that there was much of a reward materially and financially from doing this thing. And I was compounded with people on all sides, especially on the business end, especially at the Washington Post Writers Group, telling me that I had no business thinking I was going to be a success, much less be around in a year.

"The statistics of survival on the comic page are dismal. They're worse than any other profession. Worse than going to Hollywood thinking you're going to be an actor. The chances of just getting syndicated, out of the number of submissions, is like 1 in 1,000 for any one syndicate. They get a thousand submissions before they usually try to sell one.

"And out of all those submissions that are tried every year, for all the new strips that enter the market every year, one out of fifty survives. So you add that up, and these are astronomical odds.

"I ended up doing a comic strip, because it was the most effective way to make a point and get people listening, as a writer. I've always had an over-active imagination, and it could have been applied to almost any medium. I don't know if successfully, but it certainly was working when I tried out a comic strip in college. I was a writer for the paper, an avid photographer, and a columnist. I loved the idea of expressing myself in a mass medium. That became interesting to me in itself. And cartooning, in particular, drew me because when I tried it, it was clearly apparent that the potential of it was far more than the other mediums I had been trying. Photography or illustration or just writing. When you drew a figure next to your words, it had an element of attraction for people that was unimaginable to me at the time. You draw to your strengths. It was quite clear where I was getting the attention from. And so I was drawn into drawing comic strips. I knew nothing about them. I didn't understand the dynamics of a comic strip at all, and it took me years even to begin to. I'm just beginning to grasp what it is now, because, again, I'm not a fan. I'm constantly running into these people that know far more about the way comic panels work or cartoon panels work than I do. So it's been tougher for me, I think, to get into the heads of the people that really follow this stuff and care about it.

"I'm always amazed when I get these people who care about Opus ['Bloom County's' main character], and tell me that their lives have changed because of what they've seen, what experiences my characters have gone through. I'm just bowled over by that. Some cartoonists have gotten used to it. It's certainly not just distinctive of my strip. Imagine the people who have been touched by 'Peanuts' through those thirty-five years. When Charlie Brown went through some of his ordeals, there were millions of people that identified with it and felt comforted by it. And that's the kind of power that I'm just beginning to grasp and appreciate. Not that it's there in 'Bloom County,' but it's there in an element. And it's nothing that I could ever have appreciated myself."[2]

"[Trudeau's] 'Doonesbury' is the only one that had an active influence on me, especially in my college years. I hadn't read strips before 'Doonesbury.' Others had an influence on me later. 'Pogo' in its drawing; and 'Peanuts' in more subtle things such as characterization and pacing."[3]

"The only people who still consider me to be in the shadow of the Trudeau strip are Trudeau and his syndicate, really. He obviously influenced me in the beginning, but Feiffer was an inordinate influence on him—and Feiffer's upset about that. Everyone's upset about being copied."[4]

Breathed doesn't consider himself a "political" cartoonist: "A few years ago everyone was throwing around dumb political commentary on the comics page. It made me pull back. I saw it being done so badly—I mean, it's so easy to say about the politics of the day. I'd better have some unusual insight to offer. I go out of my way not to mention Reagan's name. If there's any way I can do it through metaphor or generalities, I will."[4]

"There's a distinction between my personal feelings and my role as a satirist. My feelings were not unambiguous in the strips, but expressing those feelings was clearly not the only reason for the strips. The issues dealt with are very relevant today and are being seriously debated in society. Also, I hadn't seen any other comic satire on those issues, and that made them all the more appealing as topics. It wasn't that I just wanted to get something off my chest. If I feel like that, alarm bells ring and I tend to pull back.

"I'm finding I'm now less and less interested in political commentary, even though I like politics. I'm finding politics harder and harder to write about, because most political happenings end as

A "Bloom County" strip, circa 1982.

soon as they come up, and their impact is minimal. They're too boring and transitional, and they're no more important than whoever is on the cover of *People* magazine at any given moment."[3]

"If ['Bloom County'] was truly a political strip, it wouldn't exist. Many editors won't put up with much editorial comment on the comics page. So you have to slip it under the door, through metaphor and subtlety and my particular fashion, which is silliness."[4]

In 1987, Breathed was awarded the Pulitzer Prize for Editorial Cartooning, a decision which elicited angry responses from many sources, and, in particular, the most vocal criticism from Pulitzer-Prize-winning cartoonist Pat Oliphant: "The Pulitzer for editorial cartooning was awarded to a highly derivative comic strip which has, as far as I know, not appeared on one editorial page in the country.

"The work makes no pretense of being editorial. It is on the funny pages. It does, however, make the pretense of passing off shrill potty jokes and grade-school sight gags as social commentary.

"The Pulitzer has now officially ceased to be an award for excellence in editorial and political art. Instead it has become simply a popularity contest and syndicate marketing tool. If a cartoonist wants to increase his own circulation—and who doesn't—the quickest ticket is to win a Pulitzer. From now on, to win a Pulitzer, be light, be funny, be vacuous, and be inane. Don't offend any person or institution. Don't take a stand. That's where we're headed."[5]

Breathed admitted that "it would be vastly insincere of me to try to pretend I didn't care that some of the people in the world who I admired most as artists were telling me to jump in the lake as far as my talent was concerned. There was no way that that could not be hurtful. What I didn't want to do was sound like a martyr, but I also didn't want them to think that this stuff just all rolled off like water. Of all the people that were critizing my work, or what came off or was interpreted as criticism of my style beyond the fact that I won a Pulitzer, these were the wrong people to say it, for me not to care. I don't know any artist, if he was speaking honestly, who could say that he wouldn't care that many of his peers whom he admired were critizing his work so vociferously."[2]

"I remember, specifically, the moment it occurred to me to submit 'Bloom County' to the Pulitzer committee in 1987. I was in the Evergreen, Colorado Public Library and I had just read the official requirements for winning the Pulitzer Prize for Editorial Cartooning. It was about a paragraph long and nary a mention the word 'political' or 'politics' or even editorial: just something vaguely wishy-washy about being to the benefit of society."[6]

"The Pulitzer definition, the criteria for the award, is about the most ambiguous statement I have ever seen. Technically I had all the right in the world to enter and win....But the cartoonists weren't concerned with that. They had created their own image of what or who the award should be given to, from a heritage of fifty years of them winning. So, their quest to define exactly what a correct political cartoon is, I think, dangerous. And self-defeating.

"The problem is I wear different hats all the time, that's why I like being on the comic page. If you're a political cartoonist, you've got to be hitting them every single day, and in a way, that tempers people's attention. When you're hitting every single day, different people maybe, but you're always hitting, readers approach the strip asking, 'All right, so who is he hitting today?' Like Ben Sargent says, the [preferable] ability is to pull back and not say anything nasty about anybody until they *really* do something bad. He was saying, if you're a liberal, and you've got a liberal in power, you don't have this compunction to hit him every single day. But when they *do* do something that you don't approve of, or their critics do something, then you go after them, and people perk up and pay attention. 'They must have really done something for Ben Sargent to be going down so hard on them today.' That's exactly how it is on the comics page, I think, in a related way. I'm not expected to play the editorialist or the 'graphic commentator' (as I like to say) every day until something really inspires me to do so. Or inspires my characters to do so. So the readers aren't being pummelled over their heads constantly with too much satire, or too much criticism. Essentially, graphic commentary is criticism, and too much criticism turns people off.

"I may have my characters react to administration policies one week, and then have them worried about nosejobs the next. It looks a little silly on the editorial page. What I enjoy about being on the comic page, is that you can flip back and forth. If you're on the op-ed page, the intent is for you to be serious all the time.

"The criticism that I think is perfectly fair about my strip is that it's lacking in female characters. And that's right on the money. I've had trouble

Poster for the 1989 annual festival that closes New York's Fifth Avenue, opening it to book lovers, authors, and publishers.

with female characters that were there but didn't represent womanhood in general. It's very difficult to have in this horrifically image-conscious nation. If you notice there are a lot more black characters on television shows now. And it's only recently that any ensemble show has had blacks and hispanic characters and women acting as *realistic* characters with all the problems that the rest of us have. For instance, in 'Hill Street Blues,' they had two black cops in the ensemble cast. Both of them were always the flag-bearers for honesty and reasonableness, and the tempering effect of the wild behavior of their partners. And that's typical of how television has approached minorities. I know exactly what those writers are feeling. I couldn't put black characters in my strip that acted as negative or silly as Steve Dallas. They'd become icons for something much larger; women are the same way. It's frustrating. That's not to say it *can't* be done successfully. Charles Schulz did it perfectly with Lucy. She represented women in a less than flattering light, but also in a very realistic way. An aspect of womanhood that people could identify with. It's not to excuse myself, but it is much more difficult to come up with characters that are anything but white males that have an interesting edge to them. Because they become an icon for something much larger than they're supposed to be.

"If I brought a woman in now, I'd probably bring her in as an anti-feminist—one of these women that have decided to buck the whole feminist thing entirely and go back to thinking what they really want is just a good man and old traditional values. It would be funnier to find that that image is just as false as the false feminist issue, about having it all. You're always looking for playing against society at whatever point it is. In that sense, hopefully I'm maturing in characterization."[2]

Despite the enormous popularity of "Bloom County," Breathed has kept a perspective on what it means to be a media hero. "The truth is that the only 'cult following' my comic strip (has) had…consisted of my mother. Bless her heart, she still reads it daily. She'll hand the funny page to me, point to it, scrunch her eyes together and say, 'Honey, what were you trying to say here?' If Opus spits watermelon seeds at Milo, she'll say to me, 'So this is a sort of comment on the watermelon industry?' So you see, to my publisher and to my mother, I remain a victim of unrealistic expectations."[7]

"The only time that I could begin to believe that we're having any effect or leaving an impression on people's life is in regards to how we comic strip cartoonists affect people with our characters. Completely separate from any issues we may be talking about or any opinions that are expressed, or any ironies that we reveal to the reader. The emotions and the experiences that some of our characters go through, depending on the strip, will have untoward and unimaginable effects on my readers,

BLOOM COUNTY

Breathed's July 29, 1989 strip.

BLOOM COUNTY

"Bloom County's" farewell strip, August 6, 1989.

something that I can't often fathom. I'll get letters written *to* Opus from people who really believe ninety percent that they're writing to Opus as they know him in the comic strip. Telling him how he has touched their lives in a certain way. How something that's happened to him happened to them as well and how they can better grasp and understand and deal with it better because he did it in a certain way. That's when it hits that those of us on the comic page have much more power and much more influence than anybody on the op-ed page.

"They believe [Opus] exists just like they believe Cary Grant is exactly how they saw him on the screen. They know deep down, intellectually, that he isn't, but emotionally, their right side of the brain is telling them because that's how they want to believe. When they write to Opus, they don't really think that Opus is reading it. But they don't want to write to me, they don't want to write to the reality behind Opus, they want to write to me as if I'm Opus. And I've even had journalists who called up and wanted an interview, and I told them I was unable to—I'm thinking of a specific instance—that person's reaction to me turning them down for essentially a favor was: 'I thought I was talking to Opus, I thought I was talking to the kind of person that Opus is.'"[2]

Breathed draws upon many sources for inspiration in the creation of his characters. One of the most controversial of these was the modeling of Ashley

Dashly III after Ted Turner, president of Turner Broadcasting System. "I was blown over by him. Disgusted and charmed at the same time. It was 'the world according to Ted Turner.' He was caricaturing himself with some deliberation. He is a real-life character—and they are rare these days. He succeeds in everything. He has become a large-mouthed individualist who has used his individualism as a tool to succeed where others fail."[8]

Yet unlike other cartoonists, Breathed says he never bases a character on himself. "I've never really put myself in a strip. I used to find that obnoxious when people did that, and I don't any more. A good novelist will put a large part of himself in his characters. Or even just one. Cathy Guisewite puts herself, as far as I can tell, in 'Cathy.' And I saw that almost too much in her, in drawing that much of an autobiographical strip, I found it even more intrusive than a comic strip already is in your life. You can't help but putting your own personal feelings and experiences in a comic. Sometimes I find it an invasion of privacy when I see that I'm that visible in the strip. And if I had myself there, clearly, blatantly, I would be really embarrassed. I would feel like I had no privacy left at all.

"But I've changed my view on that. I have something in mind where I'd like to create a character that I can go back in my own experiences—like any good writer, if I can presume that I could become a good writer—and pull out the ones that had an impression on me, and work it into a separate character and see if people identify with that. It's the oldest trick in the book, but if it's done well, those usually are the characters and the books that mean that much. I mean, Holden Caulfield was Salinger. For some reason people identify. I don't think he could have created that character if he hadn't pulled it from himself. They always seem to ring the truest."[2]

Breathed's process has developed over the years, and he is self-critical, even about that. "I come home with ideas every day, all sorts. But I dispose of most of them. I sit with a tablet in front of me and sketch the characters saying the dialogue. I have to see them saying it, or it makes no sense to me.

"Sometimes you'll see an advertisement in the strip, sometimes the characters will step out of character and address the comic audience as if they were an employee of me, the management of Bloom County. I want the strip to be unpredictable. Those are the only preconditions I lay out for myself."[1]

"Sometimes you lose sight of just the pure number of your readers. When you consider that fifty million people potentially are reading you every day, it makes you put a little bit more effort into what you say. In my case, I refuse to let a strip go out that is not exactly drawn perfectly as far as I'm concerned—with much more detail than it needs—because I'm thinking about all these people. I can't just spend an hour drawing this thing. I've got to spend three hours getting everything right. Of course, if I was to look at it printed the next day, I would realize why I shouldn't have. But psychologically, I have to remind myself what the influence of any one strip can be, and thus I give it the attention that it's due.

"So I'm drawing every week. I'm not drawing every day, but I have a deadline every single week. If there was a death in my family, for instance, I can't call up the syndicate and say, 'I just can't draw for the next three weeks.' That's never happened to me, nothing that bad. The only thing that's really happened to me is personal injury where I physically couldn't draw. But if my marriage was breaking up, I would have to keep drawing. And there [are] plenty of cartoonists I know who are going on through that right now. And their deadlines are expected and they're expected to meet them. So you can't look at those times and think you're going to be doing your best material. It's just going to happen. But what's nice

is that you don't have to worry about your ratings dropping. There's not ratings figures that are coming in the next week reflecting the fact that our show was bad. And you're given a lot of rope for those kinds of fluctuations in people's lives, in their creative output."[2]

Deadlines are not the only pressures with which Breathed has to contend. "Normally, if a paper in an elderly or conservative community sees a potentially offensive word or expression, the editors will pull or edit the piece, arguing that they're editing it just as they'd edit a column."[3]

"They feel completely free at taking a knife to my dialogue and putting in words that they think are more proper. And for those of us in this business, it's a complete outrage. It's hard for us to find out about it, until a fan usually notices that a strip he read today wasn't the same one that he read in another newspaper, dialogue-wise, and he'll send it to me. And at that point, we'll contact the paper and tell them that if it happens again, we'll pull the strip. We can only [make that threat], quite honestly, if the feature is strong and has a lot of public support. That's the kind of thing that drives us absolutely nuts, because for every [editor] that I find changing dialogue, there's got to be twenty more. Sometimes they just cut out a whole balloon of dialogue so you never knew that anyone was talking in that particular panel. It makes the strip make no sense at all, but it saves them the controversy of pulling the entire thing and having people call into them. They've discovered that this is the way to really handle a controversial comic strip.

"You know who the syndicates are looking for? They're looking for the dissatisfied stockbroker, sitting in his office right now, he's about thirty years old, thinking how funny it is, there's all these office things going on around him, with computers and stuff. And he can draw a little bit. *A little bit.* He's got the gags in his mind because he lived them. He's going to start drawing comic strips, and he sends the stuff off to the syndicate. Even though they're badly drawn, it doesn't matter because they're all reduced down to sub-microscopic size. And they start the comic strip. I have seen so many of these come across my desk in the past five years, and I've seen them syndicated as well. They never last very long. But they hit fast, they've got a good gimmick, they've probably got a hook that sounds good to editors. Syndicates can sell them fast.

"Now, again, I don't want to get in this business of defining what a good comic strip is. I can see the

First strip of Breathed's new comic, "Outland," September 10, 1989.

danger there. In fact, I can't even say that good artistry is complex, because 'Peanuts' has more expressiveness, or especially had in the older days, than most comics, than even 'Prince Valiant.' There's just as much expressiveness in Charlie Brown's eyes when he's laying on the baseball mound after he's been hit with a baseball, as anything you can see anywhere else. The talent that's obviously apparent in Charles Schulz is not necessarily the talent that's come into the pages these days."[2]

"Someday I'd like to draw on a local level again where I know exactly who is reading my strip and I can put them into it. If I ever get to a point of independent security, I will probably quit the national strip and go to a town like San Francisco where there are competing newspapers. That would be much more satisfying, much more fun."[1]

Breathed has considered branching out, into television, novels, and even film, but has become discouraged. "There have been plenty of producers that have gone to the networks and said, listen, we can put something together. And they said, no way. If the political cartoonists don't think 'Bloom County' is controversial or political, the networks certainly do. Very little interest. They do tend to go for the middle-of-the-road stuff.

"I've given up the idea of going into film. I can see that these poor young people who think they want to go into film don't understand Hollywood, and the frustrations from a creative point. Unless you're Spielberg, it's almost not worth your while, risking the frustrations that are inevitable in working in television or movies. The compromises you have to make are so breathtaking that you have to love it an awful lot to put up with it. After having as much freedom as I've had, I don't think I could deal with it."[2]

Ironically, in May, 1989 Breathed announced the upcoming demise of his cartoon. "A good comic strip is no more eternal than a ripe melon. The ugly truth is that in most cases, comics age even less gracefully than their creators. 'Bloom County' is retiring before the stretch marks show."[9]

"I'm. . .too young to coast. I could draw 'Bloom County' with my nose and pay my cleaning lady to write it, and I'd bet I wouldn't lose ten percent of my papers over the next twenty years. Such is the nature of comic strips. Once established, their half-life is usually more than nuclear waste. Typically, the end result is lazy, rich cartoonists. There are worse things to be, I suppose. . .lazy and poor comes to mind."[10]

Considered the cartoon of the eighties, "Bloom County" appeared in nearly 1000 newspapers nationwide, and made its final appearance on August 6, 1989. However, on September 3, 1989 Breathed's new Sunday-only strip "Outland," made its debut. He recognized the challenge that lay ahead in creating an entirely new comic strip. "I am competing with the readers' affection for a dead strip whose body is still warm. The readers and editors are mad and don't seem to be in a mood for anything but the old meadow and dandelions. But until I am booted off the page, I am having a ball. My relatives, of course, think my mind went out with last week's meat loaf."[10]

Nonetheless, Breathed is hopeful that his work continues to touch people's lives. "If someone sticks my comic strip on their refrigerator door, it's like that person [is] saying: 'This is my life, he's writing about me.'"[11]

Footnote Sources:

[1] Jon Bowermaster, "Lifestyles: Extra! Penguin's Alter Ego Wins Pulitzer," *Texas Monthly*, June, 1987.
[2] "Interview: Can Breathed Be Taken Seriously?," *Comics Journal*, October, 1988.
[3] Wayne Pacelle, "Animal Rights in Bloom: An Interview with Berke Breathed," *Animals Agenda*, July/August, 1989.
[4] Alan Prendergast, "Of Penguins and Pulitzers: No Laughing Matter," *Washington Journalism Review*, October, 1987.
[5] David Astor, "Oliphant Blasts Pulitzer Board for Picking Breathed," *Editor & Publisher*, May 23, 1987.
[6] Berke Breathed, "Pariah Speaks," *Comics Journal*, August, 1988.
[7] B. Breathed, *Bloom County: "Loose Tails,"* Little, Brown, 1983.
[8] Pat Dickey, "Nailing Ted," *Atlanta*, November, 1981.
[9] "Media," *Newsweek*, May 15, 1989.
[10] *Time*, December 25, 1989.
[11] Gail Buchalter, "Cartoonist Berke Breathed Feathers His Nest by Populating 'Bloom County' with Rare Birds," *People Weekly*, August 6, 1984.

■ For More Information See

Washington Post Book World, April 24, 1983, August 24, 1986, August 23, 1987.
Washington Journalism Review, May, 1983.
Los Angeles Times Book Review, May 15, 1983, May 13, 1984, October 5, 1986.
Playboy, December, 1985 (p. 214).
Detroit News, April 13, 1986.
Life, May, 1987 (p. 42ff).
Washington Post, May 9, 1987, November 12, 1987.
Editor & Publisher, May 16, 1987 (p. 42ff), January 30, 1988 (p. 33ff), June 18, 1988 (p. 66ff).
Publishers Weekly, June 19, 1987 (p. 58ff).
Interview, July, 1987 (p. 212).
Los Angeles Times, November 26, 1987.
Comics Journal, June, 1988, May, 1989 (p. 16).
New York Times, May 2, 1989 (p. D-25).
Time, May 15, 1989 (p. 77).

Eve Bunting

B orn Anne Evelyn Bolton, on December 19, 1928, in Maghera, Northern Ireland; came to the United States, 1959, became U. S. citizen; daughter of Sloan Edmund (a merchant) and Mary (a housewife; maiden name, Canning) Bolton; married Edward Davison Bunting (a business executive), April 26, 1951; children: Christine, Sloan, Glenn. *Education:* Methodist College, Belfast, graduate, 1945; also attended Queen's University, 1946-48. *Politics:* Democrat. *Religion:* Protestant. *Home and office:* 1512 Rose Villa St., Pasadena, Calif. 91106.

■ Career

Free-lance writer, mainly for young people, 1969—. Teacher of writing, University of California—Los Angeles, 1978, 1979, and at writer's conferences. *Member:* PEN International, California Writers Guild, Southern California Council on Writing for Children and Young People, Society of Children's Book Writers (board member).

■ Awards, Honors

Golden Kite Award from the Society of Children's Book Writers, Outstanding Science Trade Book for Children from the National Science Teachers Association and the Children's Book Council, and Notable Children's Trade Book in the Field of Social Studies from the National Council for Social Studies and the Children's Book Council, all 1976, all for *One More Flight; One More Flight* was selected one of Child Study Association of America's Children's Books of the Year, 1976, *The Big Red Barn,* 1979, *Goose Dinner,* and *The Waiting Game,* 1981, *The Valentine Bears,* 1986, and *The Mother's Day Mice,* and *Sixth Grade Sleepover,* 1987; *Winter's Coming* was named one of the *New York Times* Top Ten Books, 1977; Notable Work of Fiction from the Southern California Council on Literature for Children and Young People, and Golden Kite Award, both 1977, both for *Ghost of Summer;* Classroom Choice from Scholastic Paperbacks, 1978, for *Skateboards: How to Make Them, How to Ride Them.*

If I Asked You, Would You Stay? was selected one of American Library Association's Best Books for Young Adults, 1984; PEN Special Achievement Award, 1984, for her contribution to children's literature; Nene Award from the Hawaii Association of School Librarians and the Hawaii Library Association, 1986, for *Karen Kepplewhite Is the World's Best Kisser; The Mother's Day Mice* was selected one of *School Library Journal's* Best Books of the Year, 1986, and *The Wednesday Surprise,* 1989; Southern California Council on Literature for Children and Young People Award for Excellence in a Series, 1986, for "Lippincott Page Turners" series; Parents' Choice Award from the Parents' Choice Foundation, 1988, for *The Moth-*

er's Day Mice; Virginia Young Readers Award, 1988-89, California Young Readers Medal, 1989, and South Carolina Young Adult Book Award, 1988-89, all for *Face at the Edge of the World*; Southern California Council on Literature for Children and Young People Award for Outstanding Work of Fiction for Young Adults, 1989, for *A Sudden Silence*; Sequoyah Children's Book Award from the Oklahoma Library Association, Mark Twain Award from the State of Missouri, and Sunshine State Young Readers Award, all 1989, all for *Sixth Grade Sleepover*.

■ Writings

The Once-a-Year Day, Golden Gate, 1974.
The Wild One, Scholastic Book Services, 1974.
Barney the Beard (illustrated by Imero Gobbato), Parents Magazine Press, 1975.
The Skateboard Four, A. Whitman, 1976.
One More Flight (illustrated by Diane De Groat), Warne, 1976.
Blacksmith at Blueridge, Scholastic, 1976.
Josefina Finds the Prince (illustrated by Jan Palmer), Garrard, 1976.
Skateboard Saturday, Scholastic, 1976.
(With son, Glenn Bunting) *Skateboards: How to Make Them, How to Ride Them*, Harvey House, 1977.
The Big Cheese (illustrated by Sal Murdocca), Macmillan, 1977.
Winter's Coming (illustrated by Howard Knotts), Harcourt, 1977.
Ghost of Summer (Junior Literary Guild selection; illustrated by W. T. Mars), Warne, 1977.
Cop Camp, Scholastic, 1977.
The Haunting of Kildoran Abbey, Warne, 1978.
Magic and the Night River (illustrated by Allen Say), Harper, 1978.
Going against Cool Calvin, Scholastic, 1978.
The Big Find, Creative Education, 1978.
Yesterday's Island, Warne, 1979.
The Big Red Barn (illustrated by H. Knotts), Harcourt, 1979.
Blackbird Singing (illustrated by Stephen Gammell), Macmillan, 1979.
The Sea World Book of Sharks (illustrated with photographs by Flip Nicklin), Harcourt, 1979.
The Sea World Book of Whales, Harcourt, 1979.
Terrible Things (illustrated by S. Gammell), Harper, 1980, revised edition published as *Terrible Things: An Allegory of the Holocaust*, Jewish Publication Society, 1989.

St. Patrick's Day in the Morning (illustrated by Jan Brett), Seabury, 1980.
Demetrius and the Golden Goblet (illustrated by Michael Hague), Harcourt, 1980.
The Robot Birthday (illustrated by Marie DeJohn), Dutton, 1980.
The Skate Patrol, A. Whitman, 1980.
The Skate Patrol Rides Again (illustrated by Don Madden), A. Whitman, 1981.
Goose Dinner (illustrated by H. Knotts), Harcourt, 1981.
The Empty Window (illustrated by Judy Clifford), Warne, 1981.
The Happy Funeral (illustrated by Mai Vo-Dinh), Harper, 1981.
Rosie and Mr. William Star, Houghton, 1981.
Jane Martin, Dog Detective (illustrated by Amy Schwartz), Garrard, 1981.
Jane Martin and the Case of the Ice Cream Dog, Garrard, 1981.
The Spook Birds (illustrated by Blanche Sims), A. Whitman, 1981.
The Giant Squid, Messner, 1981.
The Great White Shark, Messner, 1982.
The Skate Patrol and the Mystery Writer (illustrated by D. Madden), A. Whitman, 1982.
Karen Kepplewhite Is the World's Best Kisser, Clarion, 1983.
The Traveling Men of Ballycoo (illustrated by Kaethe Zemach), Harcourt, 1983.
The Valentine Bears (illustrated by J. Brett), Clarion, 1983.
Clancy's Coat (illustrated by Lorinda Bryan Cauley), Warne, 1984.
Ghost behind Me (young adult), Archway, 1984.
The Man Who Could Call Down Owls (illustrated by Charles Mikolaycak), Macmillan, 1984.
Monkey in the Middle (illustrated by Lynn Munsinger), Harcourt, 1984.
Someone Is Hiding on Alcatraz Island, Clarion, 1984.
Surrogate Sister (young adult), Lippincott, 1984, published as *Mother, How Could You!*, Archway, 1986.
Face at the Edge of the World (young adult), Clarion, 1985.
Sixth Grade Sleepover, Harcourt, 1986.
The Mother's Day Mice (Junior Literary Guild selection; illustrated by J. Brett), Clarion, 1986.
Scary, Scary Halloween, (Junior Literary Guild selection; illustrated by J. Brett), Clarion, 1986.

Janet Hamm Needs a Date for the Dance, Clarion, 1986.

Ghost's Hour, Spook's Hour (Junior Literary Guild selection; illustrated by Donald Carrick), Clarion, 1987.

Will You Be My POSSLQ? (young adult), Harcourt, 1987.

A Sudden Silence (young adult), Harcourt, 1988.

Happy Birthday, Dear Duck (Junior Literary Guild selection; illustrated by J. Brett), Clarion, 1988.

Is Anybody There?, Lippincott, 1988.

How Many Days to America? A Thanksgiving Story (illustrated by Beth Peck), Clarion, 1988.

The Ghost Children (Junior Literary Guild selection; young adult), Clarion, 1989.

No Nap (illustrated by Susan Meddaugh), Clarion, 1989.

The Wednesday Surprise (ALA Notable Book; illustrated by D. Carrick), Clarion, 1989.

"Magic Circle" Series:

The Two Giants, Ginn, 1972.
A Gift for Lonny, Ginn, 1973.
Box, Fox, Ox and the Peacock, Ginn, 1974.
Say It Fast, Ginn, 1974.
We Need a Bigger Zoo!, Ginn, 1974.

"Dinosaur Machine" Series:

The Day of the Dinosaurs (illustrated by Judy Leo), EMC Corp., 1975.

Death of a Dinosaur (illustrated by J. Leo), EMC Corp., 1975.

The Dinosaur Trap, EMC Corp., 1975.

Escape from Tyrannosaurus (illustrated by J. Leo), EMC Corp., 1975.

"No Such Things?" Series:

The Creature of Cranberry Cove (illustrated by Scott Earle), EMC Corp., 1976.

The Demon, EMC Corp., 1976.

The Ghost (illustrated by S. Earle), EMC Corp., 1976.

The Tongue of the Ocean (illustrated by S. Earle), EMC Corp., 1976.

"Eve Bunting Science Fiction" Series:

The Day of the Earthlings, Creative Education, 1978.

The Followers (illustrated by Don Hendricks), Creative Education, 1978.

The Island of One (illustrated by D. Hendricks), Creative Education, 1978.

The Mask (illustrated by D. Hendricks), Creative Education, 1978.

The Mirror Planet (illustrated by D. Hendricks), Creative Education, 1978.

The Robot People, Creative Education, 1978.

The Space People, Creative Education, 1978.

The Undersea People, Creative Education, 1978.

"Eve Bunting Young Romance" Series:

Fifteen, Creative Education, 1978.

For Always, Creative Education, 1978.

The Girl in the Painting, Creative Education, 1978.

Just Like Everyone Else, Creative Education, 1978.

Maggie the Freak, Creative Education, 1978.

Nobody Knows but Me, Creative Education, 1978.

Oh, Rick!, Creative Education, 1978.

A Part of the Dream, Creative Education, 1978.

Survival Camp!, Creative Education, 1978.

Two Different Girls, Creative Education, 1978.

The 1988 Harcourt dust jacket.

Young Adult; "Lippincott Page Turners" Series:

The Cloverdale Switch, Lippincott, 1979, published as *Strange Things Happen in the Woods*, Harper, 1984.
The Waiting Game, Lippincott, 1981.
The Ghosts of Departure Point, Lippincott, 1982.
If I Asked You, Would You Stay?, Lippincott, 1984.
The Haunting of SafeKeep, Lippincott, 1985.

Under Name Evelyn Bolton; "Evelyn Bolton Horse Book" Series:

Stable of Fear, Creative Education, 1974.
Lady's Girl, Creative Education, 1974.
Goodbye Charlie, Creative Education, 1974.
Ride When You're Ready, Creative Education, 1974.
The Wild Horses, Creative Education, 1974.
Dream Dancer, Creative Education, 1974.

Under Name A. E. Bunting:

High Tide for Labrador (illustrated by Bernard Garbutt), Children's Press, 1975.

Under Name A. E. Bunting; "High Point" Series:

Pitcher to Center Field, Elk Grove Books, 1974.
Surfing Country, Elk Grove Books, 1975.
Springboard to Summer (illustrated by Rob Sprattler), Elk Grove Books, 1975.

Also author of stories for basal readers published by several educational houses, including Heath, Laidlaw Brothers, Lyons & Carnahan, Scott, Foresman, Bowmar Educational, Scholastic, and Rand McNally. Contributor to anthologies, including *Cricket's Choice*, 1975, and *Scribner's Anthology for Young People*. Contributor of adult and juvenile stories to periodicals, including *Jack and Jill*, and *Cricket*.

■ Adaptations

"How Many Days to America" (film), Coronet/MTI Film and Video, 1991.

■ Work in Progress

A middle grade novel concerning the dilemma and anguish of a twelve-year-old girl who discovers she and another child have been switched at birth due to a hospital's error.

■ Sidelights

Eve Bunting was born December 19, 1928 in Maghera, County Derry, Ireland. "When I was a child I lived with my parents in the small Northern Ireland town of Maghera. I guess we were rich, by the standards of the town. My father was the postmaster, and had a shop whose big glass window read: 'SLOAN E. BOLTON,/PRODUCE MERCHANT.'

"He sold potatoes and corn and seed and meal, and there were always farmers coming in and out of the post office/shop making deals that they sealed by spitting on their hands before they 'shook on it.'

"Yes, my father was important. And I was important enough that the men of the town always touched their caps to me, saying, 'Fine day, Miss Bolton,' or, more often, 'A terrible day altogether, Miss Bolton.' I'd nod my gracious, seven-year-old, eight-year-old head, and allow that indeed it was. I took my importance for granted. Hadn't they been touching their caps to me all my life?

"I'm not sure that my parents paid much attention to how the townspeople treated me. They certainly didn't know of my uppity ways. Not until the day when my father caught me in the act and taught me a lesson.

"My father also sold groceries—'the goods,' we called them. There was always a small crowd in the shop—women in shawls, men in muddy boots and stiff tweed caps, children with bare feet waiting to buy a pound of sugar or a packet of Lyons tea or maybe a dozen fresh herrings for Friday's dinner. But when my mother sent me to fetch 'the goods,' I never had to wait. The shop boy would spot me coming in, and greet me, 'Yes, Miss Bolton?' And I'd step straight away to the front, and give my order. I took it entirely for granted. Hadn't they been taking me first since before I was big enough to see over the counter? They had. Until that day.

"It was a soft day, I remember, and bright with rare, golden sunlight. I was planning to go on a bus 'up the mountain' with two friends. There was no bigger treat on a warm summer day than to take the Derry bus to the top of Glenshane Pass. There we would paddle in the cold bracken stream, and chase the fat, foolish sheep that roamed the slopes of Glenshane, and picnic in the heather. Tired and dirty, we would catch the Derry bus coming the other way at nightfall.

"That day, the bus had stopped outside the shop, and my friends, Maureen and Esmond, were on board already, waiting for me. But I needed a

Bunting's 1988 hardcover novel.

bottle of fizzy lemonade and a packet of chocolate biscuits and a bag of sweeties. I raced into the gloom of the shop in too much of a hurry to wait for Rollie Nelson, the shop boy, to escort me to the front of the line of customers. I pushed my way ahead, and had just issued my first, imperious, 'Give me a bottle of...' when I felt a hand on my arm. It was my father. He had been standing at the back of the shop talking with some of the men.

"'Wait your turn,' he thundered.

"'But Daddy....'

"He yanked me back. 'What makes you think you're so important, and you only a wee girl?'

"'But the bus....'

"I could see the bus, pulsing in the heat, waiting for the last passengers to board. I could see Maureen and Esmond peering out the window.

"'I think it's your turn, Mary Jane,' my father said to one of the women waiting in line. Then, 'Go on ahead, Annie.'

"'Och, sure, wee Miss Bolton can go in front of me, Sloan,' Tamany Annie said, but my father shook his head.

"People left the shop with their purchases, and new customers came in. The bus chugged away. I caught a glimpse of my two friends as it passed. They had urged me to hurry, warning that the bus wouldn't wait for me. I expect that I thought it would.

"'It's my turn now, Daddy,' I whined. 'Anyway, I don't need the lemonade. The bus....'

"His grip on my arm was unrelenting. 'You took many another person's turn, from what I can see,' he said. 'We'll just let somebody else take yours.'

"The big clock behind the counter ticked away the minutes. And the hours. There was an open crate of Jaffa oranges at the back, each piece of fruit wrapped in its own crinkly, crisp paper. The heat brought out the orange smell, and it seemed to fill the room.

Dust jacket from the 1987 Harcourt edition.

"'It's not fair,' I sniffled. 'You're cruel, so you are! My legs are sore, standing here. And that smell is making me sick.'

"Not until Rollie Nelson was getting ready to close the shop for the day did my father release me.

"The weather broke the next day. I had missed the last perfect day of summer. It was also the last day that Rollie Nelson ever took me out of turn."[1]

"At the age of nine I went off to boarding school in Belfast. Perhaps it was there, in the telling of tall tales after 'lights out,' that I got my first taste of storytelling. It was certainly there that I developed my life-long love of books and reading."[2]

"There were no radios at boarding school and we had to be content with forbidden crystal sets on which we surreptitiously listened to the Big Bands!"[3]

In 1945, Bunting graduated from Methodist College in Belfast, then went on to study for two years at Queen's University, Belfast, where she met her husband, Edward Davison Bunting. The two married on April 26, 1951 and moved to Scotland.

Nine years later, the couple moved to the United States with their three children, settling first in San Francisco, then in Pasadena. "There are always big decisions to make in life, but perhaps one of the most traumatic is the decision to wrench oneself from the roots of centuries. More traumatic when the move involves about 6,000 actual miles and incalculable culture miles from Belfast, Ireland to California! But that is what my husband and I did in 1960, trailing three small children and a string of quilts as we abandoned home, job, parents, grandparents, aunts, uncles and cousins. By jet, as by sailing ship, it's a long trip from the old world to the new.

"The rewards have been many for all of us, but for me, personally, none has been greater than the horizons opened up since I 'became a writer.'

"I had never aspired to authorship. But the educational system in Ireland is geared to the 'essay answer' in examinations, and at that I had always excelled. If I didn't have the information I could write it so it sounded as if I did and was graded accordingly.

"When I came to California and saw that a neighboring junior college offered a Writing for Publications class, I decided to take it. That was the first step to the new career. I find myself sometimes thinking what different turns my life might have taken had I not seen that junior college brochure.

"Do you believe then that writing can be taught? This seems to be the next logical question. And the answer is, yes. . .and no. Techniques can be taught. Structure and formula can be taught. A writing class can help foster the desire to succeed, can encourage self-discipline, promote good writing work habits. But the feeling for words, the driving need to tell a story, the love of the characters who constantly inhabit your mind, waiting to be born, these are the inherent things that make of us writers.

"So, here I am. A United States citizen, and, by the grace of God and Pasadena City College, a children's book author. No complaints, new world. None whatsoever."[4]

Bunting's first book entitled *The Two Giants* was published in 1972 when she was forty-three years old. "It was a story about Finn McCool, the Irish giant and how he outsmarted Culcullan, the terrible, Scottish giant. I thought everybody in the world knew that story and when I found they didn't, well I thought they should.

"There used to be Shanachies in the Ireland of long ago. The Shanachie was the storyteller who went from house to house telling his tales of ghosts and fairies, of old Irish heroes and battles still to be won. Maybe I'm a bit of a Shanachie myself, telling my stories to anyone who'll listen.

"Children often ask me which is my favorite book. That is impossible to answer. I love them all dearly and for different reasons. If I didn't, I would never have written them."[5]

Many of her books carry the word "ghost" in the title: *Ghost behind Me, Ghost of Summer*, or are about ghosts, like *Scary, Scary Halloween*. "My children had never heard of 'trick or treat.' Getting dressed up, leaving home empty-handed, returning laden with candies. . .such joy! What kind of magic land had they found where all this was permissible?

"Halloween soon became a favorite holiday, second only to Christmas. I remember Halloween as flu season in California. More than once my disappointed little devils and monsters had to stay home with fevers, their noses pressed to the window as other ghosts and goblins passed. Our smallest one, who was only two, was hard to convince that they weren't really real!

Cover from the 1986 Berkley paperback.

The 1987 Harper paperback.

"Perhaps from this genesis came: 'I peer outside, there's something there/That makes me shiver, spikes my hair....'"[3]

"When I wrote *Scary, Scary Halloween* I knew of the numerous picture books about this popular holiday. What was there to say that hadn't already been said? So I did trick or treating from a cat's point of view, a mama cat, hiding under the house with her baby kittens, waiting fearfully for the monsters, who are the children in costumes, to leave. When they do—

> It's quiet now, the monsters gone
> The streets are ours until the dawn.
> We're out, we prowlers of the night
> Who snap and snarl and claw and bite.
> We stalk the shadows, dark, unseen....
> Goodbye 'till next year, Halloween.

"A different angle? I think so, and the editor agreed."[6]

"*Ghost of Summer* did not spring from one idea but from a combination of several. On a visit home to Ireland...our two sons went off to a nearby park. There were some kids there, playing football. Our sons asked if they could join in the game. 'Are you Catholics or Prods?' one of the players demanded. 'Why?' my son asked. 'Because it depends which you are whether you can play or not,' was the reply. Our children's total lack of understanding of this attitude and of other attitudes they encountered stayed on in my mind.

"What if a boy from California went to Trallagh? A boy without religious prejudices? What would he learn? What if somehow he got involved with one of the extremist political parties? Those incredible, magical words, *what if!*

"In *Ghost of Summer* I tried to write a story that children would find exciting but that would also show them the insidious horror of prejudice and the tragedy of a people torn apart by old hatreds. I tried to be objective, to be fair in showing both sides of the Irish problem. I hope no child reading it will know if the author is Protestant or Catholic. I hope no child reading it will care. I put into *Ghost of Summer* the feelings I have for Ireland; the love and the sorrow."[2]

Bunting speaks often at schools and libraries. "Whenever I speak to groups of children, someone in the audience is sure to ask 'Mrs. Bunting, where do you get your ideas? You write so many books! How do you think of all those things to put in them?'

"Ah, well! That is never my problem. My problem is that the world is filled with so many ideas and here am I, right smack in the middle of it. I couldn't possibly write about all the interesting things I see around me or all the interesting thoughts that pop, unannounced, into my head. There aren't that many hours in a day or that many days in a year!

"I'm doing my best. So far, I have written about ghosts and giants, and about creatures with scales and fins. I've written about horses that run wild and free, and about great, beautiful birds of prey. I've written of sharks and whales and giant squid. I've written of kings and princes, of ordinary children growing up, and of young men growing old. I've written of happy families and unhappy families, of living and dying.

"What is there left? A million things. A friend once told me I should slow down and take a rest from writing for a while. How could I? For me, writing is like breathing. It's just plain necessary."[5]

"Authors have trained themselves to look for ideas. Or perhaps it comes naturally. Perhaps that's why we're authors in the first place. Because everything sparks an idea. We see stars where others see only darkness. Often I'm astonished to find that all my writer friends have clipped and saved the same items from the paper at the same time!

"I can spot a trend long before it comes. It's there, on the pages of the morning paper. As a matter of fact, we're bombarded with it by all phases of the media. Reporters pontificate. 'Sixty Minutes' runs a special report. We find little snatches of it on radio talk shows. I don't necessarily feel qualified to handle whatever the new trend may be. Nor do I always want to. But often I do.

"I would definitely say that ninety percent of my story seeds come from something I've read in my daily paper or in my weekly periodical. I take that seed and plant it in my conscious mind—maybe in my subconscious one too—and I let it germinate. I nurture it with lots of thinking time, often in the bathtub or before I go to sleep. After a time it begins to sprout. Now, this is the time to know not to grab. Leave it alone. Let it gather strength. If I yank at it, I'm going to pull it out, roots and all. When it's ready, I can take it and prune off all those shoots I don't need and transplant it from my head on to the paper.

"And because ninety percent of my ideas come from reports of current news and the other ten percent from what I see happening around me, I guess what I write has to be contemporary.

"...I have written and sold many books with contemporary characters, settings, and themes:

"*One More Flight* tells of a boy who is running away from a care center. He has run away so often that if he's caught this time he'll be sent to Juvenile Hall. Dobby is a foster child, a disturbed child, a runaway. He envies, he hates, he reaches out to belong. He is one of today's unfortunates.

"*Ghost of Summer* is set in contemporary Northern Ireland with its political upheaval, its senseless hatreds and killings in the name of religion. In it I tried to draw a parallel between the problems there and the racial problems in the United States.

"*Going against Cool Calvin* tells of a gang of young boys who beat up illegal aliens as they come across the border from Mexico, on the beach by Tijuana. I read in the newspaper about an illegal alien, a Mexican teen-ager, who was on the beach on the United States side. He was arrested when he came out of hiding to rescue an American boy who was in danger of drowning. The story seed was planted in my mind. I went down to the beach and talked to border patrol officers. I saw the place where the rescue took place. Then I took pictures so I would have no trouble visualizing the locale exactly when the time came to begin writing. The book sold to the first place to which I sent it.

"Not long ago, I presented an idea to a publisher who bought it in less than a week on the strength of two chapters and an outline....I had read about two children who found money packed into an old tin can. It was a lot of money, probably more than they'd ever seen in one lump sum in their lives. They turned it over to the police. *Two* children? Did they discuss what to do? I wondered. Did one want to turn it in and one want to keep it? Did they hide it first, and look at it, and think of all the things it could buy? I knew I had the beginnings of a story, a contemporary story—contemporary because in times past the outcome would have been apparent: virtue would naturally triumph. Good children didn't keep what didn't belong to them. The temptation would be fleeting at best. Today we are more realistic. If we write about 'what's happening,' the child protagonist must be allowed to have weaknesses, to be human. Perhaps even to succumb to temptation—for good reason.

"*Cop Camp* tells of a kid from the ghetto who likes to hassle the police and what happens when he goes to a camp run by cops and faces the doubts that arise from his inherent distrusts and his new-found awareness that cops are people. That there are good ones and bad ones. I read about a particular camp which was set up to let cops and problem kids become better acquainted. I went to police headquarters and talked to one of the officers who'd helped run the camp the year before. Again, I sent off an outline and a first chapter, and the book sold by return mail, literally."[4]

"When I began writing for children...I was told that there were certain words not to be used in books for young people; certain subjects not to be dealt with. And then, suddenly, in the 1970s 'realism' was in. Realism was not only desirable in children's books, it was necessary if the author wanted to make a sale.

"Books for children about divorce, and death, and terminal illness and abortion began appearing. It was all right to write about sex; child abuse and child molestation were perfectly acceptable subjects. Nothing was taboo, or almost nothing. Frankness was the key word.

"Many of the then current young adult books showed that nothing was too tough, nothing too sensitive, nothing too heartbreaking for our sophisticated children to handle.

"Alcoholic mothers, handicapped children, and death had all been ignored in children's books for too many years. Then they were brought out of the closet, and the early books on these subjects were timely and superior. There is now little need for more.

"None of this is to say that these and similar very real problems have vanished from our lives or that they should vanish entirely from our books. It would be dishonest to write a novel about charac-

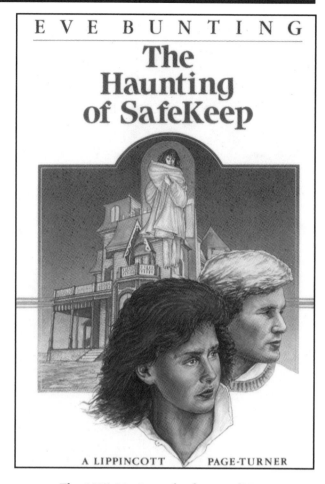

The 1985 Lippincott hardcover edition.

ters free from any problems of a serious nature. But the problems should be an integral part of the book, not the entire substance of the book.

"A young adult novel I...sold to Harper & Row tells the story of Crow, a young man who lives secretly and alone in an old apartment above the carousel on Santa Monica pier. One night, as he looks out of the window, he sees someone swimming straight for the horizon. The someone is a seventeen-year-old girl attempting to end her life. Crow saves her, heals her hurts, takes her to live with him in his secret room, and subsequently falls in love with her. The attempted suicide is a part of the plot. The haunting experiences that brought the girl, Valentine, to this crisis in her life recur and are crucial to an understanding of her character. But this is not a book about suicide. It is a story of love, of two people finding themselves and each other and making major decisions about their lives.

"It is always fascinating, and profitable, to speculate on the new trends that are appearing in children's books. But there is one thing I firmly believe: If you set out to write a book that you don't care about just because the subject matter is 'hot,' you're heading for disappointment. A hot subject is a big plus, but there also has to be that excitement, that certainty that this is what you want to write more than anything in the world, and oh! weren't you lucky and smart to come up with the idea at just the right time. Then you have the subject, the commitment, the passion, and you can write a book that is as special to you as it will be to the publisher."[7]

Most critics appreciate the realism of Bunting's themes. Lynne Rosenthal, in talking about suicide themes in young adult literature says: "[A] number of books. . .seek to help surviving peers understand that no one person is to blame for a suicide, and realize that while at times they may be depressed, they can turn to others for support. In a number of these books, the ultimate aim appears to be to help the reader separate himself from the suicide by encouraging him to identify with the main survivor, who, by the end of the book, comes to see himself as fundamentally different, stronger, more connected to others than the suicide.

"Such a book is *Face at the Edge of the World* by Eve Bunting."[8]

Bunting works at home, usually four or five hours a day, keeping up a fast pace despite the fact that she doesn't use a typewriter or word processor. "I'd never have a kid messing with drugs or messing with sex. In my books my kids are always tempted, because I think that's life. But whatever the tempting situation, kids will find a message, well-hidden I hope, that says, 'better not.'

"Each of us has a choice of what we do with our lives. I hope the children make the right choice, whatever it is, and in my books I try to help them make it."[9]

Footnote Sources:

[1] Eve Bunting, "A Lesson in Importance of Being Unimportant," *Los Angeles Times*, August 10, 1979.
[2] *Junior Literary Guild*, March, 1977.
[3] *Junior Literary Guild*, March, 1987.
[4] E. Bunting, "New Trends in Children's Books," *Writer*, April, 1979.
[5] Publicity, Harcourt, Brace & Jovanovich Profiles.
[6] E. Bunting, "Think Picture Book," *Writer*, September, 1988.
[7] E. Bunting, "What's New in Children's Books?," *Writer*, April, 1984.
[8] Lynne Rosenthal, "To Be or Not to Be: Suicide in Literature for Young People," *Lion and the Unicorn: A Critical Journal of Children's Literature*, June, 1988.
[9] Allen Raymond, "Eve Bunting: From Ireland with Love," *Early Years*, October, 1986.

■ For More Information See

Cricket, February, 1979 (p. 34).
Los Angeles Times, February 3, 1981 (section II, p. 5).
New York Times Book Review, February 19, 1984.
Jim Roginski, *Behind the Covers*, Volume II, Libraries Unlimited, 1989.

Collections:

De Grummond Collection, University of Southern Mississippi.
Kerlan Collection, University of Minnesota.

Caroline B. Cooney

Born May 10, 1947; daughter of Dexter Mitchell (a purchasing agent) and Martha (a teacher; maiden name, Willerton) Bruce; (divorced); children: Louisa, Sayre, Harold. *Education:* Attended Indiana University, 1965-66, Massachusetts General Hospital School of Nursing, 1966-67, and University of Connecticut, 1968. *Residence:* Westbrook, Conn. *Agent:* Curtis Brown Ltd., 10 Astor Pl., New York, N.Y. 10003.

■ Career

Author, 1978—. Musician (organist). *Member:* Authors' Guild, Mystery Writers of America.

■ Awards, Honors

North Carolina American Association of University Women's Award for Juvenile Literature, 1980, for *Safe as the Grave;* Romantic Book Award, Teen Romance category, 1985, for her body of work.

■ Writings

Young Adult, Except As Noted:

Safe as the Grave (juvenile mystery; Junior Literary Guild selection; illustrated by Gail Owens), Coward, 1979.

Rear View Mirror (adult), Random House, 1980.

The Paper Caper (juvenile mystery; Junior Literary Guild selection; illustrated by G. Owens), Coward, 1981.

An April Love Story, Scholastic, 1981.

Nancy and Nick, Scholastic, 1982.

He Loves Me Not, Scholastic, 1982.

A Stage Set for Love, Archway, 1983.

Holly in Love, Scholastic, 1983.

I'm Not Your Other Half, Putnam, 1984.

Sun, Sea, and Boys, Archway, 1984.

Nice Girls Don't, Scholastic, 1984.

Rumors, Scholastic, 1985.

Trying Out, Scholastic, 1985.

Suntanned Days, Simon & Schuster, 1985.

Racing to Love, Archway, 1985.

The Bad and the Beautiful, Scholastic, 1985.

The Morning After, Scholastic, 1985.

All the Way, Scholastic, 1985.

Saturday Night, Scholastic, 1986.

Don't Blame the Music, Putnam, 1986.

Saying Yes, Scholastic, 1987.

Last Dance, Scholastic, 1987.

The Rah Rah Girl, Scholastic, 1987.

Among Friends, Bantam, 1987.

Camp Boy-Meets-Girl, Bantam, 1988.

New Year's Eve, Scholastic, 1988.

Summer Nights, Scholastic, 1988.
The Girl Who Invented Romance, Bantam, 1988.
Camp Reunion, Bantam, 1988.
Family Reunion, Bantam, 1989.
The Fog, Scholastic, 1989.
The Face on the Milk Carton, Bantam, 1990.
The Snow, Scholastic, 1990.
The Fire, Scholastic, 1990.

Contributor of stories to juvenile and young adult magazines, including *Seventeen, American Girl, Jack and Jill, Humpty Dumpty,* and *Young World.*

■ Adaptations

"Rear View Mirror" (television movie), starring Lee Remick, Warner Brothers, 1984.

■ Work in Progress

The Party's Over, for Scholastic; *Miss TeenAge America,* for Bantam.

■ Sidelights

Caroline B. Cooney, a prolific author of young adult literature, is well known for her ability to create both personable and realistic heroines. Approximately half her novels are romances. "I believe that to love and to be loved are the most fierce desires any of us will ever have."[1]

"Blessed with an extemely happy childhood," Cooney grew up in Old Greenwich, Connecticut, "leading a completely ordinary, suburban life. We lived on a nice old street with lots of other kids who all knew each other from kindergarten up through high school. There was great pleasure to be had in just staying near home, playing with friends. If there were problems in the community, we certainly didn't know about them; it was a very innocent time. My parents told me and my brother that we were the most wonderful kids on earth. And we believed it.

"Starting with piano at seven, then organ at thirteen, I was fast on my way to becoming the world's greatest musician. I was also reading armloads of books. Children's books were very warm and satisfying for me; they always had happy endings. Adult books didn't, and I hated making the transition. For years I'd sneak back into the children's room of the library to get some little, comforting story. One of my favorite authors was Edward Eager, with his semi-fantasies about four children. His were very funny, sweet, family stories in which the kids were wafted off into another world.

"When I reached high school, I was one of those kids with tons of energy. In fact, I flung myself at things: I was a church organist, sang in several choirs—directed one of them, played accompaniment for the school choirs and for summer musicals, and had a job in the library.

"There I was carrying off all sorts of things, at the same time feeling I didn't have any poise. Though I had a lot of friends and was actually a very successful student, it always looked like other kids were more at the center of things, that I would never achieve the level of popularity I had daydreamed of. You have so little perspective as a teenager that you can't always see yourself clearly. I certainly didn't. Luckily, that didn't stop me from loving high school or from being good at it.

"It was college that I was bad at. I tried four times and failed; I never did finish. Having anticipated that they'd be the best four years of my life, it was quite a shock when it didn't work out that way at all. I went in as a music major, saddled with a lot of ego, only to discover that in a group of terrific kids, I didn't stand out. At eighteen, learning that my level was lower than I had dreamed proved to be quite a blow. The thought of being average had never even occurred to me, so my ego took a terrific beating.

"It was then that I realized how much easier it was to face that kind of disappointment when your parents have already helped you to a solid start. I was extremely fortunate to have developed the kind of confidence that would see me through the rough spots—no matter how awful they might have seemed at the time—and was lucky enough not to suffer the traumas so many kids experience."[1]

At the age of twenty, Cooney married. "The year was 1967, a time when marriage was still expected much earlier. I was working for a temporary agency, still braving my way through college, when we bumped into each other at work; it was all very romantic. Having such a miserable time at school, hating it so much, it seemed perfectly reasonable to get married and have children.

"Louisa was born when I was twenty-one, Sayre four years later. Sitting home with the babies, I had to find a way to entertain myself. So I started writing with a pencil, between the children's naps—baby in one arm, notebook in the other.

"I began with terrible, ghastly, short stories, many of them with no plot, no characters, no dialogue. Then at twenty-four I finished my first novel,

Scholastic's 1986 paperback edition.

Cover for the 1988 paperback edition.

absolutely confident that this book would take the
world by storm and make me a household name
before I turned twenty-five; it didn't. I went on to
write another seven adult novels that also never
found publishers. Most were set in Imperial
Rome—historical fiction. Never having gone back
to read any of them, it's difficult to say whether or
not they were any good.

"While working on these novels, I was still writing
short stories, trying every kind of writing that I
enjoyed reading. When *Seventeen* accepted one of
my humorous short stories for kids, I continued to
write for that age group and finally found the type
of writing that I could both be successful at and
enjoy. The stories really started working for me,
and I sold quite a few."[1]

Cooney's first juvenile mystery, *Safe as the Grave*,
the story of an eleven-year-old girl with a secret
project in her family's burying ground, was pub-

lished by Coward in 1979. "Having already written eight books with no luck, I wasn't interested in
wasting my time writing another unpublishable
novel. So instead I wrote an outline and mailed it
along with my short story resume to a number of
publishers, saying, 'Would you be interested in
seeing this'—knowing, of course, that they
wouldn't. Naturally, when they all said 'yes,' I was
stunned; the only thing to do was to quick write the
book. I discovered that for better or for worse a lot
of writing went into those previous eight books,
and by that time I'd finally learned my craft.
Working from my outline, I completed *Safe as the
Grave* within the course of a summer."[1]

In 1980, her first adult novel, entitled *Rear View
Mirror*, was published. The story involves a woman
who is forced into acting as a chauffeur for two
murderers. Reviewer Michele Slung of the *Washington Post* described the novel as being "so tightly

written, so fast-moving, that it's easy not to realize until the last paragraph is over that one hasn't been breathing all the while.'' Slung commended Cooney for her ability to create ''resourceful, responsible, realistic heroines.''[2]

''A wonderful thing happened when *Rear View Mirror* was reviewed. Academically speaking, there had been only one superlative teacher in my life. They used my married name in the review, but when he stumbled across it, he said to himself, 'This has to be that little kid who was in my sixth-grade class.' He telephoned and we had a reunion as writers.''[1]

Cooney started writing books for young adults, beginning with *An April Love Story,* published in 1981. Since that time, she's exclusively published books about the experiences of teenagers. ''I do a great deal of volunteer work at the school and church, see a lot of kids' pain, fear, hope, and joy. These children have been a tremendously positive influence on me, because they're the ones I'm writing to, the ones I'm writing for.

''Growing up is not necessarily any harder today than it was when I was young. Certain things haven't changed; kids' parents still remain the center of their lives. If you've got great parents who enjoy being parents and are good at it, you can still have a nice childhood. If I was young again today with the same parents, I think adolescence would be as easy as it was back then. What's unfortunate is that an awful lot of children don't have that kind of luck at home.

''There's also no question that many of today's teenagers must contend with drug abuse, alcohol abuse, and widespread sexual activity which often begins frighteningly early. Though it's ridiculous to suggest that these problems don't exist, I have the impression that kids still yearn for absolutely wholesome childhoods. They want hope, want things to work out, want reassurance that even were they to do something rotten, they and the people around them would still be alright.

''No matter what it is that they're doing, I don't think they want to have to read about it. Teenagers looking for books to read don't say, 'Oh, good, another book about rotten, depressing drug abuse.' I think they want to read about the nicer, sweeter sides of life; I think they want happy endings.''[1]

Cooney's young adult novel, *Don't Blame the Music,* provides a look into a troubled family who is struggling to pave the way to that happy ending. The story involves Susan, a high school senior, and her sister Ashley, a burnt-out failure of a rock 'n' roll singer. Ashley returns home following a three-year hiatus, forcing Susan and her family to contend with the hatred and destruction she brings back home with her.

''This book had a very definite evolution. My editor at Putnam saw a triptych by Hieronymus Bosch at the Metropolitan Museum of Art. The painting depicted a group of musicians falling backwards into the jaws of hell. She asked the curator about the theological meaning of the work, and he told her that while music must always glorify God, the musicians were trying to glorify themselves. She said she thought that teenagers today have a great yearning for fame, but that rather than thinking of fame as the by-product, they look toward it as the actual goal, anxious to glorify themselves rather than the task at hand.

''What she wanted was a book about a teenager who descended into hell through the misuse of music. I said, 'What a ridiculous idea.' To which she replied, 'Oh, and I want it to be upbeat.'

''I spent months thinking about it, getting nowhere. To begin with, you had to define hell. So I said to myself, 'What is hell? The girl's not dead yet, so it has to be hell on earth. What is hell on earth?' Then there are certain restrictions put down by the publisher—like no sex and no drugs—which cuts out a little more hell.

''My original theory was to make the one who descended into hell the heroine, but I wanted hell to be offstage, which would have been impossible; furthermore, there was nothing upbeat about it. So I decided that the one telling the story would be her sister, and very slowly, working at it everyday, I began getting a sense of the story.''[1]

Don't Blame the Music was described in the *Bulletin of the Center for Children's Books* as having, ''well-defined characters. . . .It explores the ramifications of a familial situation in which there is one member so abrasive that there is stress in all parts of the lives of others. . . .[The story] touches on issues important to adolescent development.''[3]

A disciplined author, Cooney spends five days a week writing. ''Every day I take a four-mile walk down to the beach, plotting and working things out in my head. There's so much mental work involved that doesn't take place while sitting at the typewriter or putting anything on paper, that it's difficult to say how many hours a day I actually spend working.

Lee Remick starred in the 1984 television movie "Rearview Mirror."

The 1987 Bantam hardcover.

"I can easily ponder something for a year before even beginning to get a sense of what it is I want to say—let alone a sense of the plot and characters. By the time I'm ready to write a book, I may already have taken a year or two putting the theme, characters, plot, and ending together in my head; whereas the physical writing might take only two or three months."[1]

Though at first "finding it infuriating," she has learned to work from outlines. "I never used to know what was going to happen in the story until I wrote it. Then I began doing paperbacks for Scholastic and they required outlines, largely just to ensure that two writers didn't waste time and effort on similar ideas. Before, I'd always allowed the story to develop out of the characters, but the outlines demanded that the plot and characters evolve together at the same time. Now I wouldn't do it any other way.

"There's always a stage of the work in which I don't know what I'm doing; I have an assignment and a due date but nothing that jells. However, having managed to make it work now for nearly

fifty books, I've learned to trust that though I may be anxious, it will come.

"I'm not an author who writes from pain or agony, but from joy. The writing has always been something I've wanted. I have been well-disciplined because I love what I do and take great pleasure in telling stories. There's also the minor matter of having three children to support.

"I have one daughter who wouldn't be caught dead reading a teen romance, another daughter who loves them and memorizes mine, and a son who wants to know, when each book is published, does this mean we have enough money to go to Disney World again?

"There is a phrase that is used often for kids like one of mine: 'reluctant reader.' Well, I know many of these children now, and I don't think there's any such thing as a 'reluctant reader.' They're dying to read, to be able to sit with their friends and enjoy the same Stephen King book they're reading. But they can't. The sentence never comes through to them. I have so much sympathy now for the kids for whom reading never comes, as well as for their

Cooney's 1988 hardcover edition.

Hardcover edition of the 1989 novel.

Dust jacket of the 1986 Putnam edition.

parents. When all my kids are finally off on their own, I plan to become involved with Literacy Volunteers, which has got to be one of the greatest outfits in the world."[1]

Participation in community services has helped Cooney both combat the isolation of writing and to "figure out where the reality comes in. During the week, I'm often at the school, playing piano for all the school choirs and musicals, so that I can be around kids. But in order for my life to consist of more than teenagers—real or imaginary—weekends are reserved for sociable activities among other adult human beings, hopefully to keep me from going insane.

"I also do volunteer work at the hospital in New Haven one night a week in the Emergency Room. New Haven is a very rough, very sad, big city, and my work in the E.R. allows me to see another side of life, a side I knew existed from the newspapers but which never touched me personally. It has certainly made my problems seem very minor,

giving me enough to think about for years to come."[1]

In 1987, *Among Friends* was published by Bantam. Cooney's novel stars the "Awesome Threesome," three inseparable high school girls who discover they may not be so inseparable after all. The story is told through the diary entries of six different teenagers. "This book took many revisions, many different approaches. It was very difficult to find the right voice for the story; I tried it in the second person, the third person, then from all the points of view. Finally I settled on the diary attempt in which each character speaks separately and in the first person. The problem was that by telling the story through so many voices I was running the risk that the reader would lose track, have no idea who was saying what or why; I didn't think I was going to be able to pull it off. When it finally jelled I was as pleased with *Among Friends* as with anything I've ever written."[1]

Mitzi Myers, reviewer for the *L.A. Times*, said of *Among Friends*, "Cooney's technique is particularly appropriate for her very relevant subject—academic perfection and the jealous peer pressure that inevitably accompanies it. . . .It is a pleasure to find a book for young readers that not only individualizes characters through their writing but also has wise words to say about how writing offers very real help in coping with the problems of growing up."[4]

The Fog, the first book in a horror trilogy for Scholastic, was published in 1989. "It was a lot of fun writing this series because it was so clearly a case of good guys versus bad guys, and killing off the bad guys was really satisfying. By allowing for a certain amount of fantasy and freedom that I couldn't have used in a realistic novel, these books brought out a very childlike kind of writing which I greatly enjoyed."[1]

Cooney encourages aspiring writers to "take your idea and jump in and attack it. In the beginning it may not be any good—my first work certainly wasn't—but if you pay your dues, keep on turning it out and turning it out, eventually you'll learn what you're doing. Personally I found writing to be a very difficult craft to master, but there are a lot of other people who manage to get published more quickly than I did.

"The best advice I can offer is simply to say that if you want to be a writer, you have to write. An awful lot of people get in touch with me with great ideas but with only a sentence or two on paper. When I think about my eight unpublished books, my I-don't-know-how-many short stories, it's difficult for me to be sympathetic if they're not actually writing. Becoming a writer, like any other craft, requires a long apprenticeship. Which is not to say that it is not also tremendous fun.

"Authors often make writing out to be the most ghastly profession in the world, so dreadful that it shreds your very soul; that's a lot of hooey. Writing is thrilling—every aspect of it—because there are so many rewards. I get great fan letters, kids sending pictures of themselves. For awhile we had a slew of pictures taped to the refrigerator and visitors would ask, 'Are those your nieces?' And I'd say, 'No, they live in Iowa and I don't know who they are.' Any minor difficulty that's come up during the writing is certainly paid in kind when a kid writes.

"My all time favorite fan letter came from a little girl who hated reading. Her grandmother bought her *An April Love Story* for Christmas, but she refused to touch it. Finally the grandmother put her foot down, insisting she read the book, so the little girl dragged herself through it. Then she took the time to write: '...And so, Caroline B. Cooney, I'm writing to you because I have come to an important decision. I have decided to read a second book.'"[1]

Footnote Sources:

[1] Based on an interview by Deborah Klezmer for *Authors and Artists for Young Adults*.
[2] Michele Slung, "*Rear View Mirror*," *Washington Post*, June 1, 1980.
[3] *Bulletin of the Center for Children's Books*, July-August, 1986.
[4] Mitzi Myers, "High Schoolers Learn about the Meaning of Friendship," *Los Angeles Times*, February 6, 1988.

■ For More Information See

Publisher's Weekly, June 18, 1979, September 26, 1986, August 25, 1989.

Maureen Daly

Born March 15, 1921, in Castlecaufield, County Tyrone, Ulster, Ireland; naturalized American citizen; daughter of Joseph Desmond (a salesman) and Margaret (Mellon-Kelly) Daly; married William P. McGivern (a writer), December 28, 1946 (died, November, 1983); children: Megan (deceased), Patrick. *Education:* Rosary College, B.A., 1942. *Politics:* Democrat. *Home:* 73-305 Ironwood St., Palm Desert, Calif. 92260. *Agent:* Eleanor Wood, Blassingame, McCauley and Wood, 432 Park Ave. S., Suite 1205, New York, N.Y. 10016.

■ Career

Writer, 1938—; *Chicago Tribune,* Chicago, Ill., reporter and columnist, 1941-44; Chicago City News Bureau, Chicago, reporter, 1941-43; *Ladies' Home Journal,* Philadelphia, Pa., associate editor, 1944-49; *Saturday Evening Post,* Philadelphia, Pa., consultant to editors, 1960-69; *Desert Sun,* Palm Desert, Calif., reporter and columnist, 1987—. *Member:* PEN, Writers Guild of America (West).

■ Awards, Honors

O. Henry Memorial Award, 1938, for short story "Sixteen"; Dodd, Mead Intercollegiate Literary Fellowship Novel Award, 1942, and Lewis Carroll Shelf Award, 1969, both for *Seventeenth Summer;* Freedoms Foundation Award, 1952, for "humanity in reporting"; Gimbel Fashion Award, 1962, for contribution to U.S. fashion industry through *Saturday Evening Post* articles; *Acts of Love* was selected one of *Redbook*'s Ten Great Books for Teens, 1987.

■ Writings

Young Adult Fiction:

Seventeenth Summer, Dodd, 1942, illustrated edition, 1948, new edition, 1985.
Sixteen and Other Stories (illustrated by Kendall Rossi), Dodd, 1961.
Acts of Love, Scholastic, 1986.
First a Dream, Scholastic, 1990.

Young Adult Nonfiction:

Smarter and Smoother: A Handbook on How to Be That Way (illustrated by Marguerite Bryan), Dodd, 1944.
What's Your P.Q. (Personality Quotient)? (illustrated by Ellie Simmons), Dodd, 1952, revised edition, 1966.
Twelve around the World (illustrated by Frank Kramer), Dodd, 1957.
Spanish Roundabout (travel), Dodd, 1960.
Moroccan Roundabout, Dodd, 1961.

Editor; Young Adult Except As Noted:

My Favorite Stories, Dodd, 1948.
Profile of Youth (adult), Lippincott, 1951.
My Favorite Mystery Stories, Dodd, 1966.
(And author of introduction) *My Favorite Suspense Stories,* Dodd, 1968.

Adult Nonfiction:

The Perfect Hostess: Complete Etiquette and Entertainment for the Home, Dodd, 1950.
(Under name Maureen Daly McGivern; with husband, William P. McGivern) *Mention My Name in Mombasa* (illustrated by F. Kramer), Dodd, 1958.
(With W. P. McGivern) *A Matter of Honor,* Arbor House, 1984.

Juvenile:

Patrick Visits the Farm (fiction; illustrated by E. Simmons), Dodd, 1959.
Patrick Takes a Trip (fiction; illustrated by E. Simmons), Dodd, 1960.
Patrick Visits the Library (fiction; illustrated by Paul Lantz), Dodd, 1961.
Patrick Visits the Zoo (fiction; illustrated by Sam Savitt), Dodd, 1963.
The Ginger Horse (fiction; illustrated by Wesley Dennis), Dodd, 1964.
Spain: Wonderland of Contrasts (nonfiction), Dodd, 1965.
The Small War of Sergeant Donkey (fiction; illustrated by W. Dennis), Dodd, 1966.
Rosie, the Dancing Elephant (illustrated by Lorence Bjorklund), Dodd, 1967.

Seventeenth Summer has sold over 1.5 million hardcover copies and millions in paperback editions. Author of "High School Career Series," Curtis Publishing Co., 1942-49. Writer with husband of television shows, including "Kojak," and film "Brannigan" starring John Wayne. Daly's works are included in textbooks and anthologies. Contributor to *Vogue, Mademoiselle, Cosmopolitan, Woman's Day, Scholastic, Woman's Home Companion,* and *Redbook.*

■ **Work in Progress**

Indian Summer, a story of a young Hollywood stunt woman and a young man just off the Morongo Reservation outside Palm Springs; *Hollywood People,* an adult novel about contemporary Hollywood based on Daly's working experience there.

■ **Sidelights**

Maureen Daly's first novel, *Seventeenth Summer,* written between the ages of eighteen and twenty, has remained in print for nearly half a century, selling more than seven million copies. Though originally released as an adult title, *Seventeenth Summer* is now credited as one of the first novels to begin defining the genre of young adult literature.

Living in the small town of Castlecaufield in a troubled Northern Ireland, Daly's father, both the town mayor and the owner of a small bicycle factory, ran into difficulty when he lent a bicycle to a young man carrying a message to some anti-British dissidents. "The lad was shot and my father apprehended for abetting the enemy. The British piled straw around our house, told my father if he failed to leave the country by St. Patrick's Day, the straw would be lit at an unannounced hour and the house burnt to the ground. Joseph Daly headed for America and was followed a year later by his wife and three daughters. I was two years old.

"We settled in Fond du Lac, Wisconsin because Father felt it was the only spot in America that was 'as green as Ireland.' A fourth Daly girl was born there, and my family stayed in Fond du Lac throughout our childhood years."[1]

"My sisters and I were raised as equals. There wasn't a boy in the family to deflect attention from us; maybe that's why we thrived."[2]

"My mother told us often—and shrewdly so—that we were incredibly lucky having friends right in our own home. Always someone to play with.

"We were given a lot of leeway, so discipline was never a big problem. Because our parents didn't put us in a position where we had to lie, there seemed little point to getting into trouble.

"While my mother was quite good to us, she was also very autocratic and demanding. She came from the North of Scotland where her father was an estate manager for Sir Andrew Bain, and she absorbed all the snobbery that went with the mercantile title. Since the Bains had no children, they offered my grandparents a million pounds in order to adopt her. Although they refused, it gave her an arrogance that lasted a lifetime. More than most other people, my mother knew her exact worth.

"My father was the most good-natured man in the world, with a marvelous sense of humor. He was often away during the week working as a traveling salesman, but on weekends he'd lie on the edge of

Book jacket for the first edition of Daly's 1942 award winner.

The author at the time of its publication.

our bed, reciting stories for us that he'd heard in Ireland when he was a boy.

"Sitting in his chair at night, he'd let us play hairdresser with his magnificent black curly hair. And my father loved the Irish jig; he did it so vigorously that he had to stand under a door jamb to keep the house from falling in.

"Our house was on the edge of a small town, only two blocks from beautiful Lake Winnebago. My parents acted as if they'd given us the world's most marvelous gift in that lake; we grew up thinking it was ours.

"In our family, the most important rule was always that the first one up made the coffee for everyone, including our dog, Kinkee. She preferred a little cream in her saucer with her morning coffee, and that became a bit of a family ritual. After breakfast we'd start the day by making sure the house was immaculate; there was no such thing as an untidy bedroom in those days. In the summertime we'd have the rest of the day to either swim at the lake or wander through what we called The Field—

acres and acres of open meadows with creeks and brooks. We also spent a lot of time at the public library.

"I started reading when I was very, very young. Sitting on the floor in kindergarten, I was looking up at the teacher who was writing on the board, when I suddenly realized that 'W' 'A' 'L' 'K' could spell 'walk.' It was just as if Moses had come down."[1]

"When I first began to read, Fond du Lac, like all the United States and most of the world at that time, was deep in an economic depression. But we had books. On weekly 'library day,' a van came to public schools to deliver books for selection and exchange. Our library cards were possibly the first items of personal identification most of us ever had. But it was on weekends, and during the long, hot summers, that the library meant most in our lives. . . .'The Daly Girls' were allowed to take more than the usual quota of books because we read fast and returned volumes on time. We selected what we wanted, children's or adult section. There was never advice, or censorship, from [the librarians]—and never from our parents."[3]

The Depression years took a heavy toll on the Dalys who'd been "quite wealthy in Ireland. My mother and father had brought a lot of our beautiful table linens and silver with them to America. My mother tried selling them, but with the town glutted with people trying to sell their possessions, she couldn't get enough to make it worth her while. Even in the harshest of times, we had a beautifully set table.

"In the winter—when the temperature dropped to about ten below—there was a fair degree of actual suffering, because we never heated the upstairs. I worried a lot about my father's state of mind; he was trying so hard to earn a living and just wasn't making it. But there was always a sense of hope, and as a child I didn't feel poor.

"Luckily my mother was an excellent seamstress. During the Depression, my Uncle Jack gave her yards and yards of Stuart plaid from his black and green kilt. We took out all of the pleats, and mother made us all suits and coats. For the next two seasons each of the four Daly girls looked exactly alike. We were very funny at church—a whole plaid pew.

"A lot of people in Fond du Lac didn't quite understand why we always looked a little different. When my sister, Maggie, reached her teens, my mother went to a wholesale blanket factory and bought a piece of brilliant green blanketing. She made Maggie a magnificent winter coat, trimming it with red fox fur that my Uncle Jack had brought from China; it was stunning. My mother had quite the sense of artistry and chic for our little town in Wisconsin."[1]

Daly attended high school at St. Mary's Springs Academy in Wisconsin. "We had a chapel at school—went to church occasionally on the Holy Days—but mine was not so much a religious education as it was a fine, hard-working one. I came from a religious family (my parents both slept with rosaries under their pillows) but it wore off fairly quickly for the children."[1]

Since the family had no money for tuition, Daly worked her way through school, "cleaning the gym, the auditorium, and the back stairs. I got a kick out of cleaning better than anyone else.

"I met a marvelous teacher called Sister Mary Rosita (in those days nuns always took the first name of Mary). She was a little peppery lady, a wonderful person, and a very, very strict teacher.

But she had such appreciation for the written word that she created great excitement about language for her students. When we handed in scenes and short stories, Sister Rosita marked us on any points she thought had been successful. Encouraging words were penned in the margins, followed by exclamation points: 'Good!' 'I like this!' or 'Fresh!'

"It was also thanks to Sister Rosita that we all shared a subscription to the *Saturday Review of Literature*. She or her family must have paid for it, because I know we didn't. In a small town like Fond du Lac, it was pretty marvelous to be getting something out of New York every week."[1]

Daly's first short story, "Fifteen," was written for Sister Rosita's class. "When I was fifteen years old a boy rode up on his bike and we talked and I felt that spark...and I went home and wrote about it, what we'd said, and what I'd thought. I called it 'Fifteen,' and it took fourth prize in the *Scholastic Magazine* short-story contest."[4]

The following year, she entered *Scholastic*'s contest for a second time. "One night near the end of winter I went ice-skating at a rink just a few blocks from my home. It was a week night. I didn't have anyone to go with me and I hadn't finished my homework, but the night was so wonderful—a night with a high moon and new snow—that I went anyway. That evening I ran into a Western Union boy—and to tell you the truth, I never quite got over it.

"Nothing really happened. It was just because he was a smooth boy—and the first boy. He was taller than I, wore his hat back on his head and there was just something about that uniform! Together we skated around the rink; he held my hand and put his arm around my waist. Then, after a while we sat on a snow-bank and just talked. When he walked home with me, he carried my skates over his shoulder and laughed and talked all the way as if he enjoyed being with me. When we got to my front walk he put the skates over my shoulder, smiled at me and said, 'Good night now, I'll call you.' And I was so naive at the time I thought he would.

"One evening about a week later while I was sitting at home alone waiting for the phone call that never did come through, I wrote ['Sixteen']. It wasn't meant to be a short story at all but rather I just wanted to get the experience down on paper to relieve the tense, hurt feelings inside of me."[5]

"Sixteen" took first prize in *Scholastic Magazine*'s contest in 1938 and has since been published in at least 300 anthologies and in twelve languages.

"What [I] tried to do [was] just write about the things that happened to me and that I knew about—that meant a lot to me. How you feel when you go into the drug store for a coke and a boy you like is watching you, what it is like to be at a dance and have no one dance with you for a long time while you pretend that you're doing all right....The rides in the car, the picnics, sitting in the living room waiting for the telephone to ring."[4]

"Writing that short story...and winning a prize had been a personal and blissful interlude, a stretching of skills, a playing with words and emotions that was new to me. What happened afterward was tense and awkward, something never forgotten.

"When the fifty-dollar prize money arrived from *Scholastic* magazine, my mother signed my name on the check, cashed it, and bought herself a dress costing exactly fifty dollars, a high price at that time, at an exclusive ladies' shop called Minnie Messing's. I remember clearly the dress was a soft silk in a color known as 'powder pink,' with a matching jacket in heavy lace.

"Sister Rosita canvassed the senior class for individual donations to buy me an expensive pen in black and green with my initials 'M. D.' engraved on a gold band. It was all wrong.

"I lost the honorable pen within the month, somewhere along Main Street in Fond du Lac....I just hope a doctor found it."[3]

Daly began her first novel during the summer following her high school graduation. She called the story of Angie Morrow's first love affair with Jack Duluth *Seventeenth Summer*.

"I'm mature enough now to know that this is not a corny thing to say: I was so insanely filled with joy in my seventeenth year that I had to find a way of expressing it other than screaming in the streets. With the sheer ecstacy of falling in love and of discovering sexual contact, the beauty in life was constant.

"During the summers, my sisters and I usually folded advertising brochures for the Fond du Lac Tent & Awning Company. But during this particular summer, I told my family that I was going to write a novel. By the next day my mother had already gone down to the basement and hosed out the coal house. My father went out and got one of the oldest typewriters ever made (the kind that you couldn't see what you hit until you rolled up the paper) and brought down a table and chair.

Photo of Bill McGivern, taken by Daly, after his return from overseas service in World War II.

"There was a tiny window in the coal house but no electric light, so I could only work in the daytime. I wrote almost the first half of the book down there.

"Before starting the writing for the day, I'd play Charles Trenet records and read the original Tom Wolfe. From them I learned a sense of rhythm without ever realizing what I was doing."[1]

That fall, she entered Rosary College in River Forest, Illinois. "I was writing *Seventeenth Summer* and working my way through school as a full-time housekeeper, when I saw a notice for the Intercollegiate Novel Contest sponsored by Dodd, Mead & Company on the bulletin board. They asked for three chapters, an outline, and three letters of recommendation.

"I knew that Harry Hanson was a very highly regarded reviewer in the East, and it never occurred to me *not* to find out his address and ask him for a letter of recommendation. Both he and

Dorothy Canfield Fisher submitted letters on my behalf.

"The telegram saying I'd won the contest came to the home where I was housekeeping. I called home but there was no one there. So I went down to the local church and thanked God for giving me such a chance."[1]

Between the autograph parties, interviews, and public appearances, Daly had become a prominent literary figure by the age of twenty and was doing her best "not to make my girlfriends angry with me. I rarely talked about my work to anyone."[1]

Despite the success, she continued with the responsibilities of college life. "One day I was in the nun's dining room, clearing the table when the Dean came in to get me. The entire student body applauded when I walked out. I thanked them all and went back to clean the kitchen. I've since been back to Rosary College as a writer-in-residence. Their housekeeping is not what it used to be."[1]

At the time *Seventeenth Summer* was published, young adult literature was only beginning to establish itself as a genre. "[During] the Sinatra era, when everyone from eighteen to thirty-five was in service and those above that age were immediately concerned with the war, teen-agers were publishers' favorite reading audience. Editors and writers suddenly discovered that there were a few hundred thousand teen-agers loose in the nation who had to content themselves and their minds with adult newspapers and magazines. And to top it off—the kids could read! And so the same editors and writers put their heads together, listened to juke box recordings till their brains got jivey, looked around the country at a few of the boys who liked their hats with broadrims and rolled their trousers up two cuff widths, and then put fresh ribbons in the typewriters, took a swig of Coca-Cola—and began to turn out 'teen-aged copy.' Most of that material was a super-solid line of chatter where all boys were 'joes,' all girls were 'chicks' and the high school crowd was the 'snob mob,' the 'harpy huddle' or 'the wolf pack.'

"Most of the copy was wordy, superficial stuff with plots that gave the heroine to the hero because he had a larger collection of Harry James recordings than all the other boys, all written to the background music of *One Meat Ball*. And most teen-agers read their new 'literature' hopefully, wondering what was happening to the rest of the teen-agers of the country, gave a few feeble hubba-hubbas, and went right back to reading exactly what they had been reading before becoming the nation's number one cultural project.

"There was better writing for teen-agers long before writers began 'writing for teen-agers.' There were writers and there were teachers and magazines who understood the adolescent as a 'person,' not as a 'character.'"[6]

"Actually, [*Seventeenth Summer*] wasn't written as a YA novel....It was reviewed in the *New York Times Book Review* as an adult title. The book was in print for twenty years before someone noticed that teenagers were reading it and designated it YA."[2]

In her last year at college, Daly began a career in journalism. "Eddie Johnson [news photographer for the *Chicago Tribune*] came to Rosary College for a kind of demure cheesecake picture spread on 'colleens' for St. Patrick's Day. As the only Irish-born colleen on campus, I got a picture all to myself. And Eddie Johnson said to me, 'Maybe you'd like to come to work for us someday, Miss Daly.'"[3] "The following day I went to the offices of the *Chicago Tribune*, interviewed with the city editor, and was hired to do a weekly column about young people called 'On the Solid Side.'"[1]

In 1946, she married writer William McGivern. "McGivern was a tall, husky young man—a few years older than I—witty and shy at the same time. He was a high school dropout, employed at loading freight cars in a railroad yard, I learned much later; but he wanted to be a writer, too. He came to an autographing party for *Seventeenth Summer* at Marshall Field's, Chicago's huge downtown department store. Bill bought a book and I signed it. An hour later, he came back, saying he had left the first copy in a taxi and could he buy another. He did.

"Curious the power of words to convey both love and the inner heart. It happened for me when Sergeant William P. McGivern sent me a V-mail note while he was a combatant in the famed Battle of the Bulge, stationed with an anti-aircraft crew on an isolated hill above a strategic village in Belgium. He wrote: 'On Christmas Eve, we crept down the hill behind the German tank to get to Midnight Mass. An old man closed the church doors and the organist just barely touched the keys with her fingertips to play "The Star Spangled Banner." It was so cold there were no echoes....I wish you had been there.'

"Is that a letter of love and declaration? Somehow I thought so. Bill and I were married at Holy Name

Cathedral in Chicago, more than four years after I autographed that first book for him."[3]

The City News Bureau in Chicago offered Daly her first full-time job as a journalist assigned to covering police beats. "The work was very difficult and very demanding. You were supposed to back-up every crime so that by the time big papers like the *Tribune* sent over their reporters, City News already had the story."[1]

"When I called from the scene of news stories, I was always afraid they would fire a question at me and I wouldn't have the answer. Often I'd be standing in phone booths with sweat pouring down my back."[2]

"Journalism places tremendous emphasis on detail. One time I was covering a street car accident in which there were about seven dead. It was hard enough getting the story while looking at all the blood, but to make matters worse, I called the information in to the city editor who said, 'Now go back and get their middle initials.'

"Something went wrong with the work roster and I worked straight through—every Saturday and Sunday—from June until Christmas, without ever being given a day off. I was so shy it took me that long to ask for one. I just thought I was lucky to have been hired.

"While with City News, I met the entertainment editor for one of the local papers, Eddie 'Dynamite Sokol' (Dynamite was his byline)."[1] "From Dynamite I learned that a reporter, with good manners and perhaps a few up-top introductions, can go anywhere, ask any question, and write almost anything he wishes—as long as he, or she, feels what he has learned is important, true, and has kept written notes to prove it.

"It was Dynamite who helped me to speak out on the job. He convinced me that public files were meant to be open to the public and that public officials must, within reason, remember that they *worked* for the public. 'Call 'em on the phone, baby,' he told me often. 'They got to talk to you, or call you back. You're not a kid anymore. *You're Press.*'"[3]

With a strong desire to move East, Daly interviewed for a job with the *Ladies' Home Journal*. "As a result of *Seventeenth Summer*, I'd become quite conspicuous in the writing field very early on. When I met with Executive Editor Mary Cookman Bass [now Mrs. Chauncey Newlin], I told her what I wanted and she agreed. I served as

associate editor and wrote a number of articles through the years.

"In the days before television programs like '60 Minutes' absorbed all the advertising revenue, magazines like the *Ladies' Home Journal* were power houses. We were all paid extremely well, had large budgets for research."[1] In 1952, Daly won a Freedoms Foundation Award for "humanity in reporting" for "City Girl," the story of a young black girl whose policeman father had been killed in a shoot-out. Through stories like this Daly found a voice to address prejudice—a subject for which she has maintained strong convictions.

"In the town where I grew up there were no black people whatsoever. But by reading history books, listening to my natural instincts, and following the example set by my parents, I grew up to abhor all forms of violence. In our household it was absolutely forbidden to say anything disparaging about any group of people.

"When I first met Bill McGivern, I said that there were three things I was determined to know more about: the slave question, the American Indians,

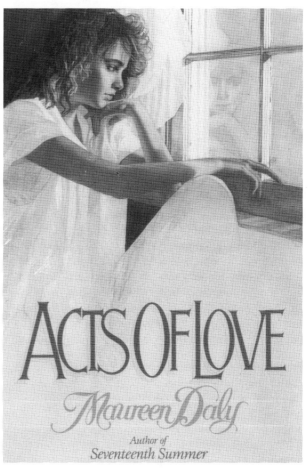

Dust jacket of the 1986 novel.

and homosexuals. At that time you couldn't just go to the Reader's Guide and look up homosexuality. And there was almost as little to be found about the American Indian.''[1]

With assignments abroad, Daly left her position at *Ladies' Home Journal* to move to Europe with her husband and two-year-old daughter, Megan. The family traveled to many different countries, living for a short time in a variety of places. ''The most pleasure I have ever had in life was being with Bill McGivern....We lived our lives the way we wanted to, and traveled all over the world.''[2]

''Bill was what the British call a 'toff.' He knew very well when his behavior was exaggerated, and he liked that. In Paris we bought a Citroen—a big two seater with a luggage rack on top—and for years he kept that car in a garage in Gibraltar. Bill said he couldn't stand to call a cab when he got off the boat, so he'd cable ahead and we'd be met by our own car. His was a tongue-in-cheek way of playing at life.

''Bill and I were very compatible but naturally there were times I'd want to do something that he didn't. When we were in Dublin I was turned on by being so close to Iceland. I told Bill I was determined to go there and he replied, 'I'm not going with you. I've just discovered that the Irish play golf in the snow with little red balls—I'm staying right here.'''[1]

The couple also lived in Rome and Germany and traveled regularly to Spain. When in Spain she ''stayed near the children, running the house, while Bill would rent a tiny house in the village to do his work.

''Since Spain was so cold in winter, we spent a great deal of time around an olive-wood fire, reading with blankets wrapped around us. The one thing that living abroad gave us was time. Not understanding a foreign language, we didn't have to become involved with other people's problems. Bill and I were amateurs in Spanish so we could turn our ears off; that gives you a lot of quiet time to yourself.''[1]

During a trip back to America, they purchased a farmhouse in Pennsylvania. ''I did all the plans, got the architects to work, and we moved back to Spain with Bill saying, 'Cable me when it's finished.' Nobody could do that sort of thing if they didn't have a wife with a literary income. We moved back to Pennsylvania when Megan and our son, Patrick, were ready for college in the mid-sixties. We loved that farmhouse for many years and left it only when a highway came through.

''Then we bought a house in Hollywood. I saw it first, asked Bill to come and look it over, and he said, 'I'll stand out by the swimming pool for twenty minutes and if a plane doesn't fly overhead, I can live there.'''[1]

''We were always looking for new experiences, as writers, as people, but we were not quite prepared when a certain new experience sought us out. We had planned to drive...to San Diego to join friends at the race-track. As Bill shaved in the early dawn, he felt a strange little lump on the side of his neck. I remember he said, 'If this doesn't go away, I don't think we should stay for the weekend.'

''We didn't stay for the weekend. Bill had cancer of the throat. With surgery and treatment, he lived nearly three-and-a-half more years, cheerful, grateful, and loving. Health was under control. He never stopped working and had a sheaf of paper and pencil near him every waking moment.

''Contracts were signed, an advance taken, a deadline set. His new book was to be titled *A Matter of Honor.* A new cancer flared up in the esophagus.

''One sad afternoon, Bill asked me if I would finish the book for him, later. He had three chapters completed, some interviews, and a lot of notes. The story had a semi-military background and I knew that a speech by a certain army general was pivotal to the plot. I brought a tape recorder to Bill's bedside and said, 'Please tell me exactly what you want the general to say. I'm not sure I can do that alone.'

'''I've got it all figured out in my mind,' he said. 'Let me tell you tomorrow.'

''By the morning, he had died.

''That was in mid-November. I clung to those who wanted to cling to me and worked, often through the saddest of tears, to finish Bill's manuscript. November, through a lonely Christmas and a lonelier New Year, into summer and the month of July. *A Matter of Honor* was completed, almost ready to send to Don Fine at Arbor House. I was at my desk, with a jar of sharpened pencils, going over the final typescript when the phone rang. It was Megan from Los Angeles.

''I knew she had not been feeling well, tired, a pain in her shoulder....Why was she so tired? She had mourned for her father, yes, and perhaps too much....

"Now Megan had something to tell. She had felt a tiny lump on her clavicle, the bone above the ribs commonly called the breastbone. She had gone with [her husband] to a hospital for a biopsy. She had cancer. Not like her father's, not related, no explanation except that she had been mourning, saddened, her immunity systems down. That was medical opinion.

"She needed us a very short time....From the beginning radiation was not effective, she became too weak for chemotherapy. Once, as she rested, I asked if she'd like to help check the galley proofs of *Honor* and I heard again those fateful words, 'Let me do it tomorrow.'

"Megan died shortly before midnight on the last day of the year, before the clocks of the world could strike twelve. I had lost both my beloved travellers."[3]

"I am more in love with them now than I was when they were alive....Both of them were so careful to make their dying easier on those they left behind. They kept a certain dignity to them....The only mistake [Megan] ever made was to get cancer. And of all the things that Bill and I tried to teach our children, one thing—courage—Megan taught herself. She died with grace.

"I started to write a book called *Megan: A Different Love Story*. I *had* to write about what she had gone through with her illness, and the way she met death. But I was in tears all the time, and I couldn't get anything done. So I put that work away, realizing that I could still write about Megan, if I could just remember a happier time."[2]

Daly moved on to *Acts of Love*, a story based on her daughter's first love affair in high school with a young, semi-cowboy. "His name was Perry Cann and he became a lifelong friend; Perry went to Vietnam from our house, came back from Vietnam to our house.

"Megan is the girl in the story named Retta Caldwell; Patrick is her younger brother, Two; Perry is the cowboy, Dallas Dobson; and Bill is the father. The highway that comes through the Caldwell's land is the same highway that came through our home in Pennsylvania."[1]

"I worked with the structure of memory, but other than the events, which are mostly true, I wanted to capture the emotions accurately—helplessness in the face of external forces. There are times in life when Fate is in control of people, and not the other way around.

FICTION
61931-4 • $2.95 • AN ARCHWAY PAPERBACK PUBLISHED BY POCKET BOOKS

The magic and wonder of first love

Seventeenth Summer
Maureen Daly

Softcover of the young adult classic.

"I wanted to show that there are people and things that we love and respond to, and yet fear. As I wrote *Acts of Love* I realized that even though Megan died so young, in her lifetime she had secret pleasures. I didn't know everything about her. I like to think that the girl in the book didn't tell her mother everything, either.

"The book is my tribute, my way of holding onto the memory of Megan and Bill's voices, their pleasures, their smiles of surprise. It is my way of keeping us together a little longer."[2]

By the time *Acts of Love* was published in 1986, forty-four years had passed since Daly's first YA novel. She found the return to fiction a refreshing change. "I felt very defiant returning to fiction. Bill was so desperate to be a novelist that I gave him the creative air of the house. He wanted to be a novelist so badly that I think I unconsciously said, 'I'll be a journalist and let you be everything you want to be.' It was only after his death that I realized how much I longed for fiction."[1] As a result, Daly completed the sequel to *Acts of Love*, entitled *First a Dream*. "The title is part of a quote from Carl Sandburg, 'Nothing happens until first a dream.' In this sequel, cowboy Dallas Dobson goes out to California as a ranch hand."[1]

Daly writes at least five days a week, preferring to work in two sessions. "Wake up time is at six-thirty. I've always got press releases to do in the morning and a lot of mail. I still handle Bill's estate—he has a lot of contract and fan mail—and that usually takes me until about ten-thirty in the morning. Then I like to work clear-headed until about one o'clock. I have a sit-down lunch, go back to the typewriter about two, work until about four-thirty.

"I live alone since Bill died, so I have a lot of time. Being my own schedule maker allows me my freedom. While writing the last of *First a Dream*, I'd often start work at six in the morning, work my regular session until about ten, and then return to work after dinner until about midnight. That's when you're excited, when you know you're coming down the home-stretch.

"Once the characters have begun to lurk in my mind, I work out the plot and succession of events on long legal pads—adding and subtracting, thickening and simplifying—until the story seems rather clear."[1]

Daly believes that "writing is one type of work that can begin as soon as you are old enough to stop drawing on the walls with crayons and turn to more serious work with pencil and paper."[4]

"Aspiring writers should read as much as possible: newspapers, good magazines, fiction, biography, and history. Writing is like training the muscles for ballet: the more you practice reading and thinking, the stronger you'll be as a writer."[1]

Looking back over the work she did when first starting out, Daly is "sometimes pleasantly surprised, impressed by some of the things I wrote when I was so young. I'm surprised I was that skilled, but that's like looking at somebody else.

"For years and years I didn't read *Seventeenth Summer*. It was just something that existed in my house. I reread it recently and thought it was perhaps the most sensual innocence I've ever come across. Librarians have told me over the years that in many editions there are three pages that are torn out: the scene in which the boy and the girl go into the woods together, pick some wild grapes, and

return to the firelight, their lips still stained dark from the wild grapes. It's as hot as Sylvester Stallone without his shirt on, but there is something about contained sensuality that is always very persuasive. The fact that at the time I didn't even know that I was being so sensual probably is what gives the book a certain magic.

"*Seventeenth Summer* has a certain universality because almost all females have experienced the same feelings."[1]

"I think that one of the reasons the book has never gone out of print is that it makes a pretty persuasive argument for love. The second reason is that teachers use it in classes. When I found out they had assigned it in Megan's school, I asked her if the students knew I had written it. She said, 'Mother, that would be sooooo embarrassing!'"[2]

"When Megan died my own agony was so great that I went to a psychologist. He asked me if I had any particular philosophy about life. English writer John Cardinal Newman once said, 'A gentleman is one who gives no pain.' That is my philosophy, and I learned it strictly from my parents. To move through life with as little pain, gossip, and retribution as humanly possible."[1]

Footnote Sources:

[1] Based on an interview by Deborah Klezmer for *Authors and Artists for Young Adults*.
[2] Kimberly Olson Fakih, "The Long Wait for Maureen Daly," *Publishers Weekly*, June 27, 1986.
[3] Maureen Daly, *Something about the Author Autobiography Series*, Volume 1, Gale, 1986.
[4] Robert van Gelder, "An Interview with Miss Maureen Daly," *New York Times Book Review*, July 12, 1942.
[5] M. Daly, "Write What You Know," *Scholastic*, March 20, 1944.
[6] M. Daly, "Writing for Young Readers," *Scholastic*, October 22, 1945.

■ For More Information See

Publishers Weekly, May 31, 1941, April 25, 1942.
Scholastic, September 15, 1941.
Current Biography, 1946, H. W. Wilson, 1947.
Harry R. Warfel, *American Novelists of Today*, American Book, 1951.
New York Times Magazine, April 28, 1957, June 16, 1957.
Muriel Fuller, editor, *More Junior Authors*, H. W. Wilson, 1963.
G. Robert Carlsen, *Books and the Teen-Age Reader*, Harper, 1967.
Nancy Larrick, *A Parent's Guide to Children's Reading*, 3rd edition, Doubleday, 1969.
Dennis Thomison, *Readings about Adolescent Literature*, Scarecrow, 1970.

Martha E. Ward and Dorothy A. Marquardt, *Authors of Books for Young People,* Scarecrow, 2nd edition, 1971.

D. L. Kirkpatrick, *Twentieth-Century Children's Writers,* St. Martin's, 1978, 2nd edition, 1983.

Contemporary Literary Criticism, Volume 17, Gale, 1981.

Collections:

University of Oregon Library.

Loren Eiseley

Born September 3, 1907, in Lincoln, Neb.; died of pancreatic cancer, July 9, 1977, in Philadelphia, Pa.; son of Clyde Edwin (a salesman) and Daisy (Corey) Eiseley; married Mabel Langdon (a poet, art teacher and educator), August 29, 1938. *Education:* University of Nebraska, B.A., 1933; University of Pennsylvania, A.M., 1935, Ph.D., 1937. *Religion:* Protestant.

■ Career

University of Kansas, Lawrence, assistant professor, 1937-42, associate professor of sociology and anthropology, 1942-44; Oberlin College, Oberlin, Ohio, professor of sociology and anthropology and chairman of department, 1944-47; University of Pennsylvania, Philadelphia, professor and chairman of the department of anthropology, 1947-59, curator of Early Man, University of Pennsylvania Museum, 1948-77, provost, 1959-61, professor of anthropology and history of science, 1961-63, chairman of department of history of science, 1961-63, chairman of department of history and philosophy of science, Graduate School of Arts and Sciences, 1961-64, Benjamin Franklin and University Professor of Anthropology and History of Science, 1961-77. Visting professor of anthropology, Columbia

University, summers, 1946, 1950, University of California at Berkeley, summer, 1949, Harvard University, summer, 1952, and University of Kansas. Hosted television program, "Animal Secrets," 1966-68. Member of presidential task force on Preservation of Natural Beauty, 1964-65. Member of board of directors, Samuel S. Fels Foundation, Philadelphia, Pa.; National Parks Division, Department of the Interior, member of advisory board, 1966-72, member of council, 1972-77.

■ Member

American Anthropological Association (fellow; vice-president, 1948-49), American Institute of Human Paleontology (president, 1949-52), American Association for the Advancement of Science (fellow; vice-president, 1969), National Academy of Arts and Sciences (fellow), National Institute of Arts and Letters (fellow), American Philosophical Society (fellow), American Academy of Political and Social Science (member of board of directors), American Association of University Professors, American Association of Physical Anthropologists, Society for American Archaeology, New York Academy of Sciences (fellow), Philadelphia Anthropological Society (vice-president, 1947; president, 1948), Phi Beta Kappa, Sigma Xi, Century Club (New York).

■ Awards, Honors

Social Science Research Council Postdoctoral Fellow, 1940-41; Wenner-Gren Foundation of Anthropology Research Grant, 1952-53; Athenaeum of Philadelphia Award for Nonfiction, 1958, and Phi Beta Kappa Award in Science, 1959, both for *Darwin's Century*; Page One Award of the Philadelphia Newspaper Guild, 1960; John Burroughs Medal, and Pierre Lecomte du Nouy Foundation Award, both 1961, both for *The Firmament of Time*; Center for Advanced Study in the Behavioral Sciences Fellowship, Stanford, Calif., 1961-62; Citation for Outstanding Service to Education from the Department of Public Instruction, Commonwealth of Pennsylvania, 1962; Philadelphia Arts Festival Award for Literature, 1962; Guggenheim Fellow, 1964-65; Bradford Washburn Award from the Boston Museum of Science, 1976, for his "outstanding contribution to the public understanding of science"; Joseph Wood Krutch Medal from the Humane Society of the United States, 1976, for his "oustanding contribution to the improvement of life and the environment in this country"; recipient of over thirty-five honorary degrees.

■ Writings

(Editor) John Moss and others, *Early Man in the Eden Valley*, University of Pennsylvania Museum, 1951.
(Editor) *An Appraisal of Anthropology Today*, University of Chicago Press, 1953.
The Immense Journey (essays), Random House, 1957.
Darwin's Century: Evolution and the Men Who Discovered It, Doubleday, 1958.
(With others) *Social Control in a Free Society*, University of Pennsylvania Press, 1958, reissued, Greenwood Press, 1975.
The Firmament of Time, Atheneum, 1960.
The Mind as Nature, Harper, 1962.
Francis Bacon and the Modern Dilemma, University of Nebraska Press, 1963, revised and expanded edition published as *The Man Who Saw through Time*, Scribner, 1973.
The Unexpected Universe, Harcourt, 1969.
The Invisible Pyramid, Scribner, 1970.
The Night Country, Scribner, 1971.
(Author of introduction) *The Shape of Likelihood: Relevance and the University*, University of Alabama Press, 1971.
Notes of an Alchemist (poems), Scribner, 1972.
The Innocent Assassins (poems), Scribner, 1973.
All the Strange Hours: The Excavation of a Life (autobiography), Scribner, 1975.
Another Kind of Autumn (poetry), Scribner, 1977.
The Star Thrower, Times Books, 1978.

Darwin and the Mysterious Mr. X: New Light on the Evolutionists (essays), edited by Kenneth Heuer, Dutton, 1979.
All the Night Wings (poems), Times Books, 1979.
K. Heuer, editor, *The Lost Notebooks of Loren Eiseley*, Little, Brown, 1987.

Contributor of verse and prose to literary anthologies. Contributor to scientific journals, including *Science, Scientific Monthly, American Antiquity*, and *American Anthropologist*, and to newspapers and national magazines, including *Saturday Evening Post, Holiday, Ladies' Home Journal, Atlantic, Reader's Digest, Harper's, Saturday Review of Literature, Scientific American, Horizon, New York Herald Tribune*, and *New York Times*. Member of editorial board, *American Scholar* and *Expedition*.

■ Sidelights

September 3, 1907. Born in the bleak farm country of Lincoln, Nebraska, the only child of Clyde, a traveling salesman, and Daisy Corey Eiseley. "I was a child of the early century, American man, if the term may still be tolerated. A creature molded of plains' dust and the seed of those who came west with the wagons."[1]

"Born. . .in the wrong time, the wrong place, and into the wrong family. I am not insensible of the paradox: It is this which made me."[2]

"I lived, like most American boys of that section, in a small house where the uncemented cellar occasionally filled with water and the parlor was kept shuttered in a perpetual cool darkness. We never had visitors. No minister ever called on us, so the curtains were never raised. We were, in a sense, social outcasts. We were not bad people nor did we belong to a racial minority. We were simply shunned as unimportant and odd."[3]

"I was born when father was forty, of a marriage that had never been happy. I was loved, but I was also a changeling, an autumn child surrounded by falling leaves."[1]

"My mother was stone-deaf; my father worked the long hours of a time when labor was still labor. I was growing up alone in a house whose dead silence was broken only by the harsh discordant jangling of a voice that could not hear itself. My mother had lost her hearing as a young girl, I never learned what had attracted my father to her. I never learned by what fantastic chance I had come to exist at all.

"There grew up between my mother and myself an improvised system of communication, consisting of hand signals, stampings on the floor to create vibrations, exaggerated lip movements vaguely reminiscent of an anthropoid society. We did not consciously work at this; we were far too ignorant. Certain acts were merely found useful and came to be repeated and to take on symbolic value. It was something of the kind of communication which may have been conducted by the map-apes of the early ice age. One might say we were at the speech threshold—not much more."[3]

"I never saw my mother weep; it was her gift to make others suffer instead. She was an untutored, talented artist and she left me, if anything, a capacity for tremendous visual impressions.

"[She] lavished affection upon me in her tigerish silent way, giving me cakes when I should have had bread, attempting protection when I was already learning without brothers the grimness and realities of the street.

"My father, a one-time itinerant actor, had in that silenced household of the stone age—a house of gestures, of daylong facial contortion—produced for me the miracle of words when he came home."[1]

"He had a beautiful resonant speaking voice. Although we owned no books, and although when I knew him in middle age a harsh life had dimmed every hunger except that for rest, he could still declaim long rolling Elizabethan passages that caused shivers to run up my back.

"He reared a son, the product of an unfortunate marriage from which he might easily have fled, leaving me inarticulate. He was kind and thoughtful with an innate courtesy that no school in that rough land had taught him. Although he was intensely sensitive, I saw him weep but twice."[3]

When still very young "I remember the mad Shepards as I heard the name whispered among my mother's people. I remember the pacing, the endless pacing of my parents after midnight, while I lay shivering in the cold bed and tried to understand the words that passed between my mother and my father.

"In the house, when my father was away and my mother's people came to visit, the Shepards were spoken of in whispers. They were the mad Shepards, I slowly gathered, and they lay somewhere in my line of descent. When I was recalcitrant the Shepards were spoken of and lined with my name.

"In that house there was no peace, yet we loved each other fiercely. Perhaps the adults were so far on into the midcountry that mistakes were never rectifiable, flight disreputable."[1]

"I did not go to church, and since the family was not agreed upon any mode of worship, I merely wondered as I grew older how it was that things came to be. In short, I would have been diagnosed today by social workers as a person suffering from societal deprivation and headed for trouble."[3]

To avoid the stress of his home, Eiseley escaped into the surrounding country, where his love of nature and animals was nurtured. The landscape of his childhood country etched into his imagination and found a place in his adult writing. "I played alone in those days. . . .I took to creeping up alleys and peering through hedges. I was not miserable. There was a wonderful compensating secrecy about these activities. I had little shelters in hedgerows and I knew and perfected secret entrances and exits into the most amazing worlds."[3]

Eiseley, age six, with his father.

"I prospected for hours alone....I still can't tell what started it. I was groping, I think, childishly into time, into the universe. It was to be my profession but I never understood in the least, not till much later. No other child on the block wasted his time like that. I have never understood my precise motivation, never. For actually I was retarded in the reading of clock time. Was it because, in the things found in the sand, I was already lost and wandering instinctively—amidst the debris of vanished eras?"[1]

"I lived, more than most children, in two worlds. One was dark, hidden, and self-examining, though in its own way not without compensations. The other world in which I somehow also managed to exist was external, boisterous, and what I suppose the average parent would call normal or extroverted. These two worlds simultaneously existing in one growing brain had in them something of the dichotomy present in the actual universe, where one finds, behind the ridiculous, wonderful tent-show of woodpeckers, giraffes, and hoptoads, some

Collecting fossils in the Badlands.

kind of dark, brooding, but creative void out of which these things emerge.

"Through the accidents of fortune, the disparity between these two worlds was vastly heightened. How I managed to exist in both I do not know....I am not unaware that I paid a certain price for my survival and indeed have been paying for it ever since. Yet the curious thing is that I survived and, looking back, I have a growing feeling that the experience was good for me. I think I learned something from it even while I passed through certain humiliations and an utter and profound loneliness. I was living in a primitive world at the same time that I was inhabiting the modern world as it existed in the second decade of this century. I am not talking now about the tree-house, cave-building activities of normal boys. I am talking about the minds of the first dawning human consciousness—about a kind of mental ice age, and of how a light came in from outside until, as I have indicated, two worlds existed in which a boy, still a single unsplit personality, walked readily from one world to the other by day and by night without anyone observing the invisible boundaries he passed."[3]

"My father, whom I admired very much and tried to model myself after...was a great teacher. He turned me loose to pursue my interests wherever they led. He bought me books on the subjects that interested me and encouraged me to browse in the town library.

"I began to read natural history and related subjects at an early age and learned a lot that had nothing to do with formal courses in school. Perhaps this kind of self-education is one source of the sense of wonder."[4]

"I did not have to go to kindergarten to learn to read. I had already mastered the alphabet at some earlier point. I had little primers of my own, the see-John-run sort of thing or its equivalent in the year of 1912. Yes, in that fashion I could read. Sometime in the months that followed, my elder brother paid a brief visit home. He brought with him a full adult version of *Robinson Crusoe*. He proceeded to read it to me in spare moments. I lived for that story. I hung upon my brother's words. Then abruptly, as was always happening in the world above me in the lamplight, my brother had departed. We had reached only as far as the discovery of the footprint on the shore.

"He left me the book, to be exact, but no reader. I never asked mother to read because her voice distressed me. Her inability to hear had made it harsh and jangling. My father read with great grace and beauty but he worked the long and dreadful hours of those years. There was only one thing evident to me. I had to get on with it, do it myself, otherwise I would never learn what happened to Crusoe.

"I took Defoe's book and some little inadequate dictionary I found about the house, and proceeded to worry and chew my way like a puppy through the remaining pages. No doubt I lost the sense of a word here and there, but I mastered it. I had read it on my own. Papa bought me *Twenty Thousand Leagues under the Sea* as a reward. I read that, too. I began to read everything I could lay my hands on."[1]

At the age of six Eiseley wrote his first book, *Animal Adventures*, about the building and care of home aquariums.

Along with the local library, the museum at the University of Nebraska became his second home. He would mold small clay skulls, fashioned from drawings he had observed, and with these set up his own museum in an abandoned barn. "Only in my museum nothing was dead. It was filled with a kind of patient, unwinking persistence—the persistence of a half-bewitched league of jack-o'-lantern faces waiting for me to come and sit with them in the green light high in the loft."[3]

By the eighth grade Eiseley had already ". . .read a great many of Charles G. D. Roberts' nature stories and those of Ernest Thompson Seton. I had also absorbed the evolutionary ideas of the early century through Jack London's *Before Adam* and Stanley Waterloo's *Story of Ab*. None of this had come from high school. It had come from the books brought home from the local Carnegie library to which I used to pedal in my coaster wagon. 'I want to be a nature writer.' How strangely that half-prophetic statement echoes in my brain today. It was like all my wishes. There was no one to get me started on the road. I read books below my age, I read books well beyond my age and puzzled over them."[1]

He worked diligently on his writing, aided by two teachers at the University of Nebraska High School.

1925. Eiseley enrolled at the University of Nebraska, majoring in zoology and literature. A serious bout of influenza forced him to drop out and spend a year in the Mohave Desert. "Another disease gnawed at my vitals. A yearlong immobility. . .had left me savage, restless, at odds with my environment. I tried, through university extension courses,

to overcome deficiencies and graduate. All failed. I prowled about like an animal. Suddenly, I vanished again. Always, as though it lingered in my blood, the ways, however wandering, lay west, not east."[1]

His wanderlust took him across an America caught in the grips of the Great Depression. "It was a time. Leave it at that. The young, the middle-ages, the old, even a few case-hardened women. We lay like windrows of leaves on sandbars beside the Union Pacific, the Rock Island, the Santa Fe, the Katy. At night our fires winked like the bivouacs of armies. We rode the empty fruit trains coming through Needles into the sand hell of the Mohave. Railroad detectives blackjacked us or turned aside in fear of numbers. We gathered like descending birds in spite of all obstacles. Like birds, some of us died because we were old and we perished, unnoticed, of cold in the high Sierras or we slipped under the wheels of freights in moments of exhaustion. If found, what remained was buried in nameless graves along the track. Cheap liquor killed us; occasionally we died by the gun and so did the railroad detectives, pushing their luck too far with sullen unknown men in the night on swaying car tops.

"It was a time of violence, a time of hate, a time of sharing, a time of hunger. It was all that every human generation believes it has encountered for the very first time in human history. Life is a journey and eventually a death. Mine was no different than those others. But this is in retrospect. At that time I merely lived, and each day, each night, was different.

"I could not get outside the ring, the ring of poverty. Like a wolf on an invisible chain I padded endlessly around and around the shut doors of knowledge. I learned, but not enough. I ran restlessly from one scent to another. Sometimes I gave up and disappeared into the dark underworld of wandering men. Or I worked at menial tasks and convinced myself I would have been content if one of them had lasted."[1]

With the money earned from these jobs, Eiseley returned intermittently to the University of Nebraska. "Some of the black marks on my college record were products of the same suspicious fears shown by my deafened mother. Other students stumbling into the wrong course or encountering inimical instructors went to their advisors and legally dropped the subject. I simply walked away and there the record stands. Bureaucracy intimidated me. I had come from the world of the night.

"I merely wanted to be left alone, but still I felt this persistent urge toward books....I tried to make whatever dream father had had of me into a reality. I found...that my appetite for wide areas of learning was insatiable, but there was no one to guide me. There was no one to say, 'Be a doctor, be a lawyer, be a teacher, a historian, a writer.' Perhaps I was none of those.

"The first English course I had ever taken at the university had turned me away from any thought of a formal career in that subject. The teacher had read my first assignment and told me bluntly, 'You didn't compose this; it is too well written.' Good or bad, it happened to be my own. The man couldn't prove his own assertion, but again, with the wary withdrawal of an animal, I merely turned away.

"This early unwarranted accusation had destroyed the pleasure of the formal subject for me. I was far on into middle age before I found a belated joy in professional literary studies. Perhaps that one belligerent sentence had something to do with my turning aside into science.

"Yet looking back I am not convinced. For a thin-skinned young man, still emerging from long isolation, encounters with the realities of the academic world were not always pleasant. My feelings for the western lands, uplifted scarps and buttes and the things contained in them, had long outweighed the written word in the emotional content of my mind. It was, perhaps, my mother's stifled vision, the visual impact of places demanding to be celebrated in essays I did not know how to write."[1]

1931. For the next three summers Eiseley was able to earn the money to help himself through school by joining excavating parties sponsored by the Nebraska State Museum. The expeditions and fossil hunts had a profound effect on him, providing him with scientific background. The majestic vastness and solitude of the land burned into his mind's eye and influenced his later writing. "I stood at the cave entrance...looking at life, at my companions, at the traffic below on the road, as though I had just arisen, a frozen man, from a torrent of melting ice. I wiped a muddy hand across my brow. The hand was ten thousand years away. So were my eyes, so would they always be, and still...I did not find a way to speak.

"The modern world was small, I thought, tiny, constricted beyond belief. A little lost century, a toy, I saw suddenly, looking upon our truck and pretentious archaeological gear with...stunned insight...and here I looked curiously and distantly upon my associates, had arisen from some kind of indefinable death amidst stalagmites and glacial mud ten thousand years removed.

"'We are dwarfed,' I muttered to myself alone, 'the tiny projection of a lantern show.'

"I have never again seen men so minutely clear, though I climbed with the others into the pickup truck and held my peace. 'Dwarfed,' I said again under my breath, seeing ourselves moving with tiny gesticulations across an infinite ice field into whose glare we finally vanished. It was like a glimpse through the slitted bone with which Eskimos protect their eyes from snow blindness. I have never had occasion in the years since to think upon us differently. Not once.'"[1]

In 1933 Eiseley earned his B.A. in anthropology and continued his studies at the University of Pennsylvania on a scholarship. His days as a drifter were over. He was awarded a Ph.D. in 1937. "When I appeared that fall before my first class in introductory sociology I realized two things as I walked through the door. I did not dare sit down. I did not dare use my notes for anything but a security blanket to toss confidently on the table like a true professor. The class was very large. A sizable portion of the football squad was scattered in the back row. I was, I repeat, an isolate....If I ever lost that audience there would be chaos. The class met every day in the week.

"Each night I studied beyond midnight and wrote outlines that I rarely followed. I paced restlessly before the class, in which even the campus dogs were welcome so long as they nodded their heads sagely in approval. In a few weeks I began to feel like the proverbial Russian fleeing in a sleigh across the steppes before a wolf pack. I am sure that Carroll Clark, my good-natured chairman, realized that a highly unorthodox brand of sociology was being dispensed in his domain, but he held his peace. By then everything from anecdotes of fossil hunting to observations upon Victorian Darwinism were being hurled headlong from the rear of the sleigh. The last object to go would be myself. Fortunately for me, the end of the semester came just in time.

"At the close of the first year I had acquired...some followers. I had learned figuratively to bow and I was destined to keep right on bowing through the next thirty years. There was no escape....An actor, and this means no reflection upon teaching, has to have at least a few adoring followers. Otherwise he will begin to doubt himself and shrink inward, or take to muttering over

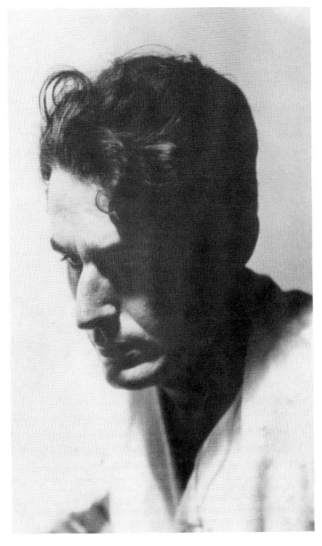

Eiseley, 1933.

Dust jacket from the 1987 Little, Brown edition.

outworn notes....I had emerged as a rather shy, introverted lad, to exhort others from a platform....For me it has been a lifelong battle with anxiety."[1]

1938. Married Mabel Langdon, a poet, art teacher and curator.

1941. The U.S. entered World War II, a time of disruption for Eiseley. "My troubles, however, were endless. I was the last of a line that had volunteered and fought in almost every war since the War for Independence. Yet here I was confronted with an utterly impossible situation. My mother, I had come to know, was committable without the care and attention of my aunt. All this had been certified and was on record. Both women were totally dependent upon my support. Moreover, my wife came home one day from the doctor's office to report a diagnosed illness which necessitated surgery. We had to borrow money.

Still I fretted, although by now four million men were under arms and the landing in Europe was drawing near. Perhaps it was foolish of me, in retrospect, but I was still young and there was a family tradition. I wanted to go. This impulse was to be suddenly augmented.

"One day I learned, in some way now forgotten, that there was a need for men capable of staffing military government in the islands of the Pacific being slowly overrun by the island-hopping technique of the Pacific war. Such an assignment would have solved the salary problem. My training and teaching in social anthropology seemed to offer some hope."[1] Failing his physical due to weak eyesight and a slight hearing impairment, he continued his work at the university.

Eiseley began experimenting; he wanted to make scientific writing more accessible to the general public. The writing began to incorporate a story-like approach and his pieces were published in *Harper's, American Scholar,* and other popular periodicals. With his intellectual prowess gaining national repute, Eiseley returned to the University of Pennsylvania as chairman of the department of anthropology and a year later as curator of Early Man in the university's museum.

Writing became paramount in his life. More magazines requested and published his varied pieces. He had found form for his writing. "A scientifically oriented magazine which had requested an article from me upon human evolution reneged in favor of a more distinguished visitor to America. Whether or not the editor realized it, I had counted heavily upon that piece. I had researched the subject considerably, but now I turned aside from the straitly defined scientific article. I had long realized an attachment for the personal essay, but the personal essay was out of fashion except perhaps for humor.

"I had done a lot of work on this article, but since my market was gone, why not attempt a more literary venture? Why not turn it—here I was thinking consciously at last about something I had done unconsciously before—into what I now term the concealed essay, in which personal anecdote was allowed gently to bring under observation thoughts of a more purely scientific nature?

"That the self and its minute adventures may be interesting every essayist from Montaigne to Emerson has intimated, but only if one is utterly, nakedly honest and does not pontificate....I shifted away from the article as originally intended. A personal anecdote introduced it, personal material lay scattered through it, personal philosophy concluded it, and yet I had done no harm to the scientific data. I sent the piece to one of the quality magazines, which accepted it. Out of the ghost world of my journeys...arose by degrees the prose world with which, it is true, I first toyed long ago, but which had been largely submerged by departmental discipline."[1]

For all his life, Eiseley would produce some of his most powerful writing during the middle of the night, when insomnia robbed him of sleep. "I do not lie and toss with doubt any longer, as I did in earlier years. I get up and write...or I read in the old chair that is as worn as I am. I read philosophy, metaphysics, difficult works that sometime, soon or late, draw a veil over my eyes so that I drowse in my chair.

"It is not that I fail to learn from these midnight examinations of the world. It is merely that I

choose that examination to remain as remote and abstruse as possible. Even so, I cannot always prophesy the result. An obscure line may whirl me into a wide-awake, ferocious concentration in which ideas like animals leap at me out of the dark, in which sudden odd trains of thought drive me inexorably to my desk and paper."[3]

1957. *The Immense Journey,* a collection of his musings on evolution, dedicated to the memory of his father, was and still is highly acclaimed, and has appeared in various editions throughout the world. "I am powerfully influenced by locale and, being geologically trained, a locale which may be projected vertically in time. My mind is stuffed with stray teeth, mammoth bones, and the lost trails of Indians and pioneers. It comes out in my writing—perhaps because my people came west in the time of buffalo grass and ox teams. I write because all these things haunt me and because, in that sense, I am the voice of things other than myself."[2]

1958. Some years earlier, at the request of an editor, Eiseley had begun exhaustive research for a book on the theory of evolution and the Darwinian epoch. Aided by a short leave of absence from the university and financial assistance provided by a foundation, Eiseley spent long periods of time in the bowels of libraries in search of forgotten or over-looked material. "In reality, there is a dust one may breathe among old books which can be just as fascinating, the heat as infernally oppressive, as any amount of crawling about in tombs and deserts.

"Contrary to the expressed opinions of the man who expounded upon the benefits of heat and dust in the field, I think I have never endured more unpleasant conditions than in those ancient library stacks.

"But the treasures. Let us come to the point. The treasures are in the mind that seeks them. Otherwise they are not recognized. Foreknowledge and preparation are needed before one blinds oneself in dark passages or wearily runs dusty thumb down the smallest news notes in some ancient and crumbling periodical.

"The scholar who descends into the catacombs of the past is endangered; he may lose his way. A given period, or a millenium, may become more real than the century he inhabits in the flesh. The documents may prove extensive; thread leads on to thread, passage to passage. My card files thickened with material tangential to the purpose with which I started. Similarly the dedicated archaeologist, laboring under an enormous compulsion, may hasten to the next tumulus carrying his discoveries only in his mortal head, while disease or a viper under a stone can suddenly erase his achievement. Equivalent perils confront the delver into libraries.

"Several years of toil passed with every spare moment occupied in a way that would have astounded and troubled the brisk young editor. I was becoming insubstantial, the present with its publishing schedules a bothersome encumbrance. My laboriously scrawled cards, which only I could decipher, continued their extension through fire-proof cases.

"I emerged ever more slowly into the light. The publishers had now waited several years. I am sure that they had given up all hope of receiving a manuscript.

"As it turned out, they were wrong. The centennial celebration of the publication of *The Origin of Species* was approaching. I owed the publishers for their advance.

"In the end I drew upon my enormous files and wrote *Darwin's Century* to discharge my obligation. I wrote till my eyes wept from stress. I slept when tired without reference to day or night, and arose and wrote again. Since my wife was visiting her parents, I had my meals from the icebox and scuttled about the halls of my apartment house like the half-wild creature I had become. A few months after publication, the book received the national Phi Beta Kappa Award in science."[1] The book is considered a basic text for students studying the history of evolutionary thought. Aside from its superb writing style and detailed documentation, the text is important because of Eiseley's rediscovery of predecesors to Darwin's theory of natural selection.

Throughout his life man and his evolution was the theme that spurred deep reflection within Eiseley. He saw a unity within the universe of life, and his love was not confined to man but to all species. "To write a book about such a mythical beast [man] demands a certain degree of detachment and a willingness to turn to the old fairy tales as well as to own oneself defeated. The sooner we come to this acknowledgement, the sooner we may be able to hold some kind of meaningful dialogue with the creature who confronts us every morning as we wake blinking in the dawn, namely that elusive changeling, ourselves.

"I have succumbed to the lure of this most restless animal, and I have learned in the hunt. It is a hunt that has taken me into ancient caverns, haunted

Softcover for the 1957 collection of essays.

tombs, and the whisperings that one hears at night in great libraries. Or again, I have felt a mocking presence in some subway face, or obscured beneath an Indian blanket. Upon one thing we can all agree: Once, so Indian mythology runs, there was a poor orphan. All Plains Indian tales have that formal opening. It is another way of saying this is the story of man. And it was to that subject that Darwin reluctantly turned in 1871."[2]

"Evolution is far more a part of the unrolling future than it is of the past, for the past, being past, is determined and done. The present, in the words of Karl Heim, 'is still in the molten phase of becoming. It is still undecided. It is still being fought for.' The man who cannot perceive that battleground looks vaguely at some animal which he expects to transform itself before his eyes."[3]

"I am not nearly so interested in what monkey man was derived from as I am in what kind of monkey he is to become."[2]

In 1960, *The Firmament of Time* was published by Atheneum. Based on a series of lectures, the book's theme is time, man's effort to understand its dimensions, and how his changing concept of time affected his place in nature.

The Mind as Nature was published in 1962. Originally given as a lecture, its subject is teaching and learning and is considered a classic. By now, Eiseley had gained a reputation as a brilliant educator. "The uses of a great professor are only partly to give us knowledge; his real purpose is to take his students beyond knowledge into the transcendental domain of the unknown, the future and the dream—to expand the limits of the human consciousness. In doing this he is creating the future in the minds of men. It is an awe-inspiring responsibility, and the men to whom this task is given should be chosen with all the care of which society is capable. The teacher is genuinely the creator of humanity, the molder of its most precious possession, the mind. There should be no greater honor given by society than permission to teach, just as there can be no greater disaster than to fail at the task. The evolution of man, which is still near to its animal beginnings, demands guidance by precept and great example. The teacher alone is in a position to supply that guidance through the long years of man's impressionable youth. He must teach men not alone to dream, but to dream so substantially that they will never in after years capitulate through weakness to the demands of a passing and ephemeral materialism. It is in the nature of man to transcend himself. All teaching which neglects this aspect of humanity will end in failure. It will fail sooner or later because it constitutes a denial, in fact, a deprivation, of human nature."[2]

1964. Eiseley received a Guggenheim Fellowship for one year to write "a kind of intellectual autobiography." "I hope to transcend the purely personal by suggesting unusual factors common to the life of man in a universe he is forced, from childhood, to try to understand.

"It is the most racking thing that I have ever attempted. Structuring it is always difficult and I am sure that a great deal will have to be reworked and thrown out before I manage to achieve anything satisfactory—assuming that I do."[2] The autobiography remained uncompleted for ten years.

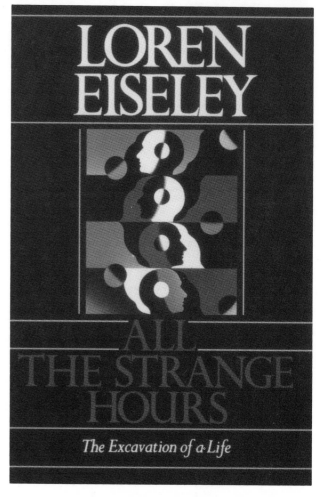

Cover for the 1975 paperback edition.

"My mother died at the age of eighty-six. The woman who in all my remembered life was neurotic, if not psychotic, whose blasted sense of beauty had been expended upon the saloon art of prairie towns, was dead. Her whole paranoid existence from the time of my childhood had been spent in the deliberate distortion and exploitation of the world about her.

"Across my brain were scars which had left me walking under the street lamps of unnumbered nights. I had heard her speak words to my father on his deathbed that had left me circling the peripheries of a continent to escape her always constant presence. Because of her, in ways impossible to retrace, I would die childless. Today, with such surety as genetics can offer, I know that the chances I would have run would have been no more than any man's chances, that the mad Shepards whose blood I carried may have had less to do with my mother's condition than her lifelong deafness. But she, and the whisperings in that old Victorian house of my aunt's, had done their work.

I would run no gamble with the Shepard line. I would mark their last earthly appearance. Figments of fantasy I know them now to be, but thanks to my mother and her morbid kin they destroyed their own succession in the child who turned away.

"For years I had expected to be drawn back to a deathbed scene of violence, without dignity and without even animal restraint. In the end it happened otherwise. Mother, who at the last had appeared the living embodiment of those witches who had terrorized the seventeenth century and among whom her own familial name was enshrined, had skipped town for the last time. She, the center of violence and contention whose ripples were still spreading toward infinity even in the lives of those who had never known her in life, had died peacefully in her sleep. The eye of the storm had passed."[2]

The Unexpected Universe was published by Harcourt, Brace & World in 1969. "There is in the universe a duality of powers in perfect equilibrium. The theme of *The Unexpected Universe* is how man in the Dark Wood has broken through this duality—so that something is loose and prowling in the fierce wood....Dante saw it long ago when he encountered himself. I saw it as a child under the bed."[2]

The book was extremely well received and the number of his dedicated followers grew. Even so, as before and with later writings, there were those in the field of science who criticized Eiseley for straying too far into literature. "*Anthropomorphizing:* the charge of my critics. My countercharge: There is a sense in which when we cease to anthropomorphize, we cease to be men, for when we cease to have human contact with animals and deny them all relation to ourselves, we tend in the end to cease to anthropomorphize ourselves—to deny our own humanity. We repeat the old, old human trick of freezing the living world and with it ourselves. There is also a sense...in which we *do* create our world by our ability to read it symbolically. But if we read it symbolically aloof from ourselves and our kindest impulses, we are returning to the pre-Deistic, pre-Romantic world of depraved Christianity—the world where man saw about him 'fallen nature,' with the devil slipping behind each tree. Modern anthropomorphizing consists in miming nature down to its ingredients, including ourselves. This is really only another symbolic reading, certainly no more 'real' than what I have been charged with."[2]

Eiseley was deeply concerned about the earth's ecology and supported the growing number of groups dedicated to its preservation. "For a couple of centuries now we have been ravagers of a continent. I have seen students who are perfectly willing to protest pollution by some large industry but who don't change by one iota their personal habits of wasteful disposal and littering. It is more fun to attack a particular industry that you don't like than to remake one's own personal habits which are part of this whole complex. This, I think, is going to be the hardest task and it will demand long educational effort. And it won't be done next year or in the next ten years.

"We can hope for progress, but change will involve more than one generation. Unfortunately, time is running out for man—in many ways he is the most recalcitrant creature in the universe."[5]

To supplement his income, Eiseley traveled the lecture circuit extensively. The time away was occasions for reflections. "My father's last years had been spent waiting alone in the solitude of hotel lobbies in the thousand little towns of the high country. Now I lay in similar beds in...college towns waiting alone to speak to university audiences of forgotten things. I pushed off the light and stared at the ceiling. There was no light there, no light at all. But somewhere in the remote darkness I could sense Halley's comet turning on its long ellipse. Hurry, I half formed the words. Hurry, or I will not be here. I did not know why I said it. Yes, I did. I wanted to return to that bare world of 1910, held in my father's arms—lay back and vanish. Pa, I said. There was no sound from the dark.

"That is my world. Pa, do you hear me? There was no answer from the dark. I lay back and tried to sleep; he had done this a thousand nights before me."[2]

1972-1973. A burst of creative energy produced two books of poetry, *Notes of an Alchemist* and *The Innocent Assassins.* "[In *Notes of an Alchemist*] I have drawn from notebooks extending into the past some poetry which my editor at Scribners persuaded me, rather reluctantly, to publish.

"When I was a very young man in college I loved the art very much and I suppose there was a time when I could have quoted off-hand any of the leading poets of the period. I had responsibilities to others, however, and because I had a somewhat omnivorous and amoeboid mind I turned aside into science. Nevertheless occasionally in professional notebooks, amidst notations on artifacts, digs, and what-not, I continued to scrawl verse, just as I have continued to enjoy the personal essay, somewhat to the discomfort of some of my colleagues. I have always been somewhat solitary and I suppose this little volume gets something off my chest. I no longer know the critical world in this domain well enough to judge its reaction or to particularly care.

"*The Innocent Assassins* being completed, I now want to turn to some prose again, although oddly enough having let this long-suppressed vice of poetry up out of the basement it is going to be difficult for me to reconcentrate my efforts.

"Retirement is looming fast upon me and...I shall have to make decisions as to whether I stay about, seek a place in the sun, or return to the long-forgotten and probably vastly changed world of my boyhood....The sense of some overwhelming autumnal sadness grows and to the best of my ability you will probably find murmurs of it in this new book."[2]

His memoirs, *All the Strange Hours: The Excavation of a Life*, were published in 1975. "I was planning to wait until I retired before I wrote it, but then I've been planning to retire since I was fifteen years old, and I haven't managed it yet.

"Is it a catharsis? Perhaps at the time but not now, not afterwards. In the end, I suppose you're writing for someone out there you feel may be similar to you. My books seem to appeal mostly to the young, or to people even older than myself—which is very old indeed. They apparently find hope in what I've written, even when I've been rather melancholy."[6]

Died of pancreatic cancer and was buried at West Laurel Hill Cemetery, Bala-Cynwyd, Pennsylvania. "I wanted increasingly to stay and wander among the sun-warmed stones representing a humanity from which harsh words and cruelty had been drained away. Perhaps a grave was the only place where things came right—except one could never get the stones to speak, only to be warm with sun if one touched them."[2]

On his and his wife's tombstone is engraved: "We loved the earth but could not stay."

1978. The Loren Eiseley Seminary and Library was dedicated at the University of Pennsylvania. It houses his personal library of over five thousand books and two thousand reprints and memorabilia in the two rooms that had been his office.

Five books of Eiseley's were published posthumously: *Another Kind of Autumn* (1977), a collection of poetry he compiled before his death; *The*

Star Thrower (1978), a compilation of his favorite writings, put together by him before his death; *Darwin and the Mysterious Mr. X: New Light on the Evolutionist* (1979), deals with the forgotton nineteenth-century naturalist, Edward Blyth; *All the Night Wings* (1979), a collection of his poetry from 1928 to 1977; and *The Lost Notebooks of Loren Eiseley* (1987), edited by Kenneth Heuer.

Footnote Sources:

[1] Loren Eiseley, *All the Strange Hours: The Excavation of a Life,* Scribner, 1975.
[2] Kenneth Heuer, editor, *The Lost Notebooks of Loren Eiseley,* Little, Brown, 1987.
[3] L. Eiseley, *The Night Country,* Scribner, 1971.
[4] Mildred Sandison Fenner, "The Editor Interviews Loren Eiseley," *NEA Journal,* November, 1966.
[5] Robert W. Glasgow, "Ego and Evolution—A Conversation with Loren Eiseley," *Psychology Today,* October, 1970.
[6] John Baker, "PW Interviews: Loren Eiseley," *Publishers Weekly,* November 3, 1975.

■ For More Information See

Harper's, October, 1947, November, 1948, May, 1951, March, 1964 (p. 51ff), November, 1971 (p. 96ff), September, 1987 (p. 27ff).
Scientific American, February, 1956 (p. 26).
Current Biography, 1960, H. W. Wilson, 1961.
Time, October 12, 1962 (p. 104).
Atlantic, June, 1963 (p. 75ff).
Wilson Library Bulletin, June, 1964 (p. 875ff), October, 1969 (p. 188ff).
New York Times Magazine, October 18, 1964 (p. 66ff).
Esquire, March, 1967 (p. 92).
Life, February 16, 1968 (p. 88ff), February 6, 1970, November 19, 1971.
Redbook, December, 1968 (p. 51ff).
Christian Science Monitor, October 16, 1969.
Washington Post Book World, November 26, 1969, July 22, 1979.
Best Sellers, December 15, 1969, December 1, 1970.
New Yorker, February 21, 1970 (p. 118ff).
Nation, March 8, 1971 (p. 312ff).
New York Times, November 10, 1971, December 18, 1975.
Detroit News, December 26, 1971.
Parnassus: Poetry in Review, fall/winter, 1973 (p. 227ff).
Today: The Philadelphia Inquirer Magazine, January 27, 1974 (p. 16).
U.S. News & World Report, March 3, 1975 (p. 43ff).
New York Times Book Review, November 23, 1975 (p. 36), July 22, 1979.
Prairie Schooner, summer, 1977 (p. 111ff).
Contemporary Literary Criticism, Volume VII, Gale, 1977.
Washington Post, July 8, 1978.
America, April 28, 1979 (p. 51ff).
Omni, June, 1982 (p. 86ff).
Leslie Gerber, *Loren Eiseley,* Ungar, 1983.

Christian Century, April 25, 1984 (p. 430ff).
Reader's Digest, November, 1987 (p. 35ff).
Gale E. Christianson, *Fox at the Edge of the Woods:
    A Biography of Loren Eiseley,* Holt, 1990.

Washington Post, July 11, 1977.
Newsweek, July 25, 1977.
Time, July 25, 1977.
Publishers Weekly, August 1, 1977.

Obituaries:

New York Times, July 11, 1977.

Dick Francis

B orn Richard Stanley Francis, on October 31, 1920, in Tenby, Pembrokeshire, Wales; son of George Vincent (a professional steeplechase rider and stable manager) and Catherine Mary (Thomas) Francis; married Mary Brenchley (a teacher and an assistant stage manager), June 21, 1947; children: Merrick, Felix. *Education:* Attended Maidenhead County School and a private school. *Religion:* Church of England. *Home and Office:* 5100 North Ocean Blvd, 609 Sea Ranch Club A, Fort Lauderdale, Fla. 33308. *Agent:* Andrew Hewson, John Johnson Authors' Agent, 45/47 Clerkenwell Green, London EC1R 0HT, England; Sterling Lord Literistic, Inc., One Madison Ave., New York, N.Y. 10010.

■ Career

Amateur steeplechase rider, 1946-48; professional steeplechase jockey, 1948-57; *Sunday Express,* London, England, racing correspondent, 1957-73; writer, 1957—; owner of horse farm, 1960-80. *Military service:* Royal Air Force, 1940-46; became flying officer (pilot). *Member:* Crime Writers Association (chairman, 1973-74), Mystery Writers of America, Writers of Canada.

■ Awards, Honors

Steeplechase Jockey Champion, 1954; Silver Dagger Award from the Crime Writers Association, 1965, for *For Kicks;* Edgar Allan Poe Award for Best Mystery of the Year from the Mystery Writers of America, 1969, for *Forfeit,* and 1980, for *Whip Hand; Reflex* was selected one of New York Public Library's Books for the Teenage, 1982; Gold Dagger Award from the Crime Writers Association, 1980, for *Whip Hand;* Order of the British Empire, 1984.

■ Writings

Mystery Novels, Except As Indicated:

The Sport of Queens (racing autobiography), M. Joseph, 1957, revised edition, 1968, Harper, 1969, large print edition, Ulverscroft, 1982.

Dead Cert, Holt, 1962.

Nerve, Harper, 1964, large print edition, Ulverscroft, 1978.

For Kicks, Harper, 1965.

Odds Against, M. Joseph, 1965, Harper, 1966, published as *The Racing Game,* Pocket Books, 1984.

Flying Finish, M. Joseph, 1966, Harper, 1967, large print edition, Ulverscroft, 1979.

Blood Sport, Harper, 1967.

Forfeit, Harper, 1968, large print edition, Ulverscroft, 1979.

Enquiry, Harper, 1969, large print edition, Ulverscroft, 1979.

Rat Race, M. Joseph, 1970, Harper, 1971.

Bonecrack, Harper, 1971.

Smokescreen, Harper, 1972, large print edition, Ulverscroft, 1978.

Slay-Ride, M. Joseph, 1973, Harper, 1974.

Knock Down, M. Joseph, 1974, Harper, 1975, large print edition, Ulverscroft, 1979.

High Stakes, Harper, 1975, large print edition, Ulverscroft, 1979.

In the Frame, M. Joseph, 1976, Harper, 1977.

Risk, Harper, 1977, large print edition, Ulverscroft, 1979.

Trial Run, M. Joseph, 1978, Harper, 1979, large print edition, Ulverscroft, 1980.

Whip Hand, M. Joseph, 1979, Harper, 1980, large print edition, Ulverscroft, 1980.

Reflex, M. Joseph, 1980, Putnam, 1981, large print edition, G. K. Hall, 1981.

Twice Shy, M. Joseph, 1981, Putnam, 1982, large print edition, G. K. Hall, 1982.

Banker, M. Joseph, 1982, Putnam, 1983, large print edition, G. K. Hall, 1983.

The Danger, M. Joseph, 1983, Putnam, 1984, large print edition, G. K. Hall, 1984.

Proof, M. Joseph, 1984, Putnam, 1985, large print edition, G. K. Hall, 1985.

Break In, M. Joseph, 1985, Putnam, 1986.

A Jockey's Life: The Biography of Lester Piggott (biography), Putnam, 1986.

Bolt, M. Joseph, 1986, Putnam, 1987, large print edition, G. K. Hall, 1988.

Hot Money, M. Joseph, 1987, Putnam, 1988, large print edition, G. K. Hall, 1988.

The Edge, M. Joseph, 1988, Putnam, 1989, large print edition, G. K. Hall, 1989.

Straight, Putnam, 1989.

Longshot, Putnam, 1990.

Compiler And Editor With John Welcome:

Best Racing and Chasing Stories (anthology), Faber, 1966.

Best Racing and Chasing Stories II (anthology), Faber, 1969.

The Racing Man's Bedside Book, Faber, 1969.

Omnibus Editions:

Three to Show (contains *Dead Cert, Nerve,* and *Odds Against*), Harper, 1969.

Across the Board (contains *Flying Finish, Blood Sport,* and *Enquiry*), Harper, 1975.

Three Winners (contains *Dead Cert, Nerve,* and *For Kicks*), M. Joseph, 1977.

Three Favorites (contains *Odds Against, Flying Finish,* and *Blood Sport*), M. Joseph, 1978.

Three to Follow (contains *Forfeit, Enquiry,* and *Rat Race*), M. Joseph, 1979.

Two by Francis (contains *Forfeit* and *Slay-Ride*), Harper, 1983.

Four Complete Novels, Crown, 1984.

Contributor To Anthologies:

Virginia Whitaker, editor, *Winter's Crimes 5,* Macmillan (London), 1973.

Joan D. Berbrich, editor, *Stories of Crime and Detection*, McGraw, 1974.

Ellery Queen's Crime Wave, Putnam, 1976.

Ellery Queen's Searches and Seizures, Davis, 1977.

Francis' books have been translated into many foreign languages, including Japanese, Norwegian, and Czechoslovakian. Contributor to periodicals, including *Horseman's Year, In Praise of Hunting, Sports Illustrated,* and *Stud and Stable*.

■ Adaptations

"Dead Cert" (motion picture), starring Scott Antony, Judi Dench, Michael Dignum, and Julian Glover, Woodfull Films, 1974.

"The Racing Game" (television series; based on *Odds Against*), starring Mike Gwilym, Yorkshire Television, 1979, appeared on "Mystery!" series, PBS-TV, 1980-81.

"Dick Francis Mysteries" (television series), Dick Francis Films Ltd., 1989.

Cassettes:

"High Stakes," Listen for Pleasure, 1980.

"Forfeit," G. K. Hall, 1983.

"Enquiry," G. K. Hall, 1983.

"Rat Race," G. K. Hall.

"Bonecrack," G. K. Hall.

"Trial Run," G. K. Hall, 1984.

"Proof," Listen for Pleasure, 1985.

"Blood Sport," G. K. Hall, 1985.

"Reflex," Warner Audio, 1985.

"In the Frame," G. K. Hall, 1986.

"For Kicks," G. K. Hall, 1987.

"Nerve," G. K. Hall, 1987.

"Bolt," Listen for Pleasure, 1987.

"The Danger," G. K. Hall, 1988.

"Slay-Ride," G. K. Hall, 1988.

"Break In," Audio Language Studies, 1989.

"Hot Money," Listen for Pleasure, 1989.

"The Edge," Listen for Pleasure, 1989.

"Straight," Listen for Pleasure, 1990.

"Flying Finish," Harper Audio, 1990.

"Dead Cert," Harper Audio, 1990.

Dick Francis, right, riding Devon Loch at the 1956 Grand National.

■ Work in Progress

Additional mystery novels; television films based on his stories and produced by Dick Francis Films Ltd.

■ Sidelights

Raised in a family of jockeys, Dick Francis rode professionally for ten years, became Champion Jockey in 1954 and nearly won the Grand National on the Queen Mother's horse, Devon Loch. Mystery still surrounds the event. Ahead by several lengths, the horse faltered and fell just before the finish line. Because Devon Loch was not injured, Francis is sure it was the deafening noise of the crowd which startled the horse.

Retiring soon after, Francis began working as a racing correspondent while writing his autobiography, *The Sport of Queens.* He followed that with mystery novels and has written one a year, with great success, ever since. Most of his books involve the world of racing and are often criticized for being too violent. But having experienced innumerable broken bones while racing, Francis feels that writing such pain into his books has helped him deal with his own injuries. He also feels that his characters become more realistic, more heroic. "During my racing days, I broke twenty-one bones. . . .As a jockey, I broke one collarbone five times and the other one six. Now it's an even dozen. I broke my nose five times. The twenty-one broken bones don't include ribs. You don't count broken ribs, and you don't say anything to the doctor about them; you just carry on. If you let people know you'd broken them, you'd miss some races. The pain stops when you get warmed up."[1]

Dick Francis was born on October 31, 1920 on the farm of his maternal grandfather, Willie Thomas, at Coedcanlas in Pembrokeshire, Wales. His paternal grandfather, Willie Francis, had been a great amateur steeplechase rider, and his father, was a professional rider and stable manager. "The fields of Coedcanlas, my grandfather's farm, sloped down to the Cleddeau estuary, and rose and fell over the surrounding hills, so that we had a large and exciting terrain for our explorations, and could get comfortably beyond the range of even the loudest grown-up voice calling us in at bedtime.

"We loved the farm. It was our mother's home, and I was born there.

"The farmhouse was large, creeper-grown, and white-washed, with solid buttressy walls six feet thick. I used to lie full length on my stomach on the window seats in the deep embrasures, looking out of the window, with my feet to the middle of the room. The house was sunk into the ground, so that one had to go down into the hall, and there was a short outside staircase which led directly, through a trellised archway covered with wisteria, to the bedrooms on the first floor. Mercifully much older than the hideous architecture which has been disfiguring the Welsh landscape for the last hundred and fifty years, it folded gently into its surroundings, instead of glaring from them aggressively in orange brick.

"Willie Thomas was a great man in the Victorian tradition. He ruled his children with a firm hand, even after they had grown up and married, and his idea of a good upbringing for his grandchildren was that they should be 'seen and not heard.' Nevertheless he was a kind man, and he often took my brother and me with him while he drove round his farm in his float.

"I remember him as being a tall man, but this is probably because I was a child looking up at him, for he died when I was ten. Certainly he was a very popular man, and as his house was open in welcome to anyone who cared to call there, it was always full of people.

"My grandmother, who usually had one or more of her five children living with her, with their husbands or wives, presided over her large and constantly changing household with astonishing calm, and everything ran with the ease of a friendly

hotel. A great deal of hard work, however, was needed to give this effect, for there was no electricity, and there were no local shops.

"Nearly all our food came from the farm itself. Butter and cheese were made in the dairy, and twice a week the great kitchen would be filled with the unique warm winy smell of bread baking. Here too the hams were smoked, the fruit and vegetables were preserved, and large barrels of good beer were brewed every month for the thirsty farm workers who sat at the long scrubbed tables every day for their dinner.

"Although the smells and warmth and friendliness of the kitchen were enticing, I spent very little time there. More exciting things, I felt, were going on outside, in the absorbing world of men."[2]

At the age of five, Francis learned to ride a donkey. "I rode without a saddle, partly because it was a pet theory of my father's that riding bareback was the best way to learn balance, but mostly because there was, anyway, no saddle to fit her high bony back.

"As soon as he saw me urging this long-suffering animal with more enthusiasm than style over a very small rail fence, my elder brother offered me the princely sum of sixpence if I could jump the fence sitting backwards. At that time I was saving all my pocket money to buy a toy farm, so this offer could not be ignored. I turned round awkwardly with my knees pressed hard into her flanks, pointed the donkey's head at the fence, and kicked.

"The donkey started off, and I went head first over her tail.

"When my brother could control his mirth at this event he collected the moke, who was fortunately too lazy to run away, and returned me to her back. We went through this programme twice more, and it became obvious that my brother's laughter was beginning to cause him considerable pain.

"However, after a pause, during which I rubbed the parts of me which had hit the ground, and my brother rubbed his stomach, gasped for breath, and wiped the tears from his cheeks, we tried again.

"He thought his sixpence was quite safe, but I wanted my farm very much.

"This time I stayed on until the donkey jumped, but we landed on opposite sides of the fence.

"Finally, with my nine-year-old brother shouting and chasing us with a waving stick, the donkey and I jumped the fence together, landed together, and came precariously to a halt.

"The sixpence was solemnly handed over, and in this way I earned my first riding fee. In my heart, from that moment, I became a professional horseman."[2]

When Francis was seven, his father became manager of W. J. Smith's Hunting Stables at Holyport and the family moved there. "I was extremely fortunate in the circumstances of my father's job, and few boys can ever have had more opportunity than I had of learning to ride every possible sort of pony. Father had about eight or nine nagsmen training the hunters under his direction, but they were too big and heavy for young and small ponies, so that Douglas and I had a clear field.

"All little boys, I suppose, like to play at doing their father's job, and at first we felt very important when we were allowed to ride the ponies in the yard. As we learned more though, the make-believe faded away, and riding became for us both a passionate and all-absorbing interest.

"For me, it was school that was the intolerable interruption of the serious business of life. I considered the long hours of arithmetic and history a thorough waste of time, and begged every day to be allowed to stay at home. Father did not care whether I went or not, so it was entirely due to Mother's firmness that I attended school at all. Employing some determination and a lot of guile, however, I managed to average only three days a week.

"For about ten years Horse Shows were my summer life, and with all that practice and Father's expert example always before me, I had every opportunity to learn how to show a horse or pony to the best advantage. In any case, when I had been at it for a year or two I began to win pony classes and riding classes, and to add my share to the collection of rosettes won by horses and ponies during their brief stay in the yard, and displayed in a glass case in the office. The only rosettes I could keep were those for riding classes; I kept them all in a drawer, for it seemed a little indecent to pin up a lot of round scarlet notices telling me I was 'Best Boy Rider.'

"I met Her Majesty the Queen for the first time when I was twelve. It was at Richmond Horse Show, where I had won the riding class and the hunting crop which was its prize. The whip was carefully presented to me by a small girl with an intent expression. I bowed to Princess Elizabeth and thanked her, and she smiled at me; I used the crop for years, and I have it still."[2]

Soon after, Francis fell off a pony named Tulip, and broke his jaw. "My smashed face was an excellent reason for a prolonged absence from school, although I was back in the show ring as soon as my skin had healed, and before I could talk properly again. The doctors earned my heartfelt thanks by telling Mother that I was not fit enough to return to Maidenhead Grammar School, and that I should be sent in the autumn to a smaller quieter place. There was no inspector to check on my attendance at the private school Mother chose, so I went less than ever.

"My accident on Tulip led to great adventures, for when he saw that I was going to be able to go to all the summer shows without classroom interruption, the great Bertram Mills [of the circus] asked Father to let me ride his show ponies for him. Father agreed, and I was ecstatic."[2]

At the age of fourteen, Francis replaced his father in a hunter class and did so well that he began to receive more invitations from owners to ride. By now he wanted to drop out of school; his mother opposed it, but his father agreed, since he was only attending school two or three days a week anyway. By fifteen, he had dropped out completely. "My father thought it was better for a boy to learn about riding than to learn about arithmetic. He thought it was more beneficial. The big hunting days were Mondays and Fridays. The school week was Monday through Friday. I used to get up early on Monday and Friday mornings. I'd see Father and ask if I could go hunting. 'Yes, boy, you can go

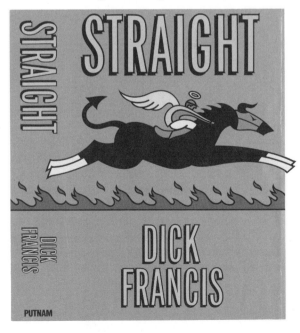

Dick Francis' 1989 novel.

hunting.' Mother used to get annoyed, but Father thought it was more beneficial to me. I think probably he was right."[3]

In 1938, his parents bought their own stables near Wokingham. "Then came the war.

"Slowly as it started, hunting as slowly declined, and the next year's point-to-point races were cancelled. Father's business began to dwindle, for with the future uncertain fewer people wanted to buy horses, and there was gradually less and less for me to do at home.

"Early in 1940 I told my father and mother that I was just off to join the cavalry. But the cavalry, I was downhearted to discover, did not want me. It seemed that to get into the cavalry I should have to wait until my age group was called up, and then trust to luck."[2]

Francis was able to enlist in aircraft maintenance; after pestering his superiors for a transfer to flight school, he was sent to Rhodesia. "At last, when I had almost given up hope, I was going to learn the one and only thing I still did not know about an aeroplane: how to fly it. I left the drab and dirty desert with barely a backward glance.

"Flying was everything I had imagined it to be, and from the moment I climbed into the open cockpit of a Tiger Moth behind the instructor I began to enjoy life again. The lightness of our little craft as it lifted off the ground, and the rushing air round my head seemed to slough off the years of grime and drudgery, and ten flying hours later, when I went up on my first solo, I felt exhilarated and whole. In solo flying, once I had passed the stage of worrying all the time I was in the air whether I would get safely down, I found again what Service life denies, the blessed peace of being alone.

"In the late autumn of 1945 I went to the wedding of my cousin Nesta.

"I had promised to be best man if I could get leave, and everything being well, I set off with Mother on the train to Weston-super-Mare, I with my mind back in my Wellington cockpit at Silverstone, and Mother chatting about which of our relations were going to the wedding too. Nothing warned me, as we trundled through Somerset in the peaceful October sunshine, of the emotional whirlwind that was waiting for me.

"Mother and I were greeted and fussed over by my aunt and cousins and a large contingent of relatives, so that it was some time before I noticed a stranger standing back a little shyly from our family reunion. A girl in a brown dress, with pale gold hair.

"My aunt said, 'Dick, I don't think you have ever met Mary? She is a friend of Nesta's who has come for the wedding.'

"Mary and I smiled at each other and to my astonishment, before we had even spoken, I found myself thinking 'This is my wife.'

"I had never believed in love at first sight, and it still seems to me an unreasonable way of choosing a companion for life, but there it was in a flash between us, and our future was pledged in a glance."[2]

Married on June 21, 1947, Francis appeared at the ceremony with his arm in a sling: he had broken his collarbone while riding.

After the war "the old impulse to be a jockey grew stronger. As the months went by, it became irresistible. Space, I said to myself as I cantered round in small circles; speed, I whispered, as I slowly popped over the jumps; stamina, I thought, as I eyed the fat nags lined up beside me.

"Although I had, I suppose, a somewhat romantic idea of racing, leaving the rails of the show ring for those of the paddock was for me a liberation and a fulfilment. As I have grown older I have discovered, of course, that in every profession one has to bear public humiliations and private heartaches, and that no competitive job is free of some wry and wistful regret for lost opportunities. Nevertheless, I have always been glad that I did at last become a jockey, and I can truthfully say that there was nothing else on earth I would rather have done."[2]

In 1948 Francis became a professional jockey, a title he held for nine seasons. That same year, Mary, who was pregnant with their first child, contracted polio. "I drove up to London fast after the races, and out to Neasden Isolation Hospital.

"Mary had certainly sounded all right, as she had said, on the telephone. But she did not look all right. Her face was yellow and grey, and she looked ill and old. It was clear that she was very far from being all right.

"The following evening she was moved into an artificial respirator. I had promised my parents I would let them know how she was, so I walked out to the telephone kiosk at the hospital gates. As I dialed the number my mind was filled with the image of Mary as I had just left her, with only her head free of the grey painted wooden box which enclosed her body while a big electric bellows

Mike Gwilym starred in the television series "The Racing Game," broadcast on PBS-TV, March 31, 1981.

pumped air in and out of her lungs. I stood trembling and shaking with the receiver in my hand, and when Mother answered and I tried to speak to her I found I was uncontrollably crying.

"I hated having to leave Mary alone and go on racing, but the doctors assured me that her life was not in immediate danger, and she herself insisted, as usual, that she was 'quite all right.' So every day, after I had ridden, I drove back to Neasden."[2]

Mary survived, and Francis was able to move her into a renovated house in Compton. Their first son, Merrick, was followed several years later by another son, Felix.

During the 1953-1954 season, Francis became Champion Jockey with seventy-six victories. "It is usual for a jockey to go straight across to greet the owner and trainer of the horse as soon as he gets into the parade ring, but when I looked round for Mr. Cazalet and Mrs. White I saw they were talking to Their Majesties the Queen and the Queen Mother, who had come to see the racing

that day and were watching the horses walk round. Lord Bicester saw my dilemma as I hovered on one foot, and beckoned me across to where he was standing with Pat Taaffe, not far from the Royal party.

"In a moment Mr. Cazalet was at my shoulder.

"'Come along,' he said. 'I am going to introduce you to the Queen.'

"I followed him over, bowed, shook hands with the Queen and the Queen Mother, and discovered how very awkward it is not to be able to take off one's hat in respect, when it is firmly tied on against the buffets of 'chasing.

"It was a cold misty day, I remember, and the Queen was wearing a fur coat and a yellow scarf. We talked about Statecraft, and, Lord Bicester having joined us, about Mariner's Log also. Then Mr. Cazalet helped me on to Statecraft, and off we went to the start. Statecraft pulled a tendon halfway through the race, and as I dismounted and walked back beside him, I had plenty of time to

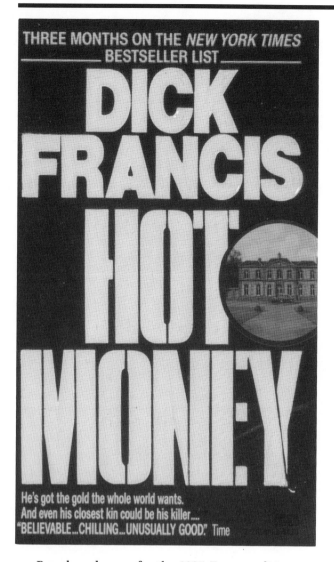

THREE MONTHS ON THE *NEW YORK TIMES*
——— BESTSELLER LIST ———

DICK FRANCIS

HOT MONEY

He's got the gold the whole world wants.
And even his closest kin could be his killer....
"BELIEVABLE...CHILLING...UNUSUALLY GOOD." Time

Paperbound cover for the 1987 Fawcett edition.

wonder at the coincidences which had led to my meeting the Queen and the Queen Mother, for I had no idea then that it was not the only time I should do so."[2]

Indeed, soon he would be riding for the Queen Mother, and his career as a jockey would culminate in his defeat on Devon Loch. "The calamity which overtook us was sudden, terrible, and completely without warning to either the horse or me. In one stride he was bounding smoothly along, a poem of controlled motion; in the next, his hind legs stiffened and refused to function. He fell flat on his belly, his limbs splayed out sideways and backwards in unnatural angles, and when he stood up he could hardly move.

"Even then, if he could have got going again he might still have had a chance, because we had been a long way clear of E.S.B.; but the rhythm was

shattered, the dream was over, and the race was lost."[2]

"If it hadn't happened, I might never have written a book, so really it was a blessing in disguise."[4]

In 1957 Francis retired as a jockey. "Within a fortnight I was offered three jobs.

"One was that of official judge. This was a then unheard-of position for an ex-professional jockey, and I accepted, feeling that I had been paid a considerable compliment. I said, however, that I would really prefer to be a starter, but was told to wait a few years until I was not so much one of the boys!

"The second job was that of race commentator. I accepted that too, and tried my hand at public race-reading at a succession of meetings like Birmingham, Fontwell and Towcester. I found it hard work to learn the colours and horses for every race, but at least twenty runners gave one plenty to say. It was the two- and three-horse affairs which had me most tongue-tied.

"The third job offer was from the *Sunday Express*. They would like four articles, they said, or perhaps a few more, which would be written by their staff to appear under my name. How about if I did them myself, I asked, and they said O.K., I could try.

"During the early summer of 1956 an elderly lady called Mrs. Johnson went to tea with my mother; and this totally ordinary and fortuitous afternoon altered the whole course of my life.

"Mrs. Johnson was accompanied by her son John, who was doing his good turn for the day by driving his aged parent to and from. To pass the time while the two ladies chatted he wandered round the room looking at books and antiques and photographs: he had a pretty sharp eye, which my mother approved, as he had worked for some time for the Arts Council.

"I was not there that day, but I've been told the same story identically by both sides. He stopped before a framed photograph of Devon Loch jumping the last fence in the National.

"'How odd,' he said, 'That you should be interested in racing. And in that horse in particular.'

"'My son rode it,' she said.

"After a very surprised pause he said, 'Has he ever thought of writing the story of what really happened?'

"'I'm sure he hasn't,' said my mother.

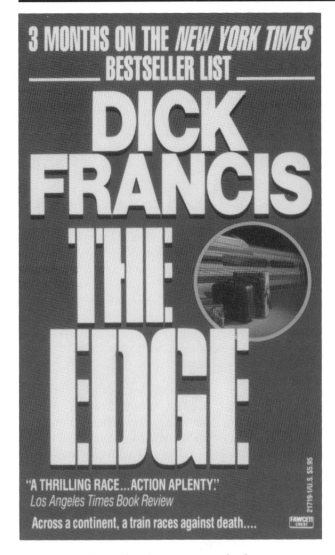

Cover for the 1988 paperback.

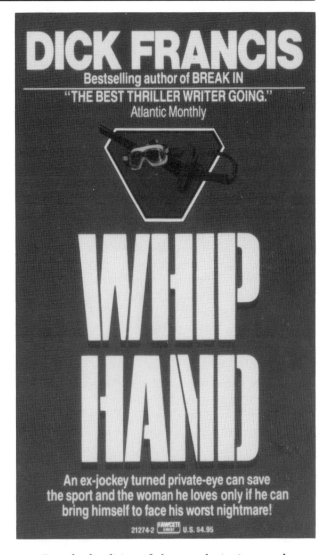

Paperback edition of the award-winning novel.

"'Do you think,' he said, 'that he would be interested in a suggestion that he should?'

"'I don't really know.'

"'Well...could you arrange that I meet him, to discuss it?'

"Mother told me, and I met him. He said he was an authors' agent. He said he could get a ghost writer. He said how about it? And the consequence was, as the schoolroom game would put it, that I had a go myself.

"I started the book...in the summer of 1956, on a boat on the Norfolk Broads. During the autumn I was told that as professional jockeys were not allowed to appear in print the book could not be published, so my enthusiasm for what had turned out to be extremely hard and unfamiliar work diminished to a standstill. If I couldn't publish, why bother to write? But by February 1957, when I

gave up racing, nearly two thirds of the book was done.

"(The rules have been changed since then, and professional jockeys may now appear in print to their hearts' content.)

"The one good thing about an autobiography as a first introduction to writing is that at least you don't have to research the subject: the story is all there in your own head. I was lucky to have my first efforts published, as most writers fill copious waste baskets before this happens, and I know that if this first book had been rejected everywhere I would never have written another. I was not filled with the burning zeal to write which survives three or four unpublished tomes and sets to work on the fifth. I would have accepted at once that I should forget about writing and do something else.

"But there we were. Michael Joseph, for whom I had ridden a few races, said he would publish the book when I'd finished it; and the *Sunday Express* printed the first article I wrote for them and said I could carry on with the others. I never really decided to be a writer. I just sort of drifted into it. For months, all through the summer of 1957, I looked upon the articles I was still producing weekly in the *Express* as only a stop-gap until I decided what to do for the rest of my life. The *Express* kept offering me a permanent job on the staff and I kept saying no, not realising how many sportswriters would have jumped at it, but by the autumn the message had got through to my sluggish brain that I really did quite like what I was doing and that this was not some temporary marking time, this was IT. In November I signed on the dotted line, and in December [my first] book came out and sold out its first (small) printing in a week, and the exchange of saddle for pen was no longer a vague possibility but a fact.

"Whatever I now know about writing I learnt from the discipline of working for a newspaper. There was small space allowed so that every word had to be worth it, and a deadline to be met so it was no good turning in a masterpiece tomorrow. For most people, writing is hard work (though those who don't do it never believe it) and actually sitting down in front of the empty sheet of paper is something to be put off whenever possible. Any publisher who gets work from me on time has the *Sunday Express*'s training to thank.

"I regret to say it was not inspiration which prompted me to start another book, but the threadbare state of a carpet and a rattle in my car: and I thought that if a novel could cover those few expenses the labour might be worth it. I underestimated twice. Writing a novel proved to be the hardest, most self-analysing task I had ever attempted, far worse than an autobiography: and its rewards were greater than I expected.

"The book, called *Dead Cert*, was accepted by the firm of Michael Joseph Ltd. (Michael himself having died) who published it in January 1962, and on publication day I received a preliminary cheque for three hundred pounds which felt like turning from amateur to professional all over again.

"Encouraged, I started anew, and *Nerve* was published two years later. Since then I have written one novel a year, and hope to continue for as long as anyone wants to read them. They have bought a new carpet or two by now, and a car or so, and of course a good deal more. I have been very lucky indeed in the rewards, but I still find the writing itself to be grindingly hard, and I approach Chapter I each year with deeper foreboding.

"The process of producing fiction is a mystery which I still do not understand. Indeed, as the years go by I understand it less and less, and I am constantly afraid that one day I will lose the knack of it and produce discord, like a pianist forgetting where to find middle C.

"People often ask me where I get ideas from, and the true answer is that I don't really know. They ask me how or why I write the way I do, and the answer is that I don't know that either. It seems to me now that one can't choose these things and that one has very little control over them. Jane Austen couldn't have written Charles Dickens, nor Charles Dickens, Jane Austen: and although I'm not in that league, I couldn't write, for instance, Tom Clancey nor he me with any sort of credibility. Books write authors as much as authors write books.

"Touching the actual technique of writing, I listen in a slight daze to people talking knowledgeably of 'first drafts' and 'second drafts,' because when I began to write I didn't know such things existed. I also didn't know that book authors commonly have 'editors,' publishers' assistants who tidy the prose and suggest changes of content: I thought that a book as first written was what got (or didn't get) published, and I wrote accordingly. The first shot had to be the best I could do.

"I still write that way. My 'first draft' is IT. I can't rewrite to any extent: I've tried once or twice, but I haven't the mental stamina and I feel all the time that although what I'm attempting may be different, it won't be *better* and may very well be worse, because my heart isn't in it. Publishers' editors have mournfully bowed to this state of affairs and resignedly ask only for a single word to be changed here or there, or for something obscure to be explained.

"When I write any one sentence, I think first of all of what I want it to say. Then I think of a way of saying it. Usually at this point I write it down (in longhand, in pencil, in an exercise book) but if I think that the form my thought has taken is a bit dull or pompous I just sit and wait, and after a while a new shape of words drifts into my head, and I write that down instead. Sometimes I rub bits out and try again, but once the sentence looks all right on paper I go on to the next one and repeat the process, and so on. It's all pretty slow as one sentence can sometimes take half an hour.

"On the following morning I read what I've written and if it still looks all right, I go on from there. If it doesn't look all right, I may despair that my work isn't good enough but all the same I don't often alter it except to add a word or two or perhaps insert a whole new sentence. When I've done a couple of chapters I type them out and it is this typescript when finished which goes to the printer.

"I start consequently at Chapter 1, page 1, and plod on to THE END; although by page 1, I have a fair idea of what the book is going to be about in general, I never know exactly what is going to happen. The story grows while I write it.

"I expect a great many authors work this way, if not most: and it is this gradual evolution of sentences, images, thoughts and plot patterns that I used to take for granted but now find increasingly mysterious."[2]

In 1962, Tony Richardson directed a movie version of *Dead Cert.* "It was ghastly. The main evil character I had in the book, Uncle George, didn't appear in the film at all. The main character in this film was a policeman. It was wrong, all wrong. They did have a royal command peformance for the initial showing. Princess Anne went to see it in London. I sat next to her. I thought she was going to enjoy it, but I'm sure she didn't. She didn't comment on it. I saw a lot of the prerelease runs being shown, and I thought it was going to be all right. But when it came to the actual showing, Tony Richardson, who had been responsible for making it, thought it was just too long and he cut the first ten minutes off. The first ten minutes had helped to unfold the story and tell the viewer what was actually happening. But the viewer didn't see it because it was just cut off. The Russians pirated *Dead Cert* many years ago. When I went to Russia [about twelve or thirteen years ago], the chap I went with arranged for a private viewing of the film the Russian television company had made of *Dead Cert.* Well, I couldn't understand a word of it, but I could follow the story far better in the Russian edition than I could in the English edition."[5]

Francis resigned from the *Sunday Express* in 1973, to devote himself entirely to his writing. "I know before I start writing what the main crime is going to be and who the culprits and victims are, but the subplots develop as I write. My crooks are an amalgam of a number of people. As for my heroes, I won't say they're autobiographical, but I wouldn't ask them to do anything I wouldn't do myself.

Cover from the 1982 paperback.

"The opening passage and paragraphs take a long time to write because I like to capture my audience straightaway when they open the book and look in. When I'm at home—I live in Fort Lauderdale now—I write about four or five hours every day, sitting outside on the veranda with a notebook. I find it easier to write over here because not so many people know my telephone number and my whereabouts. Back in England, I could never get through a day without someone telephoning and wanting to know about my social or racing life.

"My wife and I travel about the world quite a lot, and are endlessly saying: 'You know, that would be a good idea for the next story.' Wherever I go, I try to use the scenes I see....We went to the Breeders Cup at Santa Anita in California. Then we flew to Australia. We got there just in time for the Melbourne Cup on the following Tuesday. I wrote *Hot Money* around some of these places.

"Before I wrote *Blood Sport*, which was set in America, my wife and I went on Greyhound buses and traveled 7,500 miles in three weeks. The people we met around Chicago were foreigners to those who got on the bus near Phoenix: It was like going across Europe and meeting a Greek on one part of the trip and a Belgian on the other.

"As we travel, Mary takes a lot of photographs of ordinary, everyday scenes that might be of help in writing. In Oslo, for instance, we'll see the blue buses going down the road, and she'll take a picture. And she'll photograph telephone kiosks about the road, so we know that they use green boxes in Prague. We've got a big library of photographs.

"Mary is my one and only editor: If I can get something past her, I hope I can get it past the publishers. In fact, the books ought to be written by 'Dick and Mary Francis.' But I had a name to start with, and so I have carried it on like that.

"Mary loves doing research. She even took up flying for *Flying Finish*. . . .I kept going to the local flying-training school at Oxford to get up-to-date. They said: 'Why don't you start flying again? In a few hours, you'll soon get your license back.' I didn't have time, so the fellow at the school said, 'Well, send your wife along for a few lessons, and she'll help.' Mary got bitten by the bug. My accountant talked us into buying three airplanes, and we started a little air-charter business. And that was the background for the book *Rat Race*.

"Mary took up painting for another book, *In the Frame*, but she wasn't a born artist, so she didn't keep that up. We both spent a lot of time at the laboratories at UCLA to learn all about pharmacology for *Banker*. For the book I called *Proof*, we spent thirty years researching and drinking wine. Writing is hard work, but it's great fun doing the research."[6]

Film options have been taken out from time to time on most of his books, but Francis feels that the stories do not translate well to the screen. However, "television indeed seems to suit the stories fairly well and I was very pleased when Yorkshire Television used *Odds Against* as the basis for a series of six episodes, shown under the umbrella title of 'The Racing Game.' The success of this short series, due almost entirely to the skills of producer Jacky Stoller and actor Mike Gwilym, has had a direct effect on my life in many ways, not least in America, where the films were shown and repeated on public service television, coast to coast. Sales of the books themselves more than doubled in America in the year that 'The Racing Game' appeared, hoisting me into a bracket there that I had not earlier achieved.

"To Mike Gwilym also I owe the existence of the double award-winner, *Whip Hand*, since it was because the Royal Shakespeare Company actor so incredibly matched my concept of Sid Halley, chief character of *Odds Against*, that I became interested in writing a second book about the same man. Sid Halley, in *Odds Against*, lost his left hand, and in *Whip Hand* I set out to explore the mental difficulties of someone coming to terms with such a loss. In the event, it proved a most disturbing book to write, a psychological wringer which gave me insomnia for months.

"From our condominium apartment home in Fort Lauderdale, we see the generations rising, and we are both aware that in all important ways we are deeply and undeservedly fortunate."[2]

Footnote Sources:

[1] "The Talk of the Town," *New Yorker*, March 15, 1969.
[2] Dick Francis, *The Sport of Queens*, Penzler, 1957. Amended by D. Francis.
[3] Robert Cantwell, "Mystery Makes a Writer," *Sports Illustrated*, March 25, 1968.
[4] John C. Carr, *The Craft of Crime: Conversations with Crime Writers*, Houghton, 1983.
[5] *Contemporary Authors New Revision Series*, Volume 9, Gale, 1983.
[6] Alvin P. Sanoff, "Finding Intrigue Wherever He Goes," *U.S. News & World Report*, March 28, 1988. Amended by D. Francis.

■ For More Information See

New York Times Book Review, March 21, 1965 (p. 22), March 10, 1968, March 16, 1969, June 8, 1969, July 26, 1970, May 21, 1972, July 27, 1975, September 28, 1975, June 13, 1976, July 10, 1977, May 20, 1979 (p. 34ff), June 1, 1980, March 20, 1981 (p. 21), March 29, 1981 (p. 3ff), April 25, 1982 (p. 13ff), March 27, 1983 (p. 15ff), March 25, 1984 (p. 40ff), March 24, 1985 (p. 13), March 16, 1986 (p. 7).
Publishers Weekly, January 8, 1968 (p. 27ff), January 24, 1986 (p. 64), January 15, 1988, December 23, 1988.
New York Times, March 6, 1969, April 7, 1971, March 20, 1981.
Life, June 6, 1969.
Christian Science Monitor, July 17, 1969 (p. 11).
Forbes, April 15, 1970.
Family Circle, July, 1970.
Washington Post Book World, April 30, 1972 (p. 6), February 18, 1973 (p. 13), April 19, 1980, April 18, 1982 (p. 6), March 17, 1985 (p. 5).
Time, May 22, 1972 (p. 96ff), March 11, 1974, July 14, 1975, May 31, 1976, July 7, 1978, May 11, 1981.

Guardian, July 28, 1973.

Contemporary Literary Criticism, Gale, Volume 2, 1974, Volume 22, 1982, Volume 42, 1987.

London Magazine, February-March, 1975 (p. 142ff), March, 1980 (p. 95ff), February-March, 1981 (p. 143ff).

Times Literary Supplement, October 28, 1977 (p. 1258), October 10, 1980 (p. 1127), December 10, 1982 (p. 1378).

Armchair Detective, July, 1978 (p. 238ff), winter, 1986 (p. 77ff).

New York, April 21, 1980.

New York Times Biographical Service, June, 1980 (p. 810ff), May, 1982 (p. 584).

John M. Reilly, *Twentieth Century Crime and Mystery Writers*, Macmillan, 1980.

Los Angeles Times, March 27, 1981, April 9, 1982.

"Cross Country—Literature: Jockey Turned Detective," *Horizon*, April, 1981.

Newsweek, April 6, 1981 (p. 98ff).

Chicago Tribune, April 15, 1981.

Charles Moritz, editor, *Current Biography Yearbook 1981*, H. W. Wilson, 1982.

Earl F. Bargainnier, editor, *Twelve Englishmen of Mystery*, Bowling Green University Popular Press, 1984.

Architectural Digest, June, 1985 (p. 105ff).

Melvyn Barnes, *Dick Francis*, Ungar, 1986.

Writer's Digest, August, 1986 (p. 32ff).

Donna Olendorf, *Bestsellers 89: Books and Authors in the News*, Issue 3, Gale, 1989.

Writer, July, 1990.

William Golding

Kent, University of Bristol, University of Warwick, Oxford University, University of Sorbonne, and University of Kent; James Tait Black Memorial Prize for Fiction from the University of Edinburgh, 1979, for *Darkness Visible;* Booker McConnell Prize from the Book Trust (England), 1981, for *Rites of Passage;* Nobel Prize for Literature, 1983, for the body of his work.

■ **Writings**

Novels, Except As Indicated:

Poems (poetry collection), Macmillan, 1934.
Lord of the Flies, Faber, 1954, reissued, 1969, published with an introduction by E. M. Forster, Coward, 1955, casebook edition with notes and criticism, edited by James R. Baker and Arthur P. Ziegler, Jr., Putnam, 1964.
The Inheritors, Faber, 1955, Harcourt, 1962, reissued, Washington Square Press, 1981.
Pincher Martin, Faber, 1955, new edition, 1972, published in America as *The Two Deaths of Christopher Martin,* Harcourt, 1957, reissued under original title, Putnam, 1962.
(Contributor) *Sometime, Never: Three Tales of Imagination* (anthology), Ballantine, 1956.
The Brass Butterfly: A Play in Three Acts (based on story "Envoy Extraordinary"; first produced in Oxford, England at New Theatre, 1958; produced in London, England at Strand Theatre, April, 1958, produced in New York, N.Y. at Lincoln Square Theatre, 1965), Faber, 1958.
Free Fall, Faber, 1959, Harcourt, 1960.

Born September 19, 1911, in St. Columb Minor, Cornwall, England; son of Alec A. (a schoolmaster) and Mildred Golding; married Ann Brookfield (an analytical chemist), 1939; children: David, Judith. *Education:* Brasenose College, Oxford, B.A., 1935, M.A., 1960.

■ **Career**

Bishop Wordsworth's School, Salisbury, Wiltshire, England, English and philosophy teacher, 1939-40, 1945-61; Hollins College, Hollins College, Va., writer-in-residence, 1961-62; full-time writer, 1962—. Social worker at a London settlement house after graduating from Brasenose College; wrote, produced, and acted for London equivalent of "very, very far-off-Broadway theatre," 1934-40, 1945-54; honorary fellow, Brasenose College, Oxford University, 1966. *Military service:* Royal Navy, 1940-45; became rocket ship commander. *Member:* Royal Society of Literature (fellow), Savile Club.

■ **Awards, Honors**

Commander, Order of the British Empire, 1965; D. Litt., University of Sussex, 1970, University of

The Spire, Harcourt, 1964.
The Hot Gates and Other Occasional Pieces
   (nonfiction), Harcourt, 1966.
The Pyramid, Harcourt, 1967.
The Scorpion God: Three Short Novels (includes
   "Clonk Clonk," "Envoy Extraordinary," and
   "The Scorpion God"), Harcourt, 1971.
Darkness Visible, Farrar, Straus, 1979.
Rites of Passage, Farrar, Straus, 1980.
A Moving Target (essays and lectures), Farrar,
   Straus, 1982.
The Paper Men, Farrar, Straus, 1984.
An Egyptian Journal, Faber, 1985.
Close Quarters, Farrar, Straus, 1987.
Fire Down Below, Farrar, Straus, 1988.

Radio Plays:

"Miss Pulkinhorn," BBC Radio, April 20, 1960.
"Break My Heart," BBC Radio, March 19,
   1961.

Contributor to periodicals, including *Queen, Encounter, Esquire, Kenyon Review, Listener, Spectator, Times Literary Supplement,* and *Holiday.*

■ Adaptations

"Pincher Martin" (radio play), BBC, 1958.
"Lord of the Flies" (motion picture),
   Continental, 1963, Columbia, 1990,
   (cassette), Random House.

■ Sidelights

Born September 19, 1911 in Cornwall, England, William Golding descended from a distinguished line of schoolmasters. His father, Alec, was a man of exceptional learning who wrote textbooks on diverse subjects, and played several musical instruments. His relationship with his mother was extraordinary because "she and I were very like each other. We even looked like each other—poor woman—...facially we resembled each other, you see. I gave her a hell of a time, because I had a certain crude wit which I was not beyond using, I'm ashamed to say, on my own parents....She was a woman of very strong emotions, interests...I define her situation as being fond of me, but not able to stand me. I think this is quite understandable, because...as a boy I must have been—I can't think how anybody could stand me. I certainly couldn't have stood myself. I remember my father's diary...his last sentence in the diary...was his only mention of me. He says, 'Billy is the artistic member of the family. He is a little rascal.'"[1]

"My mother used to tell me...some of the ghost stories–not the ones that get into books, but the local ones, the Cornish ones, the ones she knew because she lived there...[and] I was terrified....I remember one phrase that made my hair stand on end...literally....She was telling about a girl who committed suicide...back in what my mother called 'the old days,' and that to her meant the distance which, to Cornish people, was really quite close in one sense, but vastly distant in another. It was a kind of almost Arthurian thing, but was close up....And in this time she was talking about suicides were buried at night, in ground near the churchyard, but not in the churchyard. And they went at night and buried this girl, and she had come from a farm....And my mother said, 'And as they turned away, they looked across the valley, and they saw lights moving in the farmhouse. She got back before they did.' Woosh! Hair straight up! I can still remember that 'She got back before they did'—that's pretty terrifying."[1]

Golding vacilated between the rationality of a father's desire to have his son become a scientist and his own budding fascination with myths and words. "I suppose my point of view has been diametrically opposed to what [my father] *said* he thought, but whether he actually believed what he said, I can't really tell because he was at bottom a very religious man and I think he was distressed by his own rationalism. But quite certainly I rebelled almost, one would say, intellectually. Emotionally I suppose, too, against the kind of scientific humanism of people like H. G. Wells. I think my father's mind was less rigid than I make it appear by talking about it as though it were a set thing. He lived to be eighty-three: he was a man who went through great changes in the world and in his life, and one can't just sum him up like that. But I do think that during the formative years of my boyhood I did feel myself to be in a sort of rationalist atmosphere against which I kicked."[2]

This passion for words grew into a love of literature. He devoured child and adult classics interchangeably. "I am personally stunned when I think of what a passionless pattern I made of it all. If we revisit our childhood's reading we are likely to discover that we missed the satire of *Gulliver,* the evangelism of *Pilgrim's Progress,* and the loneliness of *Robinson Crusoe.* [I] read George Alfred Henty, Ballantyne, Edgar Rice Burroughs, and Jules Verne as well, long before [realizing] that they require an innocence of approach which, while it is natural enough in a child, would be a mark of puerility in an adult.

"[Nonetheless] they held me rapt. I dived with the Nautilus, was shot round the moon, crossed Darkest Africa in a balloon, descended to the centre of the earth, drifted in the South Atlantic."[3]

1930. Upon graduation from Marlborough School, where his father served as schoolmaster, Golding entered Brasenose College, at Oxford University to study natural science for two years, intent on becoming "some sort of botanist—a microscopist, I think is the word."[1] He later switched to English.

His first work entitled *Poems* was published in 1934. To his relief, it quickly went out of print. "I don't own a copy, but I suppose there's one somewhere. Yes, at the British Museum. The Bodleian, of course. Actually, I'd rather forget it.

"The novelist is a displaced person, torn between two ways of expression....You might say I write prose because I can't write poetry."[4]

A year later, graduated from Brasenose and began a relatively short association with the London stage. "I was more or less brought up on Shakespeare and that has an influence. Only recently I decided that I'd spent my life quoting Shakespeare to people, and I'm not going to do it anymore because everything you want to say you can say by using Shakespeare's words. What a bore I must have been over a period of about sixty years, solomnly quoting Shakespeare to people. They must have said, 'Oh, God, not again, can't he find his own words?' So I've given it up, but there's no doubt that I know my Shakespeare pretty well by heart, and if you would like to consider that as denoting an interest in drama, I suppose it does.

"It was a sort of fringe theatre, I wouldn't dignify it by the name of acting. It was the Hampstead Everyman Theatre, Citizen House at Bath, and trifling things of that sort. It would be an impertinence on my part to say that I was part of the professional stage scene because I wasn't. I was a hanger-on round the fringes and finally collapsed to the side, into teaching."[2]

1939. Married Ann Brookfield, an analytical chemist, and accepted a position teaching English and philosophy at Bishop Wordsworth's School in Salisbury. "I wasn't teaching because I wanted to teach, I was teaching because it was a way of earning enough money to keep myself alive while I moved towards other things."[1]

World War II pre-empted all of Golding's plans. "I spent five years in the Royal Navy during the war against the Nazis. What did I do? I survived. I worked my way down, starting out on cruisers in the North Atlantic as an ordinary seaman and ending up in command of a rocket ship on D-Day. The war didn't last long enough for me to get a big promotion, like Admiral Nelson, who had the advantage of a longer war. All I ever rose to was *left-tenant.*"[5]

"I came to admire the navy as a structure, very much indeed. And of course there's no doubt that, if you want tradition, as long as there's been any sort of English life there's been a navy: and the traditions do date back. Yes: I was probably uncritical of it, for a time, I think. And you see I was quite old—I was twenty-eight or twenty-nine. . . .But it was very impressive. I think also that is perhaps natural to man, you know, because of this group activity thing. I think the hunting group comes out very much in that."[1]

"I was one of the sailors [involved in the pursuit of the battleship *Bismarck*]. There were thousands. We were rushing all over the Atlantic trying to find the damn thing....The nearest I got to the *Bismarck*, I blush to say, was forty miles away. I used

Golding's 1964 hardcover.

1983 NOBEL LAUREATE FOR LITERATURE

WILLIAM GOLDING

"His novels, . . . with the perspicuity of realistic narrative art and universality of myth, illuminate the human condition in the world today."
Swedish Academy Nobel Prize Citation

FREE FALL

Harcourt's softbound cover for Golding's 1959 novel.

to say that I was the sailor in the crow's nest of *Galatea* when we failed to sight *Bismarck*. . . .It is true I was in the crow's nest, but I couldn't have sighted her because she was too far away. In any case, we had radar, even in those days. So we knew where she was—at that time. She got away later on."[1] After the war, Golding returned to teaching at Bishop Wordsworth.

After writing three unsuccessful manuscripts, he began work on the story of British schoolboys marooned on a desert island—a situation similar to the one in R. M. Ballantyne's *The Coral Island*, which he had read as a boy. Golding obviously disagreed with the way Ballantyne's characters had remained good, upstanding little British citizens.

In 1954, *The Lord of the Flies* was published. "The theme is an attempt to trace the defects of society back to the defects of human nature. Before [World War II], most Europeans believed that man could be perfected by perfecting his society. We all saw a hell of a lot in the war that can't be accounted for except on the basis of original evil."[6]

"Original sin—I've been really rather lumbered with original sin. . .I suppose that. . .both by intellect and emotion—intellectually after emotionally—I'm convinced of original sin. That is, I'm convinced of it in the Augustinian way. It is Augustine, isn't it, who was born a twin, and his earliest memory was pushing his twin from his mother's breast? I think that because children are helpless and vulnerable, the most terrible things can be done by children to children. The fact that they are vulnerable, and ignorant of their own nature—can push the twin away from the breast without knowing that they are injuring themselves, without knowing that it's an antisocial action—that is ignorance. And we confuse it with innocence. I do myself. But I still think that the root of our sin is there, in the child. As soon as it has any capacity for acting on the world outside, it will be selfish; and, of course, original sin and selfishness—the words could be interchangeable. . . .You can only learn unselfishness by liking and by loving. And it seems to me that children—their love can be absolute passionate, profound love. And this is where their unselfishness comes, through their own need of love; so that anything they can do for this. . .demigod, is something they are happy to do. That is, they learn unselfishness through this extraordinary nexus between people—maybe between parents and children, nurses and children."[1]

The character of Ralph represented the civilized approach while Jack represented the bestial exhilaration of primitive hunters. Piggy and Simon were respectively the intellectual and the visionary. The conflict between Ralph and Jack mirrored the conflict of human nature. "My sympathies are with Ralph, yes. But I don't think that he will necessarily win out because he's likeable. After all it's only when you have a fairly protected society—as America has been for most of its existence–that you can develop a genuinely fair society. Athenian democracy didn't survive. Rome began as a democracy, then found out it couldn't run an empire, and finally collapsed under its own weight.

"I think all this is something Americans should deduce certain lessons from. I would have liked Ralph to 'make it,' but he couldn't. The 'nice guy' frequently loses."[7]

The book was an immediate success in England, but caught on more slowly in the United States. It also divided the critics. While some praised Golding's vision, others found it disturbing and uncomfortable.

Golding's admiration for Greek tragedy had obviously influenced the ending of the book in which the British naval officer fortuitously appears and prevents Jack's slaughter of Ralph. "I have always felt that the Athenians must have been deeply shocked by the *deus ex machina.* Here they had been watching a play with a beginning, a middle, and instead of an ending, one has a god coming down resolving everything. It's almost as if Euripides were telling his public to go see a play of Sophocles if they want tidy drama."[4]

"The whole book is symbolic in nature except the rescue in the end where adult life appears, dignified and capable, but in reality enmeshed in the same evil as the symbolic life of the children on the island. The officer, having interrupted a man-hunt, prepares to take the children off the island in a cruiser which will presently be hunting its enemy in the same implacable way. And who will rescue the adult and his cruiser?"[3]

Lord of the Flies has been analyzed on numerous levels: cultural/political, theological, and sexual. As for his political convictions, Golding once stated that: "They fit on a postage stamp. God works in ways that are impenetrable, as we all know—just like the devil, who is the leader of the opposition."[8]

While conceding to the religious undertones in his work, Golding admits that he is "...an incompetently religious man. I cannot *not* believe in God, but I do not believe in salvation and eternal life. We are provisional beings. I can accept the idea that we are going to die."[8]

He questioned the Freudian interpretations of his book, since he has never read Freud, preferring classic Greek drama. "I know people made a great deal about sexuality in *Lord of the Flies.* I wasn't aware of it, I must confess ruefully enough. Maybe if I went back and read the book I'd see it staring me in the face. But, then, I'm amazed how much sex some people can find wherever they look."[2]

Lord of the Flies eventually took its place beside J. D. Salinger's *Catcher in the Rye* as a classic. "I think both mine and Salinger's are valid pictures. My children are sub-adolescents faced with a sub-adolescent world. His hero is a post-adolescent faced with an adult world. The two are quite different."[7]

"People, I suppose, tend to think of me as the person who wrote *Lord of the Flies*, but I don't think of myself as the person who wrote *Lord of the Flies.* I'm the person who had to live with me."[2]

The film version of *Lord of the Flies*, directed by Peter Brooks, was released in 1962. A letter Golding received, from one of the children in the movie, delighted and convinced him it was perfectly cast. It read: "I think *Lord of the Flies* stinks. I can't imagine what I'm doing on this filthy island, and it's all your fault."[6] In 1990 Columbia Pictures released Jack Camp/Signal Hill Ltd.'s production of "Lord of the Flies." *Variety* feels that the original version stands miles above this "thoroughly undistinguished and unnecessary remake."

The idea for *The Inheritors* started as a rebuttal for H. G. Wells' *Outline of History*, which described Neanderthal man as an ugly brute, inferior to Homo Sapien ancestors. In his novel, Golding chose to write from the point of view of the Neanderthal, Lok, respecting his limitations of thought and communication.

"[*The Inheritors*] illustrates some of the natural, unconscious cruelty of the evolutionary theory when it is practiced. But also there's a little hope in that the good qualities of the Neanderthal people, call them the good qualities of the emergent

Paperback edition of the 1956 book.

humanity, are preserved. There is a possibility of it in this baby that is obviously going to go on and is going to be at once a source of fear and love among the new people. He will probably be a shaman or something. He obviously has powers that they will regard as unnatural, superhuman."[2]

Again, Golding surprised readers with an unorthodox approach in his third novel, *Pincher Martin*. "There's really very little point in writing a novel unless you do something that either you suspected you couldn't do, or which you are pretty certain nobody else has tried before. I don't think there's any point in writing two books that are like each other.

"I see, or I bring myself to see, a certain set of circumstances in a particular way. If it is the way everybody else sees them, then there is no point in writing a book."[3]

The book was published two years later in America as *The Two Deaths of Christopher Martin*. "That's because American publishers sometimes think they know better than the author. Also, the thing is that in England to pinch is to steal, and this is a verb which the American publishers didn't think would be instantly obvious to an American. Equally, in the Royal Navy all Martins are nicknamed Pincher, nobody knows why, just as everyone who's called Miller is called Dusty. Dusty Miller, well that makes sense, doesn't it? Or Lofty Jones is another one which doesn't make any more sense than Pincher Martin. The American publishers therefore slipped in an explanation of the whole book."[2]

The protagonist of the story, is thrown overboard in a storm, clings to a rock, and tries to survive as Golding coaxes his readers into admiration for Martin's strength and will. Gradually, the reader realizes that Martin is not at all admirable.

The end of the novel reveals that Martin had in fact died earlier in the book. "He dies on page two but he refuses to admit he's dead and constructs a universe of his own that's gradually taken to pieces. So I suppose the American editor thought that when that universe was finally taken right to pieces and all you had left was Pincher, his claws gripped like that, I suppose he thought that was the second death. In a way, it's a metaphorical second death, I suppose. But I believe afterwards they went back to calling it *Pincher Martin*."[2]

Despite Golding's penchant for originality, reviewers and critics noted similarities, as described by reviewer Bernard Oldsey: "The *tour de force* approach; here again the isolated setting, the poetic precision of detail, the allegorical mode in conjunction with the novelistic, the ambiguous and cleverly planned conclusion. Here also was the utilization of previous works of literature, for both thematic and technical purposes."[3]

As in his childhood, Golding seemed to be both poet and scientist, using his novels as experiments. "Well, I suppose the best kind of scientist works imaginatively. He says to himself, What would happen, if? But the sort of second class scientist goes on doings things until something happens. I would say that because I'm a human being—and whatever I have said about them in the past, scientists do tend to be human beings–we're bound to have things in common. The two cultures have an awful lot in common, and it's a kind of cultural chauvinism to attach oneself wholly to one or the other."[1]

Free Fall, his fourth novel, was published in 1959. Another departure, this novel's setting was contemporary society, and had no mythical substructure. In fact, its structure perplexed and exasperated many. A fact to which Golding responded, "Good. Good. Good....Splendid."[2]

The book concerned artist Sammy Mountjoy's conscious fall from grace, eventual atonement at a Nazi prisoner-of-war camp and writing of his own story. "My thesis, I think, was the fact that without a system of values, without an adherence to some, one might almost call it, codified morality, right and wrong, you are like a creature in space, tumbling, eternally tumbling, no up, no down, just in 'free fall' in the scientific sense. Also, of course, you can link it with the Miltonic idea, sufficient to have stood though free to fall; and link it, therefore, with the Miltonic concept of free will. Those two things were in my mind, but mostly the scientific one, because it's a convenient metaphor in a way, that the more science you get the more it is easy for old systems to be struck away, old supports to be knocked down and for people to find themselves in a state of free fall, just as science and technology can get you to the position where you can actually put a man into free fall. You see? I've found the metaphor adequate for my purpose, but of course also there is inherent, should be inherent in the book (whether it came off or not, I don't know) the fact that man is, I believe, by nature a moral creature, and when he's in free fall he, so to speak, stumbles over his morals without knowing they are there. He exploits people and then finds that with this comes guilt and that you can't be free of right and wrong because you know by some kind of instinct when you've exploited

The original 1963 British film "Lord of the Flies," starred Hugh Edwards and Tom Chapin.

somebody, when you've hurt somebody, when you've cheated somebody. You know when you lie and all the rest of it. It's no good saying none of these things matter. They do. They matter intensely to man because he is not just man, he is a social being."[1]

During the next few years Golding wrote book reviews for the *Spectator,* received a Master of Arts from Oxford in 1960, left teaching to devote himself full time to writing, became a writer-in-residence at Hollins College, Virginia, and went on an American college lecture tour from 1961 to 1962. "I lectured to a good many [students], of course, in every part of the country. They are all very interested, extremely interested in what I am saying. Extremely eager students, yes. But it is also perceptible that in America, age for age, they are content with a less detailed knowledge of my subject, English; than we are. They tend to have a 'digest' view of literature, you know. This is not at all true on the graduate level, of course, where details are very important.

"For fifteen years, after the war, I read nothing but classical Greek, not because it was the snobbish thing to do or even the most enjoyable, but because this is where the meat is. I don't know many American writers, unfortunately. I know my own contemporaries here, and in the States I know some. I was brought up on Mark Twain. I know and admire Robert Penn Warren and William Styron, of course. Faulkner, too. Hemmingway's *Old Man and the Sea* is a favorite, though I'm told I shouldn't like it. Robie Macauley's *Descent of Venus* is another favorite. That's about it, I'm afraid, save Salinger. . . .I like [American] writers by and large. You've got tremendous energy in your literary world."[7]

The Spire drew its inspiration from the local cathedral in Salisbury. It is the story of Dean Jocelin, a fourteenth-century clergyman, who becomes obsessed with the belief that it is his divine mission to build a four hundred-foot tower and spire over his church. The novel deals with metaphysical questions of good, evil, and hubris (again echoing Greek tragedy). "When Hilary climbed Everest he said he did it because it was there, and the Salisbury spire was there. I taught with the spire sticking up outside the window, and looking over the bowed heads of my pupils I was faced with the thing, and like Colley's adventure, it had to be explained. The more I looked at it the more incredulous I became and the more impossible it seemed that it should be there you know, and that someone should have done it. But they did it and I

had to invent the circumstances as far as I could and the sort of person who would do it."[2]

Ironically, the spire, which Jocelin does everything to preserve, survives. By the end of the story, it is Jocelin who perishes. "I would hope that God is merciful. Unless human beings build a cathedral nobody's going to, and so the cathedral has to be what human beings made of it. To that extent, yes, building always is corrupt. I don't find God driven out in that way. It's the best we can do, and I would find Him beckoned in. The mystery about the spire is (a) that anyone got so vain that he should wish to build it, (b) it's still there and (c) that, although I'm sure it wasn't meant to be, it's extraordinarily beautiful. You see, it has all these things that are very mysterious. It's the best we can do and, ah well, you have to write what it's like for corrupt human beings to do that."[2]

In 1966, Golding became an honorary fellow at Brasenose College and published his first collection of essays, *The Hot Gates and Other Occasional Pieces.* The following year, *The Pyramid,* a three-part, loosely-connected novel was published to the disappointment of most critics and readers. Denis Donoghue, in the *New York Review of Books* called it "an embarrassment, a disaster."[3]

Golding attributed the lack of enthusiasm to a misunderstanding of the book's structure and to cultural differences. "It is sonata form really, it's musical. With a scherzo in the middle, the whole business about the idiotic amateur dramatic director is the scherzo of the sonata, and then it finishes with a Beethoven set of variations, with the various pictures of Miss Dawlish in her various stages, how she comes back and back and back, and the changes in how she starts to repeat things and how she is caught in the repetitive pattern.

"[*The Pyramid*] has elements of Marlborough in it, but it's a much smaller place than Marlborough. It's much more like a village. *The Pyramid* is very English, and I'm quite aware it can't be understood in America any more than *Rites of Passage* can be understood in America. I have to bear this cross, you know."[2]

The Scorpion God, a collection of three novellas, exorcised Golding's love of Egyptology, but were not considered major works of fiction. "I had the Egyptology up my sleeve all the time. I was quite sure I was going to write something about it sooner or later. But I didn't know what it would be, and of course, the story 'The Scorpion God' is Herodotus's view of Egypt more than anybody else's, it's not received archaelogical opinion.

"Also you've got to remember, to some extent, I'm sending up the idea of history, and have my tongue in my cheek much more often than people ever suspect because I have this kind of solemn reputation. My tongue is in my cheek an awful lot of the time, and it was in those stories, it was tucked in there firmly. Herodotus says that the Egyptians do everything in public that other people do in private, and everything in private that other people do in public, so that was good enough for me. I simply tied that to the story."[2]

Darkness Visible, his next major work was published to wide acceptance. This metaphysical novel fuses the terrorism of modern headlines with elements of the *Bible.* Although American readers liked the book, Golding has refused to discuss it.

In 1980, *Rites of Passage* was published. This more socially analytical novel won the Booker McConnell Prize for Literature. "It's a black comedy with relevance to the present situation.

"It's making some urgent statements about class. Unless we can get rid of it or at least blunt the pyramid or make it a little less monumental, we're done, we're finished, and it had better happen quickly.

"I don't think the book is aimed at Britain to the exclusion of any other country which suffers from class systems, like, say, India. Or like New England, for example, that I found far more like Old England than I could have believed.

"I remember going to a party. I could go because I was a foreigner, but the person staying with us was not one of the four hundred families, or whatever it is, so he couldn't go, he had to stay at home. And then there was a receiving line of old biddies stretching from one end of the room to the other, you sort of went along, and you were in. By God, they don't have that sort of thing in England now. I aim at the English because I'm English, but there are other places."[2]

The story, set in the nineteenth century, concerns the passage of Edmund Talbot, a young snob, from England to the colonies in Australia. "I would put it round about 1812 or 1813. First, because the original, the historical incident round which I've built the story happened at that time; secondly, the Regency period is a fun period, for me; thirdly, I happened to have a great deal of source material in my head, I didn't have to bother to do any research or anything like that. And, you see, I know sailors, I know the Royal Navy.

Cover from the Putnam paperback.

"The novel was great fun for me. Again, this time, I was gently pulling the leg of the Royal Navy which is, in this country, an awful thing to do. I even shocked myself.

"Talbot is going through a rite of passage, he is growing up. He doesn't realize it because he thinks he's grown up already, but he's not. And poor old Colley fails to make the grade, but he too goes through a rite of passage. it's very much like the ceremony of crossing the line really was. After a boy had been through that he was then accepted as a sailor. He had to have been round Cape Horn before he could piss to leeward, I think it was. Before that you had to piss to windward."[2]

A second volume of essays was published in 1982, entitled, *A Moving Target.* The book betrayed some of Golding's realizations about life. "I lived for years. . .in the happy conviction that since I had the wonder in ample supply in time the wisdom would follow. I herewith deliver an interim report and announce that it is possible to live astonished for a long time; and it looks increasing possible that you can die that way too.''[9]

In 1983, he was awarded the Nobel Prize for Literature. "Twenty-five years ago I accepted the label 'pessimist' thoughtlessly without realising that it was going to be tied to my tail, as it were, in something the way that, to take an example from another art, Rachmaninoff's famous Prelude in C sharp minor was tied to him. No audience would allow him off the concert platform until he played it. Similarly critics have dug into my books until they could come up with something that looked hopeless. I can't think why. I don't feel hopeless myself. Indeed I tried to reverse the process by explaining myself. Under some critical interrogation I named myself a universal pessimist but a cosmic optimist. . . .I meant, of course, that when I consider a universe which the scientist constructs by a set of rules which stipulate that his constructs must be repeatable and identical, then I am a pessimist and bow down before the great god Entropy. I am optimistic when I consider the spiritual dimension which the scientist's discipline forces him to ignore.''[10]

The Paper Men, published in 1984, concerned the story of an aging writer's relationship with his pushy biographer. The book received poor reviews and was even called unworthy of a Nobel Prize winner.

Undaunted, Golding revived his passion for Egyptology in *An Egyptian Journal,* attributing his prolific pace to routine. "In general I'm completely disorganized, as far as work's concerned. Except when I know I've got a book. Then I sit down and write 2000 words a day until it's finished. So many pages, you see. And that is routine. And I stop in the middle of a sentence when I've filled the right number of pages, and with great relief. . . .It becomes a chore, but it's a chore I must do, and I go through with it. And sometimes it's not a chore, and one's surprised to find how much one's written, as it were by accident. But then 2000 words [are] there. I have very seldom said to myself, this is so exciting, or this is a point at which I know I can do this—very seldom gone on beyond the 2000 words. I've almost always kept rigidly to the 2000; because it's made me feel that if I write another 2000 in the same day, next day there won't be anything to write. But if I stop bang at the 2000, then next day I know I can join the next 2000 onto the other half of the sentence, or whatever it is.''[1]

Close Quarters, the sequel to *Rites of Passage,* was published in 1987. The following year, *Fire Down Below* was published, completing the voyage and the memoirs of Edmund Talbot. "In all my books I try to give some form to the universe. But there can never be an absolute parallel between a fable and the world it describes. It is true that I have mocked the naive belief in progress in an age that has seen the atomic bomb. The role of the novelist is to ask questions. I am not a sage capable of distilling truths drop by drop. I am an aging novelist mumbling at the complexities of the world.

"It is increasingly likely that some of my books will be read after my death. So?''[8]

Golding offered one piece of advice for young writers: "Have one hand holding your pen and the other firmly on the nape of the reader's neck.''[9]

Footnote Sources:

[1] John Carey, editor, *William Golding: The Man and His Books,* Faber, 1986.
[2] Bernard Oldsey, "William Golding," *Dictionary of Literary Biography,* Volume 15, Gale, 1983.
[3] James R. Baker, "An Interview with William Golding," *Twentieth-Century Literature,* summer, 1982.
[4] Bernard F. Dick, "The Novelist Is a Displaced Person: An Interview with William Golding," *College English,* March, 1965.
[5] Herbert Mitgang, "William Golding's World," *New York Times,* November 21, 1980.
[6] "Lord of the Campus," *Time,* June 22, 1962.
[7] Douglas M. Davis, "A Conversation with Golding," *New Republic,* May 4, 1963.
[8] Frederic Ferney, "Golding's Universal Truths," *World Press Review,* January, 1984.
[9] Gabriel Josipovici, "A Pragmatist and His Public," *Times Literary Supplement,* July 23, 1982.
[10] William Golding, "Nobel Lecture 1983," *Dictionary of Literary Biography Yearbook: 1983,* Gale, 1983.

■ **For More Information See**

Books:

Peter Green, *A Review of English Literature,* Longmans, Green, 1960.
Frederick R. Karl, *The Contemporary English Novel,* Farrar, Straus, 1962.
James Gindin, *Postwar British Fiction: New Accents and Attitudes,* University of California Press, 1962.
Samuel Hynes, *William Golding,* Columbia University Press, 1964.
Walter Allen, *The Modern Novel,* Dutton, 1964.
Bernard S. Oldsey and Stanley Weintraub, *The Art of William Golding,* Harcourt, 1965.
James R. Baker, *William Golding: A Critical Study,* St. Martin's, 1965.
Peter M. Axthelm, *The Modern Confessional Novel,* Yale University Press, 1967.

From the 1990 American remake of the movie "Lord of the Flies," starring Danuel Pipoly and Balthazar Getty.

Bernard F. Dick, *William Golding*, Twayne, 1967, revised edition, 1987.

Anthony Burgess, *The Novel Now: A Guide to Contemporary Fiction*, Norton, 1967.

Mark Kinkead-Weekes and Ian Gregor, *William Golding: A Critical Study*, Faber, 1967.

David Anderson, *The Tragic Past*, John Knox Press, 1969.

Howard S. Babb, *The Novels of William Golding*, Ohio State University Press, 1970.

Wilfrid Sheed, *The Morning After*, Farrar, Straus, 1971.

J. Gindin, *Harvest of a Quiet Eve: The Novel of Compassion*, Indiana University Press, 1971.

Jack I. Biles, *Talk: Conversations with William Golding*, Harcourt, 1971.

Contemporary Literary Criticism, Gale, Volume 1, 1973, Volume 2, 1974, Volume 3, 1975, Volume 8, 1978, Volume 10, 1979, Volume 17, 1981, Volume 27, 1984.

Virginia Tiger, *William Golding: The Dark Fields of Discovery*, Calder & Boyars, 1974.

John Wakeman, *World Authors 1950-1970*, H. W. Wilson, 1975.

Jean E. Kennard, *Number and Nightmare: Forms of Fantasy in Contemporary Fiction*, Archon Books, 1975.

Lawrence R. Ries, *Wolf Masks: Violence in Contemporary Fiction*, Kennikat Press, 1975.

Stephen Medcalf, *William Golding*, Longman, 1975.

J. I. Biles and Robert O. Evans, editors, *William Golding: Some Critical Considerations*, University Press of Kentucky, 1979.

Arnold Johnson, *Of Earth and Darkness: The Novels of William Golding*, University of Missouri Press, 1980.

Tyler Wasson, *Nobel Prize Winners*, H. W. Wilson, 1987.

Periodicals:

Library Journal, September 1, 1955.

Times Literary Supplement, October 21, 1955, August 7, 1959, October 23, 1959 (p. 608), June 1, 1967, November 5, 1971, November 23, 1979, October 17, 1980, July 23, 1982, March 2, 1984.

New York Times Book Review, October 23, 1955, December 10, 1961 (p. 56), April 19, 1964, November 18, 1979, November 2, 1980, July 11, 1982.

Kenyon Review, autumn, 1957 (p. 577ff).

New York Times, September 1, 1957, November 9, 1979, October 15, 1980, October 7, 1983 (p. A-1), March 26, 1984.

Time, September 9, 1957, October 13, 1967, October 17, 1983, April 9, 1984, March 20, 1989 (p 81ff).

New Yorker, September 21, 1957.

New Statesman, August 2, 1958 (p. 146ff), April 10, 1964, November 5, 1965, October 12, 1979, October 17, 1980, June 11, 1982.

Commonweal, March 18, 1960 (p. 673ff), February 22, 1963 (p. 569ff), October 25, 1968, September 26, 1980.

Nation, May 21, 1960 (p. 451ff).

College English, January, 1961, November, 1963 (p. 90ff).

Wilson Library Bulletin, February, 1963 (p. 505).

New York Post, December 17, 1963 (p. 31).

Atlantic Monthly, May, 1965 (p. 96ff), April, 1984.

Life, November 17, 1967.

Commentary, January, 1968.

South Atlantic Quarterly, autumn, 1970.

Critique: Studies in Modern Fiction, Volume XIV, number 2, 1972.

Ariel, January, 1976.

Listener, October 4, 1979, October 23, 1980, January 5, 1984.

Spectator, October 13, 1979.

Washington Post Book World, November 4, 1979, November 2, 1980, April 15, 1984.

Newsweek, November 5, 1979, October 27, 1980, April 30, 1984.

Village Voice, November 5, 1979.

New Republic, December 8, 1979, September 13, 1982.

Detroit News, December 16, 1979, January 4, 1981, April 29, 1984.

Chicago Tribune Book World, December 30, 1979, October 26, 1980, April 8, 1984.

Los Angeles Times Book Review, November 9, 1980, June 20, 1982, June 3, 1984.

Essays in Criticism, January, 1981.

London, February-March, 1981.

Washington Post, July 12, 1982, October 7, 1983.

New York Times Biographical Service, October, 1983 (p. 1204).

Chicago Tribune, October 7, 1983.

Publishers Weekly, October 21, 1983 (p. 16).

Times (London), February 9, 1984.

Structurist, number 25/26, 1985/1986 (p. 41ff).

Stan Lee

Born Stanley Martin Lieber on December 28, 1922, in New York, N.Y.; name legally changed; son of Jack (a dress cutter) and Celia (Solomon) Lieber; married Joan Clayton Boocock, December 5, 1947; children: Joan C. *Education:* Attended high school in New York, N.Y. *Residence:* Los Angeles, Calif. *Office:* Marvel Productions, 4610 Van Nuys Blvd., Sherman Oaks, Calif. 91403.

■ Career

Timely Comics (became Atlas Comics; now Marvel Comics), New York, N.Y., editorial assistant and copywriter, 1939-42, editor, 1942-72, publisher and editorial director, 1972-88; associated with Marvel Productions, Los Angeles, Calif. Marvel Entertainment Group, chairman of the board, 1989. Adjunct professor of popular culture at Bowling Green State University, Bowling Green, Ohio; lecturer on college campuses. *Military service:* U.S. Army, 1942-45; became sergeant. *Member:* American Federation of Television and Radio Artists, National Academy of Television Arts and Sciences, National Cartoonists Society, Academy of Comic Book Arts (founder and president), Friars Club.

■ Awards, Honors

Six Alley Awards, 1963-68; Award from the Society for Comic Art Research and Preservation, 1968; Eureka Award from Il Targa [Milan, Italy], 1970, for world's best comic writing; Award from the Popular Culture Association, 1974; Publisher of the Year Award from the Periodical and Book Association of America, 1978; Award from the Academy of Comic Book Arts; honorary degree from Bowling Green State University.

■ Writings

The Mighty Thor (illustrated by Jack Kirby), Lancer Books, 1966.

Spider-Man Collector's Album (illustrated by Steve Ditko), Lancer Books, 1966.

Origins of Marvel Comics, Simon & Schuster, 1974.

Son of Origins of Marvel Comics, Simon & Schuster, 1975.

Bring on the Bad Guys: Origins of Marvel Villains, Simon & Schuster, 1976.

Mighty Marvel Strength and Fitness Book, Simon & Schuster, 1976.

The Mighty Marvel Superhero Fun Book, Simon & Schuster, 1976.

The Superhero Women, Simon & Schuster, 1977.

The Best of Spidey Super Stories, Simon & Schuster, 1978.

(With John Buscema) *How to Draw Comics the Marvel Way*, Simon & Schuster, 1978.

The Incredible Hulk, Simon & Schuster, 1978.

The Silver Surfer (illustrated by J. Kirby), Simon & Schuster, 1978.

The Mighty World of Marvel Pin-up Book, Simon & Schuster, 1978.

Marvelous Mazes to Drive You Mad, Simon & Schuster, 1978.

Marvel's Greatest Superhero Battles, Simon & Schuster, 1978.

Dr. Strange, Simon & Schuster, 1979.

Omnibus Fun Book, Simon & Schuster, 1979.

The Amazing Spiderman, Simon & Schuster, 1979.

Marvel Word Games, Simon & Schuster, 1979.

The Fantastic Four, Simon & Schuster, 1979.

Captain America, Simon & Schuster, 1979.

Stan Lee Presents the Best of the Worst, Harper, 1979.

Complete Adventures of Spider-Man, Simon & Schuster, 1979.

Hulk #3, Ace, 1982.

Dunn's Conundrum, Harper, 1985.

The Best of Spiderman, Ballantine, 1986.

The God Project, Grove, 1990.

Also author of *Marvel Team-up Thrillers, The Uncanny X-Men, The Invincible Iron Man, The Story of Marvel Comics,* and "Spider Man and Power Pack Battle Sexual Abuse."

■ **Adaptations**

Marvel Comics Video Library:

"Spider Man," Marvel Productions, 1985.

"Doctor Doom," Marvel Productions, 1985

"Captain America," Marvel Productions, 1985.

"Magneto," Marvel Productions, 1985.

"The Incredible Hulk," Marvel Productions, 1985.

"The Fly," Marvel Productions, 1985.

"The Fantastic Four," Marvel Productions, 1985.

"The Sandman," Marvel Productions, 1985.

"Iron Man," Marvel Productions, 1985.

"Doctor Octopus," Marvel Productions, 1985.

"The Thing," Marvel Productions, 1985.

"The Vulture," Marvel Productions, 1985.

"Spider Woman," Marvel Productions, 1985.

"Mole Man," Marvel Productions, 1985.

"Sub Mariner," Marvel Productions, 1985.

"The Green Goblin," Marvel Productions, 1985.

"The Mighty Thor," Marvel Productions, 1985.

"The Red Skull," Marvel Productions, 1985.

"Spider Man, Volume II," Marvel Productions, 1985.

"The Mighty Thor, Volume II," Marvel Productions, 1985.

"Captain America, Volume II," Marvel Productions, 1985.

"The Fantastic Four, Volume II," Marvel Productions, 1985.

"Spider Woman, Volume II," Marvel Productions, 1985.

"The Incredible Hulk, Volume II," Marvel Productions, 1985.

Animation Production:

"Marvel Super Heroes" (included five Marvel comic book characters, including "Incredible Hulk," "Iron Man," "Sub-Mariner," "Mighty Thor," and "Captain America"), Grantray Lawrence Animation Production, 1966-68.

Television Series:

"The Amazing Spider-Man" (animated), premiered on ABC-TV, September 9, 1967, NBC-TV, September, 1981.

"The Incredible Hulk," premiered on CBS-TV, March 10, 1978.

"Spider-Woman," premiered on ABC-TV, September 22, 1979.

"Incredible Hulk Returns," NBC-TV, May 22, 1988.

Adventure Films:

"The Amazing Spider-Man," CBS-TV, April, 1978.

Dr. Strange was adapted for television in 1978. Author of a number of syndicated comic strips including "My Friend Irma," 1952, "Mrs. Lyons' Cubs," 1957-58, "Willie Lumpkin," 1960, "The Incredible Hulk," and "Spider-Man." Also editor of television scripts.

■ **Work in Progress**

An autobiography, for Harper; motion picture, "Captain America," starring Matt Salinger (actor son of J.D. Salinger) for New World Pictures.

■ **Sidelights**

One of the principal founders of Marvel Comics, Stan Lee has been celebrated as the savior of comic books, elevating them to the respectability of an art form. "Marvel Comics. Let us savor the sound of those heart-warming words. Let us bask in the glow of the pleasure they promise. Marvel Comics. Not so much a name as a special state of mind. Not so much a group of magazines as a mood, a movement, a mild and momentary madness."[1]

Joe Simon and Jack Kirby, "Captain America."
© Marvel Comics Group.

Lee, who authored and edited material on the "Captain America" strip, from its inception to 1972, is considered its definitive writer.

Lee was born and raised in New York City. After his graduation from high school at the age of sixteen, he took on several odd jobs, such as writing advance obituaries for a news service and public relations work for a hospital, before finally getting into comics. "Actually, it was a sheer accident, although I was interested both in writing and in comics. I needed a job, and I saw an ad in the paper that said a comic-magazine company needed an editorial assistant. I said, 'Wow! That sounds great,' and I applied. I must have been the only kid who applied for the job because I got it."[2]

With the change in job, came a change in name. "Myself when born was christened Stanley Martin Lieber—truly an appellation to conjure with. It had a rhythm, a vitality, a lyricism all its own. I still remember one of my earliest purchases being a little rubber stamp with my name on it, which I promptly stamped on every book and paper I owned—and even on some I didn't. So happy was I being S.M.L., and so certain that I would one day

write the great American novel, or the great American motion picture, and so young and witless was I at the time I started writing comics, that I felt I couldn't sully so proud a name on books for little kiddies. That's why seventeen-year-old Stanley Martin Lieber felt he needed a simpler sobriquet, and that's why he divided his first name into two syllables, making each syllable a name of its own. Stan Lee was for comic books. S.M.L. would be held in reserve—for greater things. Let me point out, parenthetically, that S.M.L. is still being held in reserve. . . .Anyway, just to wrap it up before it gets too sticky, I legally changed my name to Stan Lee. . .so S.M.L. is nothing more than a cherished memory—a slowly fading dream on the melancholy mattress of life."[1]

As "Stan Lee," he began his career at Timely Comics. "During the first two decades that I toiled for Timely the comic-book business was a fairly simplistic operation. If cowboy films were the rage we produced a lot of Westerns. If cops and robbers

Page 1 of *The Amazing Spider-Man #2* comic book, May, 1963.

Page from the comic book that introduced *Spider-Man: Amazing Fantasy #15*, August, 1962.

were in vogue we'd grind out a profusion of crime titles. If the trend turned to love stories, Timely (as well as the competition) became big in romance mags. We simply gave the public what it wanted— or so we thought.

"As for our audience, we all assumed that our readers primarily belonged to the bubble-gum brigade. Oh sure, there were a few iconoclastic adults here and there who might dip into a comic book upon occasion; and we knew we could always sell a certain percentage of copies to servicemen who doted upon easy-to-read escapist literature. But basically, our readers ranged from toddlers to kids the age of thirteen or fourteen—or so we thought.

"Notice how I cleverly employ the device of repeating the same provocative phrase at the end of two successive paragraphs? This is to let you know that there may be more than meets the eye contained herein. It's a device I've often used in writing comic-book scripts and I didn't want it to slip by unnoticed.

"Who were the people who actually created and produced America's comic books? To answer that burning question we must be aware that comics have always been a high-volume low-profit-per-unit business. Which is a polite way of saying that they never paid very much to the writers or artists. If memory serves me (and why shouldn't it?), I think I received about fifty cents per page for the first script I wrote in those early days. Comics have always been primarily a piecework business. You got paid by the page for what you wrote. The more pages you could grind out, the more money you made. The comic-book writer had to be a comic-book freak, he had to be dedicated to comics; he certainly couldn't be in it for the money. And, unlike most other forms of writing, there were no royalty payments at the end of the road...no residuals...no copyright ownership. You wrote your pages, got your check, and that was that.

"Perhaps this little background will serve to explain why the quality of writing in the early comic books left just a little bit to be desired. We knew we were writing for kids. (Or so we thought, remember?) The pay wasn't extravagant enough to attract too many Hemingways or Bernard Shaws. Even Mickey Spillane, who had free-lanced for Timely briefly in the 1940s, soon gave it up to seek fame and fortune in somewhat different areas.

"It wasn't much different for the artists. Their rate of pay was somewhat higher than the writers' but it took them longer to complete a page, so things seemed to even up. As a matter of fact, there were many artists who also wrote their own stories in those days—and who did the lettering and coloring as well."[1]

Lee stayed with the company through several of its name changes (Atlas Comics, Conan Publishing Co.), and some very rough years. "There was one time years ago, I think in the 1950s, when business was very bad. We had had a staff of maybe fifty or sixty or seventy people, and they all had to be fired. My publisher came down to see me, and he said, 'Stan, we've got to discontinue all the magazines, and you'll have to fire everybody.' And then he went off to Florida and I was given the job of letting everyone go. I was the only one who remained and then very slowly had to build things up from really nothing. I think that happened twice in my career because the business had many ups and downs in those first twenty years. Firing people is horrendous. They weren't just workers. They were people I had worked *with;* they were friends. Luckily, we were able to hire many of them back before too much time had passed."[2]

By the early 1960s, Lee changed the name of the company to "Marvel Comics," a name he felt had sex appeal. He was now editor, art director, and head writer. "At the moment, the trend is monster stories, so we're turning out a pandemonious plethora of BEMs and scaly-skinned scaries. Jack Kirby, he of Captain America fame when I first started at Timely, had long since left and then recently returned to the fold as our top artist. Jack and I were having a ball turning out monster stories with such imperishable titles as 'Xom, the Creature Who Swallowed the Earth,' 'Grottu, the Giant Ant-Eater,' 'Thomgorr, the Anti-Social Alien,' 'Fin Fang Foom' (I never could remember what his shtick was—if he was a he), and others of equally redeeming artistic and literary value.

"Yep, there we were blithely grinding out our merry little monster yarns. At the same time National Comics was still featuring Superman, Batman, and all their other costumed cuties. The Archie group was likewise doing business as usual with Archie, Jughead, and their fun-loving friends. Meanwhile, Harvey Publications was holding its own with Casper the Ghost and his capricious cohorts. Also in contention were the Charleton line of assorted comic-book titles, as well as the Dell and Gold Key offerings. We were turning out comics by the carload, but nothing much was happening."[1]

"In fact, I had been thinking of quitting. At that time I had been with the company more than twenty years, and I had always thought of it as a temporary job. I remember when I got married (I was about twenty-five), I said to my wife, 'I'll stay at this job until I'm thirty, and then I've got to do something else.' I was a grown man, and I'd meet people at cocktail parties and they would say, 'What do you do for a living?' And I'd say, 'I write comic books.' In those days it seemed ridiculous. And when I got to be thirty I said, 'I'll give it five more years; I'll quit when I'm thirty-five.' And then, 'Well, I'll quit when I'm forty.' Finally, when 1960 came around, I said, 'Honey, that's it. I've just got to get out and do something else. I don't want to spend my whole life with comics. It doesn't mean anything.' She said, 'You know, Stan, all these years you've said that these comics are being done the wrong way and you wish you had a chance to do them the way you want to do them.' You see, I was working for the publisher and I had to do what he wanted. 'If you're going to leave anyway, before you go, why don't you just write some books the way you feel you'd like to do them? What have you got to lose?'"[2]

"...Her little dissertation made me suddenly realize that it was time to start concentrating on what I was doing—to carve a real career for myself in the nowhere world of comic books.

"No sooner had the lovely Mrs. Lee filled me with rabid resolution than I had another talk, this time with Martin Goodman. Martin was my publisher, my friend, and my cousin-in-law...not necessarily in that order. He was also easily the best businessman, the cleverest editor, and the canniest publisher I've ever known. I suspect he'd have been a triple-threat writer as well had he been so inclined. However, Martin published a number of other types of magazines as well as comic books, and devoted most of his time to the so-called 'slicks' while I was pretty much on my own with the comics. I never knew if it was because he had unbounded confidence in me, or because he didn't think comics had much future.

"Be that as it may, Martin mentioned that he had noticed one of the titles published by National Comics seemed to be selling better than most. It was a book called *The Justice League of America* and was composed of a team of superheroes. Well, we didn't need a house to fall on us. 'If *The Justice*

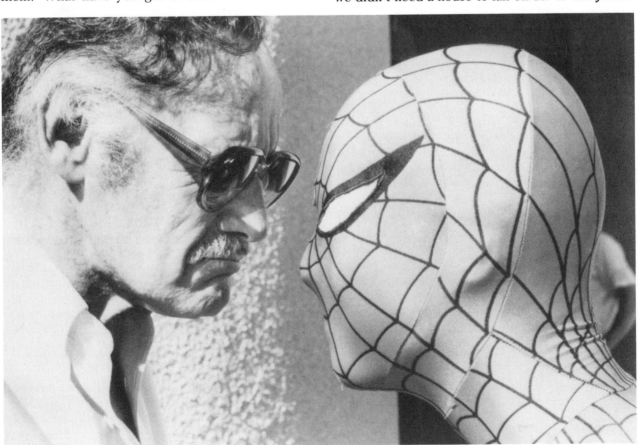

Stan Lee faces-off with Spider-Man. (Copyright © 1989 by Marvel.)

League is selling,' spake he, 'why don't we put out a comic book that features a team of superheroes?'

"His logic was irrefutable. Besides, I was tired of doing those countless monster mags. And Joan wanted me to bear down and make something of myself in the comic-book field. The timing was perfect. The elements were all at hand. Kismet.

"It was natural for me to choose Jack Kirby to draw the new superhero book that we would soon produce. Jack had probably drawn more superhero strips than any other artist and he was as good as they come. We had worked together for years, on all types of strips and stories. Most importantly, we had a uniquely successful method of working. I had only to give Jack an outline of a story and he would draw the entire strip, breaking down the outline into exactly the right number of panels replete with action and drama. Then, it remained for me to take Jack's artwork and add the captions and dialogue, which would, hopefully, add the dimension of reality through sharply delineated characterization.

"Ah, but this was not to be merely another of the hundreds of comic-strip features I had concocted in my long and lachrymose career. No, this was to be something different—something special—something to stupefy my publisher, startle my public, and satisfy my wife's desire for me to 'prove myself' in my own little sphere."[1]

"I've always believed that the only thing that will sell is quality writing, believability. The reader has to care about a character, and in order to care, he's got to believe in the character. The way you make a character believable is to flesh him out, make him three-dimensional. When I was a kid I loved Sherlock Holmes. I knew it was fiction, but a part of me felt there was a Sherlock Holmes. When I went to England, I walked down Baker Street looking for his house. I mean Conan Doyle wrote Sherlock Holmes in such a way that you had to believe this character existed; and that to me is the secret of good writing; it's the secret of good moviemaking; it's the secret of good television."[2]

"True, I would create a team of superheroes if that was what the marketplace required. But it would be a team such as comicdom had never known. For just this once, I would do the type of story I myself would enjoy reading if I were a comic-book reader. And the characters would be the kind of characters I could personally relate to; they'd be flesh and blood, they'd have their faults and foibles, they'd be fallible and feisty, and—most important of all—

inside their colorful, costumed booties they'd still have feet of clay.

"The more I thought about it, the more the concept grabbed me. All that remained was to dream up the characters, to create a team that meshed together. The first thing that came to mind was love interest. For the first time we'd have a hero and a heroine who were actually engaged. No more coy suggestions that she'd really dig the guy if only she knew his true identity. And, speaking of identities, I was utterly determined to have a superhero series without any secret identities. I knew for a fact that if I myself possessed a super power I'd never keep it secret. I'm too much of a show-off. So why should our fictional friends be any different? Accepting this premise, it was also natural to decide to forgo the use of costumes. If our heroes were to live in the real world, then let them dress like real people.

"Little by little it all took shape. We'd have the leader of the team and his lady love. She'd have a kid brother whom the readers could empathize with—but not too young. One of my many pet peeves has always been the young teenage sidekick of the average superhero. Once again, if yours truly were a superhero there's no way I'd pal around with some freckle-faced teenager. At the very least, people would start to talk. Anyway, I felt there should be one more member of our still-nameless menage—one character who was to be included for drama, for pathos, for color, and for the sheer offbeat quality he could provide. He'd be the most unlikely hero of all–ugly, morose, and totally antisocial—possessed of brute strength and a hair-trigger temper. He just had to become the most popular one of all.

"After kicking it around with Martin and Jack for a while I decided to call our quaint quartet the Fantastic Four. I wrote a detailed first synopsis for Jack to follow, and the rest is history."[1]

The "Fantastic Four" brought Lee immediate success. "...Looking back at the [first] strip...the artwork seems to be an unlikely candidate for some future Sistine Chapel, while the quality of the writing will hardly be a threat to the reputation of Dickens or Hugo.

"But if you were familiar with the comic-book genre in those halcyon days of yore, you'd possibly have reacted the way so many thousands of other startled readers did when they suddenly realized they were reading a superhero saga that was extravagantly different from those that had gone

From *The Incredible Hulk #1* comics, May 1962.

Cover of the March, 1941, issue.

before. And it was that very difference that started it all.

"For example, in the early strip we tried to give some dimension to the melancholy Moleman. Remember where he explains how he reached his underground kingdom on Monster Isle—and why? Didn't you find yourself sympathizing with him, just a bit? There he was, ostracized by his fellow man—and woman—because his physical appearance left a little something to be desired. He couldn't find acceptance in our world, so he set out to find another—one which might have a place for him. Now this was hardly reaching the dramatic heights of a Kafka, but it was almost unheard of in a comic book. Heretofore, villains were villains just because they were villains. Comics merely had good guys and bad guys, and nobody ever bothered with the whys or wherefores. But here, in the first fateful issue of the Fantastic Four, our readers were given a villain with whom they might empathize—a villain who was driven to what he had done by the slings and arrows of a heartless, heedless humanity. It was a first. It was an attempt

to portray a three-dimensional character in a world that had been composed of stereotypes. To comic bookdom, it was tantamount to the invention of the wheel.

"Similarly, the episode where Ben Grimm and Reed Richards begin to fight after their rocket ship has crash landed—and where Ben tells Reed, 'You don't have to make a speech, big shot,' as well as the other instances scattered throughout the strip where Ben is caustic and abrasive to Reed and the world in general—all these negative touches had been virtually unknown to comic books till then. Members of superhero teams were always the best of friends, with never a cross word between them. Good guys were never sarcastic, never bitter; yet here was a team with a raving malcontent, one whose paranoia was to increase with succeeding issues.

"I might as well call your attention to the dialogue, also. While it's a far cry from Paddy Chayefsky, you may notice the definite effort that was made to have people speak as much as possible like real flesh-and-blood humans, whether they were cab drivers, policemen, garage mechanics, pilots, or whatever. While reasonably natural dialogue is so much a part of writing that I feel foolish even mentioning it, you must remember that we're talking about a form of the media and a time period where 'So! You wanna play, huh?' was formerly considered a meaningful, profound exclamation when uttered by a hero in the process of being pummeled by a villain or two.

"Prior to the Fantastic Four, fan mail was almost unknown to us. Oh, we might have received a letter or two during the year, but it was always this type: 'Dear Editor, I bought a copy of Kid Colt Outlaw and there was one staple missing from the binding. I want my money back.' Hardly what you'd call a flood of fan mail.

"But no sooner did *FF* #1 hit the stands than we actually started to receive letters that said something. 'Loved your new mag. All you've gotta do is make Reed Richards less stuffy—and show us more of the Invisible Girl.' 'The Thing's the best character I ever saw. I hope he'll stop being a monster real soon.' 'How does The Human Torch burst into flame? What makes him fly? Why don't you give him his own magazine?'"[1]

"I think in the beginning at Marvel I almost went blind because I read every letter. And we received hundreds a week. I still have a compulsion to answer every letter I receive. I couldn't believe it when I learned that our competitors didn't bother reading their mail. To me, it's like having a store and competing with another store on the corner, and your customers come in and tell you everything they like and don't like about the store, and they tell you how they'd like you to display the merchandise and what goods they'd like to buy. You'd have to be crazy not to listen to them. I was getting mail from readers telling me what they liked, what they didn't like, what they'd like to see more of, what they'd like to see less of. I used to tell people after a while I didn't even need any brains to do my job; I just had to be able to read letters.

"Of course, you have to take that with a pinch of salt, too, because a lot of the mail has to be disregarded. For example, when we were doing continued stories (we were the first company ever to do that in comics), we got a tidal wave of mail saying that the kids hated the continued stories and we were ripping them off, just doing continued stories to force them to buy the next issue. And I knew they didn't mean it. The reason we did continued stories was not to make them by the next

issue particularly, but we could get better stories because by continuing the story to four or five issues, we could develop characterization and explore situations that we couldn't do with the shorter lengths. It was like writing a novel. So I felt the stories were better, and I felt that the kids must like them more. Well, despite the fact that maybe ninety percent of the letters said we should drop the continued stories, our sales almost doubled in the time that we did them. I learned later on that they really loved those stories. There's a character named Aunt May in *Spider-Man*, his old aunt who's always saying, 'Be sure to wear your galoshes when you go out in the bad weather. It looks like it's chilly out,' not knowing he's the world's strongest superhero. For years the kids have been writing in and saying, 'You've got to kill off Aunt May.' But I know damn well if I ever killed her off the book would lose something. You have to know when to listen to the fans and when not to listen."[2]

But Lee did listen to one question the letters asked with increasing frequency: "'When will you bring out another new superhero book?'"[1]

"I would have to be a little bit partial to Spider-Man only because he's become the most famous and the most successful and the most popular. I don't know whether I like him because I like him or because he's the best known. When people ask what I've written, Spider-Man is the first name that comes to my tongue. Also I guess Spider-Man is the one who's the most like me.

"He's not the luckiest guy in the world; nothing ever turns out 100 percent right for him. I shouldn't say like *me* so much as like *any* person really. I think he's probably the most human superhero. He soliloquizes, and he worries, and he agonizes and wonders why things don't turn out better for him. He's always got money problems and allergies and dandruff. I like him. I think of him as the Woody Allen of superheroes."[2]

"There I was at my desk, a brand-new sheet of paper in my typewriter, ready to begin anew the agony of creation. What kind of hero was the comic-book reading world waiting for? What could we come up with that would take fandom by storm? How about an Errol Flynn type? Or a Gary Cooper? But then that little voice kept whispering inside my head, 'Be innovative. Be original. They expect you to come up with something that's different.'

"It was patently apparent that the Thing was the most popular character in the Fantastic Four, and quite possibly in the entire comic-book field. Not

This November, 1961, comic featured four of Lee's super heroes.

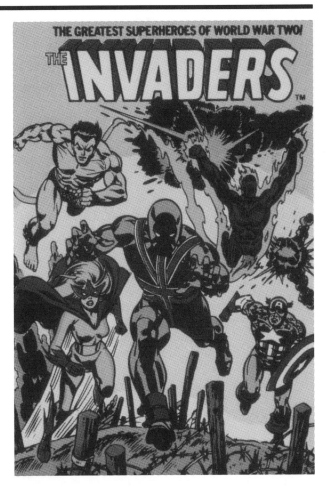

Cover from the giant-size edition of *The Invaders #1*, June, 1975.

only did the readers like him best, but he grabbed me, too. For a long time I'd been aware of the fact that people were more likely to favor someone who was less than perfect—someone. . .with whom they could identify. Why was Humphrey Bogart more popular than so many taller, smoother leading men with perfect collar-ad features—leading men whose names are now forgotten? Why the stronger-than-ever cult for the universal 'little guy,' the world's champion all-time loser, Charlie Chaplin? It's a safe bet that you remember Quasimodo, but how easily can you name any of the heroic, handsomer, more glamorous characters in *The Hunchback of Notre Dame?* And then there's Frankenstein—and he's the one I've been leading up to.

"I've always had a soft spot in my heart for the Frankenstein monster. No one could ever convince me that he was the bad guy, the villain, or the menace. It was he who was sinned against by those who feared him, by those whose first instinct was to strike out blindly at whatever they couldn't comprehend. He never wanted to hurt anyone; he

merely groped his tortuous way through a second life trying to defend himself, trying to come to terms with those who sought to destroy him.

"I suppose you can guess where we're heading. Think of the challenge it would be to make a hero out of a monster. We would have a protagonist with superhuman strength, but he wouldn't be all-wise, all-noble, all infallible. (How's *that* for a rollicking redundancy?) We would use the concept of the Frankenstein monster, but update it. Our hero would be a scientist, transformed into a raging behemoth by a nuclear accident. And—since I was willing to borrow from Frankenstein, I decided I might as well borrow from Dr. Jekyll and Mr. Hyde as well—our protagonist would constantly change from his normal identity to his superhuman alter ego and back again.

"Now all that remained was to find a name. Racking my brain for all the appellations that would describe a gargantuan creature, a being of awesome strength coupled with a dull and sluggish thinking process, I couldn't seem to find the right

Bill Bixby as Dr. David Banner transforms into his terrifying alter ego in the television series "The Incredible Hulk," presented on CBS, March, 1978-June, 1982.

word. I looked in the dictionary and the thesaurus, but nothing was on target. I knew I needed a perfect name for a monstrous, potentially murderous hulking brute who—and then I stopped. It was the word 'hulking' that did it. It conjured up the perfect mental image. I knew I had found his name. He had to be: The Hulk.

"Once again I decided that Jack Kirby would be the artist to breathe life into our latest creation. He had already gained an enthusiastic coterie of fans with his interpretation of the Fantastic Four and was more than capable of doing an additional feature strip or two. So the next time we met I outlined the concept that I'd been toying with for weeks.

"As I described him to Jack, I was envisioning a somewhat nice-looking monster, big and brutish enough to make him feared by all who met him and yet with a certain tragic appeal that would make our readers care about him and cheer him on. Not

the easiest of goals perhaps, but I had a feeling we could do it.

"Incidentally [in the first strip] I had Jack introduce a 'teenage sidekick' type of character—just the type whom I had earlier said I couldn't stand. But we did it for a reason. He was a necessary catalyst in the creation of the Hulk and he also gave me a chance to demonstrate that it was possible to introduce a teenager into a comic-book series without making him a cloying, simpy extension of the hero's personality. Remember, at Marvel we like to do things differently."[1]

The "Incredible Hulk" soon achieved the same popularity as the "Fantastic Four" and Lee turned to contemplating, arguably, his most popular character: Spider-Man.

Lee turned to Steve Ditko to draw Spider-Man. "After Spidey's premiere appearance in *Amazing Fantasy* #15 the book was dropped and we all forgot about it. I'd gotten the Spider-Man charac-

"The Amazing Spider-Man" television series starred Nicholas Hammond, and was broadcast on CBS, April, 1978-May, 1978.

ter out of my system and could now go back to our other superstars."[1]

The reaction of the readership was overwhelming, placing Spider-Man as the best-selling title for over a decade. Eventually evolving into a daily newspaper comic strip, it deals with such contemporary issues as sexual abuse. "I can't tell you the thousands of letters I've received over the years that have begun in this way: 'Dear Stan, We've never met, but I feel I've known you for years. I've got this problem, and I can't tell my father. Could you tell me, what would you do if. . .?' And, oh man, that made me feel so good."[3]

With the successes of the "Fantastic Four," the "Incredible Hulk," and the "Amazing Spider-Man," Lee realized that he had pioneered an entirely new style of storytelling. "The average comic book superhero walking down the street might say, 'Oh, a monster! I better catch him before he wipes out the city,' or something of that sort. Spider-Man would say, 'Who's that nut in the

Halloween costume? I wonder what he's advertising?'"[4]

"One day I made a bet with my publisher. He was asking me why these books were doing so well, and I said I thought we had discovered a new style of writing and drawing. He said, 'No, it can't be that. I think you're just coming up with good names, that's all. People like the names.' So I said, 'It's not just the names. I'll prove it to you. You give me a subject that can't possibly sell. Give me a type of book that you feel the kids wouldn't buy. I'll put out a book like that, and I'll give it the worst name possible, and I bet it'll sell anyway because we'll theme in the Marvel style.' At that time the Vietnam War was going on, and everybody was opposed to it. He said, 'I'll tell you what. There's no way that you can give away a war magazine. You put out a war book with a lousy title, and if it sells I'll eat my hat.' So I put out a war book called *Sgt. Fury and His Howling Commandos*, which everybody agreed had to be the worst title that had come down the pike (although secretly I loved the title), and it became one of our top-selling books. In fact, I don't like war stories that much myself, and after a few years I wanted to kill the book....We couldn't. We kept getting mail from readers; we had to keep bringing it back."[2]

Lee continued to stretch for new ideas culminating in two more series: the "Mighty Thor" and "Dr. Strange." "As far as I can remember, Norse mythology always turned me on. There was something about those mighty, horn-helmeted Vikings and their tales of Valhalla, of Ragnarok, of the Aesir, the Fire Demons, and immortal, eternal Asgard, home of the gods. If ever there was a rich lode of material into which Marvel might dip, it was there—and we would mine it."[1]

"But then there was the problem of empathy. I realized that it wouldn't be the easiest job in the world to make a reader in Hoboken develop an affinity for some long-haired nut in blue tights and helmet wings who also happens to be a Norse Thunder God. Still, one formula that's always worked in comics is the gimmick of the secret-identity hero. Also, thought I, this particular strip will be offbeat enough to allow me to employ one of the oldest cliches in the book: frail and feeble Dr. Donald Blake is in reality the most invincible immortal of them all—the mighty Thor. I wanted Blake to be a surgeon because of the dramatic possibilities it would later present. I could envision themes where Thor is needed in Asgard but Dr. Blake is needed on Earth to perform a critical operation (which none but he can perform, natch). Oh, the suspense, the tension, the choice that must be made. Besides, he could spend his spare time romping about with some ravishing registered nurse when the occasion demanded, or even when it didn't. Yep, I was convinced. Donald Blake would be a doctor, thin, lame, defenseless—the exact antithesis of his awesome Asgardian alter ego.

"When I began to write the strip, which means actually putting the words in all their little pink mouths, I decided that I wanted the hammer holder to speak more like a god. And everyone knows that gods all speak with biblical and Shakespearean phraseology. So I slowly and deliberately changed the entire style of the strip, filling it with 'thou shalts' and 'thou shalt nots' and 'so be its' and 'get thee gones' and like that. I've always been a nut about the poetic flavor of the Bible and the sentence structure and lilt of Elizabethan writing, and this was my chance to play with it....Most everyone told me that no superhero strip could

succeed if the writing were too archaic, or too stylized, or too lyrical. Well, Thor is still one of Marvel's top sellers, after all these years, and that means that [our readers are] a lot smarter and more literary than people gave [them] credit for."[1]

The aspect Lee enjoyed most about the "Dr. Strange" series was the language he had to create for the magician. "When it comes to words I'm a real cornball. I enjoy them. I relish their sound, the music made by vowels and consonants eternally jostling each other. I can lose myself completely while putting them together, trying to string them on a delicate strand of rhythm so they have a melody all their own. So, when it came to Dr. Strange I was in seventh heaven. At last I'd have a chance to be as alliterative and shmaltzy as I could wish....With Dr. Strange there were no landmarks, no points of reference. With Dr. Strange I had the chance to make up a whole language of incantations.

"Little by little it all took shape. Since I didn't know an authentic mystic chant from a Martian egg roll I had to rely on phonetics. What would sound mystical? What might a real magician say if he were intoning a genuine magical spell? There must be gods and demons in the realm of magic; surely the magician would summon them, would mutter their names in moments of crisis. Hence, my first task was to make up some authentic-sounding names for Doc to call upon. And so it began.

"The first phrase I thought of was as totally meaningless as all the others that were to follow—but I loved the sound of it: 'By the hoary hosts of Hoggoth.' No matter what he did, no matter what he wanted, no matter what he said, it always seemed to sound more dramatic when preceded by 'By the hoary hosts of Hoggoth.' Even if he was just hungry. 'By the hoary hosts of Hoggoth, I feel like a pizza.' Grabs you, doesn't it?

"Dr. Strange, which I always thought would prove exceptionally appealing to our younger readers, began to develop a cult among those at the other end of the spectrum. Suddenly the mail started pouring in—from colleges, if you will. In ever-increasing numbers students were actually devoting term papers and theses to the language of Dr. Strange, investigating the derivation of his various spells and incantations. And the payoff was—many, many of those theses explained, in detailed chapter and verse, how I had obviously borrowed from the ancient Druid writings, or from forbidden Egyptian hieroglyphics, or at least the writings of H. P. Lovecraft. Then, my correspondents would

An angry Hulk (Lou Ferrigno) finds himself trapped. The television movie, "The Death of the Incredible Hulk," was produced and directed by Bill Bixby and broadcast on NBC, February 18, 1990.

explain the relationship of Raggadorr to Ragnarok, or trace the origin of the eternal Vishanti."[1]

In 1970 Lee founded the Academy of Comic Book Artists and in 1972 became publisher and editorial director at Marvel. Through his work and many college lectures, Lee has attempted to give comics the respectability he feels they deserve as popular, modern mythology. "The problem with comics is that for so many years they were at the bottom of the barrel of the arts because everybody felt they were just for little kids who can't read anyway, and they're stupid or they wouldn't be reading comics. There were people writing them who couldn't write; there were people drawing them who were just batting them out and getting two dollars a page, and they couldn't spend more than a few minutes on each page. Even the people in the business didn't consider it a real art form. But that was years ago. Today you get good writers, good artists (I like to think we have the best), and people who really care about telling stories and doing it well, and comics are as viable a cultural entity as anything I can think of."[2]

Lee has liked some of these adaptations more than others. "With 'Spider-Man,' all of the humor, all of the wit, the satire, the life and the realism that we tried to put in the 'Spider-Man' comic book, was missing. Apparently the only thing that was emphasized was the special effects. The thing they worried about was how would they get a guy to climb a building? They did that okay. But the character was a hollow, shallow character."[3]

Lee has abandoned most of his writing chores to head Marvel Entertainment's movie and television projects in Hollywood and expresses hope that he can do for film what he has done for comic books.

Marvel Entertainment has several movies, including "Captain America," "Spider-Man," and "Dr. Strange," in various stages of development and production.

"I think there's something in the human condition that makes us love stories that are imaginative and fanciful, stories about people who are bigger and stronger and more capable than we are. We are always looking for heroes. In earlier times we had Ulysses, King Arthur, Robin Hood and Tarzan.

The 1978 television movie "Dr. Strange," based on Stan Lee's comic-book character, starred Peter Hooten.

Those were all bigger-than-life characters, and I think they embody something that will always be part of the human condition—a love for colorful heroes and villains."[2]

Footnote Sources:

[1] Stan Lee, *Origins of Marvel Comics*, Simon & Schuster, 1974.
[2] Jean W. Ross, "Stan Lee," *Contemporary Authors*, Volume 111, Gale, 1984. Amended by Lee.
[3] Tom Bierbaum, "Stan Lee's Imperfect Heroes Lifted Marvel to Top of Heap," *Variety*, September 17, 1986.
[4] David Astor, "Spidey Grows in Joke-a-Day Comic Era," *Editor and Publisher*, August 6, 1983.

■ For More Information See

New York Times Magazine, May 2, 1971 (p. 32ff).
Rolling Stone, September 16, 1971 (p. 29ff).
Arthur Asa Berger, *The Comic-Stripped American*, Walker, 1973.
Village Voice, December 23, 1974, December 15, 1975, December 13, 1976.
New Republic, July 19, 1975 (p. 26ff).
Maurice Horn, editor, *The World Encyclopedia of Comics*, Chelsea House, 1976.
Journal of Popular Culture, summer, 1976 (p. 233ff).
New York Times Book Review, September 5, 1976, November 18, 1979.
School Library Journal, January, 1977 (p. 93ff), March, 1978 (p. 144).
Quest, July-August, 1977 (p. 31ff).
Us, July 11, 1978 (p. 27).
People Weekly, January 29, 1979.
Time, February 5, 1979 (p. 138).
New York Times, December 31, 1979.
Contemporary Literary Criticism, Volume 17, Gale, 1981.
New York Daily News, February 2, 1984 (p. 4), March 17, 1985 (p. 30), Febrary 23, 1986 (p. 13ff).
Comics Journal, November, 1985 (p. 86ff).
S. Lee and Steve Ditko, *Marvel Masterworks Presents the Amazing Spider-Man*, Marvel, 1987.

Lois Lowry

A Summer to Die; Anastasia Krupnik was selected one of Child Study Association of America's Children's Books of the Year, 1979, and *Us and Uncle Fraud,* 1986; Emmy Award nomination from the National Academy of Television Arts and Sciences, 1980, for "I Don't Know Who I Am"; International Board on Books for Young People Honor List, 1982, for *Autumn Street;* American Book Award nomination (juvenile paperback category), 1983, for *Anastasia Again!;* Garden State Children's Book Award for Younger Fiction from the New Jersey Library Association, 1986, for *Anastasia, Ask Your Analyst;* Golden Kite Award from the Society of Children's Book Writers, and *Boston Globe-Horn Book* Award for Fiction, both 1987, and Child Study Children's Book Committee at Bank Street College Award, 1988, all for *Rabble Starkey; All about Sam* was selected one of *School Library Journal's* Best Books, 1988; Newbery Medal from the American Library Association, 1990, for *Number the Stars.*

Born March 20, 1937, in Honolulu, Hawaii; daughter of Robert E. (a dentist) and Katharine (a teacher; maiden name, Landis) Hammersberg; married Donald Grey Lowry (an attorney), June 11, 1956 (divorced, 1977); children: Alix, Grey, Kristin, Benjamin. *Education:* Attended Brown University, 1954-56; University of Maine, B.A., 1972, also graduate study. *Politics:* Democrat. *Religion:* Episcopalian. *Home:* 34 Hancock St., Boston, Mass. 02114; and Sanbornton, N.H. (summer). *Agent:* Harold Ober Associates, Inc., 40 East 49th St., New York, N.Y. 10017.

■ Career

Free-lance writer and photographer, 1972—. *Member:* Society of Children's Book Writers, PEN American Center, Authors Guild, MacDowell Colony (fellow).

■ Awards, Honors

Children's Book Award from the International Reading Association 1978, and Massachusetts Children's Book Award (young adult) from Salem State College, and Young Readers Medal from the California Reading Association, both 1981, all for

■ Writings

Black American Literature (textbook), J. Weston Walsh, 1973.
Literature of the American Revolution (textbook), J. Weston Walsh, 1974.
Values and the Family, J. Weston Walsh, 1977.
A Summer to Die (ALA Notable Book; *Horn Book* honor list; illustrated by Jenni Oliver), Houghton, 1977.
Find a Stranger, Say Goodbye, Houghton, 1978.

Anastasia Krupnik (ALA Notable Book),
  Houghton, 1979, large print edition, ABC-
  CLIO, 1988.
Autumn Street (ALA Notable Book), Houghton,
  1980.
Anastasia Again! (ALA Notable Book),
  Houghton, 1981, large print edition, ABC-
  CLIO, 1988.
Anastasia at Your Service, Houghton, 1982,
  large print edition, ABC-CLIO, 1989.
Taking Care of Terrific, Houghton, 1983, large
  print edition, ABC-CLIO, 1989.
The One Hundredth Thing about Caroline (ALA
  Notable Book), Houghton, 1983.
Anastasia, Ask Your Analyst, Houghton, 1984,
  large print edition, ABC-CLIO, 1989.
Us and Uncle Fraud, Houghton, 1984.
Anastasia on Her Own, Houghton, 1985, large
  print edition, ABC-CLIO, 1989.
Switcharound, Houghton, 1985.
Anastasia Has the Answers, Houghton, 1986.
Anastasia's Chosen Career, Houghton, 1987.
Rabble Starkey, Houghton, 1987, large print
  edition, G. K. Hall, 1989.
All about Sam (illustrated by D. De Groat),
  Houghton, 1988.
Number the Stars, Houghton, 1989.
Your Move, J.P.!, Houghton, 1990.

Illustrator With Photographs:

Frederick H. Lewis, *Here in Kennebunkport,*
  Durrell, 1978.

Contributor of stories, articles, and photographs to
periodicals, including *Redbook, New York Times,
Yankee,* and *Downeast.*

■ Adaptations

"I Don't Know Who I Am" (based on *Find a
  Stranger, Say Goodbye*), "Afterschool
  Special," 1980.
"Anastasia at Your Service" (cassette), Listening
  Library, 1984.
"Anastasia Krupnik" (filmstrip), Cheshire, 1987.
"Taking Care of Terrific," Wonderworks, 1988.

■ Sidelights

Not to be confused with writer Lois Duncan—
("People often confuse us. We're the same age,
sort of look alike, and even get each other's mail.
We get a kick out of it."[1]) Lois Lowry has written
books for young people dealing with subjects
ranging from the death of a sibling to the antics of

the rebellious Anastasia Krupnik. Ever present is
the author's special sense of humor.

Born in 1937 in Honolulu, Hawaii, Lowry was
originally named Cena, after her paternal grandmother. "But that name lasted only until she heard
about it. No grandchild of *hers,* she announced,
was going to bear *that name.* Hastily my name was
changed, and when at the age of eleven months I
was baptized, with a tiny lei of Hawaiian flowers
around my neck, it was with the name Lois Ann, in
honor of my father's two sisters back in Wisconsin.
Cena Ericson Hammersberg was present, having
come all the way by train and ship for the
occasion."[2]

After Pearl Harbor and the start of World War II,
Lowry's father, an officer in the Army Dental
Corps, was sent to the Pacific. "When my father
went overseas, my mother took her children back
to Pennsylvania where she'd grown up, and moved
in with her parents. My step-grandmother didn't
like children much, and I didn't like her. But I
adored my grandfather. He was the president of a
bank and very distinguished. He actually was a
question on the game show 'Jeopardy' once. The
question was: 'Bank president Merkel Landis
founded this in Pennsylvania.' The answer was:
'The Christmas Club.'

"My mother had been a teacher before her marriage, so she was very child-oriented. Like mothers
of that time, she never worked after she was
married, and was a good mom for a little girl. Since
my father was a career army officer, he was gone
during a great deal of my childhood. I remember
all these relatively normal Christmases with trees,
presents, turkeys, and carols, except that they had
this enormous hole in them because there was
never any father. I have very fond memories of
him, and I'm sure that he did come back on leave
(with no better evidence than I had a brother born
in 1943 who looks very much like my father and
not the milkman), nevertheless, he was lost to me
for a number of formative years. That's probably
why I've written a terrific father figure into almost
all of my books—sort of a fantasy of mine while
growing up."[1]

When Lowry began school in Carlisle, Pennsylvania, she "...could already read and write....I
remember that; and now; remembering too, mother tells me that I could read and write when I was
three—a saved, faded letter from a nursery school
I'd attended...confirmed that, with its terse comment: 'Her unusual ability to read and write sets
her apart from the other children.' But I have no

memory of the process of becoming literate. It just happened, I think, as I became aware that letters had sounds and if you put them together they made words, and if you put the words together they made stories.

"I *do* remember the feeling of being set apart from the other children. I hated the games they played: one in particular, where they pretended to be elephants, holding their arms like trunks, and lumbering about in line while the teacher played elephant marching music on the piano. I refused. I sat in the corner of the classroom instead, reading. An intellectual snob at the age of three; no wonder the teacher had sent home a huffy little note.

"In the first grade, in Pennsylvania, I retreated to my stubborn elitism once again. No *way* was I going to dawdle, bored, over 'See Dick. See Jane.' when back at grandfather's house there was a whole wall of bookcases filled with books.

"They got even with me. They put me into third grade, with a see-how-you-like-that attitude, and I liked it just fine—the books were more interesting....Until I was confronted by arithmetic: multiplication tables, to be exact. Multiplication tables for someone who doesn't yet know how to add or subtract.

"I was humbled. For the remainder of my official academic life I was the youngest, usually the smallest in every grade, and the one who suffered from math anxiety long before the term was invented."[2]

"I was a very shy child anyway, and would have been whatever my age in relationship to my peers, but I think the fact that I was younger by the time of junior high, became more of an issue. When you're physically less developed than the people in your class—who must wear a bra and you don't—those things are important too. It probably increased my tendency to be an introvert. I wasn't friendless or unpopular, but my friendships tended to be singular, close ones rather than large groups of giggling girls. I was never a cheerleader-type person and I'm glad, but I sort of envied them in a quiet way."[1]

Many times, Lowry would translate her experiences, often of childhood naivete and embarrassment, into the beginnings of fiction, as when her baby brother shattered the head of an antique china doll entrusted to her by an aunt. "I was heartbroken....'The brutal stranger wrest the infant from her helpless arms....' I began to create in my head.

Dust jacket of Lowry's 1987 book.

"My mother was not heartbroken. She was horrified. The doll was very valuable, and had not been given to me, merely loaned: that had been made quite clear."[2]

The shattered doll was so valuable that Lowry's mother took it to New York in an effort to find someone to fix it. "She was gone quite a while, long enough to write letters back to Pennsylvania. The one addressed to me was marked 'private' and said: 'The baby is doing well and I will be able to bring her home from the hospital very soon.'

"Short on loyalty, I completely forgot the doll in my ecstasy. Mother had given birth to a baby in New York, or perhaps (even better) she had adopted a new-born waif, an orphaned baby girl—and I was the only one who knew. She had chosen *me* as confidante....I began to create new stories, new scenes: 'The two sisters met their mother at the train station when she returned from her mysterious trip to the big city. In her arms was a squirming pink bundle. "What's that?" asked the older daughter in amazement. The younger, who had been specially entrusted with the secret, smiled knowingly. . . .'

"Once again ecstasy abruptly turned to embarrassment. On Mother's arrival home, there was no rosy-cheeked orphaned baby doll at all—just that lifeless china head with its painted-on eyes—and the private humiliation of having misunderstood.

"After a while, I began to shape it in my head, making a story of it: 'The little girl, in her excited anticipation of a baby sister, had completely forgotten about the doll. How foolish she was. . . .' I began to see the humor. Soon, even my own naivete seemed bearable as long as it had a form, a substance, and a narrative.

"Unaware, I was beginning to be a writer."[2]

Lowry also found consolation in books. "The public Library was my special place. It was better than school which was often boring, and certainly better than the Presbyterian church, where I sat restless and irritable each Sunday. The library was close by and I was allowed to walk to it alone from the time I was six or so. It had high, vaulted ceilings and dim light; voices were hushed, and shelves were dusty. The librarian—a woman—sat behind a high counter and looked down at me when I stood on tiptoe and handed her my chosen books. She did something magic to the books. Thump, thump, with her special, magical tool—pressing it definitively onto the books in a gesture only librarians are allowed to make; and then the books were mine to take home. After a while she told me in her well-modulated whisper that I was not to return them the same day. One visit to the library each day was to be my limit. So I chose more carefully, the thickest books I could find after that.

"One book that I chose when I was ten was called *A Tree Grows in Brooklyn,* and the librarian insisted that it was inappropriate, an adult book, not at all what a ten-year-old should read. I insisted, standing my ground. I took it home against her wishes, read it, and found out that librarians do not always know what they are talking about. It became one of my favorite books, it and *The Yearling.* Combining both books, I had two not-exactly-compatible dreams. I yearned to live in teeming slums, and to forge a life for myself among poverty-stricken streets. If that wasn't possible—and it seemed likely that it wasn't—my second choice was to live in a swamp and have mostly animals for friends, and one poor little crippled boy, who would die young so that I could weep at his graveside.

"In truth, there was little drama in my own life, which was quiet, well-ordered, predictable, safe, and happy.

"There were the summers at the lake where my grandparents' summer home was a massive converted nineteenth-century mill with thick stone walls and huge fireplaces. On the grounds were the ruins of the old Blacksmith's shop. . . .We were forbidden to play there because of rattlesnakes, and we obeyed—but we tested ourselves often, walking close to the forbidden ruins, daring the snakes to emerge. When we heard—or imagined we heard—a rattle, we'd run, shrieking with panic and delight. Down the dirt road was the wide-porched general store where we all would gather in the evenings, adults to gossip, teenagers to flirt, we children to eat ice cream and play tag in the twilight.

"My sister, Helen, began to move more often out of the boisterous games of tag and into the subdued, smirking, and mysterious circle of adolescents. I watched her gradual defection with puzzlement, resentment, envy, and sadness."[2]

At the end of World War II, Lowry's father remained in Japan as part of the occupation forces and in 1948 sent for his family. "I was the only kid finishing sixth grade who wasn't going to go to the local junior high but would, instead, be sailing on an ocean liner from New York, down through Panama, and across the Pacific to a place we had actually studied in our Geography textbooks. An exotic place. I gave smug oral reports on Japan in class, casually inserting the news that I soon would be living there. . .(while the rest of you, was the implied message, would still be in this boring town. . .)."[2]

Lowry spent two years in Tokyo. She and her sister attended the English-speaking Meguro School along with other military children, and wandered about the rubble of a recovering city. "There were few restrictions, and I disregarded most of the existing ones anyway. We were not to eat native food; the water was unpurified; the milk unpasteurized; and the vegetables had been fertilized with human waste. It didn't concern me a bit, since like all twelve-year-olds I considered myself probably immortal anyway, and I wandered around with my pals, all of us slurping on bacteria-ridden popsicles purchased from Shibuya street vendors, our pockets full of garish candies. I drew the line at the dried grasshoppers dispensed from big barrels from the local markets, but some of my friends even munched on those, as well. We all survived and thrived, and our parents were blissfully unaware."[2]

After the start of the Korean War in 1950 and the evacuation of all the American women and children from Japan, Lowry found herself back in Pennsylvania. She attended several schools between her freshman and senior years of high school, finally graduating from the Packer Collegiate Institute, a private school for girls in Brooklyn Heights, New York. "I never did become a joiner of clubs, to the despair of guidance counselors and advisors, who often called me in for private talks on the subject. I needed extracurricular activities, they told me, for college applications. I always nodded solemnly and said yes, I *promise* I will join the debate club, or the dramatic club, or I will try out for the operetta, *honest.* But I never did. Privately, I figured that I would find a college that didn't care about junk like that. I didn't want to go to college with a bunch of cheerleaders or yearbook editors anyway.

"Of course, there were plenty of colleges willing to look kindly on the application of a bright sixteen-year-old future novelist, whether she attended student council meetings or not. I chose Pembroke College, the women's branch of Brown University, and entered there in the fall of 1954, to study writing.

"In between dates and bridge games I worked hard at writing. I was in a special honors program for aspiring writers, and I met often with the beefy, pink-faced professor who had been appointed my mentor. He patiently read my sweet, sad stories about small children whose dogs die, and he thought of encouraging things to say to me. My grammar was impeccable, he told me. And I was, ah, *fluent.* Amazingly fluent. He puffed on his pipe and stared at me with mournful bloodshot eyes.

"I sensed that fluency and impeccable grammar weren't exactly what he wanted from me. I waited. He shifted in his chair. It seems, he suggested, finally, as if maybe you have not *experienced* very much yet.

"Like what?

"'Well, like grief.'

"I nodded diffidently, acknowledging that that was true. I had not experienced grief. Privately, I had hoped that I never would.

"He sighed. 'Love, he suggested. Love, too. It's pretty much the same as grief.'

"Now I could relax. I rose, took my paper back, thanking him for the A—he always gave me an A

because I was amazingly fluent—and headed back to my dorm. What did *he* know, an old guy like that, probably close to fifty, about love? Love was *my* department."[2]

By the end of her sophomore year, Lowry had married a newly commissioned naval officer. "That was the '50s, and that's what you did when somebody asked you to marry him; immediately gave up your academic aspirations."[3]

"One of the saddest comments I can make about those times is that to this day I don't know what any of my college friends majored in, or what their professional aspirations were. But without hesitation I could tell you which of them had some guy's fraternity pin attached to her sweater."[2]

Lowry spent the next six years moving around the country with her husband. They also started a family. "In 1963 I was twenty-six years old. I had four children under the age of five. Come to think of it, so did my husband, but he also, by then, had a law degree from Harvard, so I think he got the better end of the bargain....I don't blame him, or anyone, for that. I blame the mindless culture of

Paperback of the first book in the "Anastasia" series.

the fifties, which did a lot of damage to decent people's lives.

"My children grew up in Maine, and so did I, right along with them. For a while, when they were small, I did a lot of elephant marching: committees and boards and probably even a Tupperware party or two, before I opted out and went off and read in my own corner as I had ever since nursery school.

"There was always a dog underfoot, usually a cat or two, and a horse in the barn. There were assorted small animal graves out near the row of blue spruce trees, one with the epitaph: 'Here lies Barney Bunny, Lover of Carrots and Beloved Friend of Benjamin Lowry.' The kids were blonde and blue-eyed, energetic and funny and bright. I nagged at them to clean their rooms and they never did, and I didn't really care a whole lot. Sometimes I made rules. 'Everyone over the age of seven has to make his/her own bed,' was a rule I made once. No one

Softcover edition of the 1978 award winner.

followed it except Ben, who was proud of having just turned seven, and then suddenly he noticed that it wasn't fun to make a bed, something the rest of us had known for ages. Good old Ben. Once he even thought that he should be obedient and eat asparagus, something he hated, until the other kids explained to him that Mom only *pretended* to care about a clean plate."[2]

"I [never] really set aside the idea of writing; certainly I told stories to my kids and even wrote some down, although they are fortunately lost to posterity, I think. I went back to college when I was in my thirties and it took me four years then to complete the two years of work I needed for my degree. Then I went on to graduate school. During those six years I was writing a lot, but it was academic stuff. Nothing wrong with that, and I certainly enjoyed it, but it did postpone the time when I could just do what I wanted to do for fun—and, as it turned out, for a livelihood."[3]

In 1973 and 1974, Lowry had her first two textbooks published. These were, respectively, *Black American Literature* and *Literature of the American Revolution*. "I had a friend who was a textbook publisher and was looking for somebody to do a textbook on black American literature. I feel somewhat regretful about having done that one because I think they should have hired a black person for it. But nobody was offering me writing jobs and he did, so I did it. *Literature of the American Revolution* was written as a bicentennial textbook. Because I was offered those textbook contracts, I was able to incorporate that work into my graduate school program and get academic credit for having done them. So they did come directly out of my school experience."[3]

In graduate school, Lowry studied photography as well as literature. "I commandeered a room of the big old farmhouse in which we lived, placed my typewriter in there, and declared it off limits to bickering children and snoring dogs. I set up a darkroom in the basement and before long what had been a laundry room was strewn with enlarged prints in various stages of washing and drying.

"Photography had never been a particular interest of mine and I had begun taking courses in it only to gain some credits I needed for my degree. But it wasn't very long before I became fascinated with light and with composition: two aspects of photography which were closely connected I felt, to aspects of writing both fiction and nonfiction. What elements does the writer—or photographer—reveal (or shed light on)? And how are those elements arranged? When questions like these begin to occupy more and more of my thoughts, questions like 'What's for dinner?' became less and less absorbing."[2]

Lowry was divorced in 1977. "My kids were in college and high school and I didn't want to be a lawyer's wife anymore. I wanted to go out and work, have a career. My mother had never worked a day after she got married. She'd been the traditional 'Leave it to Beaver' mother, there in the kitchen baking chocolate chip cookies. Now, when we talk, she becomes very wistful because she never had the chance to do the things I've done. I cringe to say this, but my father never would have allowed her to. As a kid, I benefited greatly from her being there with the cookies, but was never aware that she had any desire to do anything except bake those damn things. So I've seen this from both sides. I think that my kids suffered from my desire to go out on my own, but at the same time they benefited greatly, particularly my daughters, from seeing their mother decide that she needed to do something and acting on it. My own grandson is the son of a single mother, and my daughter's gone back to school to get a degree which will lead to a better job. But she's a wonderful mother. I'm sure that he doesn't suffer from the lack of chocolate chip cookies."[1]

With the encouragement of a children's book editor at Houghton Mifflin who had liked some of Lowry's earlier stories for children, Lowry began her first novel, *A Summer to Die*, the story of two sisters, one of whom dies of cancer. "I'd worked for a number of years as a journalist, but I began writing with a certain amount of ignorance in the art of fiction, which leads me to believe that a lot of what I do is intuitive. I didn't take all those courses and workshops in 'conflict' and 'where ideas come from,' all those things on which people take notes. So I'm not sure how much that actually helped or hindered me. Sure, there are an awful lot of people who talk about writing instead of writing, but that is not to say that there aren't certain rules that one should at least be aware of. The book did come from my own experience which made it powerful. Memories and experience are probably as valuable as an 'A' in plotwriting."[1]

Lowry had based the story on her sister, Helen, who had died when Lowry was in her twenties. "That book was not strictly autobiographical. I changed a lot, but when my mother read it, she recognized the characters as my sister and me. She knew that the circumstances in the book were very

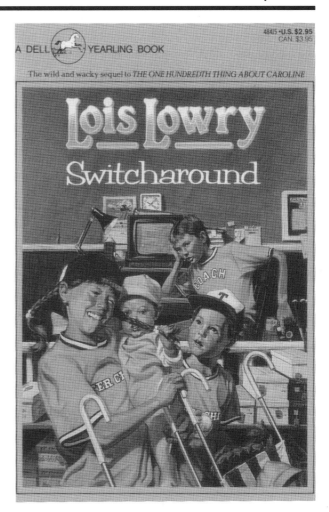

The 1985 Dell paperback.

different, but the characters had great veracity for her."[1]

Lowry continues to receive letters from readers touched by it. "Now that I get so much mail and so much of it deals with my more light-hearted books, I will confess to the reading public that I use a word processor to answer those letters because I just can't sit down and answer every one personally, although I try to personalize each one. But the letters from kids who have had a brother or a sister die, or a parent, or someone close to them, those I do sit down and answer personally."[3]

In 1978, her book of photos entitled *Here in Kennebunkport* was published. "The book on Kennebunkport was just scenery. Somebody asked me to do it and I did, but it was not the kind of thing I enjoy doing most."[3]

"I had studied photography in graduate school, and found it very handy as a journalist to supplement a magazine article I was writing with my own photos. Without realizing it, my photography began to reflect my interest in children. Gradually, I evolved into someone who specialized in children's photography. I did that for a period of time with great satisfaction. But in 1979, when I moved to an apartment in Boston, I no longer had a darkroom. When a photographer loses control over her darkroom, a lot of the pleasure goes out of it. In addition, I no longer had the time for it."[1]

At that point, writing novels became Lowry's main focus. Her second novel, *Find a Stranger, Say Goodbye* was published. This novel dealt with adopted children and the desire to find their real parents. Like *A Summer to Die*, this book became popular and elicited a strong reaction from readers. Though this book did not come directly from her own experience, Lowry believed that her years as a mother qualified her to speak on the subject. "I'm sure my four children. . .would not mind my revealing to the world that when they were teenagers they put me through every conceivable problem that one can have with adolescents. I dealt with that in some cases well and in some cases very badly. Certainly I learned from all of those experiences, and maybe it's because of having watched my own kids go through the torture of becoming adults, and having suffered through it as a parent, that I think those kinds of issues are important and it's important to deal with them in a sensitive and compassionate way."[3]

"Besides, by the time I began writing for kids, my own kids had become old enough and independent enough that I don't think they were embarrassed by anything I wrote. I never borrowed a lot of specifics anyway, and they were living their own lives. I don't think it's been a problem for them."[1]

Memories of her own childhood, plus her experiences as a parent, have led Lowry to one of her most popular characters: Anastasia Krupnik, the spunky, rebellious, and often irreverently funny adolescent who has blossomed into a series of books, the first published in 1979. "Until I was about twelve, I thought my parents were terrific, wise, wonderful, beautiful, loving, and well-dressed. By age twelve and a half, they turned into stupid, boring people with whom I didn't want to be seen in public. Often when I talk at schools, I'll ask the thirteen-year-olds, 'Have you noticed how suddenly your mother has turned into a stupid and boring person?' and they all light up with a sense of recognition, but also with a sense of humor about it. That happens to all kids, and to the kids in my books as well."[1]

"[Anastasia's] probably a composite of my two quite nutty daughters. But she actually started out as a short story. . . .I was working on the book *Autumn Street,* which is a more serious book, and just as comic relief I wrote a short story that turned out essentially to be the first chapter of the Anastasia book, thinking I would just sell that to a children's magazine. But after I'd finished it I had become so fond of that little character that I decided she was worth extending into a book, and that's when I continued writing the first book about her. I did not intend to make it into a series but. . .I have the feeling that she's going to go on forever—or until I get quite sick of her, which hasn't happened yet. I'm still very fond of her and her whole family."[3]

"I also modeled Anastasia after Jimmy Carter's daughter. When I started writing this book, he was still president. Amy was a really neat little kid in that she always appeared on television, in newspapers, and in magazines, to be a normal kid, having tantrums and misbehaving. I liked that because I had grown up in the era of the perfect Nixon daughters. My own daughters have always been very independent. I admire that in anybody, though I must add that it's sometimes difficult to be the parent of a child like that. My oldest daughter was the first person in the history of her high school to turn down an invitation to join the National Honor Society. She asked me, 'What's the purpose of joining an organization that doesn't do anything?' and I sympathized with her. She stood her ground though the school officials were very embarrassed. So while I admire that spunk, I sometimes wish it was somebody else's daughter I admired—but that's what I meant by nutty. Nutty in an interesting, often admirable, yet frustrating way.

"My current thinking is that Anastasia will not get any older than thirteen. Kids write me letters asking, 'Please can she be in high school?' What they don't realize is that she would not be as much fun for children their age if she became older. Thirteen is such a neat combination of ingeniousness and sophistication that it's a great age to write about."[1]

Despite that, Lowry doesn't write for a particular age group. "When I am writing, I become the age of the main character and therefore include what would be relevant and appropriate to the character. I don't think of potential audience. That's what the publisher gets stuck doing—marketing. I just don't think in those terms."[1]

For this reason, her book *Autumn Street,* published in 1980, was reviewed both as a children's and as an adult book. In this autobiographical story, set in her grandparent's house in Pennsylvania, Lowry described the murder of their housekeeper's young son, and of the painful lessons the heroine learns. "That's the book about which I get letters from adults. They come across it by accident because a child has to read it in school or brings it home; then the forty-five-year-old women pick it up and find that it evokes their childhood in them. It does cross those boundaries, and although that affects me in a negative way in that it doesn't sell thousands of copies the way an Anastasia book does, I don't mind that; while I do make my living by writing, my aspirations are not to become a millionaire. I'm glad special people come along and find *Autumn Street* and it becomes special to them."[3]

Lowry's books have occasionally become controversial to others. "What usually happens is that one of my books will be called into question by a parent or parents' group and then be reviewed by the committee of a library or school. As far as I know, every time that's happened, my books have been reinstated. The process seems to work for me. I really can't think of a better way to deal with it.

"I have a hard time reconciling my distaste for censorship with the knowledge of some of the crap that's put out there to influence kids. I sympathize with parents whose feeling of helplessness sometimes leads them to make illogical decisions. They have legitimate reason to be terrified that their kids will be doing crack at twelve, or be pregnant at thirteen. However, I don't believe that books contribute to that; moreover, I think that good books can help to prevent those tragedies.

"Besides, we have some wonderful teachers and librarians fulfilling roles that my teachers never did. When I went to school in the forties, my teachers were, almost without exception, grim-mouthed spinsters. They arrived at nine a.m. and, while we sat rigid in our desks, stood in front of the class until three o'clock with only a little break for lunch. They didn't like us and we didn't like them. Today when I visit schools, I see that the relationship between teachers and children has become a much more human and personal one, which helps to fill the need created by the dissolution of families."[1]

Lowry's next book, *The One Hundredth Thing about Caroline,* published in 1983, explored themes of family and displayed Lowry's familiar style of humor. Followed by *Switcharound* in 1985,

Paperbound edition of the 1983 adventure novel.

this book established another series for her. "The most important things to me in my own life, as well as in my books, are human relationships of all kinds. Although my books deal largely with families, I also attach a great deal of importance to friendships. Those are the things young people should pay attention to in their lives.

"The third book in that series is called, *Your Move, J.P.!.* I think I made a mistake in that the titles don't make it clear that these books are all about the same family, so kids happen on that realization by accident. Obviously, it's too late to change that."[1]

Ideas come to Lowry in different ways for different books. "For the 'Anastasia' books, all I usually have to do is think of a new plot or a new problem for her to handle. My publisher is always very eager for new 'Anastasia' books because they have a built-in audience, so they automatically sell more than a book about a completely new set of characters. My other books, very often, will more likely begin from a combination of character and setting.

"Since I have a flower garden at my house and I'm often thinking about pulling up and fertilizing things, the idea of compost comes to mind when I discuss the beginnings of books. I toss little tidbits of character and setting onto the compost heap in my mind and they ferment in the same way as my garbage and old tulip bulbs. All that fertilization takes place without my being aware of it. Sometimes it stinks, but if I'm lucky, I'll end up with something productive.

"For example, my book *Rabble Starkey* had a very strong sense of place because my brother lives down in the mountains of western Virginia. The more I visited him, the more I began to have a feel for that region, its speech, and its geography. I also think that I'm affected subliminally by things I see or hear in the news, especially when it concerns kids. During that period, I was hearing a lot about the large number of pregnant teenagers; children having children. So I began to think about the logical extension of that: a girl who finds out she is pregnant and has decisions to make. But often in writing, it works better when you reverse the obvious. So I began to think about writing the book from the point of view of a kid who has been born to a kid. I factored that into my compost along with my impressions of West Virginia: the simplicity of values as compared to a sophisticated Boston where 'Anastasia' and I live, and all those elements came together."[1]

From an International Reading Association Award for her first novel, *A Summer to Die,* to the 1990 John Newbery Medal for *Number the Stars,* Lowry's writing has earned her a multitude of awards. Still, she feels that writers for young people are occasionally somewhat slighted. "Even people I know well and love dearly continue to say to me, 'Gee, do you think you'll ever write a...?' They don't say 'a real book' but that's what they mean....I think it represents the funny kind of attitude people have toward children's books. And as people who write them know, they're just as tough to write as adult books."[3]

Lowry maintains a fairly workman-like approach to her writing. "When I'm home I sit down every day at my desk and work. I do a lot of traveling because, like most writers, I have to go and speak at schools and conventions and libraries all around the country. But when I'm home I work about five hours a day. That's not all working on books. But I do sit down regularly at my desk. I don't wait around for inspiration to strike or I'd never get a thing written."[3]

"I don't write a whole book and then rewrite it from the beginning. Back when I used a typewriter, it was easy to say 'I did three rewrites of this novel,' because the three manuscripts were sitting there. Now that I use a word processor, I sort of rewrite along the way and end up not knowing how many times I've rewritten because I haven't printed it out every time. What I'll do is write a chapter and before going onto the next, revise it. Then I'll write the next and rewrite the first two before going onto the third. It's an on-going process.

"Part of it also is that, unlike many writers, I don't have an outline or know what's going to happen in the story until I write it. So sometimes I'll realize that something has to happen in chapter eight, but for it to happen I have to change something in chapter two. It's a very disorderly way to write a book. It would be more orderly for me to write it with a set of index cards so that I'd know beforehand what will happen in chapters two, eight, and sixteen. But I'm not sure it would be better."[1]

Find a Stranger, Say Goodbye was adapted as an "Afterschool Special" titled: "I Don't Know Who I Am" and was nominated for an Emmy Award in 1980. "Because of my background as a photographer and my keenly-developed visual sense, I have always had a fantasy about becoming a filmmaker. But after a dinner with Bruce Brooks, another young adult author, I changed my thinking. I mentioned my interest in filmmaking to him and he asked me what aspect of it appealed to me. I answered: the writing, and the set design, and the cinematography, and the directing....He looked at me and said, 'You sound like somebody who ought to be a writer.' He was absolutely right. When I sit at my desk, I do all those things, plus casting, costume design, etc. I realized I didn't need to have that fantasy because I was, in a way, doing it already. And after taking a course in screenwriting, I became aware of the hideously frustrating limitations placed on the screenwriter.

"When I saw [it], I was very disappointed. But the things that disappointed me were things which were a necessary outcome of the medium. Since it was cheaper to film in Southern California, they changed the setting. So New England disappeared from the story. It would have been very frustrating for me to live with those restrictions in the production. I have since turned down several offers to make the 'Anastasia' books into a television series because I don't want to see the books destroyed in that way, which would be almost inevitable.

"Nonetheless, I hope I haven't given the impression that I dislike the medium because I'm an enormous film fan. I have my own private film festivals; I'll watch all Australian films for a week because it's my Australian film festival, or I'll watch all the films of a particular director or screenwriter. My favorite is Horton Foote. A lot of his stuff is little known because it's introspective. He adapted a short story of Faulkner's which was gorgeous. The film was called 'Tomorrow,' but no one's ever heard of it because the average guy who likes 'Rambo' doesn't want to go see this slow-moving, beautiful, black-and-white film. It's the kind of film that I would make, and nobody would go to see."[1]

In addition to writing fiction and watching movies, Lowry enjoys traveling. "I do a lot for business purposes, but I've been all over the world. I enjoy it because I can combine it with photography, just for my own pleasure.

"I'm also interested in architecture and am remodeling my ancient farmhouse in New Hampshire. I still read a lot, although not books by other young adult authors. My main enjoyment comes mostly from memoirs and biographies of literary figures, books by people sifting through their own childhood as if they're looking at old maps and picking out the landmarks, I guess because it relates to my own work.

"I also grow flowers, a typical grandmotherly pursuit."[1]

Lowry has observed another change from the days when she lived at her grandfather's house in Pennsylvania. "Though my grandfather was wonderful, he was nonetheless reserved and distant. Grandparents didn't feel compelled in those days to get down on their knees and build towers of blocks with their grandchildren. Now, fifty years have passed and I recently visited my six-year-old grandson who had been set to the task of looking up and learning a new word every day by his mom, my youngest daughter. While I was there, his mother asked him what word he had learned for today and his eyes darted around the room. Obviously he'd forgotten. But he caught sight of the cover of the *TV Guide* and quickly said, 'Drama. Drama is my word for today.' We looked it up in the dictionary, but he still didn't understand the definition very well. So grandmother took it upon herself to demonstrate drama to him and did a scene from 'Little Red Riding Hood,' playing all the parts. My daughter said that if he liked the drama he could cheer and clap, but if he didn't like it, he could hiss and boo and throw rotten tomatoes. So of course my grandson went immediately into the kitchen to look for rotten tomatoes. Fortunately, there weren't any available. Had my grandfather played the role of the big bad wolf, which he never would have done because bank presidents don't do those things, I never in a million years would have considered throwing a tomato at him. But it was my grandson's first thought. And if he had done so, I would have found it wonderful."[1]

Footnote Sources:

[1] Based on an interview by Dieter Miller for *Authors and Artists for Young Adults.*

[2] Lois Lowry, *Something about the Author Autobiography Series*, Volume 3, Gale, 1987.

[3] Jean W. Ross, "Lois Lowry," *Contemporary Authors New Revision Series*, Volume 13, Gale, 1984.

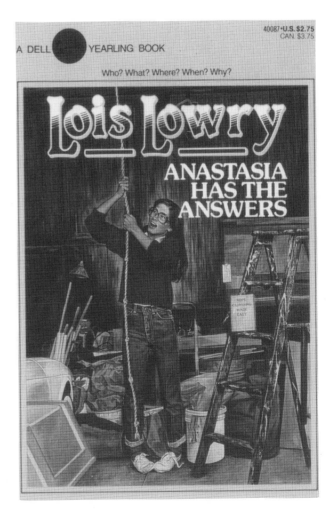

The 1986 Dell softcover.

■ For More Information See

Publishers Weekly, February 28, 1977, June 20, 1977 (p. 72), May 15, 1978, March 26, 1979, September 24, 1979, April 11, 1980 (p. 78), July 27, 1984, February 21, 1986 (p. 152ff), June 26, 1987 (p. 50).

School Library Journal, May, 1977, May, 1978 (p. 77ff), October, 1979 (p. 152), April, 1980 (p. 125ff), October, 1981 (p. 144), November, 1982 (p. 87ff).

Horn Book, August, 1977 (p. 451), June, 1978 (p. 258), December, 1979 (p. 663), August, 1980 (p. 409), October, 1981 (p. 535ff), December, 1982 (p. 650), June, 1983 (p. 304), March/April, 1987 (p. 181ff).

New York Times Book Review, September 18, 1977, February 28, 1982 (p. 31), April 11, 1982, May 17, 1987 (p. 33).

Language Arts, October, 1977, May, 1982, March, 1983 (p. 360).

Kirkus Reviews, March 1, 1978 (p. 248), December 15, 1979 (p. 1430), June 15, 1980 (p. 779), March 15, 1983 (p. 310).

Kliatt, April, 1979, April, 1982.

Junior Bookshelf, August, 1979 (p. 224ff), August, 1980 (p. 194).

Times Literary Supplement, March 28, 1980 (p. 356).

New Yorker, December 1, 1980.

Children's Literature Review, Volume 6, Gale, 1984.

Glen Estes, *Dictionary of Literary Biography,* Volume 52, Gale, 1986.

''A Visit with Lois Lowry'' (videotape), Houghton, 1986.

Writer, July, 1987 (p. 16ff), May, 1990 (p. 7ff).

Collections:

Kerlan Collection at the University of Minnesota.

Bobbie Ann Mason

Born May 1, 1940, in Mayfield, Ky.; daughter of Wilburn A. (a dairy farmer) and Christie (a dairy farmer; maiden name, Lee) Mason; married Roger B. Rawlings (a magazine editor and writer), April 12, 1969. *Education:* University of Kentucky, B.A., 1962; State University of New York at Binghamton, M.A., 1966; University of Connecticut, Ph.D., 1972. *Residence:* Pennsylvania. *Agent:* Amanda Urban, International Creative Management, 40 West 57th St., New York, N.Y. 10019.

■ Career

Writer, 1960—; *Mayfield Messenger*, Mayfield, Ky., writer, 1960; Ideals Publishing Co., New York, N.Y., writer for magazines, including *Movie Stars, Movie Life,* and *T.V. Star Parade*, 1962-63; Mansfield State College (now Mansfield University), Mansfield, Pa., assistant professor of English, 1972-79. *Member:* PEN, Authors Guild, and numerous animal rights organizations.

■ Awards, Honors

National Book Critics Circle Award nomination, American Book Award nomination, and Ernest Hemingway Foundation Award for Best First-Fiction, all 1982, PEN-Faulkner Award for Fiction nomination, 1983, and American Academy and Institute of Arts and Letters Award for Literature to encourage new writers, 1984, all for *Shiloh and Other Stories;* National Endowment for the Arts Fellowship, 1983; Pennsylvania Arts Council Grant, 1983; Guggenheim Fellowship, 1984; *In Country* was selected one of *School Library Journal*'s Best Books, and one of American Library Association's Best Books for Young Adults, both 1985, and nominated for the Colorado Blue Spruce Young Adult Book Award, and received Award from the Vietnam Veterans of America for contribution to the arts, both 1989.

■ Writings

Nabokov's Garden: A Nature Guide to Ada, Ardis, 1974.
The Girl Sleuth: A Feminist Guide to the Bobbsey Twins, Nancy Drew, and Their Sisters, Feminist Press, 1975.
Shiloh and Other Stories, Harper, 1982.
In Country (novel), Harper, 1985.
Spence & Lila (illustrated by sister, LaNelle Mason), Harper, 1988, large print edition, Thorndike, 1989.
Love Life (short stories), Harper, 1989.

Contributor:

Hortense Calisher and Shannon Ravenel, editors, *Best American Short Stories, 1981,* Houghton, 1981.

Anne Tyler and S. Ravenel, editors, *Best American Short Stories, 1983*, Houghton, 1983.

Bill Henderson, editor, *The Pushcart Prize: Best of the Small Presses*, Volume VIII, Pushcart, 1983.

O. Henry Prize Collection, Doubleday, 1986.

O. Henry Prize Collection, Doubleday, 1988.

Contributor of short stories to numerous magazines, including *New Yorker, Atlantic, North American Review, Washington Post Magazine, Ascent, Boston Review, Virginia Quarterly Review, Boston Globe Magazine, Story, Paris Review*, and *Mother Jones*.

■ Adaptations

"In Country," (motion picture; starring Bruce Willis and Emily Lloyd), Warner Brothers, 1989, (cassette), Harper, 1990.

■ Work in Progress

Short stories and a novel.

■ Sidelights

"'Born to Run'. . .that's my whole history, and my whole psychology, and all my subject matter. I grew up 150-200 miles from any city. You simply didn't have much connection with the outside world. So my dreams were always to get out."[1]

Bobbie Ann Mason was raised on a fifty-four acre dairy farm in rural Kentucky. Confined to an isolated childhood without any "playmates," she was "personally very shy, and probably pathologically shy."[1]

For adventure, she looked to mystery books like "The Bobbsey Twins" and "Nancy Drew" stories. "Those were the only books I had read until I was about eighteen and so they influenced me a great deal; they formed my life and my expectations. The Bobbsey twins. . .went on a vacation every single book and I had never been on a vacation in my life, so they led me to expect a great deal out of life."[2]

"Nancy [Drew] had a car and went out and did things. . . .She filled my head with dreams of escape and adventure and being somebody."[3]

By the age of ten Mason began writing mystery stories of her own, imitating the children's books she was reading at the time. Neither of her parents graduated from high school, but they insisted that their daughter attend the "city school" in Mayfield rather than the country school for a better educa-

tion. It was at Mayfield High that Mason got her first taste of the tensions between city and country life. "City people tended to look down on country people. . . .Maybe not as much as the country people thought they did, but the country people felt very awkward around city people—and of course we're talking about a town of 8,000. In that part of the world I think there's a special kind of class difference, not so much between the upper and the lower class as between the people who live in town and the people who live in the country."[1]

While still a teenager, Mason "held a national office, published a journal, was interviewed on television and radio, and traveled widely to places like Cincinnati and Detroit and Blytheville, Arkansas. I was a. . .backward, anti-social kid. . .but I was ambitious and determined to hit the big time—or at least meet somebody famous.

"From the time I was a child singers impressed me more than movie stars did. I listened to the radio constantly."[4]

"[The] stations that were playing rhythm and blues really got to me very deeply. The Hilltoppers, a white group, were in that period, just before rock-and-roll, and they were a kind of safe, clean-cut embodiment of the outside world in their music, something for me to aspire toward that summed up my feelings about longing and wanting to escape and be somebody. But the reason they appealed to me really was because they were from Kentucky. And it gave me the notion that somebody, even though they were from Kentucky, could do something in the world."[1]

"The Hilltoppers made me feel there was an answer—some release from the cycle of the seasons, the planting and harvesting.

"I started a Hilltoppers fan club, and the day that the package of membership cards, autographed glossy eight-by-ten photographs, and buttons ('I AM A HILLTOPPERS FAN') arrived was the turning point in my life.

"Over the next year, I diligently worked my way up through the Hilltoppers' power structure. . .and at last became National President of the Hilltoppers Fan Clubs. As National President, I wrote and mailed a newsletter to three hundred fan-club chapters on an addressographed list—most addresses in the exotic environs of New York City.

"In time, my mother and I traveled to Cincinnati to see the Hilltoppers perform. It was my first trip anywhere. The ride took sixteen hours, overnight, on a bus that jolted miserably around the curves

BOBBIE ANN MASON

SHILOH
AND OTHER STORIES

"Mason is a full-fledged master of the short story...her first collection is a treasure." —ANNE TYLER, THE NEW REPUBLIC
BY THE AUTHOR OF IN COUNTRY

Softcover edition of the multi-award-winning novel.

along the Ohio River. I remember waking up at each stop and checking the town on the map, so I could say I had been there."[4]

To Mason's delight, she and her mother got to know the members of the Hilltoppers quite well. "Mama and I traveled many places to see the Hilltoppers. We went to Centralia, Illinois; Princeton, Indiana; Herrin, Illinois;...and Cape Girardeau, Missouri, as well as St. Louis and Detroit. Daddy had to milk the cows and couldn't go. The Hilltoppers welcomed us....They were boyish, modest, and funny. I adored them. Being a groupie in the fifties was as innocent as the Girl Scouts.

"I hadn't told the Hilltoppers about the ESP experiments I had been trying (they involved sending telepathic messages to d.j.s to play Hilltoppers tunes). I wanted them to think I was normal.

"In Memphis, I visited Vicki Woodall, the National President of Pat Boone's fan club, and a photo of me with Pat and Vicki appeared later in *Sixteen Magazine*. (After she graduated, Vicki went to

Hollywood to be Pat's secretary. Something like that was my ambition; the only alternative I could see was working at the Merit, a clothing factory.)"[4]

With a growing interest in ESP and parapsychology, Mason received little encouragement at school to pursue any course of unorthodox study. "I had read 'Reincarnation: A Hope of the World,' and it impressed me. I was filled with philosophical questions and I wrote a paper for English class on agnosticism. My teacher, Miss Florence, summoned me to her office and accused me of plagiarism. 'Young lady, you have no business entertaining ideas like this,' she said. 'Where did you get such an idea?'

"I quaked. 'I read about it. I read lots of philosophy,' I said, which was only partly a lie. Reincarnation was philosophy, sort of. I told her I had read John Locke, which *was* a lie. But I hadn't plagiarized. I really believed it was possible that God did not exist, and furthermore it seemed likely that there was no way to know whether he did or not.

IN COUNTRY

A NOVEL

BOBBIE ANN MASON

Author of Shiloh and Other Stories

Jacket from Mason's novel that deals with the moral fallout of Vietnam.

"'Take my advice,' she said, growing softer. 'Give up these strange ideas of yours. Your field is mathematics. That's what you're good at. Stay away from these peculiar questions, because they're destructive. And stick with the Bible. That's all the philosophy you'll ever need.'

"I was silent, rigid with fury—too intimidated to speak.

"'You have a lot of big ideas, but they will lead you astray,' Miss Florence said in dismissal.

"I immersed myself in my presidential duties, publishing my bimonthly newsletter, *Hilltoppers Topics.* In Mayfield, I was an outcast, but in the greater world I was suave and self-important.

"That summer [following high school graduation], I picked blackberries in the early-morning dew with rock-and-roll songs like 'Get a Job' by the Silhouettes and Eddie Cochran's 'Summertime Blues' blasting in my mind, and in the afternoons I trudged down the dusty lanes through the fields with the dog to round up the herd of cows. In the evenings, I worked at the Rexall. I went out with boys—boys who wanted to settle down and work in the new factories—but I wasn't impressed. I was always dreaming. Our house was close to Highway 45, which ran straight south to Tupelo, Mississippi, where Elvis was born. I knew he had dreamed the same dreams.

"Miss Florence refused to write me a recommendation to Duke University, where I wanted to study parapsychology with the famous Dr. J. B. Rhine, so in the fall I went away to the University of Kentucky, in Lexington....All the mysteries of the universe lay before me, and I couldn't learn fast enough. I read *Brave New Word* and *1984* and *On the Beach* and *Mandingo* and *Elmer Gantry.* I studied French and psychology and philosophy and volleyball....Buddy Holly died that winter. Elvis was in the Army."[4]

Mason took journalism classes and reported for the school newspaper, *Kentucky Kernel.* Upon graduation, she moved to New York and worked on a movie magazine in the early 60s. After about fifteen months she went to graduate school, attending first the State University of New York at Binghamton and then the University of Connecticut.

"I've never felt that I decided much of anything....Like 'decided' to go to New York. I just sort of did what came along, what was available. There weren't all these choices laid out like, do you want to be a nurse, do you want to be a doctor, or do you want to go into marketing? I didn't know about any of those things. All I knew was I could work in a factory, but if I went to a college then I might not have to go to work in a factory, and then maybe I could get work in an office. And work in an office meant being a secretary maybe, or some kind of clerical work. And nothing was very clear. Nobody explained anything."[1]

She received her Ph.D. in English in 1972, later publishing her dissertation on Nabokov's novel *Ada.* During graduate school, Mason met her husband, Roger Rawlings, and they moved to northern Pennsylvania, both teaching at Mansfield State College (now Mansfield University). It was not until 1976 that Mason began writing in earnest.

"For several years after college, I stopped writing. I tried a story once in a while, but I didn't really know what to do. I tried writing a novel in 1967. I didn't finish it. And then I got out of graduate school [and] I just had no direction whatsoever.

"What I was doing mainly was reading mystery books. I was, I think, exhausted by graduate school, and at that time I wrote a little critical study of the girls' mystery series that I had grown up on....It was called *The Girl Sleuth.* And that was sort of the beginning of my understanding that you could go back and start all over again and come full circle. It was then that I started to realize a lot about where I'd come from, and then it took a few years to realize that that was the source of my experience and my material for my fiction."[1]

Mason went to work writing about her past in western Kentucky, and then around 1978 she realized that she could write contemporary stories. "That was the big move for me. And about the second story I wrote, I sent to the *New Yorker.*

"I got a note of rejection from [*New Yorker* fiction editor] Roger Angell and I kept sending in stories and getting letters from him. He took an interest in my writing—apparently I had been picked out of the slush pile. This was so exciting that I worked very hard and started writing very fast. And in the space of a year and a half I sent in twenty stories— and the twentieth story was the one they purchased."[1]

In 1982, *Shiloh and Other Stories* was published by Harper & Row. The book, a compilation of sixteen stories set in rural western Kentucky, looks at the people of a changing South. "I feel that my characters are on the threshold of possibility....Their lives are being changed, and they're very excited by it. They're getting a chance maybe

From the 1989 Warner Brothers film "In Country," starring Bruce Willis and Emily Lloyd.

for the first time in their lives to get somewhere and to prove something and to do something. Many of my characters are caught up in the myth of progress; from their point of view it means liberation, the promise of a better life."[1]

"It seemed to me that in graduate school all I ever read was about the artist hero in American literature, the alienated hero who suffered because he was superior to society. I was so sick of that when I got out of graduate school that it was almost as if I made a conscious decision...to write about anybody *but* the artist hero.

"A lot of contemporary fiction had not only been about the artist hero, it had been about English teachers. I thought there was something deadening about writing literature about literature or about literary matters. I wanted to write about real people. Characters like mine are not always taken seriously in the culture....It's only some kind of elitism that doesn't give them what they're due and doesn't treat them seriously....There are more people like my characters than not in this world.

"I write about people who if they go to Lexington they'll head to McDonald's because it's familiar."[2]

"The characters in my world don't have the guidance or perspective to know that there might be this *other* view of television or malls. They're in that world and they like television fine, thank you. And they love the malls, and I don't judge them for it. When they go to the shopping mall, and many of them go just to window shop, they're looking at deliverance from a hard way of life."[1]

"I guess I'm bothered by snobbish attitudes toward shopping malls the most. Shopping malls mean a great deal to a lot of people. It's where they get they're entertainment, it's the replacement for their community, it's where the teenagers hang out on Friday night. People point out a lot how I write about the K-Mart. And I guess I figure that not everybody can afford to shop at Sax Fifth Avenue.

"I'm interested in portraying in fiction some of the qualities of experience and the desires and the emotions of people who are less privileged than others."[2]

"The kind of responses I was getting from the people in the cities or the people in publishing, it was almost as if this was a novelty, this was a whole world they hadn't known about. They'd say, 'Who

Dust jacket from Mason's 1989 collection of short stories.

are these people and why haven't we heard about them before?' But in the South, I was getting responses like, 'Yeah, these are people we all know and they're very familiar.'

"It was almost as if. . .people in the cities and in modern life feel cut off from something authentic, and they feel like they're hearing about it through something like the current fiction about ordinary people.

"I think people who are interested in reading about laborers and farmers may in a way romanticize it themselves. They wouldn't want to be in that position, but it's comforting somehow to read about it, because they get a sense that those lives are more authentic.

"In fact, I think laborers and farmers have as much existential anguish as anyone else."[5]

"I'm the first person in my family to go to college. . . .And so I'm the first person in my family, and one of the few people in my region and generation, to speak for all those people. Before

this, their experiences were ignored, were not considered suitable for fiction."[1]

"[I'm] not trying to solve anything or even analyze it but to present some people's dreams and to show the validity of that."[2]

The characters who populate Mason's fiction are "kind of naive and optimistic for the most part: they think better times are coming, and most of them embrace progress. But I think they reflect that tension that's in the culture between hanging onto the past and racing toward the future. . . .One story I wrote, 'Residents and Transients,' really was the focal point for the main theme of the [Shiloh] stories: there are some people who would just never leave home, because that's where they're meant to be; and others are, well, born to run."[6]

Her stories usually begin taking shape with "something quite insignificant: an image or a detail, a line of dialogue, something that sparks my interest and gets me going on a kind of journey of discovery to find out what it connects to.

"You really can just start with the first line and see where it goes. Things will fall into place, patterns emerge. . .a subject announces itself, and all the stuff that doesn't belong kind of falls away.

"When I began writing stories. . .I was writing pretty steadily for the first two or three years and usually what would happen is that about every three weeks I would feel this creative urge, and [knew I could] write a new story. . . .That was a period of great excitement. Obviously I had stored up a lot of stuff over the years that could come out very rapidly now."[2]

Praise for *Shiloh* was nearly unanimous. Robert Towers for the *New York Review of Books* remarked, "Vision and technique come exhilaratingly together in Bobbie Ann Mason's collection of stories. . . .She is one of those rare writers who, by concentrating their attention on a few square miles of native turf, are able to open up new and surprisingly wide worlds for the delighted reader."[7]

Anne Tyler commented, "[To say that Mason] is a 'new' writer is to give entirely the wrong impression, for there is nothing unformed or merely promising about her. She is a full-fledged master of the short story."[8]

"I think that if I had been writing all along, steadily. . .collecting rejection slips [and] learning gradually. . .I probably wouldn't have been any further along. . . .I think it took that number of years to get the experience so that I would know what to write about and how to write about it...and to get the right perspective on the material. I don't think the craft had a whole lot to do with it....I didn't need ten years of learning the craft exactly; I needed ten years of learning who I was."[2]

In 1985, Mason's first novel, *In Country*, was published by Harper & Row. "The term 'in country' was the term the American soldiers used in Vietnam to mean being in [the war]. They would talk about being 'in country' six months or a year...as opposed to being back in the world."[2]

The story involves a seventeen-year-old girl named Sam who is struggling to come to terms with the effects of the Vietnam War. "How do you find out what really went on? How do you know who you really are, what your legacy is, and how this event shaped the world you live in? I think Sam goes through a lot of those questions that Americans went through historically in examining the war.

"I'm trying to portray—with some credibility I hope—an emotional experience. This story is everybody's story. Everybody in America has their version of [it]. And Vietnam affected everybody in some way....It's the big story of our generation.

"All kinds of books are coming out about Vietnam and the whole subject is exploding wide open...it's as if we needed this period of time to reflect on it, to be able to reconsider it and figure it out....There were years when it was hard for the country to deal with it; probably that's true for writers....It's taken this amount of time to wake up to it, to the effects that it's had on the communities and to the experiences the veterans have gone through."[2]

Mason began writing her ideas about the main characters *In Country* and then set out to find their story. "It was one of the few times I had really started with a group of characters. Usually I discovered the characters after backing into the story through some other entrance....The novel went through so many transformations before I finally settled on what it was about, where it was going.

"I had this character, a young girl—just graduated from high school—named Sam, and she lived with her Uncle Emmett. Her mother had gotten married again, gone off to Lexington and had a new baby....And Sam had a boyfriend [named] Lonnie.

"At some point well into the whole thing, I discovered that the Uncle was a Vietnam Veteran. Then I wrote for a long time and didn't do anything

with that information....[but] it was there, and I had to deal with it sooner or later. It kind of crept up on me....The breakthrough came when I realized that her father had been killed in Vietnam and that she was of an age to start finding out about her father and what the Vietnam war was all about. I knew at that point that I had something to go on.

"It took a long time to get to the point where I was really involved with [the book] to the point that I looked forward to going at it everyday.

"Toward the end when it started coming together,...when I started to realize that I was actually going to do it after all, it got so incredibly exciting. Writing a story was never quite that intense....It was worth all the meandering and boredom I went through trying to get into it at the beginning. Toward the end I realized that I'd grown so fond of my characters that I didn't want to let them go. That was a real reward—to get that intense about what I was writing."[2]

Dust jacket of the 1988 hardcover.

In Country is filled with references to popular American culture: from Coca-Cola and McDonald's to "Mash," and Rock 'n' Roll. Because her characters spend their free time watching television, going to shopping malls, or eating at McDonald's, Mason has occasionally been criticized for creating characters too shallow for fiction.

"I think that what happens with literary-minded readers. . .is that they're used to reading fiction in which allusions to popular culture are almost like code words. These words carry a derogatory, condescending attitude, a negative feeling about what some people call the American trash culture.

"Take the idea of eating breakfast at McDonald's every morning or watching 'Dynasty' on TV. . . .Typically in American fiction, when we run across allusions like that we seem to know they refer to a culture we're supposed to criticize and rise above, because supposedly we're more sophisticated than that.

"But in fact there's a whole mass culture out there that thrives on TV and junk food, and I guess I'm saying I take that seriously, because I think there are some people who think that's all right, and who do get something positive out of it.

"In their town of Hopewell, Kentucky, [these characters are] just beginning to feel the effects of shopping malls and junk food, and they like it. To them it's the outside world they've been isolated from for so long coming into their lives at last.

"So in my fiction I'm not using those allusions as negative or condescending code words, because if I did, I would have to accuse my characters of being small minded and shallow. I don't think they are, and certainly they aren't the ones to *blame* for this junk culture. But I think they are blamed, and that's a typically elitist attitude about our culture.

"When I grew up, a Coca Cola was a great treat, and going out for a hamburger was just bliss, so I think I can understand the sources of that dream."[9]

"It's very real, it means something to a whole lot of people, and I can't ignore that. People have a lot of affection for these images on the screen, names of songs, things that are a familiar part of their lives. If you're writing about people who watch 'Mash' all the time, as I did, then you've got to know why they watch it, what they feel about it, what place it has in their lives. . . .I'm not so interested in what it means ultimately—whether 'Mash' is a good show or not, whether television is ruining our lives, whether we're being manipulated by these images.

I'm just after the quality of experience in everyday life. Things like that have significance."[6]

Like so many of her characters, Mason is a rock 'n' roll fan, and she listens to music as she writes. "I just have a radio station on kind of low, and turn it up if there's something I like. . .Bruce Springsteen.

"Writing is my version of rock-and-roll. . . .I identify with Bruce Springsteen's songs, and of course I'm not alone in this. I like the way his songs are stories with characters. He writes about the disintegration of lives due to social forces. But his people keep striving, hoping."[1]

"More than anyone performing or writing today [he] is authentic in carrying on the tradition of rock 'n' roll and expressing the desires and aims of people who don't have what they ought to have.

"Rock-and-Roll is a very important dimension of this book. . . .In Sam's world where there's not a whole lot that's solid and real and traditional. . . .Rock-and-Roll is one thing that. . .she has a connection to and knows something about. It's important in that way."[2]

When beginning a project, Mason is hesitant to think in terms of themes, perferring to "think pretty literally [about] who these people are, what they're wearing, what their jobs are, and what they want to do. Other people can decide what it all means."[2]

The novel soon became a bestseller, bringing Mason much publicity. "When I read my name in the paper or read something about what I've written, it's not really about me. . . .You wrote something, and it's very private because you do it alone. And then suddenly you find perfect strangers have heard of it and have read it and have had a response to it, and that's very gratifying. But it's always surprising."[5]

Spence & Lila was published by Harper & Row in 1988. Unlike her previous work, the main characters of this novel are older people, a farmer and his wife. The story focuses on Lila's bout with cancer and the ways in which the couple learn to deal with her illness. Mason describes the book as semi-autobiographical "with many things changed."[1] In 1985 her mother had her own dealings with the disease.

"It's my journey back home. . . .In a way, I've always done everything—everything—to please my parents. I think that's not an unusual thing that people do. I have found that the act of writing has been a way of growing up, doing whatever one does to finally be accepted as an adult by one's parents. That was something that started to happen with me when I began publishing my stories. I think the thing that always drives me back to Kentucky is that I always resisted the notion I would leave my roots, which would mean abandoning my parents, and I'm too close to them to ever do that.

"I basically consider myself an exile. . . .And I have been one for years. And that's what gives me the distance to look back to where I'm from and to be able to write about it with some kind of perceptiveness. And I guess that's why I identify with Nabokov [Russian author of *Lolita* in exile]. Because it seems to me that an exile has a rather peculiar sensibility—you're straddling a fence and you don't know which side you belong on. I don't know if that comes through in the fiction, but I think it's probably what gives the strength to the fiction."[1]

"I think that if [my parents] could have had the words for it or really visualized it, this is what they would have thought I'd do. They thought I was smart, and they encouraged me. They thought I would do something smart to get me famous.

"The biggest reward in writing, the real reward, has been fulfilling that dream for them."[5]

As her character Spence Culpepper looks out over his farm, Mason writes: "This is it. This is all there is in the world—it contains everything there is to know or possess, yet everywhere people are knocking their brains out trying to find something different, something better. . . .Everyone always wants a way out of something like this, but what he has here is the main thing there is—just the way things grow and die, the way the sun comes up and goes down every day. These are the facts of life. They are so simple they are almost impossible to grasp."[10]

Footnote Sources:

[1] Mervyn Rothstein, "Homegrown Fiction," *New York Times*, May 15, 1988. Amended by B. A. Mason.

[2] Kay Benetti, "Interview with Bobbie Ann Mason," American Audio Prose Library, 1985. Amended by B. A. Mason.

[3] Andrea Chambers and David Hutchings, "Bobbie Ann Mason's *In Country* Evokes the Soul of Kentucky and the Sadness of Vietnam," *People Weekly*, October 28, 1985.

[4] Bobbie Ann Mason, "Reaching the Stars: My Life as a Fifties Groupie," *New Yorker*, May 26, 1986. Amended by B. A. Mason.

[5] Paul Nussbaum, "Re-Creation of Western Kentucky," *Los Angeles Times*, November 29, 1985.

[6] Wendy Smith, "PW Interviews Bobbie Ann Mason," *Publishers Weekly*, August 30, 1985.

[7] Robert Towers, "American Graffiti," *New York Review of Books*, December 16, 1982.

[8] Anne Tyler, "Kentucky Cameos," *New Republic*, November 1, 1982.

[9] Patricia Holt, "On Literary Elitism and the Junk Culture," *San Francisco Chronicle*, October 1, 1985.

[10] B. A. Mason, *Spence & Lila*, Harper, 1988.

■ For More Information See

Washington Post, February 5, 1976 (p. H6).

San Francisco Chronicle, October 31, 1982, September 30, 1985.

Washington Post Book World, October 31, 1982 (p. 3ff), September 8, 1985 (p. 3).

Village Voice Literary Supplement, November, 1982, February 1986 (p. 10ff).

Newsweek, November 15, 1982.

New York Times Book Review, November 21, 1982 (p. 7ff), December 19, 1982, September 15, 1985 (p. 7).

New York Times, November 23, 1982 (p. C14), March 11, 1983 (p. C21), April 15, 1984 (p. A50), September 4, 1985 (p. C20), March 15, 1987 (p. F62), June 11, 1988 (p. A18), August 28, 1988 (p. B23ff).

Time, January 3, 1983, January 10, 1983 (p. 60ff).

Chicago Tribune Book World, January 23, 1983.

Times (London), August 11, 1983.

Times Literary Supplement, August 12, 1983, April 18, 1986 (p. 416).

Peggy Whitman, *Women Writers of the Contemporary South*, Southern Quarterly, 1984.

Christian Science Monitor, September 6, 1985 (p. B2).

Wilson Library Bulletin, December, 1985.

School Library Journal, March, 1986, April, 1986.

Contemporary Literary Criticism, Gale, Volume 28, 1984, Volume 43, 1987.

Southern Literary Journal, spring, 1986 (p. 76ff), spring, 1987 (p. 21ff).

New York Times Magazine, March 15, 1987 (p. 62).

Harry Mazer

Born May 31, 1925, in New York, N.Y.; son of Sam (a dressmaker) and Rose (a dressmaker; maiden name, Lazevnick) Mazer; married Norma Fox (an author), February 12, 1950; children: Anne, Joseph, Susan, Gina. *Education:* Union College, B.A., 1948; Syracuse University, M.A., 1960. *Home and office:* Brown Gulf Rd., Jamesville, N.Y. 13078; 330 Third Ave., New York, N.Y. 10010. *Agent:* Curtis Brown Ltd., 575 Madison Ave., New York, N.Y. 10022.

■ Career

New York Construction, Syracuse, N.Y., sheet metal worker, 1957-59; Central Square School, Central Square, N.Y., teacher of English, 1959-60; Aerofin Corp., Syracuse, welder, 1960-63; full-time writer, 1963—. Has also worked as a bus driver, longshoreman, and railroad worker. *Military service:* U.S. Air Forces, 1943-45; became staff sargeant; received Purple Heart and Air Medal. *Member:* Writers Guild, Civil Liberties Union.

■ Awards, Honors

Snowbound was selected one of American Library Association's Best of the Best Books, 1970-73, received Preis der Lesserratten for the German edition from the Second German TV Network, 1975, and selected one of *Booklist*'s Contemporary Classics; Kirkus Choice Award, 1974, for *The Dollar Man; The Solid Gold Kid* was selected one of American Library Association's Best Books for Young Adults, 1977, *The War on Villa Street,* 1978, *The Last Mission,* 1979, *I Love You, Stupid!,* 1981, *When the Phone Rang,* 1985, and *The Girl of His Dreams,* 1987; Children's Choice from the International Reading Association and the Children's Book Council, 1978, for *The Solid Gold Kid; The Last Mission* was selected one of *New York Times* Outstanding Books of the Year, 1979, and one of American Library Association's Best of the Best Books, 1970-1983.

New York Public Library Books for the Teen Age, 1986, and Young Adult Choice from the International Reading Association and the Children's Book Council, 1987, both for *Hey, Kid! Does She Love Me?; The Girl of His Dreams* was selected one of American Library Association's Books for Young Adult Reluctant Readers, and one of New York Public Library's Books for Teen Age, both 1988; West Australian Young Readers Book Award, 1989, for *When the Phone Rang; Hearbeat* was selected one of New York Public Library's Books for the Teen Age, 1989; *City Light* was selected one of American Library Association's Books for the Reluctant Young Adult Reader, 1989.

■ Writings

Guy Lenny, Delacorte, 1971.

Snowbound: A Story of Raw Survival, Delacorte, 1973.

The Dollar Man, Delacorte, 1974.

(With wife, Norma Fox Mazer) *The Solid Gold Kid*, Delacorte, 1977.

The War on Villa Street (novel), Delacorte, 1978.

The Last Mission, Delacorte, 1979.

The Island Keeper: A Tale of Courage and Survival (Junior Literary Guild selection), Delacorte, 1981.

I Love You, Stupid!, Crowell, 1981.

(Contributor) Donald R. Gallo, editor, *Sixteen: Short Stories by Outstanding Writers for Young Adults*, Delacorte, 1984.

Hey, Kid! Does She Love Me?, Crowell, 1985.

When the Phone Rang, Scholastic, 1985.

Cave under the City, Crowell, 1986.

The Girl of His Dreams, Crowell, 1987.

City Light, Scholastic, 1988.

(With N. F. Mazer), *Heartbeat*, Bantam, 1989.

Someone's Mother Is Missing, Delacorte, 1990.

Snowbound has been published in Germany, France, and Finland.

■ Adaptations

"Snowbound" (movie), NBC-TV Special, 1978, (cassette), Listening Library, 1985.

"The Last Mission" (cassette), Listening Library, 1985.

■ Sidelights

Mazer came from a family of hard-working Polish-Jewish immigrants. Both parents worked in factories, and a young boy's dream of becoming a writer was not given much credence. "Reading was my great pleasure. I was very interested in every library I ever entered, and I remember it was like a rite of passage for me to go from the juvenile section to the adult section of a library."[1]

But Mazer did make many serious attempts at writing. "...A lot of sporadic attempts. I was never very successful. (I had, I don't know precisely where they came from, standards well beyond any reading I had done.) I know we had some books in the house; I think we got them through a newspaper promotion: the complete set of Dickens and a complete set of Mark Twain, a set of Jack London. One book used to come every month or so and it would be a big moment. I made attempts at writing, but they were...not really satisfactory, and I didn't publish things in high school. I really didn't think I could write; my standards were too

high and anything that I attempted just looked so awful to me that I couldn't carry on with it....I didn't know what the world of writing was like. All I had were the classics, and they just told me I was hopeless. So it took me many years before I began to write."[1]

Mazer served in the U.S. Air Force during World War II. He subsequently graduated from Union College and soon thereafter married Norma Fox. She, too, wanted to write. It was with her encouragement ten years into their marriage that both began writing in earnest. "While the kids were growing up, Norma insulated me from them. (I've only gradually become liberated in my thinking.) I remember very well, at times she'd be writing in the dining room, with all of them right around her. [She had] these great powers of concentration. I'd be working in another room with the door closed....We tended to keep the same working hours at night and early in the morning. When we were just beginning to write, I was doing other kinds of work. Norma, the year when she was pregnant with our fourth child, was waking up at 3:30 in the morning, and she thought it was a great idea for both of us to get up and write.

"And that worked well. I have enjoyed the discipline of having someone else keeping the same schedule."[2]

"I was in my mid thirties. It had taken me all that time to...develop the *sitzfleisch* I needed just to keep me down in a chair long enough even to begin to think about writing. I naively believed that if I sat in front of that blank paper long enough I'd sure write something.

"And finally it happened. I wrote a line, and then another. I don't know why I wrote them or what I had in my mind.

"I wrote: 'Isabel, you'll never know what you did to me. How could you? I never spoke to you.'

"Isabel was a girl in my sixth-grade class in PS 96 in the Bronx, a tall, skinny girl with long hair. I followed her slavishly around for weeks. My sixth-grade picture shows me a big fat kid, in need of a haircut, the only one wearing a dark shirt in a field of white shirts and blouses.

"I never spoke to Isabel. I never talked to anyone about her. Not my friends, certainly not my parents. I followed her around everywhere. She lived on the third floor of an apartment house on Bronx Park East. In the evening after supper, I used to stand across the street from her house and look longingly up at the lighted windows and wonder which one was hers.

"Once I boldly crossed the street, and went up the stairs, and stood outside her door. What was I doing there? What did I want? What would I have done if she had opened the door? What if it was her father? The moment I heard a noise at the door I fled.

"She noticed me only once. I was across the street one day. She was with a girl friend. When they saw me they threw their arms around each other and started laughing and jeering at me.

"That was the story I started writing when I finally sat down to write, more than twenty years after the event. 'Isabel, you'll never know what you did to me.' How I loved that line. The poet Auden wrote, 'A sentence uttered makes a world appear/where all things happen as it says they do.' As I wrote, I spoke to Isabel as I could never have spoken to her then. 'You'll never know what you did to me.' I wrote of desire, longing, frustration, bewilderment. I made everything more intense—the building taller, the steps steeper and darker; Isabel cooler and more inaccessible. The light blazed from her window. I made things happen with an intensity of detail and emotion that they'd never truly had. In a word, I made a story of it.

"Here it is forty years later and that puppy-love incident I call Isabel still works itself into my books."[2]

Mazer soon quit his job and the couple devoted all their energies to writing; supporting themselves by selling articles and short stories to confession magazines.

He began to concentrate on writing for young people. "It was partially a conscious decision. I had an agent at the time and she encouraged me to write in this area. The readers were there with a great hunger for books. But I don't think that would have been enough if I didn't feel attracted to writing for young people. It's such an alive period of life. People have a lot of hope, wanting, desire for love, desire for discovery; and I find that in spite of my age I remain very interested in beginnings: how people get started, all the freshness and hope you feel when you're young. So I continue to enjoy writing in this area. I keep telling people that I'm going to do a grown-up book someday, but so far all my books have been for young people. There's a lot of freedom. I can do just about anything I want. My books are welcome; there's an interest in them. Once you are

Harper's 1987 hardcover novel.

successful in a particular area, in a sense it becomes difficult to break out."[1]

In 1971 Mazer published his first book, *Guy Lenny*, and two years later, *Snowbound: A Story of Raw Survival.* It was always in his mind to write a survival story. "There is no end to uncertainty. We all live with it, we are all forced to consider events over which we have no control. And we all wonder...What if?...What would I do?...Will I be ready? We all have the survivor's mentality, perhaps none so much as the young, knowing so much of the awfulness of life and having still done so little."[3]

In 1978 *Snowbound* was adapted for television and aired on NBC-TV. "I had mixed feelings about it. I was glad that it was done. A television production will tend to bring readers to the book. In the book *Snowbound* the protagonist is about thirteen or fourteen years old, and in the movie they turned him into a kind of Robert Redford eighteen-year-old lookalike. They gave him a girl friend, which he certainly didn't have in the book. They frame the movie with this other relationship. They bring the girl friend in at the beginning and again at the end. Then they added scenes: they had a fire, which I didn't write; they had a helicopter—things that probably were useful in scripting the movie. But what kids—and adults—who read the book and saw the movie said was that they liked the book more than the movie. And I suppose that's my feeling as well. But in general my reaction was positive.

"I think that if another of my books were taken for a television or movie production, I would try to get involved. I would hope it would give me a little more control over what happens.

"Before I got into the writing that I'm doing now, I did write some television scripts that were directed at various shows that were popular at the time but are gone now. I know the form. It's just a very difficult area to get into. At the time I was told that if I would come to California, which is where most of these movies are made, it would be possible to write for television. But where I was in New York State, I really couldn't get started."[1]

After completing *The Dollar Man*, Mazer co-authored a novel, *The Solid Gold Kid*, with his wife. "Though we have collaborated...most of our literary work is separate. However, we talk about everything. We discuss every stage of the writing, read the other's work, encourage and support each other, make editorial suggestions, celebrate each other's successes, comfort the other in times of doubt and adversity.

"But then we get into ego things. Norma's second book, *A Figure of Speech*, received a National Book Award nomination, and I wasn't getting any special awards. That was hard to take. Then she had a book...called *Dear Bill, Remember Me?*, a collection of short stories which got a lot of rave reviews, and I was having trouble finishing *The War on Villa Street*. Well, we talked. You really have to say those awful things you're feeling, things that you're ashamed to say out loud: you're angry, you're jealous. Once you are able to voice what you feel, it tends to dissipate. This is what we've had to do at every turn in our writing lives, a lot of talking. It's brought us much closer than we were before I came home and started writing."[1]

"*The War on Villa Street* took me longer to write than any of my other books. With hindsight, I think this was because the book deals with two strong ideas: The relationship of Willis Pierce, a lonely, tense boy, and his father, who's an alcoholic; and that between Willis and Richard Hayfoot, a retarded boy, who in some ways is more fortunate than Willis.

"The strange thing is that Willis came to light in a previous book of mine, *The Dollar Man*. In that book Willis plays a minor role, and not a sympathetic one. Willis is a skinny little spider of a kid who clings to the fence of the Prescott Street playground, tormenting Marcus Rosenbloom. 'Jump on those bars again, Rosen Balloon, I want to see you bend them.'

"Marcus hates Willis, and for good reason....In *The Dollar Man* there's nothing likeable about Willis Pierce. I didn't like him, myself.

"Toward the end of *The Dollar Man* there's a scene where Marcus, standing on the roof of an apartment house, looks down into the lighted windows of another building. Marcus, who hungers for the love of the father he's never known sees Willis and his father sitting at a table across from each other. When I began to think about the story that became *The War on Villa Street*, that rooftop scene came back to me. I kept thinking about it, coming back to it. Maybe it was what Marcus thought that interested me. 'He was seeing Willis in a secret way, a way he wasn't supposed to, but one that was more truthful than all the other ways.' As a writer this is what intrigues me. As much as telling a good story, I want to show my readers that behind the facade that we all throw up to protect ourselves, there exists a human heart.

"Once I began to think about the real Willis Pierce, my attitude toward him changed. I had been looking at him through Marcus's eyes, seeing him as a nasty, little, dried-up punk, without an ounce of goodness in his body. Then I began to understand him as a very lonely, deprived, and suffering kid, whose real, good core was hidden behind a tough guy exterior.

"What Marcus saw when he stood on the roof in *The Dollar Man* became the final scene of *The War on Villa Street*. I was no longer outside looking in, but in the Pierce's apartment, in Willis's mind and heart, seeing all the love and hate he felt for his father.

"That scene between Willis and his father, for me, was at the heart of *The War on Villa Street*. I wrote it before I wrote anything else. In fact, although the book was written and rewritten several times before I got it right, that last reconciliation scene survived all the rewrites with little change."[4]

Mazer's realistic novels have been highly praised and successful. He deals frankly and insightfully with the problems that beset the youth of today: divorce, war, unwed mothers, the homeless, and

From the NBC-TV movie "Snowbound," produced by Learning Corporation of America, 1978.

drugs among others. His protagonists are shown in problematic situations from which they run, and eventually deal with head-on. "The problems in my books have more to do with the problems of constructing a novel: the need for conflict, the need for something important to be at stake, something that's not easily resolved. You can't do a book that deals with superficial questions. So I really don't think that I'm specifically answering questions about alcoholism and brutality; what I'm very much concerned with is survival, in one form or another. If I have a message, it's that you, too, can cope; you can get through this period in your life. You have the strength in yourself. Very often in my books the character becomes disillusioned, particularly with the father, and realizes that he must and can face the world on his own strength."[1]

His protagonists are usually boys, but in *The Island Keeper*, a young girl is the central character. "At first, thinking about the idea of *The Island Keeper* (and that was always the title), I imagined a boy on a river in a leaky wooden boat, discovering a tiny island that he claims for his own. Then an old crazy woman appeared on the island, more interesting to

me than the boy. Then the old woman disappeared, to be replaced by a girl, Cleo Murphy.

"Why a girl? This is my first book in which a girl is the principal protagonist; in fact, for much of the book, the only character. Will boys read a story with a female protagonist? I think, given the chance, the answer is—and should be—yes. Why should it make any difference if the hero is male or female? It's the story that must hold the reader. Is the story suspenseful? Does the character show courage, wit, enterprise? Is it a good book? Isn't that finally what matters, not that it's a 'girl's' book or a 'boy's' book, but simply a good book?

"It was [the] phrase. . .—the island keeper—that made me imagine the old woman and then the girl. The female keeper of the island, keeper of the shrine, of the sacred places, protector of Old Truths. The female has always had a connection to earth and life that is closer than the male's."[3]

"I think much of what I write comes out of my own memory of myself. Also I've had four children, and I've watched them rather carefully and thought about them. But I think really what informs my writing and keeps me in this field is an interest in the secret parts of a character, not what people say and do so much as what they think and feel: the areas where they feel deprived, their longings, their feelings of separation, isolation. Much more than anything else I write out of a memory of those feelings.

"There are some writers who say they remember everything. I would hardly say that: I think I've *forgotten* everything. I've certainly forgotten the details. But I think I know the feeling, and that's what I really write out of. Then there's the perspective that comes from getting older, looking at things from a different angle. Everything is the ultimate for a young person. There's no perspective; there's no time when you're young."[1]

"From time to time when I meet people I get the feeling that they're eyeing the gray in my chin and wondering, what's that middle-aged man doing writing for the young? How does he know what's

"There is such charged energy in Mazer's work ... that you care, very much, what happens."
—*The New York Times Book Review*

Cover for the Dell paperback.

going on? They come right out with it sometimes: 'How do you keep in touch with what's happening, the changes in language, dress, and manner, I mean, man, what gives you the right?'

"And not only strangers. My own kids, too, have let me know plenty of times. 'Dad, you don't know...you don't know what it's like.'

"'It's like liquor,' I suggest. This on the subject of dope.

"'No,' my son says. 'You don't know.'

"'You don't understand,' one of my daughters says when we discuss the proprieties of visiting a boy in his room. 'Why can't we close the door? What's wrong with that?'

"It wasn't so bad when I was a welder. Ironworkers aren't expected to understand kids. But writers are. The way kids talk, and act. They have their own language, their own dress, their own rituals. It is as if the world were newly created with them. And of course they're right.

"But where does that leave me as a writer? How do I know? What do I know about kids today? Thirty-two years out of high school. And all those revolutions.

"But how many books are there written by writers under twenty, or twenty-five, for that matter? A handful maybe. There's a rightness in the old—I mean, of course, the mature—writing for the young. The young, after all, are young, they're impatient, they've got ants in their pants. I wonder if they can sit still long enough to give form to their own thoughts and feelings. (At that age I couldn't.) Maybe the trappings of dress and manner have changed, but the emotions of the young are not a foreign country. We've all been there. We recognize our ties to the young, even when they don't recognize their ties to us."[2]

"It's true that the problems change, but I think the underlying emotions remain the same. My generation knew about alcohol, but we didn't know about drugs. But that's what your imagination is for. If I have to, I'll research and I'll interview. There are so many things you don't know that you have to learn about. The other side of it is that you really don't want to be too much in the mode when you're writing. You can't hope to keep up with trends, because a book takes a year to write. Trends change sometimes faster than that. You can just write yourself out of style if you try to keep in style.

"To write about a character, you have to live with that character to feel comfortable with him and to experience the events of his life. Yes, I would say that at the moment I'm writing, I *am* that character. I don't think that when I leave the typewriter I remain the character. There may be moments when I'm not thinking, when I flip back—start thinking through certain problems or certain situations—into the mind of the character. Of course that's very good when that happens. I must say that I don't feel there's any great difference between the mind of a child and the mind of an adult. Children have the same desire we do for recognition and admiration, a desire to be unique."[1]

"The inner life joins us all: girl, boy, middle-aged woman and old man. We all live two lives simultaneously. The visible life in which we grow up, marry, take jobs, acquire homes and cars. And the other life—the secret life—of our fantasies, longings.

"As a writer, I'm primarily interested in my characters' inner life. Not the trappings of character but their feelings, their dreams and fantasies, the way they distort reality, their hopes and disappointments.

"That kind of insight into people is not often revealed. Not many volunteer the information. The writer has to do it himself. To get in touch with his characters he must get in touch with himself.

"The things I never knew I knew or felt or thought of till I started writing. I don't mean know yourself the way, say, an analyst does, with all his preconceptions, theories, categories. I mean 'know' only in the sense of 'being aware,' turning a ready ear to that sometimes dimly heard inner voice. A voice persistent nonetheless, demanding, often outrageous—a voice that won't be stilled.

"It's the inner life that makes the connection possible between the middle-aged writer and his young reader. The inner life that connects us all. I address myself to the reader at thirteen, at thirty, at seventy-two, to the reader in myself. As a writer for the young, the limitations I accept are not limitations of language or of subject matter, but only those imposed by the necessarily narrowed experience and outlook of my young protagonists. Not looking down at that young person, but looking out at the world through his eyes.

"I share the writer's conceit that what interests me will interest you, that what arouses emotion in me will arouse emotion in you. With good fortune, I'll touch the reader, leave him or her with a sense that

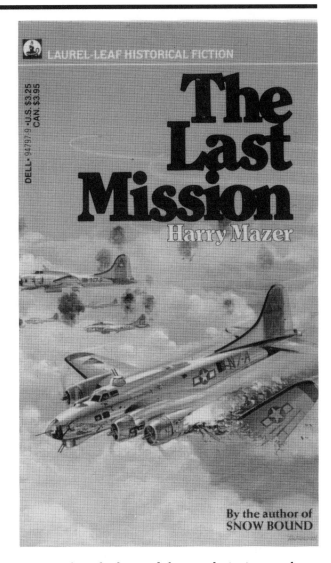

Paperbound edition of the award-winning novel.

what he's read is perhaps something that he's always known but hasn't quite expressed."[2]

With his use of strong language and occasional treatment of pre-marital sex, Mazer touches off controversial sparks. He acknowledges the special problems involved in writing for young people. "There is a very strong censorious element that doesn't exist in the adult field, what I call the guardians looking very carefully. Their concern is legitimate, but sometimes it goes too far. Censorship is wrong. It affects an author's work. There is pressure still to prettify the world that you present to the young reader, to present the realities you see in a somewhat sugarcoated fashion. You'd hardly think that from some of the titles that appear, but a lot of these titles and a lot of the subjects that are dealt with have their problems getting into the schools and school libraries.

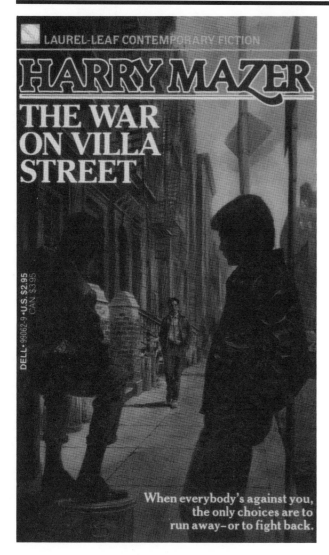

The 1978 Dell paperback.

"I don't like books that are much ado about nothing. Often people write books where you get a lot of chatter, no real penetration of character. I want to know about the character. I like to feel that the person I'm reading about is distinct, different. Very often you get serviceable types of characters that all seem to come out of the same can. As in any other field of fiction, there are many mediocre books, many that are really good, and a few that are outstanding.

"Good fiction has form. Some of the things I look for are strong sympathetic characters, development, change. A book has to have form: a beginning, a middle, and an end.

"For a beginning writer, I think it's wise to read widely in the area of children's books being done today. Get a feeling of what's being done and how it's being done. And then I'd say, write the book that is in *you*, that hasn't been done, the one that only you can write.

"Beyond that, a beginning writer should recognize that writing requires a long apprenticeship. This is something that I didn't know when I was young, which is what kept me from writing. Desire makes up a great part of being a writer, and then there's work: writing, writing—and writing badly, of course, before you write well. I would pay close attention to any professional advice or criticism received along the way, and then revise and revise. Nothing is right the first time. That's another thing I didn't recognize in the beginning. Revision, attention to detail, is going to make your book. That's what I think is the hardest."[1]

Footnote Sources:

[1] *Contemporary Authors,* Volumes 97-100, Gale, 1981.

Dust jacket from the hardcover edition.

[2] "Harry Mazer: On Writing for the Young," *Notes from Delacorte Press*, summer/fall, 1975. Amended by H. Mazer.

[3] Harry Mazer, "Island Within and Without: Thoughts about Writing *The Island Keeper*," *Notes from Delacorte Press*, winter, 1980/spring, 1981.

[4] H. Mazer, "*The War on Villa Street*," *Notes from Delacorte Press*, winter, 1978/spring, 1979.

■ For More Information See

New York Times Book Review, August 12, 1974, November 17, 1974 (p. 8), December 2, 1979 (p. 4), September 13, 1981 (p. 50).

Washington Post Book World, July 10, 1977 (p. H10).

New York Times, December 4, 1979.

Voice of Youth Advocates, February, 1983 (p. 19ff), August, 1985 (p. 187).

Sally Holmes Holtze, editor, *Fifth Book of Junior Authors and Illustrators*, H. W. Wilson, 1983.

Wilson Library Bulletin, March, 1985, February, 1986, November, 1986, October, 1988.

Alleen Pace Nilsen and Kenneth L. Donelson, editors, *Literature for Today's Young Adults*, 2nd edition, Scott, Foresman, 1985.

Children's Literature Review, Volume 16, Gale, 1989.

Norma Fox Mazer

Born May 15, 1931, in New York, N.Y.; daughter of Michael (a truck driver) and Jean (a sales clerk; maiden name, Garlen) Fox; married Harry Mazer (a novelist), February 12, 1950; children: Anne, Joseph, Susan, Gina. *Education:* Attended Antioch College, 1949, and Syracuse University, 1958-59. *Home and office:* Brown Gulf Rd., Jamesville, N.Y. 13078; 330 Third Ave., New York, N.Y. 10010. *Agent:* Elaine Markson, 44 Greenwich Ave., New York, N.Y. 10011.

■ Career

Writer, 1964—. *Member:* Authors Guild, PEN.

■ Awards, Honors

National Book Award Finalist, 1974, for *A Figure of Speech;* Lewis Carroll Shelf Award from University of Wisconsin, 1976, for *Saturday the Twelfth of October;* Christopher Award, one of *New York Times* Outstanding Books of the Year, one of *School Library Journal*'s Best Books of the Year, and one of American Library Association's Best Books for Young Adults, all 1976, and Lewis Carroll Shelf Award, 1978, all for *Dear Bill, Remember Me?; The Solid Gold Kid* was selected one of American

Library Association's Best Books for Young Adults, 1977, and a Children's Choice from the International Reading Association and the Children's Book Council, 1978; *Up in Seth's Room* was selected one of American Library Association's Best Books for Young Adults, 1979, and *Someone to Love,* 1983.

Up in Seth's Room was selected one of New York Public Library's Books for the Teen Age, 1980, and one of American Library Association's Best of the Best Books, 1970-1983; Austrian Children's Books Honor List, and German Children's Literature Prize, both 1982, both for *Mrs. Fish, Ape, and Me, the Dump Queen;* Edgar Allan Poe Award for Best Juvenile Mystery from the Mystery Writers of America, 1982, and California Young Reader Medal (junior high division), 1985, both for *Taking Terri Mueller; Downtown* was selected one of New York Public Library's Books for the Teen Age, one of American Library Association's Best Books for Young Adults, and one of *New York Times* Outstanding Books, all 1984; *Someone to Love* was selected for the University of Iowa's Books for Young Adults List, 1984.

Iowa Teen Award from the Iowa Educational Media Association, 1986, for *When We First Met;* Children's Choice from the International Reading Association and the Children's Book Council, 1987, for *A, My Name Is Ami;* Newbery Honor Book from the American Library Association, one of *School Library Journal*'s Best Books of the Year, one of the Association of Booksellers Best Books for Young Adults, and Canadian Children's Book Council Choice, all 1988, all for *After the Rain; Silver* was selected one of American Library Association's Best Books for Young Adults, and one of New York Public Library's Books for the Teen Age, both 1989; *Heartbeat* and *Waltzing on Water* were each selected one of New York Public Library's Books for the Teen Age, 1989.

■ Writings

Fiction:

I, Trissy (juvenile), Delacorte, 1971.

A Figure of Speech (young adult), Delacorte, 1973.

Saturday, the Twelfth of October (young adult), Delacorte, 1975.

Dear Bill, Remember Me? and Other Stories (young adult; ALA Notable Book), Delacorte, 1976.

(With husband, Harry Mazer) *The Solid Gold Kid* (young adult), Delacorte, 1977.

Up in Seth's Room (young adult), Delacorte, 1979.

Mrs. Fish, Ape, and Me, the Dump Queen (juvenile), Dutton, 1980.

Taking Terri Mueller (young adult), Avon (paperback), 1981, Morrow (hardcover), 1983.

When We First Met (young adult; sequel to *A Figure of Speech*), Four Winds, 1982.

Summer Girls, Love Boys and Other Short Stories (young adult), Delacorte, 1982.

Someone to Love (young adult), Delacorte, 1983.

Downtown (young adult), Avon, 1983 (paperback), Morrow (hardcover), 1984.

(Contributor) Donald R. Gallo, editor, *Sixteen: Short Stories by Outstanding Writers for Young Adults*, Delacorte, 1984.

Supergirl (young adult; novelization of screenplay by David Odell), Warner, 1984.

A, My Name Is Ami (young adult), Scholastic, 1986.

Three Sisters (young adult), Scholastic, 1986.

(Contributor) *Short Takes: A Short Story Collection for Young Readers* (juvenile), Lothrop, 1986.

(Contributor) Donald R. Gallo, editor, *Visions: Nineteen Short Stories by Outstanding Writers for Young Adults*, Delacorte, 1987.

B, My Name Is Bunny (young adult), Scholastic, 1987.

After the Rain (young adult; ALA Notable Book; *Horn Book* honor list), Morrow, 1987, large print edition, G. K. Hall, 1989.

Silver, Morrow, 1988.

(Editor with Margery Lewis) *Waltzing on Water: Poetry by Women*, Dell, 1989.

(With H. Mazer) *Heartbeat*, Bantam, 1989.

Contributor of stories and articles to magazines, including *Jack and Jill, Ingenue, Calling All Girls, Top of the News, Children's Activities, Child Life, Boys and Girls, Redbook, English Journal, Voya, Signal, Writer*, and *ALAN Review*.

■ Adaptations

(Also coauthor of filmscript) "When We First Met" (motion picture), HBO, 1984.

"Taking Terri Mueller" (cassette), Listening Library, 1986.

"Dear Bill, Remember Me?" (cassette), Listening Library, 1987.

"After the Rain" (cassette), Listening Library, 1988.

■ Work in Progress

A novel for young adults.

■ Sidelights

"I grew up, the middle of three sisters, in a small town in the foothills of the Adirondack Mountains."[1]

"I am first-generation American on both sides. My parents came to this country with their parents at a very young age. And, growing up, I was always aware of that.

"My father's family came from the Ukraine...but he was born in London. A strange and wonderful place, it always seemed to me, for the...son of Ukrainian-Jewish parents to be born. Somehow, growing up myself...in a town *Look* magazine called Hometown U.S.A., I didn't quite believe in the reality of English Jews. Russian Jews, yes. Polish Jews, yes. Even German Jews. I knew those people. But English Jews? Yet there was my father, an English Jew by birth. And, indeed, in my eyes, it lent him an added enchantment.

"The Fox family (they may originally have been the Ochs family, renamed by immigration officials) came here when my father was about three years old; that would have been 1901.

"My father...was always a difficult person, moody, tense. And shy! My mother says that when they were first married if people came to visit he would sit in the room and never say a word. 'I would sweat buckets,' he told me. 'I was shy and aggressive at the same time.'

"He did become easier on himself, easier to be with as he got older, but he never fully lost that shyness. For instance, it was like pulling teeth to make conversation with Dad on the phone. Well, one ordinarily didn't make small talk with him, anyway. He was interested in politics, the world around him, facts, hard solid things he could bite into, remember, absorb, mull over.

"I remember him sitting close to our radio at home, his head bent, absorbed, twisting the dial to catch the foreign-language stations, although English and Yiddish were the only languages he knew.

"My father...had a strong character; he also had principles, he believed in things like loyalty and family and working hard."[2]

Mazer's mother, Jean, was born in a small town in Poland and her family escaped to the U.S. during the years of the persecution of the Jews by the Cossacks.

Both parents left school in the eighth grade to begin working. They met and married in New York City, where Mazer and her older sister were born. "My father drove a milk truck for Sheffield Farms. Then there was a strike and my father (that shy man!) was pinpointed as one of the leaders. He didn't think of himself as a leader. He just got mad once and stood up and said what he had to say. What he had to say was heartfelt, rousing, and made sense to the other men. It was influential in getting the strike vote. But later on, he was blacklisted. Which meant no job would open for him, and this was 1935, the middle of the Depression. So my uncle, my mother's brother, asked him to come upstate to drive a bread truck for the [family] bakery, which had passed to him.

"For me, growing up in Glens Falls meant, as much as anything, my uncle Charlie's fresh bread every day: dark pumpernickel, Jewish rye bread, crusty rolls, the holiday Challahs, braided and shiny.

"My mother worked in department stores, a sales clerk. I used to visit her sometimes after school, look at the cashmere sweaters piled softly in the don't-touch glass cases—that was as close as I'd ever get to cashmere. At various times Mom sold sweaters, baby clothes, women's dresses. At the end of the day, she'd come home and cook supper—vegetable soups from scratch, nothing out of a can, baked potatoes I could mash with beets or peas, and always on Friday nights, chicken."[2]

"I think my parents never felt completely at home in this country, because of their immigrant backgrounds, and I suppose I picked up on that. I don't know if I write about outsiders consistently, but I do an awful lot of it. Sometimes I'm conscious of it, and sometimes it's there when I'm not conscious of it. The whole working-class thing is also a very strong influence."[3]

"My older sister, Adele (named for our grandmother, Udell), was beautiful, smart, and admired throughout the family. My younger sister, Linda, was a cutie pie with freckles, blonde braids, and a swift, sassy mouth. My uncle called her Dynamite. And there I was, caught between these two sisters, one wonderful, one (when she wasn't in trouble) adorable.

"Well, I did some things, too. I taught myself to read and my first-grade teacher, Miss Dooty, loved me. Never again did a teacher love me as much. I put Miss Dooty in a short story I wrote, called 'Why Was Elena Crying?'

"We were a family of readers. There were always books in our house, shelves of them in the living room and more in the hall."[2]

Jacket of the 1976 multi-award winner.

"Mother didn't allow comics in our house....Nothing else printed was off limits. I read everything, without discretion, as long as it contained words: my parents' books, the Sue Barton nurse series from beginning to end, *Gulliver's Travels*, and dreadful *Pollyanna* whom I adored, all in the same big gulp. But no comics. I had to go across the street to Buddy Wells' house and read his *Wonder Woman* and *Elastic Man* on the sly."[4]

Mazer vividly remembers one moment in her childhood. "A girlfriend and I are playing near...wooden steps. I have forgotten the game, although I made it up, but not her words. 'Norma Fox! What an imagination!' And perhaps it was precisely then that I realized that my imagination had some other function than to torment me with witches in doorknobs and lurking figures in the shadows of the stairs.

"I was a famous crybaby. In the family they called me the faucet. They said, 'You only have to look at Norma cross-eyed and she cries.' I cried if the boys teased me. I cried if someone hit me. I cried if I did something wrong. I cried if I was scared. Or sad. Or happy.

"Perhaps my sense of myself lurking around the edges of adult society comes from...the summers I spent working in Seven Keys [a camp on Loon Lake in the Adirondacks for adults owned and run by an uncle] working and looking at people, watching, listening, making up stories about those people, making up stories about myself, living in a dream, the dream of 'Someday I'll show them...' and 'When I...' and 'They'll all pay attention to me when....'

"It was around this time, too, that I was newly defined in the family: I was now the Cold One, the Selfish One. (My younger sister had metamorphosed from the Cute One to the Brat, the Bad One. My older sister remained responsible, beautiful, and bright: the Good One.)

"My being called cold and selfish had a certain dreary justification. In my teens, I was more and more in my own world, at once shiveringly aware of everything going on around me and keeping it all away with an invisible wall. So many things hurt....I saw myself as clumsy, shy, awkward, stiff; but to others, so I heard years later, I appeared cool, poised, and self-contained.

"The sense of myself as different became something I lived with, almost unnoticed, yet I was never free of its effects. I felt an outsider, someone poised on this earth, but not solidly planted. I even felt an outsider in the small Jewish community in Glens Falls: we Foxes weren't religious, we were radicals politically, and we didn't mix a whole lot (except for my mother).

"Were I to be asked to use one word to describe myself then and for years afterward, it would be— eyes. There's a picture of me around thirteen, sitting in a high-backed leather chair, looking out of the corner of my eyes, looking around, watching, a little frightened smile on my face. Along about then, it struck me, a bone-aching truth, that grown-ups—adults, these powerful mysterious people—were all play-acting; they weren't, in fact, any older, any more grown-up than I was.

"It was harder to watch kids my own age. All those 'in' girls, the sorority girls, the prom-queen types with their long, smooth, tawny legs and strings of pearls and cashmere sweaters, those magic girls whose boyfriends were always presidents of the senior class or played football for Glens Falls High. I never went to a pep rally in my life. My legs were impossibly short and solid. I blushed when a boy I liked spoke to me or even passed me in the hall, not a sweet, pale blush, but a bright red, fiery blush that covered my neck and face."[2]

Mazer tried to fit in, "to have all the right opinions, to be nice and to say all the nice things.

"I think that from the time I was very young I was the kind of person who had strength inside, but I was also very frightened; it took a long time to get past that layer of fear and to be independent and strong."[3]

"In grade school I had confided to my diary that I wanted 'adventures' or, failing that, to be a nurse. By the time I went into junior high, there was something else: a longing, a need to write, so palpable it seemed it must always have been with me. I hooked up right away with the school newspaper and for the next six years the newspaper was the focus of my school existence.

"What did I learn as a writer for the school newspaper? On reflection, not much. To begin a story with the five W's: who, what, when, where, and why. I can't remember anything else. It didn't matter. I was around print, I was a reporter. I wrote feature stories and sports stories and editorials and headlines. I stayed late in school and 'put the paper to bed,' and when the issue came out I sniffed the good clean ink smell and knew I was as close to heaven as I was going to be allowed to get.

"But I wanted to write more than newspaper articles. There was a longing in me, vague, incho-

From the movie "When We First Met," produced by Learning Corporation of America, 1984.

ate, but real, almost an ache. Once I wrote about a storm. An A plus from my English teacher. Another time I wrote about an old man seen on the street. Again A plus. My English teachers sighed contentedly over my compositions. I helped out my friends with their essays and themes and wondered why it was so difficult for them to do what was so easy for me. But nobody told me anything about writing. No hints, no encouragement, no advice, no direction. There just wasn't anybody around to do that sort of thing.

"The year I was fifteen I met a friend of my newly married older sister. He was twenty-one, tall, curly haired, a veteran of the air force. I came home and reported to my best friend that I'd met an incredibly handsome guy, name of Harry Mazer, too bad he was so—ughhh—*old.* Two years later, in the fall of my seventeenth year, I met him again. He was still six years older than I, but by one of the lovely miracles of nature, not *that* old anymore. By then. . .three or four other young men had fallen in love with me. My confidence had risen a little. I decided that I would let Harry Mazer fall in love with me, also.

"Unfortunately for my plans, he thought I was too young. I had to work some to make him notice me. I did. He did. We fell in love. Out of love. In love. I went off to college, Antioch; fell out of love. Then in love again. We quarreled and made up, and quarreled and made up. We decided to get married. An uncle, aghast at the thought of his baby eighteen-year-old niece getting married said, 'For God's sake, live with the guy, don't marry him!' But that was 1950 and I was deeply insulted by such advice and wondered if I could ever forgive my uncle."[2]

Leaving Antioch after one semester, the newlyweds moved to New York City where she was accepted at Hunter College. The noise and crowds of the city proved intolerable and the Mazers moved to upstate New York. "We talked about books and writing and literature. We also talked about politics, unions, injustice, the atom bomb, the cold war. We were radicals and ready to reform (re form) the world, if not in ninety days, then in five years. Five years—good god, it was a lifetime! If we couldn't straighten out the world in five years, then things were really in a bad way.

"In between all this talk, we refinished furniture, laid tiles in our tiny kitchen, went to movies and plays, worked at boring jobs, and tried to learn to cook. Neither of us knew how, but he knew more than I did. . . .I wished the first year of being

married would hurry up—it dragged on endlessly. I was tired of being a bride: I didn't like bride jokes, I wanted to get on with my life, I wanted to be an old married lady.

"Eventually, in the way of these things, I got my wish. If not yet old (my conception of old having radically altered in my twenties), I was well married and had three children [1958]: Anne, then about five, Joey, two, and Susan, the baby. I went around with a little pad stuck in my jeans pocket, taking down the clever things my kids said. They were all fascinatingly different.

"I was Mommy; I had almost forgotten Norma. One day, looking around at the houseful of kids and listening to the never ending cries of Mommy! Mom! Mama!, it occurred to me that the day I'd been both putting off and waiting for—the day when I was all grown up—had arrived without my noticing. Indeed, it must have been here for quite a while. And that famous question 'What are you going to do when you grow up?' had not gone away. What *was* I going to do when I grew up? I'd gone on fooling around with writing, beginning stories, jotting down ideas and nifty little perceptions. But that wasn't being a writer. That was being 'someday when I am a real writer.'

"Along about this time, things were happening to Harry, too. Some of the same stuff—wondering why, now that he was a grown-up, he was doing work he didn't like, not making his old dreams come true. We talked. Our best talks always came with long walks.

"We both knew what I wanted—to be a writer. But then something surprising happened. Harry began to talk about his longing to be a writer, a dream he'd harbored—or hidden–since he was in his teens. And I hadn't known anything of it. I thought we talked about everything. Maybe I vaguely knew he was interested in writing. There were all those notebooks he kept, yet he had never actually said the words: I want to be a writer.

"Now that he'd said it, I think he looked at me in amazement when I didn't fall over laughing at the idea. But why would I laugh? As far as I could tell, my own longing to become a writer was no less arrogant than his.

"But if arrogant, I was also practical. Since we both wanted to become writers, wasn't it about time we did something real about it? I thought that what I needed—what we both needed—was to develop the habit of writing. Not to write only when we could squeeze in a few minutes here or there. Not to write only when 'inspiration' struck. But to write something every day.

"I remember sitting down and opening my green notebook to its first fresh page. I tried to fashion the events of the morning into a little story. It was clumsy, it was crude, but I sat there and finished it.

"Every night, after supper, after the kids had been bathed and read to and had been brought the requisite number of glasses of water, and after we had found each child's particular stuffed animal or blanket necessary for good sleep—every night after Harry had spent a day working in a factory and I had spent a day taking care of the kids, we sat down across from each other at the old oak table in the dining room with our notebooks and pens.

"We stuck to our schedule, an hour a day, at the end of the day, for about three years. Little as it was, it made a difference. I was writing, finishing what I began, learning about rewriting. The notebooks didn't last long; typewriters took their place. Writing and kids filled our lives. During the day I could think about the story I was working on. At the end of the day we'd take a walk, talk about the kids and writing. We read other writers and tried to analyze what they did, how they achieved their effects. I wonder now how we found time to write between the kids and talking. Half our talk was dreaming still. Would we ever make it? Were we any good? Wouldn't it be wonderful if we could write for a living? Was it even possible? Maybe...since there were two of us. . . .

"I sold a few things—we both did. I sold a few little quizzes and anecdotes, a story here and there."[2]

The first thing Mazer ever sold "...wasn't a book or even a story. It was an 'out of the mouths of babes' item to *Parents* magazine. About three lines, and they paid me three dollars. A dollar a line—big money. If I had been less in need of that three dollars, I would have framed it. Opening that envelope, seeing that check which signified that I was going to be published was total joy. Words that I had written printed in a bona fide magazine. Never mind that they were words my clever little son had uttered. I was the one who had heard them, who had copied them down, who had typed them up, who had sent them into *Parents* magazine. And that was *my* name in print underneath those words. Not even on a ketchup bottle, but in a real magazine."[5]

In 1963 "I was pregnant again—despite the scorn of a friend who told me I evidently didn't care

The 1981 Morrow hardcover.

about overpopulating the world. Yes, I did! Only I so much wanted another baby. I was restless during that pregnancy, I didn't sleep well and often found myself in the middle of the night, wandering forlornly around the house, wondering what to do all by myself. Maybe I should put in some time writing? Weird hour, but since I was awake. . . .

"I suggested to Harry that he might want to get up with me in the middle of the night and write, too. Just think, I said, how tired you are at night after working all day. How hard it is to sit there and put the words down on paper. Now think how good you feel in the morning, how much energy you have then.

"We began to get up at 3:30 a.m. and write for the two or three hours before the official day began. We did this for almost a year. The dark winter mornings were the hardest times.

"And then something unexpected happened. A few years before, there had been an accident. I had been driving with my mother and a couple of my kids when another car ran a stop sign and slammed into us on the driver's side. My kids and my mother were okay. I came out with an enormous bruise on my left hip and a whiplash that affected me off and on for the next fifteen years. That was the bad news. The good news was that, now, there was a settlement—twenty-five hundred dollars. It seemed like a fortune to us. With care, day-old bread, and thrift-shop clothes, we could live on that for six months.

"Gina, our fourth child, was two months old. We had four children under the age of ten and twenty-five hundred dollars. Harry left his job in the factory and we became free-lance writers. It was mildly terrifying. I had some days when I sat in front of the typewriter and shook because I couldn't think of what to write next.

"We decided we would write for the women's romance and confession market. It was a steady, reliable market that needed plenty of stories, and the bulk of them, despite lurid titles, were stories of relationships: men and women, parents and children, brothers and sisters. Someone—the narrator or the chief character—made a mistake, did something wrong, 'sinned.' Every action had a reaction, a consequence. The world of these stories was strict and moral. Being human, a character would surely do wrong, but never go unpunished, unrepentant or, finally, unenlightened.

"The stories were all published without a byline. They were all written in the first person and the readers were meant to think that the events of the stories had been lived by the 'people' who wrote them. Eventually there were issues of magazines in which as many as three or four stories had been written by Harry and/or me. One story might be in the voice of a sixteen-year-old girl, another in the voice of a thirty-five-year-old woman, and still another 'by' a nineteen-year-old boy.

"The stories were typically about five thousand words long and paid by the word—two to five cents per word. To earn enough for our family, week in and week out, for years each of us wrote a story. Coming up with ideas and writing at that pace meant long hours and no days off. Early on, we got the habit of writing seven days a week. But it also meant doing what I wanted to do and learning while I was doing it. Writing story after story forced me to learn how a story is constructed, how to hold a reader's attention, how to write dialogue and narration, how to do simple, yet previously baffling things like transitions.

"We tried other kinds of writing: short stories, screenplays, a first attempt at a novel for children. We were both anxious to break out of romance writing, but not at all tired of living the life of free-lance writers. Although my housekeeping had gone steadily downhill since I went to work side by side with Harry to earn our living, my spirits had gone steadily uphill. But I was still dreaming about the future. If only I had the time to write a novel....One little problem: to write a novel, I needed time away from the pulp fiction. To get that time, I needed money. To get money, I had to write the pulp fiction. For some years, it was our own version of Catch-22.

"Then in 1970 I scraped together the time to write *I, Trissy*. I had fun writing that book. I used a variety of literary techniques to tell the story of a girl who was quite stubbornly unhappy about her parents' separation. Trissy, volatile, spirited, and outspoken, seemed to me entirely unlike myself. (But now, I think perhaps Trissy is not so much the me I never was, as the me I had actually once been and forgotten about.)

"In December of 1970 I sent the manuscript of *I, Trissy* off to my agent and prepared myself for a long wait, a long series of submissions and rejections. I expected to wait at least one year, possibly two years. But Delacorte Press accepted the manuscript less than a month later."[2]

"The call from my agent saying that Delacorte wanted to publish *I, Trissy* gave me cold chills. Those were chills of excitement. Not too long after, I was assailed by another kind of chill—the chill of fear, the will-I-ever-write-another-book terror."[5]

"Two years after *I, Trissy* came *A Figure of Speech*. This was quite a different book...much more of a real novel—longer, more serious, more sustained."[2]

In this novel, young Jenny struggles against her parents' decision to place her grandfather in a nursing home. "All the time I was writing it, I was thinking, is this the way you write a novel? Is this what you do?"[3]

This fear did not leave Mazer for several years. "I went on writing pulp fiction to earn money, squeezing in time here and there to write my books. For a long time I had been fascinated by the lives of tribal peoples. I had read and reread Colin Turnbull's *The Gentle People* about the pygmies of the Ituri forest, and Laurens van der Post on the Bushmen of the Kalihari. And always, as I read, the thought behind my eyes was, What if I could live with these people? What would life be like for me?

"Then, by chance, I saw a film on public TV about the discovery of a group of Stone-Age people, the Tasaday, on the Philippine island of Mindanao. The Tasaday lived in caves, quiet, gentle, gathering their food; one generation after another had gone on without change for ten thousand years.

"Watching the Tasaday, I almost jumped out of my skin with excitement. That night I couldn't sleep and began to imagine a story about a girl, an ordinary girl from this world of ours, somehow finding herself among Stone-Age people. It would be utterly different from my first two books, a time-travel book, aspects of science fiction and fantasy, a book as far from 'reality' as the Stone-Age people were from our twentieth century.

"It was not an easy book to write. I researched, mostly by reading the reports of anthropologists who had lived with tribal peoples. I wrote and rewrote. The manuscript was rejected and I had the first anxiety attack of my life, sitting up in bed at night, gasping for air, wondering if I could carry off this story. I've written [more] books since then but none as difficult as *Saturday, the Twelfth of October*. It's unlike any of my books and it's one of my favorites.

"After *Saturday*, I wanted very much to write some short stories and hoped Delacorte would publish them as a collection. Some of these stories had been waiting around for at least fifteen years for me to write them, but when I mentioned this project to my editor, his first reaction was negative. 'Kids,' he said, 'don't read short stories. Short stories are shelf-sitters. Everyone knows this.' But, thinking about it, he went on to say, 'Well, maybe now's the time for a change. Why don't you go ahead and write them.'

"The short stories I wrote became the book *Dear Bill, Remember Me?*... During the months I spent working on the stories, I somehow lost the secret fear that I was only masquerading as a writer. For the first time, I began to believe fearlessly in the endless vitality of that mysterious source from which my imagination is constantly replenished. Writers have different names for it. Some call it dipping into the well. Some speak of being guided by another hand, or simply putting down what a voice tells them to. I've heard my husband refer to it as though it were a buried coil of rope on which he pulls, bringing out one surprise after another, and no one more surprised by the surprises than he."[2]

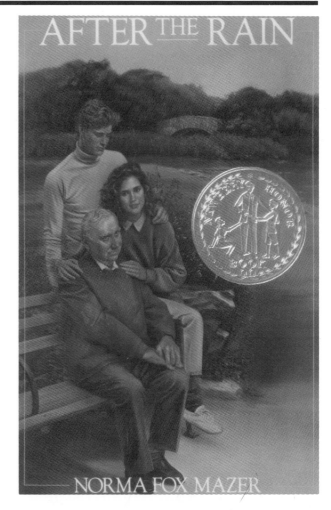

Dust jacket of the 1988 Newbery Honor Book.

By now, Harry Mazer was also a published writer of novels for young adults. "Harry and I have been each other's first and most trusted readers for over twenty years. Not a book, article, or story that either of us has written has ever gone out into the world without the other's blessing."[6]

They collaborated on the novel, *The Solid Gold Kid*, about the kidnapping of a wealthy boy. It was received with enthusiastic reviews. In 1989 they made another joint effort with *Heartbeat*, also well received. "I wrote more books: *Up in Seth's Room, Someone to Love, Downtown, Taking Terri Mueller.* Each one, in its own way, took me over. I lived in the world I was creating; it became real to me. Sometimes I'm asked about 'writer's block.' I don't have it and I don't fear it. Those years of writing pulp fiction taught me that there are always more words. And writing my novels taught me that there are things inside me waiting to come out that I hardly know are there."[2]

"That adolescent me, that girl who was, as I remember her, insecure, unsure, dreaming, yearning, longing, that girl who was hard on herself, who was cowardly and brave, who was confused and determined—that girl who was me—still exists. I call on her when I write. I am the me of today—the person who has become a woman, a mother, a writer. Yet I am the me of all those other days as well. I believe in the reality of that past.

"I believe there is more than one reality. Our memories are real. Our dreams are real. Our fantasies are real. All the life of our mind is real. No wonder we are eternally fascinated, charmed, troubled, and moved by stories. This is because, at its best, the story springs from inside ourselves and speaks to the inner life of the listener or reader.

"When I first began writing, I wrote blindly, wanting only to put down words on paper. The first real lesson I learned about writing was that I needed to—and did—have something to say. Something was there, inside me, waiting to be called out. The struggle, I think—not only for the writer, but just for living in this world with self-respect—is to find what's uniquely one's own: the real, the true things one thinks, which reflect one's own view of the world, one's own experiences, one's own perceptions and visions.

"When I start asking myself that most basic question—What do I really believe?—the emphasis is on *really*. I need to get past the first thoughts, the surface slog, the pat phrases, the pet ideas, the banal and the slick, the easy answers.

"My method, if it can be called that, when I'm thinking, when I'm planning a book, when I'm working out characterizations, or when I want to know what I think this book is really saying, is to talk to myself on paper. This means all barriers down, no 'writerly' stuff, no looking for the right word, the phrase that will resound, the beautifully constructed sentence. It means pouring out what's in my mind, what's beneath the surface, all those unique, not nice, and but-what-if-no-one-else-agrees-with-me thoughts.

"Out of days of sitting frozen in front of the typewriter years ago, tears coming because I knew I'd never make it and our dream would shatter, came this method of 'get it out.' It's still the way I draft—get it out, get it on paper. Never mind what it sounds like, just get it down so I have something to work with, so I can rewrite, so I can clear my mind for other things to enter.

"Any writing that intends to make an impression has to be informed by what the writer believes, not what she thinks she ought to believe. Every word, every sentence she puts down ought to be laid on the solid foundation of her point of view. Point of view, what the writer thinks, should never be spelled out in a novel, yet it is intricately, I should say inextricably, tied to the development of plot and the working out of character. And those two, in turn, are so closely intertwined for me that I am at a loss when someone asks me which comes first, plot or character.

"I think my first duty as a writer is to know how to tell a story, how to capture and entertain my readers. I want to write good books, I don't want to write products. I don't want to write books that fit neatly into slots, interchangeable books–we're seeing a lot of those these days. Product books which have less and less to do with the writer and more and more to do with marketing. I assume these books are, in the most basic sense, entertaining. That is, they do have story in its elemental form. I want to entertain, too; I don't consider that a dirty word. The story, the line of the story, the plot, if you will, is the basic ingredient of entertainment.

"But a book written only to entertain, only to distract, a book without something worth saying underlying the story will have a robotlike quality. It will lack the heart beating at its center that is so necessary for a story to be more than a diversion, that will keep the story living in the reader's mind.

"I love stories. I'm convinced that everyone does, and whether we recognize it or not, each of us tells stories. A day doesn't pass when we don't put our lives into story. Most often these stories are ephemeral, of the moment. They are the recognition, the highlighting of the minutiae of our daily lives.

"But other stories embed themselves in our hearts. A story isn't an event, but the telling of the event. . .and not the bone-dry factual telling, but the event as seen through the eyes and heart of the teller.

"I believe that stories and storytelling are as basic to human life as singing and dancing. . .that stories are as essential to our lives as food and water, as sleep, dreams, and love."[5]

Always an experimenter in her writing, Mazer's basic theme, through all her critically acclaimed books, is that one must find one's own way, work through problems, and not give in to defeat.

Her stories tackle problems that young people face. In *Up in Seth's Room,* Mazer deals with the issue of sex and youth. "Had I written this book

The 1984 award-winning novel.

and without guilt. Sex is good, sex is nice, sex is easy. Well, yes. . .and no.

"The problem is that sex (by which we usually mean intercourse) demands a high degree of responsibility and responsiveness, at the very time when the young are besieged by all kinds of problems and decisions, when they are most changeable and volatile. No, it just is *not* as easy as the books have been telling us.

"Nevertheless, the young *are* full of passion, longing, and desire. They want, they need, they *should have,* a sexual life. I said 'a sexual life.' We tend to use the word 'sex' narrowly.

"Books for young adults have carried on the idea that 'sex' is synonomous with 'doing it.' But sex, in fact, covers a whole range of activity and behavior. I read an article that said fifty-seven percent of high school girls have had intercourse. I thought,

Paperbound edition of the 1973 novel.

while I was growing up, or even years after, it would have been easy. Nice girls didn't. (They didn't even *think* about *it*.) So we were told by our mothers, and so we were told by the books we read. We all wanted to be nice girls (boys married *them*, not the other kind), and in front of our parents and teachers we all *acted* like nice girls.

"But what was happening in private? In the cars we parked in with our boyfriends? In the hallways and beneath trees in secluded parks? Well, the same thing that has always been happening—sex. And though most of us tried valiantly, despite our longing, our curiosity, and our delight, to remain *nice girls,* some of us didn't succeed. But we only whispered about that.

"Things have changed. No one is whispering anymore. Everyone talks about sex. Everyone writes about sex. And everyone seems to be 'doing it.' In book after book for young adults, the characters not only have sex, but have it with fewer problems than most adults. The message is that sex is here to stay, and the young should have it and enjoy it as well as anyone else, without remorse what about the other forty-three percent? Who are they? What are *they* doing? Are they happy? Or are they feeling guilty because they aren't enjoying guilt-free 'sex?'

"I knew that my heroine, Finn, felt she wasn't ready for intercourse. 'Too young, too soon, too important,' she says. Finn is a strong-minded character. Seth is older; he's made love with other girls, and he wants to make love with Finn. He's putting on the pressure. A classic situation. In the 'olden days' it was clear what happened when *he* wanted it and *she* didn't. She lost him, of course; but never mind, a *really* nice boy (one who 'respected' her) would be waiting in the wings.

"I knew Finn was a loving, warm, responsive, *sexual* person. I also knew she was going to stick to her guns. And I didn't want her to lose Seth. (I liked him too much; I couldn't see a terrific guy like Seth throwing over a girl he loved because she wouldn't sleep with him.)

"Well, what to do? How to keep these kids together without pulling strings? I never want to write a book where I'm a puppet-master. So Finn and Seth worked out their own problems. They fought a lot, they loved each other, and they found out something I wish a lot of kids would find out: You *can* love someone fully, you *can* have a sex life that will satisfy both of you, and you *can* do it without. . .'doing it.'"[7]

"I believe that the young do, indeed, need a literature of their own. A literature that doesn't avoid the painful truths of our world, but which will provide affirmation as well.

"I should like in my writing to give meaning and emotion to ordinary moments. In my books and stories, I want people to eat chocolate pudding, break a dish, yawn, look in a store window, wear socks with holes in them. . . ."[8]

"When my children began to read, I decided they could read anything, including comics. I hewed to the line that no printed word, sentence, or story ever killed or maimed anyone, that reading leads to more reading, and that, finally, given time, the kids would develop their own tastes which, hopefully, would include much more than comics.

"Today there's a rather strong current alive in our country devoted to screening, censoring, banning, and in some cases even burning books that our children read. And the cry for censorship rings out not just against sex, for instance, but against books which contain certain words people find offensive, certain attitudes and points of view.

"As a writer for the young, as a reader, a parent, I despise all censorship, even including things that enrage and pain me. I want to bite nails when I read yet another portrait of a silly, simpering, weepy, noncapable girl. I find, even in a book for the young that I otherwise admire, a gratuitous, racist remark about Jews. And in a book which has been widely acclaimed, a black woman character who might have come off the pancake box: unmarried, working faithfully for a white family, deeply understanding, and always there when needed by the white children.

"I don't like these things, I hate the blindness that persistently ties us to such stereotypes, but I wouldn't keep these books out of the hands of children who want to read them. And this is because I believe that children are people with as much sense and an equal ability to sort out things for themselves as adults.

"Children are not imperfect copies of ourselves who magically come into the possession of our superior adult reasoning powers at a certain fixed age. Children, in fact, have remarkable sense from quite a young age and lack, most of all, experience. It's experience, I believe, which separates 'us' from 'them.'

"Of course there are other differences. The young are more intense, emotional, impatient, lusty, and zestful. Their time sense is quite different. And they can throw themselves into life in a wonderful way which we adults gradually lose.

"Today, writers for adolescents are giving them stories about things that used to be verboten. . . .Writers are discovering that death, sex, love, war, divorce, and so on are part of the lives of the young. Some books, it's true, are written, it seems, merely to be in the swim, to be realistic because 'realistic' is in vogue. But others are literature; they're real, passionate, felt books. They may deal, on one level, with social problems, but they are primarily about the human condition, about the way we feel and how we live with others."[4]

To the young aspiring writer, Mazer says: "Write. Write letters. Keep a journal. Only write something every day. Don't ever write what you think you ought to write, but only what you feel, think, and observe for yourself."[1]

Footnote Sources:

[1] Sally Holmes Holtze, editor, *Fifth Book of Junior Authors and Illustrators*, H. W. Wilson, 1983.
[2] Norma Fox Mazer, *Something about the Author Autobiography Series*, Volume 1, Gale, 1986.

³ S. H. Holtze, *Presenting Norma Fox Mazer*, Twayne, 1987.

⁴ N. F. Mazer, "Comics, Cokes, and Censorship," *Top of the News*, January, 1976.

⁵ N. F. Mazer, "Growing Up with Stories," *Top of the News*, winter, 1985. Amended by N. Mazer.

⁶ N. F. Mazer, "'I Love It! It's Your Best Book!,'" *English Journal*, February, 1986.

⁷ N. F. Mazer, "*Up in Seth's Room*," *Notes from Delacorte Press*, winter, 1979/spring, 1980.

⁸ Anne Commire, editor, *Something about the Author*, Volume 24, Gale, 1981.

■ For More Information See

New York Times Book Review, March 17, 1974 (p. 8), October 19, 1975 (p. 12ff), November 14, 1976, January 20, 1980 (p. 30), March 13, 1983.

Horn Book, April, 1974 (p. 152ff), February, 1977 (p. 58ff), August, 1977 (p. 451ff), December, 1982 (p. 660ff).

New York Times, December 21, 1976.

Contemporary Literary Criticism, Volume 26, Gale, 1983.

Washington Post Book World, April 10, 1983 (p. 10).

Writer, February, 1986 (p. 15ff).

Zibby Oneal

Born Elizabeth Bisgard, March 17, 1934, in Omaha, Neb.; daughter of James D. (a thoracic surgeon) and Mary Elizabeth (a housewife; maiden name, Dowling) Bisgard; married Robert Moore Oneal (a plastic surgeon), December 27, 1955; children: Elizabeth, Michael. *Education:* Attended Stanford University, 1952-55; University of Michigan, B.A., 1966. *Politics:* Democrat. *Religion:* Episcopalian. *Home and office:* 501 Onondaga St., Ann Arbor, Mich. 48104. *Agent:* Marilyn Marlow, Curtis Brown Ltd., 575 Madison Ave., New York, N.Y. 10022.

■ Career

Writer, 1954—; University of Michigan, Ann Arbor, lecturer in English, 1976-85. Member of board of trustees, Greenhills School, 1975-79. *Member:* PEN, Authors Guild.

■ Awards, Honors

Friends of American Writers Award, 1972, for *War Work; The Language of Goldfish* was selected one of American Library Association's Best Books for Young Adults, a *Booklist* Reviewers Choice, and one of *School Library Journal's* Best Books, all

1980, and one of American Library Association's Best of the Best Books, 1970-82; *A Formal Feeling* was selected one of American Library Association's Best of the Best Books, 1970-1982, one of American Library Association's Best Books for Young Adults, a *Booklist* Reviewers Choice, and one of *New York Times* Best Books, all 1982, and Christopher Award, 1983; *Boston Globe-Horn Book* Award for Fiction, and one of American Library Association's Best Books for Young Adults, both 1986, both for *In Summer Light.*

■ Writings

War Work (juvenile; ALA Notable Book; illustrated by George Porter), Viking, 1971.
The Improbable Adventures of Marvelous O'Hara Soapstone (juvenile; illustrated by Paul Galdone), Viking, 1972.
Turtle and Snail (juvenile; illustrated by Margot Tomes), Lippincott, 1979.
The Language of Goldfish (young adult novel; ALA Notable Book), Viking, 1980, large print edition, Thorndike Press, 1989.
A Formal Feeling (young adult novel; ALA Notable Book), Viking, 1982.
Maude and Walter (illustrated by Maxie Chambliss), Lippincott, 1985.
In Summer Light (young adult novel; ALA Notable Book; *Horn Book* honor list), Viking, 1985.
Grandma Moses: Painter of Rural America (biography; illustrated by Donna Ruff and with paintings by Grandma Moses), Viking, 1986.

A Long Way to Go, Viking, 1990.

■ Work in Progress

Young adult novel; biography of novelist Willa Cather.

■ Sidelights

Zibby Oneal was born on March 17, 1934 in Omaha, Nebraska. "My mother loved books, both for their content and because they are beautiful objects. Our house was full of them. She read aloud to us a great deal. I can remember finding it miraculous that she could look at the strange black marks on a page and see a story there. I planned to fill pages with black marks of my own as soon as I learned how to make them. Wanting to write goes back that far anyway."[1]

"[Our] house...was full of paintings as well, and though I am no artist, I think in terms of color and composition. All my books have begun with a picture in mind—a character and a place visualized. When I can see these things clearly—almost as if they were a painting on a wall—and then I can begin to write about them."[2]

While her friends learned to jump rope and roller skate, Oneal spent much of her childhood and adolescence writing. "I learned to ride a bike....Got through sixth grade, then eighth, then high school, writing all the time. In those days I mainly wrote stories having to do with love (which I didn't know much about), set in places I'd never seen. From time to time somebody would suggest that I try writing about something I knew. But what did I know? Nothing interesting.

"In college I took writing courses, and once—just once—a professor praised a story. It happened to be a story about my sister and myself, about the day I realized that she was still a child but that I was not. This was something I knew about. I remembered the day, the sunlight on my sister's fine hair, her doll with its missing eye. I remembered the smell of the grass being cut and of strawberries being boiled into jam. Most importantly, I remembered how I *felt*. And so it turned out to be a pretty good story.

"It would be nice to say that I learned something from that. I didn't, or only much later. *Then* I just went back to writing about love affairs in Hong Kong and collecting rejection slips."[1]

On December 27, 1955 she married Robert Moore Oneal, a plastic surgeon. "It was only after I'd married, had two children, and had begun to write stories for them that I discovered what I both liked and could do. The first books came out of these stories created expressly for them."[1]

War Work is a story of three young people living in a Midwestern town during World War II. Their detective efforts help uncover black market activities and a plot to blow up a local bomber plant. The book received the Friends of American Writers Award.

A year later *The Improbable Adventures of Marvelous O'Hara Soapstone* was published. It is the story of Marvelous, the pig, who meant to win a blue ribbon for the Soapstones, but blows her chance by biting the judge at the fair.

In *Turtle and Snail*, published in 1979, Oneal tells several episodes of friendships between a turtle and a snail.

"I began writing for children when my own two were small. My characters aged along with them. Eventually everyone reached adolescence, but my characters remained there, because I found I was deeply interested in exploring this brief time of life, these few years when everything is in the process of becoming what it will be."[2]

"I feel a responsibility to make children understand that adolescence is a self-absorbed world—this may be why I always have islands in my books—but it's not a place you can stay forever. The movement away and out into the world, into concern for other people, has to happen; you aren't an adult until you make that move. Sure, explore your feelings, because if you're hung up on your problems you're never going to be able to move on. So work that out, but then get out into the world."[3]

"At the heart of adolescence is a period of making choices and decisions. I...[want] in my writing to leave my readers with a feeling of hope—a feeling that they do have control and will be able to handle certain emotional situations successfully."[2]

"There is a magnificent blindness involved in writing. You don't know exactly what you're doing until you've done it. At least I don't. I am convinced of that. Too often now people have pointed out things that clearly I have said but didn't recognize I was saying. I am always astonished when this happens, always grateful. It makes writing as wonderfully mysterious to me now as it was when stories were only strange black marks on paper."[1]

Oneal began to teach writing at the University of Michigan, Ann Arbor, and found the classroom a good change from the solitude of the typewriter.

The Language of Goldfish, her first novel for young adults, was published in 1980. It chronicled the attempted suicide of thirteen-year-old Carrie Stokes and her subsequent recovery. "I found one day that a thirteen-year-old girl was on my mind. She began to haunt me. Thinking about her made me remember adolescence and what a difficult time that can be. Eventually I began to write about her, investing imagined events with remembered feelings, sorting things out for myself.

"As my wonderful editor pointed out, it's a book about change. I hadn't seen that, but it makes sense that it should be. At the heart of adolescence is change, and change can be disturbing."[1]

"I get too involved in a story to stand back and look at it. I don't know: Have I said enough? Have I not said enough? Is this going to be clear to anyone but me? [My editor] is invaluable, because she looks at it with an objective eye. It's a collaborative process.

"To me, what's hard is the time I wonder where on earth I'm going, if anywhere! But [my editor] is very good to work with on revisions, because she's so meticulous. It would kill me to have somebody go through it in a slapdash way and say, 'This is fine.' I want that very detailed sort of editing, because that means we're really communicating about the character and the situation. That's how I write, and that's how I want to be edited."[3]

In *A Formal Feeling*, sixteen-year-old Ann Cameron contends with emotions following her mother's unexpected death. The novel's title is from an Emily Dickinson poem, "After great pain, a formal feeling comes—." "Both *The Language of Goldfish* and *A Formal Feeling* are about people who resist change but learn finally to accept it. So, too, I now realize, was the story I wrote about my sister and me so long ago."[1]

A Formal Feeling published in 1982 was initially conceived as a much larger work, and was, in fact, split into a second book, *In Summer Light*, published three years later. Her editor, Deborah Brodie, has a "very vivid picture of the moment when the book split. Zibby was working on a book and she sent me the manuscript, saying, 'It's kind of ready to be worked on.' There are certain moments you always remember in a working relationship and this was one of them. It was as though somebody had handed me an orange and

Paperback edition of the 1985 award winner.

said, 'This is a whole orange,' and I took it and split it. It was two books: one of them was all about summer and heat and sweat and light, and the other had ice and cold and winter. I wrote to Zibby and said, '*Winter* is ready to be worked on, and *Summer* needs more time. How would you feel about a two-book contract?' *Winter* became *A Formal Feeling*, and *Summer* was *In Summer Light*.

"It was. . .January," remembered Brodie, "and I was working at home in my daughter's room, because she has a big desk. I had the last three drafts spread out—one on the desk, one on the floor, one on the bed—and I was cutting and pasting, using the second draft as the master. I was working very intensely, because my time was so limited. And when I was finally finished and I got up to stretch, I looked out the window and I couldn't believe there was snow and ice! I was so full of the feeling of summer, heat and light.

"We had another good meeting on *In Summer Light*" says Oneal. "There's a scene in the book where Kate comes down to the studio and says to Ian [the graduate student she's fallen in love with], 'Take me to Boston.' Well, that phrase came right from Deborah; she said that it would be more dramatic than Kate just saying she loved him. I thought it over and said, 'Yes, of course.' Very important things are added that are Deborah's suggestions."[3]

In Summer Light won the *Boston Globe-Horn Book* Award for fiction. "The landscape existed in my imagination long before I saw it for the first time. I recognized it at once. For me it was the landscape of fairy tale. When the prince comes riding to claim his princess, he rides through just such meadows of wild roses, through just such forests of dappled shade. At least that was the way I imagined it, always. How natural, then, that *In Summer Light*, born as it was of this magical landscape, should have turned out to be a fairy tale. How curious that I, having spent many months in the writing, should

Jacket from the Viking hardcover.

never have noticed. But I didn't notice. It was only later, well after the book was published, that I saw how much *In Summer Light* shared with tales.

"One day a friend and I were talking about the way that themes from certain tales reappear in present-day children's books in one disguise or another. I remember having a theory I was eager to argue for. While this might be true for some tales, I said, it wouldn't continue to be true for all. Surely certain tales—'Cinderella,' for instance, 'Snow White,' 'Rapunzel'—were no longer relevant to the present day. Surely these passive heroines, content to wait for their princes to arrive, had become anachronisms in the wake of the women's movement. How could these tales continue to interest modern girls, intent on careers and achievement? How could the themes found in these stories mean anything to them at all? It was at about this point that I faltered, as suddenly it occurred to me that, in fact, I had just written something suspiciously like 'The Sleeping Beauty' myself.

"One doubts the relevance of tales at one's peril, as I have discovered. It is foolish to argue with their wisdom, even if that wisdom seems, at first glance, hopelessly out-of-date. The tales clearly tell us that though young boys must go off to slay dragons in the pursuit of maturity, young girls must be content to sit and wait. To my astonishment, apparently I agreed. At least I had chosen to tell this ancient tale again, albeit unwittingly.

"Suppose I were to tell you the story of *In Summer Light* in this way. Once upon a time on an island off the coast of Massachusetts there lived a famous painter and his wife. Now to this couple was born a daughter, and they named her Kate. All went well with them for a time, but then came the year that Kate was seventeen, and she fell into a curious state of lethargy. She began to languish there on the island, hedged all around by a thorny tangle of childhood memories. It was not from a jealous fairy's spell that Kate suffered. Rather it was from a thoroughly modern malady called mononucleosis, but the symptoms were much the same. Drowsy, dozing, full of lassitude, Kate rested, deep among the thorns and brambles of the family thicket. In time, of course, a prince arrived. He came riding one day to the place where Kate slept, not on a fine and spirited palfrey but in a car with broken-down springs. A graduate student from California, this prince had neither wealth nor title, yet he succeeded in awakening Kate. Much as I would have liked to deny it at first, I had to admit that the parallels were persuasive. Disguised in modern trappings, the old tale was there.

"I had thought I was making use of a quite different model. Shakespeare's play, *The Tempest*, had been on my mind. I wanted to write about a powerful, arrogant, magical father and about his daughter's involvement with him. I wanted to talk about how a girl begins to move away from this intense childhood involvement; about how it is when, like Miranda in *The Tempest*, she is able to gaze for the first time on a man besides her father.

"I wonder now whether the old tales about adolescent girls may not, themselves, be speaking of some such time. When Snow White and Beauty, Cinderella and Rapunzel gaze for the first time upon their princes, they are prepared to ride away. They are no longer the obedient and sequestered young girls they have been. Something has changed. We credit the prince with effecting the change, but I wonder whether his kiss is not meant to be more like an acknowledgement of something already accomplished. I wonder whether the change may not have ocurred, in fact, earlier–during that time among the cinders or in the tower or deep in sleep. When at last the prince awakens these girls, they are ready to go with him. They have left childhood behind. So, too, it is with my Kate. By the time that she can name her feelings for her prince, she has moved beyond childhood preoccupations. She has left behind those things which prevent her becoming a woman. And she has done this while seeming to do nothing at all.

"Passivity, then, is an illusion. Growing up is not a passive undertaking. If we do not see the process in tales—or only a metaphor for process—I do not think we are meant to assume that no effort has been expended, that no struggle has taken place. While boys journey off to seek their fortunes, the girls set off on a journey of another kind. It is a quiet, dreaming, inward journey, but who is to say that the dragons encountered are not equally fearsome or that the arrival at the destination has not been just as dearly won? Surely Kate has struggled by the time she wakes. During her long sleepy summer, she has fought a dragon or two. While doing nothing, she has done much. When at last her eyes are open, it is a young woman—not a child—gazing through them.

"Fairy tales are shorthand. They are metaphors, models, myths. We carry them in our heads like patterns, and they tell us what we need to know about how humans grow and change and prosper. How very unsurprising, then, that we should sometimes turn to them when we have a story to tell, should sort among them for a pattern to fit our

Jacket from Oneal's multi-award-winning novel.

intention. That this should happen, as it did for me, unconsciously, seems only proof of how deep within us these patterns lie. Wanting to tell the story of an awakening, I turned intuitively to the oldest story of awakening I know. I could not have turned to it in any other way, prevented by all my rational arguments. Fortunately I seldom write with both eyes open—fortunate because it is the closed eye, the dreaming eye, that leads me places I might never otherwise go."[4]

Footnote Sources:

[1] Zibby Oneal, "Author's Commentary" (publicity), Viking Press, 1982.
[2] "Meet the Author" (publicity), Delacorte.
[3] Wendy Smith, "Working Together," *Publishers Weekly*, February 21, 1986.
[4] Z. Oneal, "*In Summer Light*," *Horn Book*, January-February, 1987.

■ For More Information See

Reader's Digest, August, 1975 (p. 43ff).
Best Sellers, April, 1980 (p. 39).

New York Times Book Review, April 27, 1980 (p. 52ff), November 14, 1982 (p. 48), November 24, 1985 (p. 21).

Washington Post Book World, October 10, 1982 (p. 6).

Contemporary Literary Criticism, Volume 30, Gale, 1984.

Alleen Pace Nilsen and Kenneth L. Donelson, *Literature for Today's Young Adults,* Scott, Foresman, 1985.

Globe & Mail (Toronto), February 8, 1986.

New Statesman, October 10, 1986.

Times Literary Supplement, October 30, 1987.

Gerald J. Senick, editor, *Children's Literature Review,* Volume 13, Gale, 1987.

Sally Holmes Holtze, *Sixth Book of Junior Authors and Illustrators,* H. W. Wilson, 1989.

Gene Roddenberry

Born Eugene Wesley Roddenberry, August 19, 1921, in El Paso, Tex.; son of Eugene Edward (a master sergeant in U.S. Army) and Carolyn Glen (Golemon) Roddenberry; married Eileen Anita Rexroat, June 20, 1942 (divorced July, 1969); married Majel Barrett (an actress), August 6, 1969; children: (first marriage) Darleen R. Incopero, Dawn R. Compton; (second marriage) Eugene Wesley, Jr. *Education:* Los Angeles City College, A.A., 1941; attended University of California, Los Angeles, University of Miami, and Columbia University. *Politics:* Democrat. *Religion:* American Humanist Association. *Residence:* Beverly Hills, Calif. *Agent:* Leonard Maizlish, 10573 Pico Blvd., Suite 246, Los Angeles, Calif. 90064. *Office:* c/o Paramount Pictures, 5555 Melrose Ave., Hollywood, Calif. 90038.

■ Career

Pan American Airways, pilot, 1945-49; Los Angeles Police Department, Los Angeles, Calif., 1949-53, began as police officer, became sergeant; creator, producer, and writer of television programs and motion pictures, 1953—. President of Norway Productions, Inc. Member of board of directors, National Space Society, Los Angeles Police Band Associates. *Military service:* U.S. Army Air Corps, 1941-45; became captain; received Distinguished Flying Cross and Air Medal. *Member:* Writers Guild of America, West (past member of executive council); Science Fiction Writers of America; World Future Society; Academy of Television Arts and Sciences (former member of board of governors); American Civil Liberties Union; Caucus for Producers, Writers, and Directors; Explorers Club (New York City); Planetary Society; L-5 Society; Academy of Science Fiction, Fantasy, and Horror Films.

■ Awards, Honors

Commendation from the Civil Aeronautics Board for rescue efforts; Writers Guild of America Award for Best Teleplay of the Year, 1958, for "Helen of Abiginian," an episode of "Have Gun Will Travel"; Golden Reel Award from the Film Council of America, 1962, for "The Lieutenant," and 1966, for "Star Trek"; Special Award from the Twenty-fourth World Science Fiction Convention, 1966, for "Star Trek"; Hugo Award for Best Dramatic Presentation from the World Science Fiction Society, 1967, for "The Menagerie," and 1968, for "The City on the Edge of Forever," both episodes of "Star Trek"; Brotherhood Award from the National Association for the Advancement of Colored People (NAACP), 1967; Gold Medal from *Photoplay* for Most Popular Television Show, 1968, for "Star Trek"; Special Plaque from the Twenty-sixth World Science Fiction Convention, 1968, for "Star Trek"; Image Award from the NAACP, 1969, for "Star Trek" (television series).

D.H.L. from Emerson College, 1973; Emmy Award for Children's Entertainment Series from the Academy of Television Arts and Sciences, 1975, for animated series "Star Trek"; D.Litt., from Union College, 1977; Freedom through Knowledge Award from the National Space Club, 1979, for lifetime achievement; American Freedom Award from the National Space Club, 1980, for lifetime achievement; D.Sc. from Clarkson College, 1981; Star on Hollywood Walk of Fame, 1985; three Emmy Awards and the Peabody Award for the Best of the Best, all 1987, all for "Star Trek: The Next Generation"; Jack Benny Memorial Award for lifetime achievement from the March of Dimes, 1990.

■ Writings

(With Stephen E. Whitfield) *The Making of "Star Trek,"* Ballantine, 1968.
Star Trek—The Motion Picture, Simon & Schuster, 1980.
(With Susan Sackett) *The Making of "Star Trek: The Motion Picture,"* Simon & Schuster, 1980.

Television; Creator, Writer, and Producer:

"The Lieutenant," National Broadcasting Co. (NBC), 1960-61.
"Star Trek" (series), NBC-TV, 1966-69.
"Genesis II" (movie), CBS-TV, 1973.
"Planet Earth," ABC-TV, 1974.
"The Questor Tapes" (movie), NBC-TV, 1974.
"Spectre" (movie), NBC-TV, 1977.

Television; Creator and Executive Producer:

"Star Trek: The Next Generation" (series), Fox (for syndication), 1987.

Motion Pictures; Creator, Writer, and Producer:

"Pretty Maids All in a Row," Metro-Goldwyn-Mayer, (MGM), 1970.
"Star Trek: The Motion Picture," Paramount, 1979.

Motion Pictures; Executive Consultant:

"Star Trek II: The Wrath of Khan," Paramount, 1982.
"Star Trek III: The Search for Spock," Paramount, 1984.
"Star Trek IV: The Voyage Home," Paramount, 1986.
"Star Trek V: The Final Frontier," Paramount, 1989.

Also author of over eighty scripts for television programs, including "Goodyear Theater," "The Kaiser Aluminum Hour," "Chevron Theater," "Four Star Theater," "Dragnet," "The Jane Wyman Theater," "Naked City," and "Have Gun Will Travel." Contributor of articles to aeronautical magazines, and of poetry to *Embers* and *New York Times.* Poems included in anthologies.

■ Adaptations

"Star Trek" (animated cartoon series), NBC-TV, September 8, 1973-August 30, 1975.

"Star Trek" Series; Videocassettes:

"Star Trek I" ("The Menagerie"), RCA VideoDiscs.
"Star Trek II" ("The City on the Edge of Forever" and "Let That Be Your Last Battlefield"), RCA VideoDiscs.
"Star Trek III" ("The Trouble with Tribbles" and "The Tholian Web"), RCA VideoDiscs.
"Star Trek IV" ("Space Seed" and "The Changeling") RCA VideoDiscs.
"Star Trek V" ("Mirror, Mirror" and "Balance of Terror"), RCA VideoDiscs.
"Star Trek: Space Seed," Paramount Home Video.
"Star Trek: A Taste of Armageddon," Paramount Home Video.
"Star Trek: Amok Time," Paramount Home Video.
"Star Trek: Arena," Paramount Home Video.
"Star Trek: Balance of Terror," Paramount Home Video.
"Star Trek: Catspaw," Paramount Home Video.
"Star Trek: Charlie X," Paramount Home Video.
"Star Trek: Court Martial," Paramount Home Video.
"Star Trek: Dagger of the Mind," Paramount Home Video.
"Star Trek: Errand of Mercy," Paramount Home Video.
"Star Trek: Friday's Child," Paramount Home Video.
"Star Trek: I, Mudd," RCA VideoDiscs.
"Star Trek: Journey to Babel," Paramount Home Video.
"Star Trek: Metamorphosis," Paramount Home Video.
"Star Trek: Miri," Paramount Home Video.
"Star Trek: Mirror, Mirror," Paramount Home Video.
"Star Trek: Mudd's Women," Paramount Home Video.

"Star Trek: Operation Annihilate," Paramount Home Video.

"Star Trek: Shore Leave," Paramount Home Video.

"Star Trek: The Alternative Factor," Paramount Home Video.

"Star Trek: The Apple," Paramount Home Video.

"Star Trek: The Changeling," Paramount Home Video.

"Star Trek: The City on the Edge of Forever," Paramount Home Video.

"Star Trek: The Conscience of the King," Paramount Home Video.

"Star Trek: The Corbomite Maneuver," Paramount Home Video.

"Star Trek: The Deadly Years," Paramount Home Video.

"Star Trek: The Devil in the Dark," Paramount Home Video.

"Star Trek: The Doomsday Machine," Paramount Home Video.

"Star Trek: The Enemy Within," Paramount Home Video.

"Star Trek: The Galileo Seven," Paramount Home Video.

"Star Trek: The Man Trap," Paramount Home Video.

"Star Trek: The Menagerie Parts I and II," Paramount Home Video.

"Star Trek: The Naked Time," Paramount Home Video.

"Star Trek: The Return of the Archons," Paramount Home Video.

"Star Trek: The Squire of Gothos," Paramount Home Video.

"Star Trek: This Side of Paradise," Paramount Home Video.

"Star Trek: Tomorrow Is Yesterday," Paramount Home Video.

"Star Trek: What Are Little Girls Made Of?," Paramount Home Video.

"Star Trek: Where No Man Has Gone Before," Paramount Home Video.

"Star Trek: Who Mourns for Adonais," Paramount Home Video.

"Star Trek: A Piece of the Action," Paramount Home Video.

"Star Trek: A Private Little War," Paramount Home Video.

"Star Trek: By Any Other Name," Paramount Home Video.

"Star Trek: Obsession," Paramount Home Video.

"Star Trek: Patterns of Force," Paramount Home Video.

"Star Trek: Return to Tomorrow," Paramount Home Video.

"Star Trek: The Cage," Paramount Home Video.

"Star Trek: The Gamesters of Triskelion," Paramount Home Video.

"Star Trek: The Immunity Syndrome," Paramount Home Video.

"Star Trek: The Trouble with Tribbles," Paramount Home Video.

"Star Trek: Wolf in the Fold," Paramount Home Video.

"Star Trek: All Our Yesterdays," Paramount Home Video.

"Star Trek: Day of the Dove," Paramount Home Video.

"Star Trek: Elaan of Troyius," Paramount Home Video.

"Star Trek: For the World Is Hollow and I Have Touched the Sky," Paramount Home Video.

"Star Trek: Let That Be Your Last Battlefield," Paramount Home Video.

"Star Trek: Plato's Stepchildren," Paramount Home Video.

"Star Trek: Requiem for Methuselah," Paramount Home Video.

"Star Trek: The Cloud Minders," Paramount Home Video.

"Star Trek: The Empath," Paramount Home Video.

"Star Trek: The Lights of Zetar," Paramount Home Video.

"Star Trek: The Mark of Gideon," Paramount Home Video.

"Star Trek: The Savage Curtain," Paramount Home Video.

"Star Trek: The Tholian Web," Paramount Home Video.

"Star Trek: The Way to Eden," Paramount Home Video.

"Star Trek: Turnabout Intruder," Paramount Home Video.

"Star Trek: Whom Gods Destroy," Paramount Home Video.

"Star Trek: Wink of an Eye," Paramount Home Video.

"Star Trek Volume 1" ("The Menagerie"), Paramount Home Video.

"Star Trek Volume 2" ("Amok Time" and "Journey to Babel"), Paramount Home Video.

The original crew of the Starship *Enterprise*.

"Star Trek Volume 3" ("Mirror, Mirror" and "The Tholian Web"), Paramount Home Video.

"Star Trek Volume 4" ("The Trouble with Tribbles" and "Let That Be Your Last Battlefield"), Paramount Home Video.

"Star Trek Volume 5" ("Balance of Terror" and "The City on the Edge of Forever"), Paramount Home Video.

"Star Trek Volume 6," Paramount Home Video.

"Star Trek Volume 7," Paramount Home Video.

"Star Trek Volume 8," Paramount Home Video.

"Star Trek Volume 9," Paramount Home Video.

"Star Trek Volume 10," Paramount Home Video.

"Star Trek Volume 11" ("A Taste of Armageddon" and "Space Seed"), Paramount.

"Star Trek Volume 12" ("The Devil in the Dark" and "Errand of Mercy"), Paramount.

"Star Trek Volume 13" ("The Alternative Factor" and "The City on the Edge of Forever"), Paramount.

"Star Trek Volume 14" ("Operation—Annihilate!" and "Amok Time"), Paramount.

"Star Trek Volume 15" ("Who Mourns for Adonais?" and "The Changeling"), Paramount.

"Star Trek Animated Series," Paramount Home Video.

"Star Trek" Motion Pictures; Videocassettes:

"Star Trek: The Motion Picture," Paramount Home Video.

"Star Trek II: The Wrath of Khan," Paramount Home Video.

"Star Trek III: The Search for Spock," Paramount Home Video.

"Star Trek IV: The Voyage Home," Paramount Home Video.

"Star Trek V: The Final Frontier," Paramount Home Video.

Roddenberry (behind Uhura), film crew, and cast on the set of "Star Trek III."

■ Sidelights

Gene Roddenberry spent his boyhood in Los Angeles and was educated at L.A. City College and U.C.L.A. During World War II he served in the Army Air Corps as a second lieutenant, flying B-17 bombers out of Guadalcanal. During this time he began selling stories to flying magazines. As a civilian he flew for Pan Am, and briefly ran an import-export business before his stint with the L.A. Police Department.

Throughout the years, he wrote and produced several television programs and motion pictures. "I think that the purpose of all writing is to reach people and say something you believe in and think is important. You may do it as a scientific or philosophical tract, but with fiction and drama and a certain amount of adventure you reach them easier and you reach more of them and you can infiltrate your messages into them. I think people forget too often that literature—usually fiction—is responsible for more changes in public opinion

than news articles or sermons. An excellent example of this is *Uncle Tom's Cabin*—actually it's not a very good book—which probably did more to propel us into the Civil War than any other writing of the time. So historically this has been true of literature and whether we like it or not, television is literature. It may not be very good literature usually, but of course not everything that is printed is very good, either.

"I'm a storyteller. And producing is merely an extension of the storytelling function. There's no difference between writing that 'he spoke slowly, uncertainly, unsure of himself' and being a director who makes sure the actor does it that way, or being the producer who hires an actor who is capable of doing it that way.

"When I first began writing, and I think many beginning writers go through this, I felt that the director and the producer and the actors were the enemy. They took, it seemed to me, these priceless visions I had in my head, these lovely, lovely sonnets that I had written and put them on the screen and destroyed them. Or warped them. As I became a more and more professional writer I began to realize that actors and directors indeed were taking some fairly average things that I had done and were making them very much better. So the longer you're in the business, the longer you're in television and film, the more you begin to respect all of the creative levels for what each of them brings to it. I had some strange ideas about Hollywood when I first came here. I had read these stories of the orgies and the pink Cadillacs and the flaming passions that erupt on set and all of that. But actually television and most independent motion picture production people are a group of very hardworking, dedicated, sensible people. This is not to say that we don't have our moods and arguments and disagreements, and often violent ones. But I think probably no more than take place at the top echelon of U.S. Steel or Prudential Life Insurance Company. Naturally people that care have strong feelings."[1]

In 1964, Roddenberry developed a pilot for television entitled "The Cage." He had envisioned it as a kind of "Wagon Train" or "Gunsmoke" in outer space. "The Cage," starred Jeffrey Hunter as Captain Christopher Pike, whose second in command was played by Majel Barrett, an old friend of Roddenberry's who was later to become his second wife. "'The Cage' was turned down in 1964 and the reasons were these: too cerebral, not enough action and adventure. 'The Cage' didn't end with a chase and a right cross to the jaw, the way all manly films were supposed to end. There were no female leads then—women in those days were just set dressing. So, another thing they felt was wrong with our film was that we had Majel as a female second-in-command of the vessel. It's nice now, I'm sure, for the ladies to say, 'Well, the men did it.' But in the test reports, the women in the audience were saying, 'Who does she think she is?' They hated her. It is hard to believe that in twenty years, we have gone from a totally sexist society to where we are today—where all intelligent people certainly accept sexual equality.

"We also had what they called 'a childish concept'–an alien with pointy ears from another planet. People in those days were not talking about life forms on other worlds. It was generally assumed by most sensible people that this is the place where life occurred and probably nowhere else. It would have been all right if this alien with pointy ears, this 'silly creature,' had the biggest zap gun in existence, or the strength of 100 men, that could be exciting. But his only difference from

the others was he had an alien perspective on emotion and logic. And that didn't make television executives jump up and yell, 'Yippee!'

"At that time, space travel was considered nonsense. It wasn't until we were off the air three months that man landed on the Moon and minds were changed all over. The Talosian planet's 'ridiculous' premise of mind control annoyed a great many people and the objection, of course, overlooks the fact that the most serious threat we face today in our world is mind control—such as not too long ago exercised by Hitler, and what's now exercised by fanatical religions all over the world and even here in our own country. Mind control is a dangerous subject for TV to discuss because the yuppies may wake up someday and be discussing it and say, 'Well wait a minute, television may be the most powerful mind control force of all,' and may begin taking a very close look at television. And so most executives would like to avoid that *possibility*.

"It took me a second pilot to start 'Star Trek.' And after they removed the female second-in-command, I told Majel, 'We really want to keep you on the show, and if we could change your name, your look, your hair and everything, we'll put you in as a nurse.' And she didn't want to be a nurse. It's hard, you know, after you're second-in-command and a co-star. So, I tried to figure out how I could get her to take the part, and I said, 'Majel, I'll promise you something: this nurse is in love with Mr. Spock.' And she said, 'Sounds kind of interesting.' I think she has always been sweet on Leonard. I double-crossed her though, I never told her until the series was on the air that Vulcans come in heat only once every seven years. The second pilot ('Where No Man Has Gone Before') seemed to have great concepts: humans turning into gods. But they were nice safe gods, gods who go 'Zap! You're punished.' Kind of like the guys you see on those Sunday morning shows.

"Anyway, the biggest factor in selling the second pilot was that it ended up in a hell of a fist fight with the villain suffering a painful death. Then, once we got 'Star Trek' on the air, we began infiltrating a few of our ideas, the ideas. . .folks have all celebrated. 'Star Trek' fans are people who are ready for 23rd century dreams now. And I wish to God our leaders could catch up with them.

"'Trek' means walking, voyaging. And the name 'Star Trek' really means voyaging from star to star. I knew it was the right title because when I first

The 1982 Paramount movie "Star Trek II: The Wrath of Khan" featured Kirstie Alley as Saavik.

mentioned it to the network executives, they said, 'We don't like it.'"[2]

"I made 'Star Trek' for two reasons. One was that I thought science fiction hadn't been done well on television and it seemed to me, from a purely selfish, career point of view, that if I did it well I would be remembered. I suppose if a Western or a police story hadn't been done to my satisfaction I might have done that, too. The second reason is that I thought with science fiction I might do what Jonathan Swift did when he wrote *Gulliver's Travels*. He lived in a time when you could lose your head for making religious and political comments. I was working in a medium, television, which is heavily censored, and in contemporary shows I found I couldn't talk about sex, politics, religion,

and all of the other things I wanted to talk about. It seemed to me that if I had things happen to little polka-dotted people on a far-off planet I might get past the network censors, as Swift did in his day. And indeed that's what we did."[1]

"Science fiction wasn't popular. Hardly anyone in the networks or studios read science fiction. They thought science fiction was a terrible idea. I was able to get it started because I had gone to Desilu, where they hadn't sold a single pilot for about seven years. They had tried everything. I think they finally reached a point where they said, 'Oh hell, we'll even try Roddenberry's crazy idea.'"[3]

Roddenberry's "crazy idea" debuted as a television series on September 8, 1966. The developing U.S. space programs made space exploration more

Christopher Lloyd is the villain, Kurge, in "Star Trek III: The Search for Spock," Paramount, 1984.

William Shatner and Leonard Nimoy demonstrate comedic byplay in the 1986 Paramount movie "Star Trek IV: The Voyage Home."

realistic and appealing, and Roddenberry gave the program a pioneering theme which evoked America's history and myths about exploring the unknown.

The cast included William Shatner and Leonard Nimoy as Captain Kirk and Mr. Spock, respectively, with DeForest Kelley as Dr. McCoy, and Majel Barrett as Chapel, the nurse. "The reason for the creation of the three main characters—Captain Kirk, Dr. McCoy, and Mr. Spock—was that one thing you don't have in film literature that you do have in novels is stream of consciousness. In a novel you can get inside the character's mind and you can read, 'He thinks, "Well should I do this or that, and there's this to say on this side and there's something else to say on the other side."'" So in 'Star Trek' the Captain would say, 'Which way shall we face up to this threat?' And Spock would say, 'Well, from the logical point of view we'll do this.' The doctor would say, 'As a man of action I'm bound by my orders.' They could have the whole

discussion right there that in the novel would have been stream of consciousness.

"There are certain principles that I have and that other writers have that they will not violate even to get a show on the air. I don't like too much violence. I refuse to have the future run by the United States of America because I don't think that's the way it will be. I refuse to have an all lily-white, Anglo-Saxon crew. And I think if they had said, 'This ship really has to be an instrument of the CIA of the future, of keeping the galaxies safe for democracy,' I certainly would have said, 'You can shelve the whole project.'

"If there was one theme in all of 'Star Trek' it was that the glory of our universe is its infinite combinations of diversity. That all beauty comes out of its diversity. What a terrible, boring world it would be if everyone agreed with everyone else. And if there weren't different shapes and colors and ideas. When we are truly wise—and my test for a wise human is when they take a positive delight when someone says, 'I disagree with you because....' My God, what an opportunity this opens for dialogue, discussion, learning.

"I get a huge charge out of doing a 'Star Trek' episode that demonstrates that petty nationalism must go if we're to survive and so on. Although there are certainly many network executives who are moral men, who give to charities and raise their children decently, and who worry about these things too, this is not the main thrust of their jobs. Since they belong to a corporation, the main thrust of their jobs is to produce so many viewers for each sponsor and to turn a profit to the stockholders every year. So many of the arguments and fights that we have with them come out of just two different viewpoints, two different goals. I suppose that if writer/producers could have their way totally, I would try to do lovely things that would maybe attract an audience of two million people instead of the necessary eighteen million, and the network, of course, would go broke.

"The way you win in this game is you must be unimaginably stubborn and keep doing it over and over again, hoping that the break comes and the way you get your break is you have to be unimaginably lucky. If you're a writer or you like storytelling as a producer or director, whatever, probably the worst place you can start is in television. Because your chances are so few."[1]

"If I were to start all over again now, I would try to begin in paperback books, areas like that where you have a much better chance. Eventually, if you're good, you'll get to television. But television's impossible—you probably could win the Irish Sweepstakes easier than you could go out and get a job in television. I had figured that I had an even chance because I'm even more stubborn than the next guy, and I figured I would write it, rewrite it twenty times until I got it right. Terrible, terrible ordeal."[2]

"Star Trek" did not have good ratings, and it was only the tremendous support of the fans that kept it on the air for three seasons. Roddenberry felt that one of the reasons for its failure was that too much of the project was delegated. "As long as the original creator stays with the show, it gives it a certain unity. When other minds become involved, it's not that they are lesser minds or not as clever writers, but you lose the unity of that one driving force.

"But I had no choice. The only way I could get people like Gene Coon to come in and produce—and I needed a producer, more helping hands—

was to become executive producer, actually a supervising producer. Today, it would be different. No one would object to a very complex show having two, three, or even four line producers with a supervising producer over them. In those days, it was unheard of, but I just *had* to get some extra people in any way I could. I had found myself working twelve or fourteen hours a day and I could no longer do it. Everyone on our staff was in the hospital at least once during those three years just from total exhaustion. We were doing half a science-fiction movie every week. Imagine what a burden that is. Science-fiction movies usually take twenty weeks to do. We were doing one every week!"[3]

Roddenberry quit the show in the third season to protest the time slot the network had given "Star Trek." "The first year we were on at 8:30 P.M. on Thursdays. If we'd kept that time slot and evening I think our ratings would have slowly built because we built them all through that year. The second year, though, they put us on Friday, at 9 o'clock, which was a bad time. Our ratings dropped again. We slowly, all year, fought to build them back up again. NBC was going to cancel us and then the fans protested, had marches all over the country, sent in over a million letters, and they put us on for a third year, but then they gave us Friday at ten o'clock, which is even worse. But it was the first time the fans had ever forced a network to keep a show on the air. But I went to the network and said, 'If you'll give us a decent time slot, I'll come back and personally produce the show.' I was at the time executive producer. 'And not only that, I will guarantee to work as I've never worked before to really make the show a hit.' And they said, 'Fine. We'd like you to come back and oversee it. Become the producer again and we'll give you Monday at seven,' I believe it was. A great time slot. And so I proceeded to prepare for the next season. But as they began to line up their schedules, a show came along called 'Laugh-In' that they felt they had a big bid on, and so they said, 'We're going to put "Laugh-In" there and we're going to give you Friday night at ten.'

"Well I knew this was death for the show. When you bargain with a network you have to use the only clout you have, the only single thing I had was agreeing to personally produce the show. And so, in an attempt to force them to give us some time period that would work, I said, 'I will not personally produce a show if you put it on Friday night at ten o'clock. There's just too much labor and effort and ultimate disappointment. If you do that I will

From the 1989 Paramount movie "Star Trek V: The Final Frontier."

stay executive producer. And, in fact, knowing that it's going to die, I'll be spending part of my time lining up what I'm going to do in the following year.' As it turned out, the network elected to keep us on at that time. And having made this threat, I felt that I had to stay true to my word, otherwise how could I, in the future, ever again make a bargain from any position of strength? It turned out it wasn't such a position of strength because they left it there."[1]

Roddenberry examined the reasons for the show's continued popularity. "First, we had real heroes, almost old-fashioned heroes, people who believed in their work, believed in honor, who believed that things must be done even at the cost of great danger and sometimes your life. Second, 'Star Trek' was an optimistic show that said, 'There is a future for us humans, the human adventure is just beginning.' In a time when so many people were saying 'In twenty or thirty years, it's all gonna go boom,' it was a breath of fresh air to turn on the TV and hear them say, 'Hey! We've just begun. Most of our adventures are ahead of us.' It's that spirit of optimism.

"And third, 'Star Trek' stories are *about* something. They aren't inane-running around with sound and fury and bang, bang car chases, things

that add to nothing. One of our very, very early ones, the Horta story ('The Devil in the Dark'), made a very strong statement—that just because something is ugly doesn't mean it is bad or dangerous. Every episode makes a statement of some sort. And people are hungry for statements."[3]

"Star Trek" went off the air in 1969 and Roddenberry was out of work. "It was a hard time for me. I was perceived as the guy who made the show that was an expensive flop, and I couldn't get work. Thank God, college kids discovered the show because I made enough money lecturing to pay the mortgage."[4]

In 1973, Roddenberry wrote "Genesis II" a movie for television which starred Mariette Hartley and Alex Cord. A twentieth-century NASA scientist is buried in suspended animation until he is resuscitated in the future. "Our civilization as we know it had been destroyed. It had fallen apart. It had not been, however, due to nuclear warfare. Really, nuclear warfare is not necessary to cause a breakdown of society. You take larger cities like Los Angeles, New York, Chicago—their water supply comes from hundreds of miles away and any interruption of that, or food, or power, for any period of time and you're going to have riots in the streets.

"Our society is so fragile, so dependent on the interworking of things to provide us with goods and services, that you don't need nuclear warfare to fragment us any more than the Romans needed it to cause their eventual downfall. It's important to know that I wasn't saying that 'Star Trek's' future, which would occur several hundred years after 'Genesis II,' never happened; I'm saying that humanity has always progressed by three steps forward and two steps back. The entire history of our civilization has been one society crumbling and a slightly better one, usually, being built on top of it. And on mankind's bumpy way to the 'Star Trek' era, we passed through this time, too.

"'Gensis II' we almost sold. CBS had it pencilled into their schedule. Fred Silverman had seen 'Planet of the Apes' and he thought the monkeys were so cute that he cancelled doing 'Genesis II' and decided to go for the monkeys. Several of us tried to warn him that it was a one-time joke. He didn't listen and it was a disaster and cost them many millions of dollars. It's a pity, too, because 'Genesis II' had the makings of a very exciting show. It had one thing in common with 'Star Trek' and that was that you could bring in a good writer and say to him, 'What bothers you about the world?' then go and invent a place in this new world and have it happening there. It's a tragedy that opportunities like this to do exciting things and to talk about exciting things are pulled out by the roots by business executives who have no desire at all to give writers, directors and actors a chance to explore and elevate the art of film and television. And it could have been more exciting than the monkeys which captured his attention, but he seemed to be incapable of looking beyond and seeing the potential of something new and different."[1]

In September, 1976, the first U.S. space shuttle was named *Enterprise* (after the spaceship in "Star Trek") by President Ford over the objections of NASA administrator John Fletcher. Roddenberry was at the launch.

In 1979 "Star Trek" was made into a movie, "Star Trek: The Motion Picture," directed by Robert Wise and starring the original television cast. "I had been arguing with the studio for seven years, saying 'Star Trek' could make a huge success as a movie. They kept saying, 'You're crazy! Science fiction doesn't work. The mass audience does not like SF.' When 'Star Wars' came out, they suddenly got very excited. They said, 'Wow, we were wrong.' Well, they never said they were *wrong*. They just said, 'Wow, we've got "Star Trek," let's

go with it.' Then, they wanted to go with it too fast."[3]

"I guess my biggest fear was that it would not be 'Star Trek.' I knew I couldn't go into a major picture with a fine director like Robert Wise and say to him, 'Don't change *anything*.' But at the same time, we had to ask ourselves, 'What are the things that made "Star Trek" what it was that we *don't* want to change?' That was a very tenuous and narrow path to walk, but I think we've done it successfully.

"Almost from the beginning we decided that we wanted to keep our characters intact; because we felt that in a time when the anti-hero seems most popular, we wanted to keep the old-fashioned type of heroes—people with great integrity. I personally feel that people tend to do what they see; and if you make integrity fashionable, I think maybe we could get rid of a lot of our problems.

"Bob Wise and I both believed that a story ought to be about people; and it doesn't matter whether it's set in the future, or in the past, or in the present. So we've put the same amount of effort into the movie as we did in the television show to make sure that the crew are alive. We didn't design this picture as a vehicle for spectacular opticals....If you believe that there are real people there and can identify with them, then you can believe the rest."[5]

Roddenberry served as executive consultant for the film. "I invented the term 'executive story consultant,' and set the rules: That they have to show me everything they do...from the first lines (through) all the rewrites and the dailies.

"I can comment, but the rule I make for myself is that they have no obligation to do what I tell them to do.

"If (Captain Kirk and company) land on a planet and they start zapping things because they're ugly, then that's the day I call a press conference and announce my way out."[6]

"When we had a press meeting to announce that we were going to make a 'Star Trek: The Motion Picture,' there was a table over there and when they introduced me, the applause just kept going on and on at this one table, and I looked over and I finally recognized the people there—all the second level actors, the dear people who really held the show together. Not that the stars were not fine people, but these people understood and cared. And, wow, that was a moment, that was a chill moment."[2]

The movie was a tremendous success, earning almost twelve million in its first three days. In the same year, Roddenberry, with his executive assistant, Susan Sacket wrote a book entitled *The Making of Star Trek: The Motion Picture.*

Two years later, "Star Trek II: The Wrath of Khan" appeared, directed by Nicholas Meyer with Roddenberry as executive consultant. It earned close to fifteen million in its first three days. "I think it was an exciting picture. I had many problems with it though. I thought they were very lucky they had the actor they did in Ricardo Montalban to play Khan, since it was not a well-written part. 'I will chase you through the moons of Jupiter' and so on, in the hands of almost any other actor would have gotten snickers from the audience. Montalban saved their ass. Khan was not written as that exciting a character, he was rather flimsy. The Khan in the TV episode was a much deeper and better character than the movie Khan, except that Montalban pulled it off.

"I also objected to other little things. Remember when the eel came out of Chekov's ear? What did Kirk do? He had a look of disgust on his face and grabbed his phaser and went 'zap.' Now, how dare he destroy a life form that had never been seen before! It needs studying. They had him act like an old woman trampling on a tarantula. Now that's not the Kirk we built up for three years. So many of those fine little things in the episodes, hundreds of them, are what gave 'Star Trek' its quality. Unfortunately, they began doing those things incorrectly in that movie. There was also a great deal of violence. But yes, it was exciting—exciting photographically. I'm grateful that it did what it did."[3]

"Star Trek III: The Search for Spock" was directed by Leonard Nimoy, as was "Star Trek IV: The Voyage Home." Roddenberry again consulted with both movies. "Emotionally ['Star Trek III'] was the best, and, it used *all* of our characters—our band of brothers and one sister—really for the *first* time.

"What I want is a final say where I can be sure no future producer or director will have them land on a planet and start zapping creatures because they look ugly or different. I write them memos about how they should do it, and over a period of time, they're beginning to accept more and more of them. There seems to be a feeling now that, 'Hey, wait! Maybe "Star Trek" is a legend because someone did something right. Maybe we should consider a little more seriously the things he suggests.'"[3]

The cast of the 1987 television series, "Star Trek: The Next Generation."

Roddenberry became executive producer for a new television series, "Star Trek: The Next Generation" which debuted in October, 1987. The new program is set seventy-eight years into the future of the original series. New characters including Captain Jean-Luc Picard, Commander William Riker, Lieutenant Commander Data, and Counselor Deanna Troi were introduced. The old enemies, the Klingons, were now members of the Federation and a new starship *Enterprise* was designed. "When Paramount came to me. . .and asked me to do the sequel, I said absolutely not, no way. The first show took too much out of me. I didn't see my family for two years. It was only when the Paramount people agreed with me and said a sequel was probably impossible anyway that my interest was piqued."[4]

He couldn't resist the offer to air the program on independent television stations which limits censorship. And, after a twentieth anniversary party for the series, he agreed to produce the new series. "The philosophy of the first series was to move forward and that's what I'm doing too. I'm hopeful and optimistic that people won't be disappointed.

"The new series is an evolution of the original show. Captain Kirk, Spock and Dr. McCoy will all be legends to the new Starfleet and be remembered fondly.

"But the new crew has *new* challenges.

"'Star Trek' celebrated friendship and never doubted that man would have a future. This won't change.

"I never want to preach. But if a truth can be slipped in here and there, well, that's okay."[7]

Unfortunately, there were conflicts with some of the writers, several of whom quit over disagreements with Roddenberry. "I'm very sorry that it has happened, but I don't know any other way to do a series this complex. You have to have one point of view—you can't put it together by committee. I rewrote the first thirteen episodes of the original show also."[4]

Footnote Sources:

[1] "Star Trek's Gene Roddenberry," *Penthouse*, March, 1976.
[2] "At the Salute: Gene Roddenberry," *Starlog*, November, 1986.
[3] Ian Spelling, "Gene Roddenberry: Homeward Bound," *Starlog*, July, 1986.
[4] David Schonauer, "'Star Trek' Sails Boldly On," *New York Times*, March 27, 1988.
[5] Don Shay, "Star Trek: The Motion Picture," *Cinefantastique*, spring, 1979.
[6] "Roddenberry Reserves the Right to Comment on 'Star Trek' Pictures," *Variety*, December 17, 1986.
[7] Jill Brooke, "Sci-fi Master Moves Forward," *New York Post*, October 5, 1987.

■ For More Information See

Books:

David Gerrold, *The World of "Star Trek,"* Ballantine, 1972, reissued, Bluejay Books, 1984.
Jacqueline Lichtenberg, Sondra Marshak, and Joan Winston, *"Star Trek" Lives!*, Bantam, 1975.
Karin Blair, *Meaning in "Star Trek,"* Anima Books, 1976.
Betsy Caprio, *"Star Trek": Good News in Modern Images*, Sheed Andrews & McMeel, 1978.
Susan Sackett, Fred Goldstein, and Stan Goldstein, *'Star Trek Speaks!,'* Pocket Books, 1979.
Contemporary Literary Criticism, Volume 17, Gale, 1981.

Periodicals:

Saturday Review, June 17, 1967 (p. 46), February 2, 1980.
New York Times, October 15, 1967, August 25, 1968, February 18, 1969, June 4, 1969, January 21, 1979, November 23, 1979 (p. C12), December 8, 1979, January 14, 1980, October 9, 1980, December 23, 1981, May 23, 1982, June 8, 1982, June 27, 1982, July 4, 1982, September 8, 1982.
Popular Science, December, 1967.
Newsweek, January 29, 1968, December 19, 1979.
Show Business, May 9, 1970.
Daily News, February 16, 1973 (p. 76), August 12, 1973 (p. 17), May 27, 1981 (p. 44), October 19, 1986.
New York Post, March 15, 1973.
TV Guide, April 27, 1974 (p. 3).
Variety, August 25, 1976 (p. 38), June 12, 1985 (p. 46), October 7, 1987 (p. 70).
Journal of Popular Culture, spring, 1977 (p. 711ff), fall, 1979 (p. 310ff).
Starlog, March, 1978 (p. 25ff), November, 1980 (p. 43ff), October, 1981 (p 36ff), January, 1983, March, 1986 (p. 9).
Time, January 15, 1979, December 17, 1979, June 7, 1982, April 18, 1988.
Daniel L. Smith, "The Voyage of Starship Enterprise," *Saturday Evening Post*, May, 1979.
Science Fiction and Fantasy Book Review, December, 1979 (p. 151ff).
Science Digest, December, 1979.
Detroit News Magazine, December 9, 1979.
Cincinnati Enquirer, December 16, 1979.
New Yorker, December 17, 1979 (p. 167ff), June 28, 1982.
New York, December 24, 1979, June 21, 1982.
New Republic, December 29, 1979.
Christian Century, January 16, 1980, August 18-25, 1982.
Washington Post Book World, January 27, 1980.
Progressive, March, 1980 (p. 52ff).
Stereo Review, March, 1980 (p. 130).
VOYA, April, 1980, August, 1980.
School Library Journal, May, 1980 (p. 71).

Best of Starlog, Volume 2, 1981.
Maclean's, June 14, 1982.
Rolling Stone, July 22, 1982, September 2, 1982,
   December 3, 1987 (p. 42).
Nation, August 21-28, 1982.
USA Today, September 1982.

Film (London), September, 1984 (p. 3).
Futurist, February, 1985 (p. 39).
People Weekly, March 16, 1987 (p. 111ff).
Video, September, 1987 (p. 74ff).
Analog, November, 1988 (p. 158).

Aranka Siegal

Born June 10, 1930, in Beregszasz, Czechoslovakia; came to the United States, 1948; daughter of Ignac and Rise (Rosner) Davidowitz; married Gilbert Siegal (an attorney), February 3, 1952; children: Rise, Joseph. *Education:* Attended State University of New York College at Purchase, 1974-77; State University of New York Empire State College, B.A., 1977. *Religion:* Jewish. *Home:* 390 Carrollwood Dr., Tarrytown, N.Y. 10591. *Agent:* Jean Naggar, Jean Naggar Literary Agency, 216 East 75th St., Suite A, New York, N.Y. 10021.

■ Career

Worked as a model in Bridgeport, Conn., and New York City, 1948-51; writer, 1975—. Host of "Remembering Komjaty," a series on WBAI-Radio, New York City, 1975-76. *Member:* Authors Guild, PEN.

■ Awards, Honors

Janusz Korczak Award from B'nai B'rith Anti-Defamation League, and one of *School Library Journal*'s Best Books of the Year, both 1981, *Boston Globe-Horn Book* Award for Nonfiction, and Newbery Honor Book from the American Library Association, both 1982, Prix de L'association des Libraires Specialises Jeunesse, 1988, and Academie des Lecteurs Je Bouquine First Prize, all for *Upon the Head of the Goat; Grace in the Wilderness* was chosen one of Child Study Association of America's Children's Books of the Year, 1985, and a Notable Children's Trade Book in the Field of Social Studies by the Children's Book Council and the National Council for Social Studies, 1986.

■ Writings

Upon the Head of the Goat: A Childhood in Hungary, 1939-1944 (novel; ALA Notable Book; *Horn Book* honor list), Farrar, Straus, 1981.
Grace in the Wilderness: After the Liberation, 1945-1948, Farrar, Straus, 1985.

Upon the Head of the Goat has been published in England, France, the Netherlands, Germany, and Japan, and *Grace in the Wilderness* has been published in France and the Netherlands.

■ Adaptations

"Upon the Head of the Goat: A Childhood in Hungary, 1939-1944" (filmstrip with cassette; listening cassette), Random House, 1983.

■ Work in Progress

A novel about two generations, war-tossed by the upheaval in Europe.

■ Sidelights

Aranka Siegal was born on June 10, 1930 in Beregszasz, Czechoslovakia. Her early childhood was divided between two distinct cultures. She spent most of the year with her family enjoying the city life of Beregszasz, while summers were spent with her grandmother, Babi, in the Ukrainian farming community of Komjaty. When the borders closed at the beginning of World War II, Aranka spent a year in Komjaty unable to rejoin the rest of her family. "The open fields, the river, and the forest of this Ukrainian village became my playground. The color of the wild flowers, the feel of the forest, the sound of the water, the humming of the insects, the warmth of the animals—these experiences became the play from which I learned so much.

"What seemed strange at first—the people, their clothes and habits—quickly became familiar. Their language was Ukrainian, but Babi spoke to me in Yiddish. 'No, not Hungarian, or Ukrainian,' said Babi; 'you must learn Yiddish.' Soon I could ask questions in three languages.

"In 1939, when I was nine, the impending war in the rest of Europe still seemed far away from us and my mother had sent me to Komjaty to spend the spring holidays with Babi.

"A few days after I arrived, a major battle over disputed borders broke out between Hungary and the Ukrainian Resistance Fighters trying to hold on to their independent state. [We] could hear bursts of gunfire from the border most of the day. The women, children, and old people huddled together in their small whitewashed and straw-thatched houses. The animals had been gathered and locked in the barns. Babi sat in her chair in the kitchen, with her shawl around her, fingering the worn pages of her prayer book as her mouth moved in silent prayer.

"I was frightened and cried, wishing I were home in the safety of my own city in Hungary. Babi's house seemed small and exposed, set in the midst of her flat fields. The fence around it was only waist-high and the gates were without locks. The front porch didn't have a gate and led right to the kitchen entrance. The kitchen was the center of the house, flanked on each side by a bedroom. The larger of these served as dining and sitting room, as well as our bedroom. The guest bedroom on the other side was used mainly for storage. None of the rooms seemed very secure to me; anyone could easily enter at any time.

"'I want to go home,' I said.

"'Don't be afraid,' comforted Babi. 'Nothing bad will come to us. Our house is full of His books, and they will protect us.'

"In the morning when I awoke, I immediately went over to the window and looked out: I was curious to see if Komjaty had changed overnight under the Hungarian occupation.

"I put on my sheepskin coat and red rubber boots and went out into the woods.

"As I started. . .back to Babi's house, I could hear the loud gushing of the river and went to look at it.

"My attention was caught by a log floating toward me. As the current carried it closer, I realized that it was not a log but a body. It was a body clad in a Ukrainian uniform, face up, approaching head first. . . .The face, puffy with death, was that of a boy between eighteen and twenty.

"I saw two more soldiers in the river before I turned my back. These bodies, in the middle of the river, were being thrown from rock to rock. The bodies all had one thing in common; they were all missing hats and boots. Thinking of my stepfather, whom I had so often seen in his officer's uniform, and of my baby brother, Sandor, who would grow up to wear one, I started running again and did not stop until I reached Babi's warm kitchen.

"'They are at peace now,' she said."[1]

This was the first of countless encounters with violence Aranka would come to endure. Like her autobiographical heroine, Piri Davidowitz, in *Upon the Head of the Goat*, Aranka began to learn what it meant to be a Jew during Hitler's rise to power. "When [Babi] spoke her voice was soft. 'I should have told you all this before, Piri, but I was hoping that your generation would be spared. A Jew always hopes; it is his nature. But I am afraid that we now have another madman, that Hitler stirring up all of Europe. He marches over others' lands like a plague. . . .They've already started taking jobs away from the Jews. That's today, and tomorrow, who knows?

"'As long as there are wars they will always need scapegoats, and as long as we are here, we will be chosen.'

"My mind whirled in the confusion of trying to understand all the things Babi had said. . .pogroms, scapegoats—was this what being a Jew meant?

"Somewhere in my heart I had known that my Christian friends were different from me; that I lived in their world, not they in mine; that the laws came from their world, not mine; that school closed for Christmas and Easter, not Hanukkah and Passover. I had accepted these rules without thinking much about them, just as I accepted having to wash my face and brush my hair. The code was part of my awareness, but I did not dwell on it."[1]

When the borders reopened and train service resumed, Aranka's family traveled to Komjaty for Passover Seder. Babi tried to convince Aranka's mother, Rise, to send the children to America so that they would be safe from the impending war, but Rise could not be persuaded.

When her family returned to Beregszasz, Aranka stayed on with her grandmother in Komjaty for several months. She returned after her mother had given birth to her sixth sibling. "It was exciting to be back in Beregszasz; the big house and city people generated a kind of energy that was absent in Komjaty. My whole family turned out to welcome me at the train station.

"When school began in September, life resumed its routine for Iboya [my older sister] and me. Politics seemed remote from us all as we were kept busy with our studies in school and with our chores and projects at home.

"One day, instead of coming straight home from school, Iboya and I stopped. . .to get some notebooks. . . .It was already dusk. . . .We had reached the little synagogue on the other side of Tinodi Street when we heard loud shouting and saw several old men, prayer shawls still over their shoulders, running from the courtyard into the street. Three boys were among the men with sticks in their hands.

"'Stop,' I screamed, 'or I'll get the police.'

"Seeing us directly across the street from the synagogue, they yelled, 'There are two of those Jew girls,' and then came toward us. We started to run as fast as we could. Our schoolbags smacked against our backs, and we could hear the boys gaining on us.

"'Dumb Jew bitches, we'll pound your asses, you won't get away. Get the one with the pigtails, the one who yelled she would call the police.' They mimicked my voice. 'What police is she going to tell? As if they cared about our beating up some old Jews.'

"Just then two men stepped out of the shadows at the corner. . . .They walked into the street, putting

Jacket for the 1981 hardcover edition.

themselves between us and the three boys, but Iboya and I kept running, not even looking back to see how they stopped the boys."[1]

As conditions grew steadily worse, Babi sold part of her land to send the grandchildren to America. By the time Rise consented, it was too late to get them out. "A few days later we returned home from school [when] Mother came in. . .dressed in her best clothes. . . .She sat down heavily on one of the kitchen chairs and began to speak. 'I ran my feet off, going to all the places where people told me I could get visas to send you girls to America. People don't know what they are talking about. You can't get passage on a boat no matter what. . . .I pleaded, I cried, I tried to bribe. Nothing made an impression.'

"The spring of 1941 also brought some changes to our school routine. Instead of play during recess, we now had drills and group gymnastics like soldiers. We had to buy navy shorts and white shirts; they gave us large wooden hoops and batons, and we were taught to do tricks with them.

We learned to do push-ups, to jump through hoops, and to use the batons as swords in fencing exercises."[1]

With many runaways on the streets seeking refuge in a Jewish home, Aranka, now only eleven years old, began escorting people to a neighbor's house where Jews were cared for secretly. "I learned to recognize them from a distance. Most of them were women, some older, some younger, but their posture showed that they were refugees. Their bodies drawn in almost to a curl, they moved fast, yet hesitated a few seconds, scanning the space around them. Sometimes they asked me for help and sometimes I went over and whispered swiftly in Yiddish, 'Follow me at ten paces behind, and I will take you to shelter.' [They followed me] straight to Mrs. Silverman's [our neighbor]. She no longer asked me what I wanted when she opened her gate, but beckoned the runaway behind me in as she searched the street, and then pushed me out with a whispered, 'Be careful.'

"In the fall [of 1942], a few days before school was to open, we heard that Jewish children would no longer be permitted to attend the public schools. Mrs. Gerber [a family friend] decided to give [us] lessons in Hungarian, German, and history. Iboya and I went to her house every morning, coming home at lunchtime. We had to walk past the schoolhouse on our way home, at the time that the other children were in the yard on recess, and it felt strange looking in from the outside to see them practicing gymnastics.

"By October, the Jewish teachers, who had been barred from teaching in the public schools, opened a makeshift school in the Sunday-school room of the big synagogue on Main Street. The students in the room Iboya and I were assigned to ranged from fifth to tenth grade. The teachers at first attempted to teach all the school subjects, but soon gave up in despair and decided instead to concentrate on math, reading in Hebrew and Hungarian, and Jewish history.

"A few days after our makeshift school had started its second year, I was in the kitchen helping Mother prepare our dinner. The door opened and Iboya, drained of color and energy, came through it, a newspaper tucked under her arm. Mother put down the tray of potatoes and took the paper from her. Her back stiffened as she read the headlines.

"'Hungary is right in line with Czechoslovakia, Poland, and Germany in carrying out Hitler's orders against Jews. They are all the same, and we are all Jews, and nobody cares.' Iboya spoke in a bitter tone.

"Mother threw the paper on a chair and turned back to the potatoes. Iboya took off her jacket, hung it up, and began to set the table. I took the newspaper from the chair and opened it. 'JEWS MUST WEAR THE STAR OF DAVID.'

"The next morning, the town crier appeared at our street corner....Clearing his throat, he stretched out his neck and started to read.

"'By the end of this month, September 30, 1943, it will become mandatory for all Jews in Hungary so defined by Article 270 to wear a yellow star sewn on the left side of their outerwear. A curfew will also be in effect, Jews may not leave their homes before 10 a.m. or after 3 p.m.'

"The curfew was related to rationing, Mother explained when she returned home from the market with an empty basket. 'After 10 a.m., there is nothing left.'

"Eichmann had divided Hungary into six zones, and the first to be evacuated would be our area and the surrounding villages....A word from any one of us and we would have started to cry. It was enough just to be close to one another.

"Early the following morning, we were awakened by strange sounds of movement in our street. We came out onto the porch in our nightshirts to see our street lined with slowly moving wagons and walking refugees—mostly women....In the wagons, heaped high with bundles, rode the infants, the old, and the sick. Hungarian policemen and German soldiers with bayonets fixed to their rifles walked alongside the wagons. After watching this procession in uncomprehending silence for about fifteen minutes, Mother stopped one of the Hungarian policemen and asked, very politely, where all of these people were from and where they were being taken.

"'Jews from the villages outside of Beregszasz,' he said scornfully. 'They are being taken to the brick factory, now the ghetto.'

"'What is a ghetto?' I asked Mother.

"'It is a place for people who have been separated from the rest of the community.'"[1]

It was not long before Aranka's family was relocated. "Two young men with arm bands met us on the other side of the gate and helped us with the parcels. The younger of the two smiled at me as he bent to pick up a bundle.

"'You'll be staying in number 6,' he said.

"We followed the two men, carrying the rest of our sacks and looking at the faces of the women and few men we passed.

"We entered one of the sheds of the brickworks, but this was not the brick factory I remembered. The busy workers had been replaced by crowds of idle families....Nothing but bundles and people crowded this shed, which had no walls, only a clay-tiled roof held up by wooden pillars. People either sat on their bundles or stood around in clusters. Some of the elderly were propped up, lying on the earth floor of the shed.

"The two young men came to an empty spot on the left side of shed number 6 and dropped our bundles on the ground.

"'This area between these two posts will be your home. You'll have to confine yourselves within its boundaries. We are running out of space,' the older of the two said.

"They turned and walked away, leaving us standing there in the area, which was two and a half by three meters.

"Closing my eyes at the end of this first day in the ghetto, I told myself that the five of us were still together and that was the most important thing."[1]

Several weeks passed as the Jews were told that their stay in the ghetto would be brief, and that trains would soon be arriving to take them to Germany where they would receive better care. "Suddenly we were aware of a rustling sound around us....Throughout the barracks, people were stirring, standing up from their hunched positions and moaning as they stretched their stiff bodies.

"Iboya, Judi [my friend], and I were just walking back from our turns at the latrine when we heard the clacking sound of the train approaching the brick factory. I heard it with all of my being—not a sound, but as a total experience—and was filled with terror. A tremor shook my body. We tried to run but found ourselves planted in the ground, and as the train pulled into view, we saw that it was not the kind of train we had expected. Instead of the usual passenger cars with windows and seats, it consisted of a long line of rust-colored cars like the ones cows were loaded into. The cars of the train were tall, closed up, with only small openings near the roofs.

"'We are all God's children,' Babi used to say, meaning both Jews and Christians. Did she mean Germans, too? I wished that I could ask her. They did not look like anybody's children, and they looked not at us, but through us as if we didn't exist."[1]

Upon the Head of the Goat ends as Piri and her family board the cattle cars for transport to Auschwitz. Aranka continued her story in her second book, *Grace in the Wilderness: After the Liberation, 1945-1948*, which tells how she and Iboya survived. The two sisters had seen their mother, younger brother, and younger sister for the last time when the family arrived in Auschwitz on May 9, 1944. "I could see Mother so clearly there, in the bright sunlight. She got out of the cattle car first. Then Iboya handed down [brother] Sandor and [sister] Joli before jumping down herself. Everyone had gotten out, but I was still standing at the ledge, looking outward, wondering what kind of factory they had brought us to.

"Mother's face was exhausted as she looked up at me. '...Jump,' she called. Her voice was anguished and panic-stricken. It was a big drop. She stretched out her arms to catch me. There were hundreds of people around us, pushing and shoving, not knowing which way to go. Children were crying to be picked up, scared of being trampled.

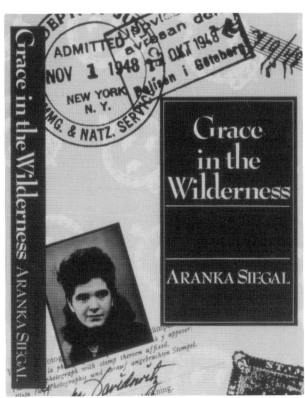

Jacket for the 1985 Farrar, Straus edition.

"Male prisoners tried to organize us. One came over and, speaking Yiddish, asked how old I was. 'Thirteen,' I said.

"'Nein, nein!' he said, 'Du bist sechzehn [16].' Turning to Iboya, he repeated the question. When she said she was sixteen, he told her to say she was seventeen, and rushed over to some other teenagers.

"A woman with a shrill voice was shouting orders through a megaphone in Hungarian with a German accent: 'Men to the right—women and children to the left; keep the lines moving.' The five of us stayed together. 'Don't be alarmed. This is a temporary separation. You will be reunited on Sunday.'

"I walked along bewildered, not noticing that the lines in front of us were being divided, till we faced four SS men. One of them held an officer's baton. Another asked Iboya and me our age. We replied as we had been warned. The one with the baton extended his arm like a fencer's and let it fall between Mother and the two little ones, pushing them away from her. Mother stood petrified while seconds passed. Then, leaving us, she rushed to pick up Joli and took Sandor by the hand. 'They need me more,' she told the hostile and annoyed SS man with the stick. Turning to us, her eyes murky, she said, 'Be brave and look after each other.' It was her last act as our mother, setting an example to last us a lifetime."[2]

In September of 1944, Aranka and Iboya left Auschwitz for the concentration camp at Christianstadt where the inmates worked in a munitions factory. "Our last day in Auschwitz...during the selection, Iboya was picked as part of a transport to go to Christianstadt and I was left back with the discards—the weak and the sick no longer fit for work. At the last minute, as the transport was moving toward the bathhouse, we spotted Mrs. Berger, a friend of mother's from Beregszasz, who was returning from her work as a sorter of clothing. This was a very privileged work detail—she wore a white kerchief to set herself apart. Sometimes she found food among the belongings of the new arrivals and would share it with us, as on this occasion.

"Secretly passing a small parcel to Iboya in the moving line, she asked why Iboya was crying.

"'We have been separated; Piri is over there.' Iboya pointed to where I stood crying convulsively.

"Mrs. Berger looked around and, in the flash of a second, managed a miracle. With one hand, she pulled a crying mother out of the transport and deposited her back with her daughter, while with her other hand, she swung me over into the moving line. I slowly worked my way up toward Iboya as inconspicuously as possible, controlling my relief and joy at being reunited. Even when I was finally alongside her, trying to keep up the pace five abreast, I only communicated silently with my puffy eyes.

"Not till the lines were halted outside the bathhouse, to wash away the soot of Auschwitz before our departure, did we dare to speak. Iboya reached out and took my hand. 'We are leaving this godforsaken place together.'"[2]

They remained in Christianstadt until January 1945 when the Russians were rapidly approaching, and the Germans forced them to walk to Bergen-Belsen. The journey took until the beginning of March. On April 19, 1945, Bergen-Belsen was liberated by Field Marshal Montgomery's First Army. "We were awakened by distant gunfire. With a burst of new found energy, we rushed out in the dim light to watch the exchange of fire between the fleeing Germans and the approaching British army. I ran up to the gate, praying that this would be the end of our imprisonment. Male prisoners filtered in through the clusters of women, some speaking excitedly, others crying. A few stood repeating the Shema—'Hear, O Israel, the Lord our God, the Lord is One'—not in the traditional way of prayer, but in demanding voices, calling on God to witness the confrontation with their despairing, wasted women.

"The men looked worse than we did. They shouted over one another, telling us who they were, asking where we were from. Husbands, sons, brothers, fathers. They were looking for Hana, Sara, Frida, Bella, Samu, Fage....The names were endless.

"Exhausted, I sat down propped against the south wall of the barrack while Iboya went off talking with some people. The April morning sun felt warm, and I dozed off. Toward midafternoon, I was awakened by a tumultuous uproar. The first British tanks approached our gate. They were halted by the mass of prisoners that ran to greet them. I joined the welcomers.

"Under their flat caps the eyes and faces of the soldiers registered shock and horror as they stood in the tanks and looked us over. Many hands reached toward them and voices begged for food. English, German, Hungarian, Polish, Dutch, Czech, Romanian, and other languages blended in the shouting.

"We. . .watched the camp fill with soldiers. Some of them had cameras and took pictures. Then they discovered the stacks of corpses behind the barracks and brought out movie cameras. When the Germans realized they were losing the war, they had stopped hiding their victims.

"Iboya and I lined up with the groups in front of the ten-foot-high stacks being filmed. I hoped that I would be discovered by a lost member of our family. A Yiddish-speaking English soldier who asked us questions said, 'This film will be shown in newsreels, so the world will know what has taken place.' He was crying. 'My dear children, your suffering must be known.'

"I was gratified by his emotion, and a new feeling surfaced inside me—a sense of importance, that we mattered to the outside world. My eyes welled with tears and suddenly I was sobbing. The soldier came over and embraced me, taking no notice of my dirty appearance and lice-infested clothes. He asked my name.

"He searched his pockets for something to give me. Finding only cigarettes, he took the whistle from around his neck and hung it on mine."[2]

That evening Aranka became terribly ill after eating rich food. "By morning I was too weak to stand up. Iboya carried me over to the door so I could get some air, then went in search of help. She came back dragging a medic and pleading, 'My sister is dying. You must take her or it will be too late.'

"The soldier checked my pulse and marked my forehead with a red cross. As soon as he turned his head, Iboya knelt down beside me. She moistened the red mark with spittle and pressed her forehead like a blotter over mine. 'I'm not going to let them separate us now,' she whispered. When they came to put me on a stretcher, she lay down on it alongside me."[2]

In the Red Cross ward, Aranka suffered from typhoid, dysentery, and malnutrition. Iboya unsuccessfully attempted to track down the other family members, but when no one could be found and Aranka's health had improved, the sisters were sent to Sweden with the Red Cross. "It was just after my fifteenth birthday, toward the middle of June, when the Red Cross lady reappeared. Iboya and I were still in bed. Leaning against the washstand dividing our beds, she announced, 'You will be starting your journey for Sweden right after breakfast.'

"We both sat up, wide awake.

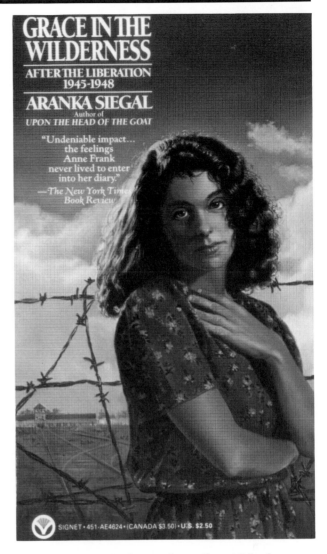

Paperbound edition of Siegal's 1985 book.

"'What is Sweden like?' I asked.

"'A country not touched by war, where life will be good for you.' I could not imagine such a place."[2]

While in Sweden, they settled in Varnamo where they worked in a raincoat factory. Though the hours were long and gruelling, they were well cared for by many Swedish families. "Iboya soon got accustomed to our new schedule, but my energy would run out in midafternoon. I often got into bed as soon as we arrived home from the factory at 5:30 p.m. I had to stand on my feet all day, by a long workbench. There would be tall stacks of raincoat collars waiting for me every morning. The woman at the bench in front of mine would fold over and double the pattern given to her by the cutter, then glue them on the wrong side. My job was to run a small roller over each collar to get out the bubbles, then turn it right side out and roll it again on the outer edges so it would lie perfectly smooth when it was sewn onto the coat. After I became more skillful, I was allowed to work on sleeves and belts, rolling the glued seams and turning them right side out.

"As soon as winter approached I developed a fever and spent many weeks in the hospital. Iboya visited me every day....The doctors were so awed and fascinated by my experiences that they took turns examining me, not believing that there was nothing more wrong than my heart murmur and digestive difficulties.

"The worst of winter was over by the time I was released, and Iboya informed me that...we would be moving to Jonkoping, where we would be working in a match factory. As much as I hated to be uprooted again, I was not sorry to leave the raincoat factory with its constant fumes of rubber and glue.

"I was assigned to a machine that made boxes for wooden matches. As the boxes came off a conveyor belt, I had to pick out the bad ones and guide the rest into cases. It needed complete concentration and electric speed. If I idled for a second, the boxes would pile up, choking the machine.

"My machine and I stood in a vast room with eleven other women, each one responsible for different stages of manufacturing. There were daily fires sparked by the phosphate. Fire extinguishers were in constant use. Smoke and phosphate odor hung in the room like a permanent curtain, exceeding the rubber and glue fumes at the raincoat factory many times over. The workers coughed, cursed, and carried on with resigned acceptance."[2]

While at the match factory, the sisters received a letter from an aunt who had emigrated to America before the war and had managed to locate the two girls. She promised to find a way to get them from Sweden to America. "Iboya and I exploded with joy. We hugged and danced about our room."[2]

It was quite awhile before their relatives in America could secure passage for them, and in the meantime, Aranka went to live with a Swedish family in Astorp, Skane. "I...arrived in Astorp toward the middle of May, and a week later there was a party in my honor. All the family and their minister were invited.

"The Rantzows' house was on a quiet street with neighbors close by. It had three bedrooms upstairs, a living room, dining room, and kitchen on the main floor, with a front and rear entrance, and the brand-new indoor bathroom had a toilet and a sink. They were very proud of that. Not everybody in Astorp had indoor plumbing. It felt good living in a house again."[2]

By the time passage was booked, Aranka had grown very attached to her Swedish family and had fallen in love with a Christian boy in Astorp. The decision to leave was a difficult one, but she was determined to emigrate and join the uncles and aunts who awaited their arrival. She left Astorp behind in order to rejoin her sister for the ten-day boat trip to America. "I was not aware that I was the only passenger boarding the 10:08 train from Astorp until I looked back and realized that the people on the platform were all waving to me. It looked desolate and eerie....The woman next to me tried to cheer me up. 'Trains that take you away also bring you back.'

"The trains I had traveled on had not made many return trips in my past. They seemed to have gone one way—away from my home and the people who mattered most to me. I had always been an optimist, but I was starting to believe that everything was transitory. I made a vow that in the future I would not hold back my affection from the people I cared about."[2]

On October 22, 1948, the sisters finally set sail for America. "Aboard the *Gripsholm*, people were milling around in a frenzy of excitement. Every passenger had someone to see them off. They attempted to call and shout to one another across the distance separating them. The well-wishers on the shore were growing small and remote. Soon the sound of the ship's horn drowned out the voices. I waved to everyone and no one in particular. Another stage of my life was in the past."[2]

Aranka was eighteen when she arrived in New York City. She supported herself by modeling in the garment district while attending night school to learn her sixth language, English. She married Gilbert Siegal on February 3, 1952, and later had a daughter, Rise, and a son, Joseph.

As she never finished elementary school, Siegal yearned for a formal education, but it was not until both children were away at college that she was able to enroll as a full-time student at the State University of New York College at Purchase. Her interest in the cultural similarities and dissimilarities led her to the study of social anthropology. She was writing anthropological vignettes about the countries she had lived in when she met a producer on campus for the radio station WBAI. He asked her to host a radio show, telling the stories of the places she had seen.

When the radio show met with favorable public response, Siegal decided to take material from the show for her first book, *Upon the Head of the Goat*. "I wanted to bring the story to human proportions....No one ever knew who we were as people. My idea was to present a family like any other family. Girls growing up to be ladies, dreaming about wearing fancy clothes. People who had dreams in a normal sense. I wanted to show what it was like to be an individual, and I tried to relate on a one-to-one basis.

"I'm proof that anybody who wants to do anything has to really persevere....For me, writing was difficult, like a lame person trying to dance. I was writing in a foreign language, in long hand with carbon paper between the pages of my legal pad. I do not type, so I had to get a typist who could read my writing. The book took four years. But I always had the story in me. In a way it's a memorial. I don't even have a picture of my parents. There is no grave. Nothing."[3]

"Since *Upon the Head of the Goat* is autobiographical, my motivation was to share the experience and enlighten the younger generation, in hopes of a future world without prejudice and without scapegoats. I believe in the importance of my message and its inherent truth as history."[4]

Footnote Sources:

[1] Aranka Siegal, *Upon the Head of the Goat: A Childhood in Hungary, 1939-1944*, Farrar Straus, 1981.
[2] A. Siegal, *Grace in the Wilderness: After the Liberation, 1945-1948*, Farrar Straus, 1985.
[3] Lydia S. Rosner, "Portrait of a Family in Holocaust Days," *New York Times*, January 31, 1982.
[4] *Contemporary Authors*, Volume 112, Gale, 1985.

■ For More Information See

Baltimore Sun, December 27, 1981.
Newsweek, January 18, 1982 (p. 91).
St. Louis Post-Dispatch, January 31, 1982.
Los Angeles Times, February 7, 1982.
Minneapolis Tribune, February 28, 1982.
Gannett Westchester Newspapers, March 28, 1982.
Cosmopolitan (London), September, 1982.
Daily Mail (London), September 9, 1982.
Times (London), October 9, 1982.
New Yorker, December 6, 1982.
Catholic Herald, December 17, 1982.
Jewish Monthly, January, 1983.
Observer (London), January 30, 1983.
Media & Methods, February, 1983 (p. 12).
Jerusalem Post, November, 1983.
Sally Holmes Holtze, editor, *Fifth Book of Junior Authors and Illustrators*, H. W. Wilson, 1983.
Times-Picayune (New Orleans), January 1, 1984.
School Library Journal, December, 1985 (p. 100).
Horn Book, March-April, 1986 (p. 225).

Collections:

Kerlan Collection at the University of Minnesota.

William Sleator

S urname rhymes with "later"; born February 13, 1945, in Havre de Grace, Md.; son of William Warner, Jr. (a professor) and Esther (a physician; maiden name, Kaplan) Sleator. *Education:* Harvard University, B.A., 1967; studied musical composition in London, 1967-68. *Politics:* Independent. *Home:* 77 Worcester St., Boston, Mass. 02118. *Agent:* Sheldon Fogelman, 10 East 40th St., New York, N.Y. 10016.

■ Career

Royal Ballet School, London, England, accompanist, 1967-68; Rambert School, London, accompanist, 1967-68; writer, 1970—; Boston Ballet Company, Boston, Mass., rehearsal pianist, 1974-83.

■ Awards, Honors

Bread Loaf Writers' Conference Fellowship, 1969; *Boston Globe-Horn Book* Award, and Caldecott Medal Honor Book from the American Library Association, both 1971, and American Book Award for Best Paperback Picture Book, 1981, all for *The Angry Moon; Blackbriar* was selected one of Child Study Association of America's Children's Books of the Year, 1972; *House of Stairs* was selected one of American Library Association's Best Books for Young Adults, 1974, *Interstellar Pig*, 1984, *Singularity*, 1985, and *The Boy Who Reversed Himself*, 1987; Children's Choice from the International Reading Association and the Children's Book Council, for *Into the Dream; The Green Futures of Tycho* was selected one of *School Library Journal's* Best Books of the Year, 1981, *Fingers*, 1983, and *Interstellar Pig*, 1984; Golden Pen Award from the Spokane Washington Public Library, 1984, and 1985, both for "the author who gives the most reading pleasure."

■ Writings

The Angry Moon (picture book; ALA Notable Book; *Horn Book* honor list; illustrated by Blair Lent), Little, Brown, 1970.
Blackbriar (juvenile novel; ALA Notable Book; illustrated by B. Lent), Dutton, 1972.
Run (mystery), Dutton, 1973.
House of Stairs (juvenile; science fiction), Dutton, 1974.
Among the Dolls (illustrated by Trina Schart Hyman), Dutton, 1975.
(With William H. Redd) *Take Charge: A Personal Guide to Behavior Modification* (adult), Random House, 1977.
Into the Dream (Junior Literary Guild selection; illustrated by Ruth Sanderson), Dutton, 1979.
Once, Said Darlene (illustrated by Steven Kellogg), Dutton, 1979.
That's Silly (easy reader; illustrated by Lawrence DiFiori), Dutton, 1981.

The Green Futures of Tycho (young adult),
  Dutton, 1981.
Fingers (young adult), Dutton, 1983.
Interstellar Pig (young adult; ALA Notable
  Book; *Horn Book* honor list; Junior Literary
  Guild selection), Dutton, 1984.
Singularity (young adult; Junior Literary Guild
  selection), Dutton, 1985.
The Boy Who Reversed Himself (young adult),
  Dutton, 1986.
The Duplicate (young adult), Dutton, 1988.
Strange Attractors (young adult), Dutton, 1990.

Writer of musical score for animated film, "Why
the Sun and Moon Live in the Sky," in collaboration with Blair Lent; also composer of scores for
professional ballets and amateur films and plays.

■ Adaptations

"The Angry Moon" (cassette), Read-Along-
  House.
"Interstellar Pig" (cassette), Listening Library,
  1987.

■ Work in Progress

A novel about a Thai student who comes to the
United States.

■ Sidelights

With his works consistently nominated for "Best
Book" honors on subjects ranging from the occult
to the scientific study of chaos, William Sleator has
become a popular sci-fi author for young-adults.
"Everybody in my family is a scientist except me. I
always liked science but was never good enough to
be a real scientist; I was the dumbest person in the
advanced class. Still, I learned a lot. I prefer
science fiction that has some basis in reality:
psychological stories, time-travel stories, but especially stories about people. My book *Singularity* is
about several things—including the idea of time
speeding up or slowing down in relation to gravi-
ty—but it's also about the relationship between
two brothers. My best books have a physical
reality.

"What I don't like are space operas which are
violent war stories that take place with spacemen
in rocket ships instead of gunslingers on horses."

Sleator was born on February 13, 1945, in Havre
de Grace, Maryland, "because at that time, my
father was doing research on ballistics for the army
during the war. Then he got a job at the University
in St. Louis and we moved there. I was raised in a

Jewish suburb of St. Louis, which was great. The
schools were good, and everybody around was
smart.

"My parents always encouraged us to be whoever
we were. I hated sports, and of course sports are a
big deal when you're a teenager (the girls only like
the athletes), but my parents didn't push me to fit
into any particular pattern."

One thing his parents did impose on Sleator and his
siblings was music lessons. "You had to play an
instrument. The attitude was that learning an
instrument was much easier when you're young
and would be something you'd have your whole
life. They realized, however, that left up to the
kids, they would not want to learn. So my parents
insisted.

"In my case it was the piano. They started me at
six, but I was too young and quit. So they said 'fine'
and tried again when I was eight. That time I liked
it. They never intended for me to be a concert
pianist, so I didn't practice five hours a day. It was
more like one hour, and since I didn't go out for
sports, that didn't interfere with my life."

His parent's house was full of books as well as
music and Sleator also felt drawn toward reading.
"I learned how to read easily and read all the time.
I wasn't a particularly good student, but my friends
were always the intellectuals. We were the first
hippies in my high school. I graduated around
eighty-fifth in my high school class, while all my
friends were first, second, or third. That had
nothing to do with ability. I spent all my time doing
extra-curricular activities.

"We made a movie once, a little fantasy called 'The
Magic Chalk,' starring my younger brothers, similar to the film, 'The Red Balloon.' This was before
video, so it was very unusual for high school kids to
get together and make a movie. It was a heart-
warming film, with a supernatural element.

"Everything I did, the stories I wrote, the music I
played, had an element of weirdness to it. I
suppose it came from the kind of stories, mostly
science fiction, I read as a kid. For instance, once I
had to write a story about Easter, which I called
'The Haunted Easter Egg.' I even made Easter sort
of sinister. My parents thought it was great. Of
course, that was before they realized that I was
going into this bizarre career without any security,
but they encouraged me at the time.

"I wasn't a complete nerd. I rebelled with drugs,
sex—all the things every kid goes through. My

Jacket of Sleator's 1985 novel about twin brothers.

parents weren't happy about it, but they were looser about it than most."

After graduation from high school, Sleator reluctantly entered Harvard. "I was accepted, and when you're accepted at Harvard, you go. My mother would have committed suicide if I hadn't. I started with music, but they threw me out of the department. I had been composing music for a long time. I'd even composed music for our 'Magic Chalk' film and the high school orchestra. At Harvard I couldn't study musical composition before suffering through a rigid structure of courses. We had to study theory and make copies of Bach chorales. I was lousy at that, so I finally majored in English, which was fine because English had always been easy for me.

"There were several things that bothered me about Harvard—if you wanted to be an artist, Harvard was not the place to go. It's a very academic school that teaches you how to be a scholar and study the arts, but not how to create. I hated it so much that I wanted to get it over with. In terms of preparing me for my career, I can't think of anything it did.

Publishers don't care if you have a degree, and a B.A. in English doesn't mean very much anyway."

The decision not to enter graduate school shocked Sleator's parents. "Their encouragement had backfired. When I first said I was going to be a writer, my parents thought I was nuts. I had to publish about six books before they began to take me seriously."

Instead, Sleator went to London to study musical composition. "That was my chance to study music. I also worked as a pianist in ballet schools. I rented a room from the secretary of one of the schools where I worked. She was about fifty-five and I was twenty-two. Her only son had moved to Australia. I soon began to realize that I was fulfilling that role in her life. She wanted to know what I was doing every minute, where I was going, who I was with. I was more restricted as a college graduate, than I had been as a high school student in my parent's house. I had to struggle for independence. I'm a non-assertive person, but that year I learned to assert myself.

Dutton 1984 hardcover edition.

"She had this isolated cottage in the country where we went every weekend. You had to have a jeep to get there; there wasn't a road leading to it. This place had at one time been used as a pest house, isolating people with smallpox. It hadn't changed in 200 years—no plumbing, heat, or electricity. Of course, I didn't want to go there every weekend; I wanted to go to parties. But there was so much hard physical work, she needed to have a man along, and that was my other function in her life. If I didn't go, and she couldn't drag somebody else, we'd be stuck in that apartment in London all weekend, and she would hate me.

"But the place was interesting, way out in the middle of the woods, and eerie with graffiti from 1756 on the walls. There were burial mounds nearby where druids were buried and festivals were held. The whole thing was like a Gothic novel. So there was my first book, *Blackbriar*, handed right to me.

"I've always kept a journal, and when I wrote letters to people, I'd keep carbons, which would function similarly to a journal. That's how I remembered what it was like in that place. *Blackbriar* was about that house and the struggle for independence between this kid and his guardian. I was able to write the novel because I didn't have to invent very much. The things I did make up, when I think of it now, were sort of cornball and trite, like witches and devil worshipers.

"Parents today are concerned that their kids will read about the occult and become instant devil worshipers. I don't agree with that. There's nothing wrong with writing about the occult. I feel that the book would have been much better if I could have kept it more realistic. That's why I've called it a 'stumbling first effort,' because I had to resort to cliches in order to get a plot.

"The first draft took a long time because I didn't plot it out. I didn't know what was going to happen next. So when it was finished, it didn't make sense. The first editor to see it rejected it. She didn't think it was publishable, but suggested I get another opinion."

Sleator turned to his illustrator friend, Blair Lent, for advice. Lent had provided Sleator with the opportunity to publish his first book by allowing him to write the text for the children's book, *The Angry Moon.* "Blair sent my manuscript to Ann Durell, an editor in New York he had worked with. She wrote back saying that the book had potential but, of course, had problems as well. I rewrote it a couple more times. It wasn't easy, but I was lucky to work with an editor who helped me learn what it meant to write a book.

"You might think that after sixteen books I wouldn't need as much editing, but that isn't the case. It doesn't get any easier. I still need a lot of feedback. I might have a picture in my mind of who the characters are, but the problem is writing it so that the reader will see everything the way I do. It helps to have another point of view."

After his return from England, Sleator divided his time between writing novels and working as a pianist for the Boston Ballet. "For a while, working for the ballet was interesting because it was so different from being a writer. Some people become writers because they like being isolated or because they're shy, but I'm neither. At the ballet, I worked with other people. I liked that. Putting on performances and going on tours seemed sort of glamorous, at first.

"The dancers had an hour-and-a-half class every day to keep themselves in shape and their technique sharp. I played the piano for this class and heard all the gossip. After that, they would use an audio tape for rehearsals because it was cheaper than paying me. That was ideal because I could go in from ten to eleven-thirty in the morning and then go home to write.

"When famous people came to direct the ballet, I played for the rehearsals, too. It was easier for them, because they wouldn't have to keep rewinding the tape. Instead, they could say, 'Go back to this particular dance step,' and I would know where in the music that step came. A good rehearsal pianist knew the whole ballet. The person running the rehearsal wouldn't really have to say much to the pianist at all.

"Class was much different from rehearsal. In class, I could choose whatever music I wanted as long as it worked with what the dancers were doing. I quickly became bored with the usual stuff and began playing all sorts of crazy jazz and rock and roll. The dancers liked that because it was livelier and more fun for them. In rehearsal, I played the music of that particular show. Many of the dancers didn't know a thing about music. I had to learn to count it the way they did. Sometimes, if they were jerks, and a lot of them were, they would blame the pianist if they made a mistake. The pianist was the low man, so they would just say the music was too fast or too slow. I had to be alert enough to see their tempo for that day and play the music accordingly. You had to have a natural talent for it. I learned.

"The ballet was very dramatic, especially as we got closer to the performance. Tensions would mount and everybody would go a bit crazy. The first time we performed in New York, we did a ballet in which the second act began with people flying. In the dress rehearsal, everything went wrong. One girl, who was being flown by a wire, got stuck. There she hung from the ceiling and we started wondering if she was going to be there for the whole act. Things like that happened all the time. Dancers even fell into the orchestra pit. We also worked a lot with Rudolph Nureyev who is very temperamental and would actually spit at people on stage."

Touring with the company provided different experiences. "It wasn't glamorous, because we worked under conditions that weren't ideal. There was only one person who had to go to every rehearsal: me. We'd tour these fantastic cities in Europe and I'd be in rehearsal for eight to ten hours, playing the same music over and over again. Meanwhile, each group would come in for their one-hour rehearsal and then go out to the museum or the beach.

"On tour I basically saw the inside of the theater or rehearsal room, and spent a lot of time on the bus with the same dancers, each with three suitcases. The funny thing about dancers is that they pack heavy. They're the best-dressed people in the world, but that's their job—to look perfect. But most dancers don't know much of anything else. They've spent their lives, since they were eight years old, dancing five hours a day. They couldn't read a menu or even begin to try and say a word in a foreign language. There was a woman who paid them all in the currency of whatever country we were in because they didn't know how to change money. They were taken care of in every way. It was like kindergarten. You'd get on the bus and there'd be roll call.

"The things that were not great about ballet highlighted the good things about being a writer, such as independence. Dancers never make a decision. They're screamed at, told what to do every second. As a writer, I could do whatever I wanted. Plus a dancer's career is very short, similar to that of an athlete. Once a dancer turns thirty, he feels like he's on his way down. As a writer, you usually get better. I began to appreciate all those things."

Sleator left the ballet in 1983. "I began to make more money from my books and didn't need the

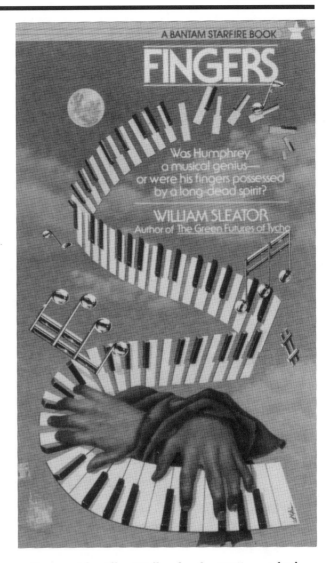

Cover art by Allen Welkes for the 1985 paperback.

job anymore. I was beginning to get offers to speak and my work for the ballet interfered with that.

"Since I left, I've lost all interest in the ballet. I never go. So now I have all this material that just doesn't interest me. In the whole company, there were two or three smart dancers who were fun to be with and I miss them. But I do a lot of traveling and speaking which has taken the place of ballet. The difference is that now, at least I'm the star, being treated and paid like one. What's there to miss, really?"

Sleator feels that writing and musical composition are ultimately different processes. "Whether composing music or writing words, you're making decisions. 'Should I use this note or should I use this word?' You must constantly decide what to do next and in that sense, they are similar. The times that I've been inspired—where something just flew out of me (which has happened once in my whole life)—is when composing and writing can be very similar. But in another sense, they're completely opposite. Words are symbols; they mean something. Music is not a symbol. It's sound and abstraction."

Sleator has established a schedule which allows him to write more easily. "It's like exercising. The way to get yourself to exercise is to make it a routine. Then when you miss the routine, you can't stand it. I treat writing the same way. It's like an addiction. I love to work on books, and I miss it when I'm not. I've worked out an entire work schedule.

"I must know that I have as much time ahead as I need and that nothing will interrupt or stop me. It's very hard to get started if I know I have to stop after a couple of hours. So I set up three or four days a week in which I write. I compartmentalize my life so that on writing days there will be nothing besides writing, and on the other days I can write letters, run errands, go to the gym. People ask me, 'How can you have the discipline to do that?' I answer that it's just something you train yourself to do."

Sleator's writing has become increasingly personal. "At the beginning, I was copying other things, but with each book, I've learned to tap deeper into my subconscious. The more books I write, the more they represent who I really am. I used to be afraid to tell anybody if I had an idea for a book because I didn't want to give anything away. Now, my feeling is that nobody can steal an idea from me because anybody else who used that idea would write a completely different book.

"Also, my style has improved; I'm a better writer, but that goes up and down. I wrote one book that was published in 1983 called *Fingers*, which I think is my best book, stylistically. I don't think I've improved on that one."

Sleator feels that the *The Green Futures of Tycho*, named for his brother, was his watershed book. "I really got in touch with my weirdness in that one. That was the first book into which I was able to inject humor, and I feel humor is important. Even in a basically serious, or even a scary piece, there must be comic relief to reduce the tension. Humor is also very attractive to kids.

"The big competition is television. Obviously, I'm not seriously competing with television—I've lost that one. All writers have. But if we can at least get them to realize that reading is also fun, maybe they'll find something in books just as good as what's on television, if not better.

"I try to make my books exciting. I also provide incentives in the sense of giving kids a more active role in the story. Of course, reading is more active than watching television to begin with, but I will frequently have an ending in which the reader must think a little to participate. A kid will have to use his own imagination to solve the plot, which never happens on television. So in a book, I can get kids more involved. One other ingredient is irony: letting the reader know something the character doesn't, letting the reader know that the bomb in that room is going to go off in five minutes, but not telling the character. That really involves them."

Although there's been movie interest in several of Sleator's books, *Singularity* came the closest to being realized, then fell through. "Now my attitude is that once I actually have the check in my hand, I'll believe it. Film has always interested me, ever since I made that movie as a kid. The whole editing process is especially interesting, along with film music. But I'm very realistic about the small odds of having a film made. I realize that movies are a different art form and if they want to make a movie, I will have to let them do anything they want with it, (at least the first time). Most producers wouldn't even consider one of my books if I held out for any kind of control. I don't blame them; I can understand why they want to do that. If they made a couple of movies based on my books and they were successful, I'd have more clout."

But novels remain Sleator's preference. "My goal is to entertain my audience and to get them to read. I want kids to find out that reading is the best entertainment there is. If, at the same time, I'm also imparting some scientific knowledge, then that's good, too. I'd like kids to see that science is not just boring formulas. Some of the facts to be learned about the universe are very weird."

In his works, Sleator has done his best to illustrate the absurdity inherent in the world. "I wish that I could put humor into everything I write, but it's harder to be funny on the page than to be scary. *Interstellar Pig* is my funniest book. There were a lot of opportunities for humor in it."

Interstellar Pig is the name of an intergalactic board game which sixteen-year-old Barney plays with his new neighbors, only to realize that the neighbors are aliens and that the game reflects actuality. "The trouble is that I can not turn my sense of humor on and off, and there are some subjects to which humor just doesn't apply.

"I thought that *The Duplicate* would be very funny. Instead, it turned out to be very unfunny. The shock value of certain moments in that book was very effective." The narrator of the book, sixteen-year-old David, discovers an object labeled "Spee-Dee-Dupe" lying on the beach and uses it to duplicate himself, leading to dire consequences. "I think the moment when the second duplicate shows up worked out very well. Again, it goes back to irony. If somebody had noticed everything happening up until then, they would have said, 'I bet there's a second duplicate,' even though the main character hadn't realized it. I gave the readers enough clues so that once it happened, they could go back and say, 'Now I understand.' At the same time, I don't think I totally gave it away."

Each plot has required a varying degree of research. "*The Duplicate* didn't require much research because there was only one scientific element in that book, the fact that David makes a duplicate of himself, which is scientifically impossible. I felt that wasn't the interesting part anyway, so I got that out of the way and let the rest of the book explore what it would be like to have a duplicate.

"For my latest book, *Strange Attractors*, I did a lot of research on chaos. I laughed when my brothers told me that chaos was a field of scientific study. Then I discovered that they're studying not so much chaos, as the exact process of how any normal system goes from stability into chaos. It's very complicated with a pattern called 'period doubling.' As it turns out, all these different systems exhibit this same pattern when you examine them closely. I thought this order behind chaos was ominous. There was a good story there and that became the idea behind the book. I researched enough for ten different books and tried to put it all in one. Then I had to rewrite it."

Way-out plots are not Sleator's sole interest in writing. "Many times critics will say that I handle the plots and scientific aspects of my books very well, but that my characterizations tend to be weak. I think that's funny because one of the main things that interest me are situations between people—how they treat each other. In any idea for a book, I want to see how I can explore the personal relations that would manifest from that idea.

"The characters in my work who put themselves in other people's shoes are the most successful in the end. In *House of Stairs*, the kids who refused to become conditioned by hate were being human in the end, as opposed to trained animals. I always stress that. I'm not saying to be nice to other people because it's good; I'm saying think about how other people feel because it's practical. I'm not making any moralistic, goody-goody kind of point. You will get along better with people if you are able to understand them.

"*The Boy Who Reversed Himself* deals with peer pressure. I read a lot of science-fiction stories about the fourth spatial dimension when I was a kid. One day I realized that this would be a great idea for a young-adult book. My first version was told from a boy's point of view, but then I said to myself, 'There's only one female in this whole book and she's a grotesque, four-dimensional witch.' I couldn't do that. So I turned the main character into a girl. That made the book much more interesting. She likes a certain boy but has to deal with peer pressure: 'Don't go out with this creep because you'll look like a creep, too.' Of course, it turns out at the end that the creepy guy is really the stronger and better person.

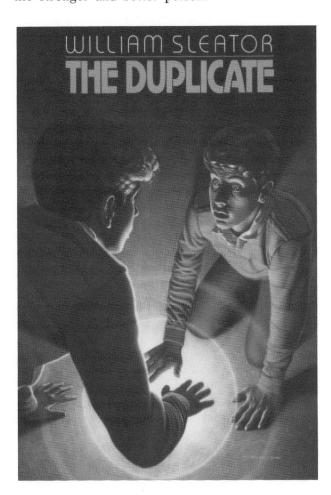

The 1988 Dutton hardcover.

Jacket from the 1986 novel.

"That's one of the few moral issues I try to communicate to kids: someone could be an oddball, but that doesn't mean he's a jerk."

Despite the criticism he has received, Sleator has suffered little controversy over his works or ideas unlike many other young-adult authors. "Since my stories take place in a science-fiction world, parents might be less afraid of them because they think their kids won't be influenced by any of it. Of course, I don't think that's true. In a way, Robert Cormier might be taking more of a chance than me because he writes about these ultra-realistic situations, but it certainly hasn't hurt his career or book sales.

"Another reason I haven't had trouble is that I don't write much about sex. That eliminates one area that people are dying to censor. Norma Klein had nerve; I really respect her. One community had a hearing about whether to take one of her books off the shelf. The story was about a relationship between this guy and girl who slept together but weren't really in love. That's what they objected to. Norma went to the hearing. I thought that

was gutsy. Of course, it turned out that most of the people who were against the book hadn't read it.

"I find it interesting that adults are not afraid of their children reading the violence in my books. They're much more afraid of people loving each other than of people hating each other. That shows a warped system of values. They'll use obscenities around the house; they'll allow their kids to watch all sorts of violence and sex on television. But when they see a hint of sexuality in a book, they want it taken off the shelf. People think the only place kids are going to learn about sex and bad words is in a book. That seems peculiar, but I have a theory about it. Without realizing it, these people are saying that a book can be more influential than a television show–they're recognizing the power of literature."[1]

Footnote Sources:

[1] Based on an interview by Dieter Miller for *Authors and Artists for Young Adults.*

■ For More Information See

Sally Holmes Holtze, editor, *Fifth Book of Junior Authors and Illustrators,* H. W. Wilson, 1983.

Hardcover edition of the 1974 book.

Jim Roginski, *Behind the Covers: Interviews with Authors and Illustrators of Books for Children and Young Adults,* Libraries Unlimited, 1985.
Bulletin of the Center for Children's Books, June, 1985, January, 1987, April, 1988.

Publishers Weekly, November 28, 1986, October 30, 1987.
School Library Journal, February, 1987, October, 1987, March, 1989.
VOYA, April 1988, August, 1988.
Wilson Library Bulletin, September, 1989.

Richard Wright

guished American Novel from the American Writers Congress, 1942, both for *Native Son; American Hunger* was selected one of New York Public Library's Books for the Teen Age, 1980, 1981, and 1982.

■ Writings

Uncle Tom's Children: Four Novellas, Harper, 1938, expanded edition published as *Uncle Tom's Children: Five Long Stories*, 1940, reissued, 1969.

Native Son (novel), Harper, 1940, reissued, 1969.

Twelve Million Black Voices: A Folk History of the Negro in the United States (nonfiction; illustrated with photographs selected by Edwin Rossham), Viking, 1941.

Black Boy: A Record of Childhood and Youth (autobiography), Harper, 1945.

The Outsider (novel), Harper, 1953.

Savage Holiday (novel), Avon, 1954.

Black Power: A Record of Reactions in a Land of Pathos (nonfiction), Harper, 1954.

The Color Curtain: A Report on the Bandung Conference (nonfiction), World, 1956.

Pagan Spain: A Report of a Journey into the Past (nonfiction), Harper, 1957.

White Man, Listen! (nonfiction), Doubleday, 1957, reissued, Greenwood Press, 1978.

The Long Dream (novel), Doubleday, 1958.

(Contributor and editor) *Quintet* (short stories), Pyramid Books, 1961.

Eight Men (short stories), World, 1961.

Lawd Today (novel), Walker, 1963.

Born September 4, 1908, near Natchez, Miss.; died of a heart attack, November 28, 1960, in Paris, France; buried in Pere Lachaise, Paris, France; son of Nathan (a mill worker) and Ellen (a teacher; maiden name, Wilson) Wright; married Dhimah Rose Meadman, August, 1938 (divorced); married Ellen Poplar, March 12, 1941; children: Julia, Rachel. *Education:* Attended school in Jackson, Miss.

■ Career

Novelist, short story writer, poet, and essayist. Worked at odd jobs in Memphis, Tenn., and other cities; clerk at U.S. Post Office in Chicago, Ill., during 1920s; associated with Works Progress Administration Federal Writers' Project, Chicago, and New York, N.Y., 1935-39.

■ Awards, Honors

Prize from *Story* magazine, and Best Work of Fiction by a Works Progress Administration writer, both 1938, both for *Uncle Tom's Children;* Guggenheim Fellowship, 1939; Spingarn Medal from the National Association for the Advancement of Colored People (NAACP), 1940, and Most Distin-

(With Louis Sapin) "Daddy Goodness" (play), first produced Off-Broadway at St. Mark's Playhouse, June 4, 1968.

The Man Who Lived Underground (novella), Aubier-Flammarion, 1971.

(Contributor) Hiroshi Nagase and Tsutomu Kanashiki, editors, *What the Negro Wants*, Kaitakusha, 1972.

Farthing's Fortunes, Atheneum, 1976.

American Hunger (autobiography), Harper, 1977.

The Richard Wright Reader, edited by Ellen Wright and Michel Fabre, Harper, 1978.

The Life and Work of Richard Wright, edited by David Ray and Robert M. Farnsworth, University of Missouri, 1979.

(Contributor) Calvin Skaggs, editor, *The American Short Story*, Volume I (contains "Almos' a Man"), Dell, 1985.

Editor of *New Challenge* (formerly *Challenge*), beginning 1937. Contributor of articles, essays, short stories, and poems to magazines and newspapers, including *Atlantic Monthly*, *Saturday Review*, *New York Post*, *New Republic*, *Negro Digest*, *Daily Worker*, *New York World Telegram*, and *New Masses*.

■ Adaptations

(Also author with Paul Green) *Native Son (The Biography of a Young American): A Play in Ten Scenes* (first produced on Broadway at the St. James Theatre, March 24, 1941, produced at Perry Street Theatre, March 21, 1978), Harper, 1941, revised edition, Samuel French, 1980.

(Also author) "Native Son" (screenplay), Classic Films, 1951.

"Native Son" (filmstrip with cassette), Current Affairs Films, 1978, (cassette), Caedmon, 1973, rereleased, 1989.

"Black Boy" (cassette), Caedmon, 1973, rereleased, 1989.

"Almos' a Man" (musical drama), first produced in New York City at Soho Rep, April 12, 1985, (filmstrip with cassette), Random House.

■ Sidelights

Richard Wright was born September 4, 1908 in Adams County, Mississippi. "I was born too far back in the woods to hear the train whistle, and you could only hear the hoot owls holler."[1]

In an effort to improve their economic situation, Wright's parents boarded a boat and moved the family to Memphis. "For days I had dreamed about a huge white boat floating on a vast body of water, but when my mother took me down to the levee on the day of leaving, I saw a tiny, dirty boat that was not at all like the boat I had imagined. I was disappointed and when time came to go on board I cried and my mother thought that I did not want to go with her to Memphis, and I could not tell her what the trouble was. Solace came when I wandered about the boat and gazed at Negroes throwing dice, drinking whisky, playing cards, lolling on boxes, eating, talking, and singing. My father took me down into the engine room and the throbbing machines enthralled me for hours.

"In Memphis we lived in a one-story brick tenement. The stone buildings and the concrete pavements looked bleak and hostile to me. The absence of green, growing things made the city seem dead. Living space for the four of us—my mother, my brother, my father, and me—was a kitchen and a bedroom. In the front and rear were paved areas in which my brother and I could play, but for days I was afraid to go into the strange city streets alone.

"It was in this tenement that the personality of my father first came fully into the orbit of my concern. He worked as a night porter in a Beale Street drugstore and he became important and forbidding to me only when I learned that I could not make noise when he was asleep in the daytime. He was the lawgiver in our family and I never laughed in his presence. I used to lurk timidly in the kitchen doorway and watch his huge body sitting slumped at the table. I stared at him with awe as he gulped his beer from a tin bucket, as he ate long and heavily, sighed, belched, closed his eyes to nod on a stuffed belly. He was quite fat and his bloated stomach always lapped over his belt. He was always a stranger to me, always somehow alien and remote."[2]

In Memphis as they did in Mississippi, the Wrights lived in poverty. "Hunger stole upon me so slowly that at first I was not aware of what hunger really meant. Hunger had always been more or less at my elbow when I played, but now I began to wake up at night to find hunger standing at my bedside, staring at me gauntly. The hunger I had known before this had been no grim, hostile stranger; it had been a normal hunger that had made me beg constantly for bread, and when I ate a crust or two I was satisfied. But this new hunger baffled me, scared me, made me angry and insistent. Whenever I begged for food now my mother would pour me a cup of tea which would still the clamor in my stomach for a moment or two; but a little later I would feel hunger nudging my ribs, twisting my empty guts until they ached. I would grow dizzy and my vision would dim. I became less active in my play, and for the first time in my life I had to pause and think of what was happening to me."[2]

Not long after, Wright's father walked out on his wife and children. "As the days slid past the image of my father became associated with my pangs of hunger, and whenever I felt hunger I thought of him with a deep biological bitterness.

"To keep us out of mischief, my mother often took my brother and me with her to her cooking job. Standing hungrily and silently in a corner of the kitchen, we would watch her go from the stove to the sink, from the cabinet to the table. I always loved to stand in the white folks' kitchen when my mother cooked, for it meant that I got scraps of bread and meat; but many times I regretted having come, for my nostrils would be assailed with the scent of food that did not belong to me and which I was forbidden to eat. Toward evening my mother would take the hot dishes into the dining room where the white people were seated, and I would stand as near the dining room door as possible to get a quick glimpse of the white faces gathered around the loaded table, eating, laughing, talking. If the white people left anything, my brother and I would eat well; but if they did not, we would have our usual bread and tea.

"Watching the white people eat would make my empty stomach churn and I would grow vaguely angry. Why could I not eat when I was hungry? Why did I always have to wait until others were through? I could not understand why some people had enough food and others did not.

"I now found it irresistible to roam during the day while my mother was cooking in the kitchens of the white folks. A block away from our flat was a saloon in front of which I used to loiter all day long. Its interior was an enchanting place that both lured and frightened me. I would beg for pennies, then peer under the swinging doors to watch the men and women drink. When some neighbors would chase me away from the door, I would follow the drunks about the streets, trying to understand their mysterious mumblings, pointing at them, teasing them, laughing at them, imitating them, jeering, mocking, and taunting them about their lurching antics. For me the most amusing spectacle was a drunken woman stumbling and urinating, the dampness seeping down her stockinged legs. Or I

First edition cover of the 1953 novel.

would stare in horror at a man retching. Somebody informed my mother about my fondness for the saloon and she beat me, but it did not keep me from peering under the swinging doors and listening to the wild talk of drunks when she was at work.

"One summer afternoon—in my sixth year—while peering under the swinging doors of the neighborhood saloon, a black man caught hold of my arm and dragged me into its smoky and noisy depths. The odor of alcohol stung my nostrils. I yelled and struggled, trying to break free of him, afraid of the staring crowd of men and women, but he would not let me go. He lifted me and sat me upon the counter, put his hat upon my head and ordered a drink for me. The tipsy men and women yelled with delight. Somebody tried to jam a cigar into my mouth, but I twisted out of the way.

"'How do you feel, setting there like a man, boy?' a man asked.

"'Make 'im drunk and he'll stop peeping in here,' somebody said.

"'Let's buy 'im drinks,' somebody said.

"Some of my fright left as I stared about. Whisky was set before me.

"'Drink it, boy,' somebody said.

"I shook my head. The man who had dragged me in urged me to drink it, telling me that it would not hurt me. I refused.

"'Drink it; it'll make you feel good,' he said.

"I took a sip and coughed. The men and women laughed. The entire crowd in the saloon gathered about me now, urging me to drink. I took another sip. Then another. My head spun and I laughed. I was put on the floor and I ran giggling and shouting among the yelling crowd. As I would pass each man, I would take a sip from an offered glass. Soon I was drunk.

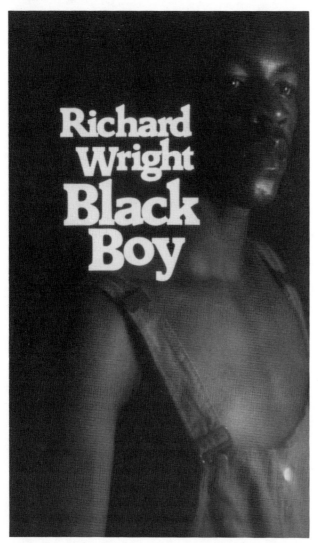

Paperbound cover of Wright's autobiography.

"A man called me to him and whispered some words into my ear and told me that he would give me a nickel if I went to a woman and repeated them to her. I told him that I would say them; he gave me the nickel and I ran to the woman and shouted the words. A gale of laughter went up in the saloon.

"'Don't teach that boy that,' someone said.

"'He doesn't know what it is,' another said.

"From then on, for a penny or a nickel, I would repeat to anyone whatever was whispered to me. In my foggy, tipsy state the reaction of the men and women to my mysterious words enthralled me. I ran from person to person, laughing, hiccoughing, spewing out filth that made them bend double with glee.

"'Let that boy alone now,' someone said.

"'It ain't going to hurt 'im,' another said.

"'It's a shame,' a woman said, giggling.

"'Go home, boy,' somebody yelled at me.

"Toward early evening they let me go. I staggered along the pavements, drunk, repeating obscenities to the horror of the women I passed and to the amusement of the men en route to their homes from work.

"To beg drinks in the saloon became an obsession. Many evenings my mother would find me wandering in a daze and take me home and beat me; but the next morning, no sooner had she gone to her job than I would run to the saloon and wait for someone to take me in and buy me a drink. My mother protested tearfully to the proprietor of the saloon, who ordered me to keep out of his place. But the men—reluctant to surrender their sport— would buy me drinks anyway, letting me drink out of their flasks on the streets, urging me to repeat obscenities.

"I was a drunkard in my sixth year, before I had begun school. With a gang of children, I roamed the streets, begging pennies from passers-by, haunting the doors of saloons, wandering farther and farther away from home each day. I saw more than I could understand and heard more than I could remember. The point of life became for me the times when I could beg drinks. My mother was in despair. She beat me; then she prayed and wept over me, imploring me to be good, telling me that she had to work, all of which carried no weight to my wayward mind. Finally she placed me and my brother in the keeping of an old black woman who watched me every moment to keep me from running to the doors of the saloons to beg for whisky. The craving for alcohol finally left me and I forgot the taste of it."[2]

Because Wright's mother could not afford proper clothes for him, Wright began school several years late. "In the immediate neighborhood there were many school children who, in the afternoons, would stop and play en route to their homes; they would leave their books upon the sidewalk and I would thumb through the pages and question them about the baffling black print. When I had learned to recognize certain words, I told my mother that I wanted to learn to read and she encouraged me. Soon I was able to pick my way through most of the children's books I ran across. There grew in me a consuming curiosity about what was happening around me and, when my mother came home from a hard day's work, I would question her so relentlessly about what I had heard in the streets that she refused to talk to me.

"One cold morning my mother awakened me and told me that, because there was no coal in the house, she was taking my brother to the job with her and that I must remain in bed until the coal she had ordered was delivered. For the payment of the coal, she left a note together with some money under the dresser scarf. I went back to sleep and was awakened by the ringing of the doorbell. I opened the door, let in the coal man, and gave him the money and the note. He brought in a few bushels of coal, then lingered, asking me if I were cold.

"'Yes,' I said, shivering.

"He made a fire, then sat and smoked.

"'How much change do I owe you?' he asked me.

"'I don't know,' I said.

"'Shame on you,' he said. 'Don't you know how to count?'

"'No, sir,' I said.

"'Listen and repeat after me,' he said.

"He counted to ten and I listened carefully; then he asked me to count alone and I did. He then made me memorize the words twenty, thirty, forty, etc., then told me to add one, two, three, and so on. In about an hour's time I had learned to count to a hundred and I was overjoyed. Long after the coal man had gone I danced up and down on the bed in my nightclothes, counting again and again to a hundred, afraid that if I did not keep repeating the numbers I would forget them. When my mother returned from her job that night I insisted

First edition of Wright's 1940 award winner.

that she stand still and listen while I counted to one hundred. She was dumbfounded. After that she taught me to read, told me stories. On Sundays I would read the newspapers with my mother guiding me and spelling out the words.

"I soon made myself a nuisance by asking far too many questions of everybody. Every happening in the neighborhood, no matter how trivial, became my business. It was in this manner that I first stumbled upon the relations between whites and blacks, and what I learned frightened me. Though I had long known that there were people called 'white' people, it had never meant anything to me emotionally. I had seen white men and women upon the streets a thousand times, but they had never looked particularly 'white.' To me they were merely people like other people, yet somehow strangely different because I had never come in close touch with any of them. For the most part I never thought of them; they simply existed somewhere in the background of the city as a whole. It might have been that my tardiness in learning to sense white people as 'white' people came from the fact that many of my relatives were 'white'-looking people. My grandmother, who was white as any 'white' person, had never looked 'white' to me. And when word circulated among the black people of the neighboorhood that a 'black' boy had been severely beaten by a 'white' man, I felt that the 'white' man had had a right to beat the 'black' boy, for I naively assumed that the 'white' man must have been the 'black' boy's father. And did not all fathers, like my father, have the right to beat their children? A paternal right was the only right, to my understanding, that a man had to beat a child. But when my mother told me that the 'white' man was not the father of the 'black' boy, was no kin to him at all, I was puzzled.

"'Then why did the "white" man whip the "black" boy?' I asked my mother.

"'The "white" man did not *whip* the "black" boy,' my mother told me. 'He *beat* the "black" boy.'

"'But why?'

"'You're too young to understand.'

"'I'm not going to let anybody beat me,' I said stoutly.

"'Then stop running wild in the streets,' my mother said.

"I brooded for a long time about the seemingly causeless beating of the 'black' boy by the 'white' man and the more questions I asked the more bewildering it all became. Whenever I saw 'white' people now I stared at them, wondering what they were really like."[2]

After Wright's mother's efforts to wrest child support from her estranged husband ended in a humiliating courtroom scene, she became so sick and depressed she was unable to care for her two sons. Wright and his brother were placed in a public orphanage. "The orphan home was a two-story frame building set amid trees in a wide, green field. My mother ushered me and my brother one morning into the building and into the presence of a tall, gaunt, mulatto woman who called herself Miss Simon. At once she took a fancy to me and I was frightened speechless; I was afraid of her the moment I saw her and my fear lasted during my entire stay in the home.

"The house was crowded with children and there was always a storm of noise. The daily routine was blurred to me and I never quite grasped it. The most abiding feeling I had each day was hunger and fear. The meals were skimpy and there were only two of them. Just before we went to bed each night we were given a slice of bread smeared with molasses. The children were silent, hostile, vindictive, continuously complaining of hunger. There was an over-all atmosphere of nervousness and intrigue, of children telling tales upon others, of children being deprived of food to punish them.

"The home did not have the money to check the growth of the wide stretches of grass by having it mown, so it had to be pulled by hand. Each morning after we had eaten a breakfast that seemed like no breakfast at all, an older child would lead a herd of us to the vast lawn and we would get to our knees and wrench the grass loose from the dirt with our fingers. At intervals Miss Simon would make a tour of inspection, examining the pile of pulled grass beside each child, scolding or praising according to the size of the pile. Many mornings I was too weak from hunger to pull the grass; I would grow dizzy and my mind would become blank and I would find myself, after an interval of unconsciousness, upon my hands and knees, my head whirling, my eyes staring in bleak astonishment at the green grass, wondering where I was, feeling that I was emerging from a dream."[2]

Wright ran away from the orphanage, for which he was severely whipped by the Directrice. In despair, Wright's mother brought her son to confront her husband on his refusal to help support the family. They found him living in a shack with another woman who tauntingly flipped the starving child a nickel. When Wright's mother refused the coin out of pride, his father pocketed the five cents, laughing. "We left. I had the feeling that I had had to do with something unclean. Many times in the years after that the image of my father and the strange woman, their faces lit by the dancing flames, would surge up in my imagination so vivid and strong that I felt I could reach out and touch it; I would stare at it, feeling that it possessed some vital meaning which always eluded me.

"A quarter of a century was to elapse between the time when I saw my father sitting with the strange woman and the time when I was to see him again, standing alone upon the red clay of a Mississippi plantation, a sharecropper, clad in ragged overalls, holding a muddy hoe in his gnarled, veined hands—a quarter of a century during which my mind and consciousness had become so greatly and violently altered that when I tried to talk to him I realized that, though ties of blood made us kin,

Victor Love and Geraldine Page starred in the 1986 film version of "Native Son."

though I could see a shadow of my face in his face, though there was an echo of my voice in his voice, we were forever strangers, speaking a different language, living on vastly distant planes of reality. . . .

"He asked easy, drawling questions about me, his other son, his wife, and he laughed, amused, when I informed him of their destinies. I forgave him and pitied him as my eyes looked past him to the unpainted wooden shack. From far beyond the horizons that bound this bleak plantation there had come to me through my living the knowledge that my father was a black peasant who had gone to the city seeking life, but who had failed in the city; a black peasant whose life had been hopelessly snarled in the city, and who had at last fled the city—that same city which had lifted me in its burning arms and borne me toward alien and undreamed-of shores of knowing."[2]

Wright's "undreamed-of shores of knowing" were to include struggles with his own racist demons born of the environments in which he was forced to live. "Having grown taller and older, I now associated with older boys and I had to pay for my admittance into their company by subscribing to certain racial sentiments. The touchstone of fraternity was my feeling toward white people, how much hostility I held toward them, what degrees of value and honor I assigned to race. None of this was premeditated, but sprang spontaneously out of the talk of black boys who met at the crossroads.

"It was degrading to play with girls and in our talk we relegated them to a remote island of life. We had somehow caught the spirit of the role of our sex and we flocked together for common moral schooling. We spoke boastfully in bass voices; we used the word 'nigger' to prove the tough fiber of our feelings; we spouted excessive profanity as a sign of our coming manhood; we pretended callousness toward the injunctions of our parents; and we strove to convince one another that our decisions stemmed from ourselves and ourselves alone. Yet we frantically concealed how dependent we were upon one another.

"We were now large enough for the white boys to fear us and both of us, the white boys and the black boys, began to play our traditional racial roles as though we had been born to them, as though it was in our blood, as though we were being guided by instinct. All the frightful descriptions we had heard about each other, all the violent expressions of hate and hostility that had seeped into us from our surroundings, came now to the surface to guide our actions. The roundhouse was the racial boundary of the neighborhood, and it had been tacitly agreed between the white boys and the black boys that the whites were to keep to the far side of the round-house and we blacks were to keep to our side. Whenever we caught a white boy on our side we stoned him; if we strayed to their side, they stoned us.

"Our battles were real and bloody; we threw rocks, cinders, coal, sticks, pieces of iron, and broken bottles, and while we threw them we longed for even deadlier weapons. If we were hurt, we took it quietly; there was no crying or whimpering. If our wounds were not truly serious, we hid them from our parents. We did not want to be beaten for fighting. Once, in a battle with a gang of white boys, I was struck behind the ear with a piece of broken bottle; the cut was deep and bled profuse-ly. I tried to stem the flow of blood by dabbing at the cut with a rag and when my mother came from work I was forced to tell her that I was hurt, for I needed medical attention. She rushed me to a doctor who stitched my scalp; but when she took me home she beat me, telling me that I must never fight white boys again, that I might be killed by them, that she had to work and had no time to worry about my fights. Her words did not sink in, for they conflicted with the code of the streets. I promised my mother that I would not fight, but I knew that if I kept my word I would lose my standing in the gang, and the gang's life was my life."[2]

The pressures of poverty, continual struggle, and discouragement told on the health of Wright's mother. She suffered several strokes, which left her crippled, sometimes paralyzed, and chronically depressed. "My mother's suffering grew into a symbol in my mind, gathering to itself all the poverty, the ignorance, the helplessness; the pain-ful, baffling, hunger-ridden days and hours; the restless moving, the futile seeking, the uncertainty, the fear, the dread; the meaningless pain and the endless suffering. Her life set the emotional tone of my life, colored the men and women I was to meet in the future, conditioned my relation to events that had not yet happened, determined my attitude to situations and circumstances I had yet to face. A somberness of spirit that I was never to lose settled over me during the slow years of my mother's unrelieved suffering, a somberness that was to make me stand apart and look upon excessive joy with suspicion, that was to make me self-conscious, that was to make me keep forever on the move, as though to escape a nameless fate seeking to overtake me.

"Until I entered Jim Hill public school, I had had but one year of unbroken study; with the exception of one year at the church school, each time I had begun a school term something happened to dis-rupt it. Already my personality was lopsided; my knowledge of feeling was far greater than my knowledge of fact. Though I was not aware of it, the next four years were to be the only opportunity for formal study in my life.

"I studied night and day and within two weeks I was promoted to the sixth grade. Overjoyed, I ran home and babbled the news. The family had not thought it possible. How could a bad, bad boy do that? I told the family emphatically that I was going to study medicine, engage in research, make discoveries. Flushed with success, I had not given a second's thought to how I would pay my way through a medical school. But since I had leaped a grade in two weeks, anything seemed possible, simple, easy.

"I was now with boys and girls who were studying, fighting, talking; it revitalized my being, whipped my senses to a high, keen pitch of receptivity. I knew that my life was revolving about a world that I had to encounter and fight when I grew up. Suddenly the future loomed tangibly for me, as tangible as a future can loom for a black boy in Mississippi.

"I now saw a world leap to life before my eyes because I could explore it, and that meant not going home when school was out, but wandering, watching, asking, talking. Had I gone home to eat my plate of greens, Granny would not have allowed me out again, so the penalty I paid for roaming was to forfeit my food for twelve hours. I would eat mush at eight in the morning and greens at seven or later at night. To starve in order to learn about my environment was irrational, but so were my hungers. With my books slung over my shoulder, I would tramp with a gang into the woods, to rivers, to creeks, into the business district, to the doors of poolrooms, into the movies when we could slip in without paying, to neighborhood ball games, to brick kilns, to lumberyards, to cottonseed mills to watch men work. There were hours when hunger would make me weak, would make me sway while walking, would make my heart give a sudden wild spurt of beating that would shake my body and make me breathless; but the happiness of being

SOHO REP PRESENTS THE PREMIERE OF

Almos' a Man

chip lopez

A MUSICAL DRAMA BY
PARIS BARCLAY
BASED ON A SHORT STORY BY
RICHARD WRIGHT
DIRECTED BY
TAZEWELL THOMPSON

Poster for the stage adaptation of Wright's short story, which premiered at Soho Rep (New York City), April 12, 1985.

free would lift me beyond hunger, would enable me to discipline the sensations of my body to the extent that I could temporarily forget."[2]

In order to eat more regularly, Wright decided to get a job. It consisted of house and outside work for a white family who gave him moldy, rotten food. "I can't eat this, I told myself. The food was not even clean. The woman came into the kitchen as I was putting on my coat.

"'You didn't eat,' she said.

"'No, ma'am,' I said. 'I'm not hungry.'

"'You'll eat at home?' she asked hopefully.

"'Well, I just wasn't hungry this morning, ma'am,' I lied.

"'You don't like molasses and bread,' she said dramatically.

"'Oh, yes, ma'am, I do,' I defended myself quickly, not wanting her to think that I dared criticize what she had given me.

"'I don't know what's happening to you niggers nowadays,' she sighed, wagging her head. She looked closely at the molasses. 'It's a sin to throw out molasses like that. I'll put it up for you this evening.'

"'Yes, ma'am,' I said heartily.

"Neatly she covered the plate of molasses with another plate, then felt the bread and dumped it into the garbage. She turned to me, her face lit with an idea.

"'What grade are you in school?'

"'Seventh, ma'am.'

"'Then why are you going to school?' she asked in surprise.

"'Well, I want to be a writer,' I mumbled, unsure of myself; I had not planned to tell her that, but she had made me feel so utterly wrong and of no account that I needed to bolster myself.

"'A what?' she demanded.

"'A writer,' I mumbled.

"'For what?'

"'To write stories," I mumbled defensively.

"'You'll never be a writer,' she said, 'Who on earth put such ideas into your nigger head?'

"'Nobody,' I said.

"'I didn't think anybody ever would,' she declared indignantly.

"As I walked around her house to the street, I knew that I would not go back. The woman had assaulted my ego; she had assumed that she knew my place in life, what I felt, what I ought to be, and I resented it with all my heart. Perhaps she was right; perhaps I would never be a writer; but I did not want her to say so."[2]

Wright held several other jobs all of which ended distastefully. "The eighth grade days flowed in their hungry path and I grew more conscious of myself; I sat in classes, bored, wondering, dreaming. One long dry afternoon I took out my composition book and told myself that I would write a story; it was sheer idleness that led me to it. What would the story be about? It resolved itself into a plot about a villain who wanted a widow's home and I called it 'The Voodoo of Hell's Half-Acre.' It was crudely atmospheric, emotional, intuitively psychological, and stemmed from pure feeling. I finished it in three days and then wondered what to do with it.

"The local Negro newspaper! That's it....I sailed into the office and shoved my ragged composition book under the nose of the man who called himself the editor.

"'What is that?' he asked.

"'A story,' I said.

"'A news story?'

"'No, fiction.'

"'All right. I'll read it,' he said.

"He pushed my composition book back on his desk and looked at me curiously, sucking at his pipe.

"'But I want you to read it now.' I said.

"He blinked. I had no idea how newspapers were run. I thought that one took a story to an editor and he sat down then and there and read it and said yes or no.

"'I'll read this and let you know about it tomorrow,' he said.

"I was disappointed; I had taken time to write it and he seemed distant and uninterested.

"'Give me the story,' I said, reaching for it.

"He turned from me, took up the book and read ten pages or more.

"'Won't you come in tomorrow?' he asked. 'I'll have it finished then.'

"I honestly relented.

"'All right,' I said. 'I'll stop in tomorrow.'

"I left with the conviction that he would not read it. Now, where else could I take it after he had turned it down? The next afternoon, en route to my job, I stepped into the newspaper office.

"'Where's my story?' I asked.

"'It's in galleys,' he said.

"'What's that?' I asked; I did not know what galleys were.

"'It's set up in type,' he said. 'We're publishing it.'

"'How much money will I get?' I asked, excited.

"'We can't pay for manuscript,' he said.

"'But you sell your papers for money,' I said with logic.

"'Yes, but we're young in business,' he explained.

"'But you're asking me to *give* you my story, but you don't *give* your papers away,' I said.

"He laughed.

"'Look, you're just starting. This story will put your name before our readers. Now, that's something,' he said.

"'But if the story is good enough to sell to your readers, then you ought to give me some of the money you get from it,' I insisted.

"He laughed again and I sensed that I was amusing him.

"'I'm going to offer you something more valuable than money,' he said. 'I'll give you a chance to learn to write.'

"I was pleased, but I still thought he was taking advantage of me.

"'When will you publish my story?'

"'I'm dividing it into three installments,' he said.

"'The first installment appears this week. But the main thing is this: Will you get news for me on a space rate basis?'

"'I work mornings and evenings for three dollars a week,' I said.

"'Oh,' he said. 'Then you better keep that. But what are you doing this summer?'

"'Nothing.'

"'Then come to see me before you take another job,' he said. 'And write some more stories.'

"A few days later my classmates came to me with baffled eyes, holding copies of the *Southern Register* in their hands.

"'Did you really write that story?' they asked me.

"'Yes.'

"'Why?'

"'Because I wanted to.'

"'Where did you get it from?'

"'I made it up.'

"'You didn't. You copied it out of a book.'

"They were convinced that I had not told them the truth. We had never had any instruction in literary matters at school; the literature of the nation or the Negro had never been mentioned. My schoolmates could not understand why anyone would want to write a story; and, above all, they could not understand why I had called it 'The Voodoo of Hell's Half-Acre.' The mood out of which a story was written was the most alien thing conceivable to them. They looked at me with new eyes, and a distance, a suspiciousness came between us. If I had thought anything in writing the story, I had thought that perhaps it would make me more acceptable to them, and now it was cutting me off from them more completely than ever.

"At home the effects were no less disturbing. Granny came into my room early one morning and sat on the edge of my bed.

"'Richard, what is this you're putting in the papers?' she asked.

"'A story,' I said.

"'About what?'

"'It's just a story, granny.'

"'But they tell me it's been in three times.'

"'It's the same story. It's in three parts.'

"'But what is it about?' she insisted.

"I hedged, fearful of getting into a religious argument.

"'It's just a story I made up,' I said.

"'Then it's a lie,' she said.

"'Oh, Christ,' I said.

"'You must get out of this house if you take the name of the Lord in vain,' she said.

"'Granny, please. . .I'm sorry,' I pleaded. 'But it's hard to tell you about the story. You see, granny, everybody knows that the story isn't true, but. . . .'

"'Then why write it?' she asked.

"'Because people might want to read it.'

"'That's the Devil's work,' she said and left.

"My mother also was worried.

"'Son, you ought to be more serious,' she said. 'You're growing up now and you won't be able to get jobs if you let people think that you're weak-minded. Suppose the superintendent of schools would ask you to teach here in Jackson, and he found out that you had been writing stories?'"[2]

"In the end I was so angry that I refused to talk about the story. From no quarter, with the exception of the Negro newspaper editor, had there come a single encouraging word. It was rumored that the principal wanted to know why I had used the word 'hell.' I felt that I had committed a crime. Had I been conscious of the full extent to which I was pushing against the current of my environment, I would have been frightened altogether out of my attempts at writing. But my reactions were limited to the attitude of the people about me, and I did not speculate or generalize.

"I dreamed of going north and writing books, novels. The North symbolized to me all that I had not felt and seen; it had no relation whatever to what actually existed. Yet, by imagining a place where everything was possible, I kept hope alive in me. But where had I got this notion of doing something in the future, of going away from home and accomplishing something that would be recognized by others? I had, of course, read my Horatio Alger stories, my pulp stories, and I knew my Get-Rich-Quick Wallingford series from cover to cover, though I had sense enough not to hope to get rich; even to my naive imagination that possibility was too remote. I knew that I lived in a country in which the aspirations of black people were limited, marked-off, yet I felt that I had to go somewhere and do something to redeem my being alive.

"I was building up in me a dream which the entire educational system of the South had been rigged to stifle. I was feeling the very thing that the state of Mississippi had spent millions of dollars to make sure that I would never feel; I was becoming aware of the thing that the Jim Crow laws had been drafted and passed to keep out of my consciousness; I was acting on impulses that southern senators in the nation's capital had striven to keep out of Negro life; I was beginning to dream the dreams that the state had said were wrong, that the schools had said were taboo.

"Had I been articulate about my ultimate aspirations, no doubt someone would have told me what I was bargaining for; but nobody seemed to know,

and least of all did I. My classmates felt that I was doing something that was vaguely wrong, but they did not know how to express it. As the outside world grew more meaningful, I became more concerned, tense; and my classmates and my teachers would say: 'Why do you ask so many questions?' Or: 'Keep quiet.'

"I was in my fifteenth year; in terms of schooling I was far behind the average youth of the nation, but I did not know that. In me was shaping a yearning for a kind of consciousness, a mode of being that the way of life about me had said could not be, must not be, and upon which the penalty of death had been placed. Somewhere in the dead of the southern night my life had switched onto the wrong track and, without my knowing it, the locomotive of my heart was rushing down a dangerously steep slope, heading for a collision, heedless of the warning red lights that blinked all about me, the sirens and the bells and the screams that filled the air."[2]

Desperate for money with which to go North, Wright allowed himself to be manipulated by his white employers to fight a "cockfight" with another young black man named Harrison. Neighborhood whites bet on the match; a share of the "pot" was to go to the two fighters. "The fight took place one Saturday afternoon in the basement of a Main Street building. Each white man who attended the fight dropped his share of the pot into a hat that sat on the concrete floor. Only white men were allowed in the basement; no women or Negroes were admitted. Harrison and I were stripped to the waist. A bright electric bulb glowed above our heads. As the gloves were tied on my hands, I looked at Harrison and saw his eyes watching me. Would he keep his promise [to fake the fight]? Doubt made me nervous.

"We squared off and at once I knew that I had not thought sufficiently about what I had bargained for. I could not pretend to fight. Neither Harrison nor I knew enough about boxing to deceive even a child for a moment. Now shame filled me. The white men were smoking and yelling obscenities at us.

"I lashed out with a timid left. Harrison landed high on my head and, before I knew it, I had landed a hard right on Harrison's mouth and blood came. Harrison shot a blow to my nose. The fight was on, was on against our will. I felt trapped and ashamed. I lashed out even harder, and the harder I fought the harder Harrison fought. Our plans and promises now meant nothing. We fought four hard rounds, stabbing, slugging, grunting, spitting, cursing, crying, bleeding. The shame and anger we felt for having allowed ourselves to be duped crept into our blows and blood ran into our eyes, half blinding us. The hate we felt for the men whom we had tried to cheat went into the blows we threw at each other. The white men made the rounds last as long as five minutes and each of us was afraid to stop and ask for time for fear of receiving a blow that would knock us out. When we were on the point of collapsing from exhaustion, they pulled us apart.

"I could not look at Harrison. I hated him and I hated myself."[2]

At nineteen, Wright discovered writer H. L. Mencken. "...Denouncing everything American, extolling everything European or German, laughing at the weaknesses of people, mocking God, authority. What was this?...Trying to realize what reality lay behind the meaning of the words....Yes, this man was fighting, fighting with words. He was using words as a weapon, using them as one would use a club. Could words be weapons? Well, yes, for here they were. Then, maybe, perhaps, I could use them as a weapon? No. It frightened me. I read on and what amazed me was not what he said, but how on earth anybody had the courage to say it.

"Occasionally I glanced up to reassure myself that I was alone in the room. Who were these men about whom Mencken was talking so passionately? Who was Anatole France? Joseph Conrad? Sinclair Lewis, Sherwood Anderson, Dostoevski, George Moore, Gustave Flaubert, Maupassant, Tolstoy, Frank Harris, Mark Twain, Thomas Hardy, Arnold Bennett, Stephen Crane, Zola, Norris, Gorky, Bergson, Ibsen, Balzac, Bernard Shaw, Dumas, Poe, Thomas Mann, O. Henry, Dreiser, H. G. Wells, Gogol, T. S. Eliot, Gide, Baudelaire, Edgar Lee Masters, Stendhal, Turgenev, Huneker, Nietzsche, and scores of others? Were these men real? Did they exist or had they existed? And how did one pronounce their names?

"I ran across many words whose meanings I did not know, and I either looked them up in a dictionary or, before I had a chance to do that, encountered the word in a context that made its meaning clear. But what strange world was this? I concluded the book with the conviction that I had somehow overlooked something terribly important in life. I had once tried to write, had once reveled in feeling, had let my crude imagination roam, but the impulse to dream had been slowly beaten out of me

by experience. Now it surged up again and I hungered for books, new ways of looking and seeing. It was not a matter of believing or disbelieving what I read, but of feeling something new, of being affected by something that made the look of the world different.

"My trips to the library became frequent. Reading grew into a passion. My first serious novel was Sinclair Lewis's *Main Street*. It made me see my boss, Mr. Gerald, and identify him as an American type. I would smile when I saw him lugging his golf bags into the office. I had always felt a vast distance separating me from the boss, and now I felt closer to him, though still distant. I felt now that I knew him, that I could feel the very limits of his narrow life. And this had happened because I had read a novel about a mythical man called George F. Babbitt.

"The plots and stories in the novels did not interest me so much as the point of view revealed. I gave myself over to each novel without reserve, without trying to criticize it; it was enough for me to see

Expatriate Wright in Luxembourg Gardens shortly before his death. (Photo by Gisele Freund.)

and feel something different. And for me, everything was something different. Reading was like a drug, a dope. The novels created moods in which I lived for days. But I could not conquer my sense of guilt, my feeling that the white men around me knew that I was changing, that I had begun to regard them differently.

"Whenever I brought a book to the job, I wrapped it in newspaper—a habit that was to persist for years in other cities and under other circumstances. But some of the white men pried into my packages when I was absent and they questioned me.

"'Boy, what are you reading those books for?'

"'Oh, I don't know, sir.'

"'That's deep stuff you're reading, boy.'

"'I'm just killing time, sir.'

"'You'll addle your brains if you don't watch out.'

"I read Dreiser's *Jennie Gerhardt* and *Sister Carrie* and they revived in me a vivid sense of my mother's suffering; I was overwhelmed. I grew silent, wondering about the life around me. It would have been impossible for me to have told anyone what I derived from these novels, for it was nothing less than a sense of life itself. All my life had shaped me for the realism, the naturalism of the modern novel, and I could not read enough of them.

"Steeped in new moods and ideas, I bought a ream of paper and tried to write; but nothing would come, or what did come was flat beyond telling. I discovered that more than desire and feeling were necessary to write and I dropped the idea. Yet I still wondered how it was possible to know people sufficiently to write about them? Could I ever learn about life and people? To me, with my vast ignorance, my Jim Crow station in life, it seemed a task impossible of achievement. I now knew what being a Negro meant. I could endure the hunger. I had learned to live with hate. But to feel that there were feelings denied me, that the very breath of life itself was beyond my reach, that more than anything else hurt, wounded me. I had a new hunger.

"In buoying me up, reading also cast me down, made me see what was possible, what I had missed. My tension returned, new, terrible, bitter, surging, almost too great to be contained. I no longer *felt* that the world about me was hostile, killing; I *knew* it. A million times I asked myself what I could do to save myself, and there were no answers. I seemed forever condemned, ringed by walls.

"If I went north, would it be possible for me to build a new life then? But how could a man build a life upon vague, unformed yearnings? I wanted to write and I did not even know the English language. I bought English grammars and found them dull. I felt that I was getting a better sense of the language from novels than from grammars. I read hard, discarding a writer as soon as I felt that I had grasped his point of view.

"I knew of no Negroes who read the books I liked and I wondered if any Negroes ever thought of them. I knew that there were Negro doctors, lawyers, newspapermen, but I never saw any of them. When I read a Negro newspaper I never caught the faintest echo of my preoccupation in its pages. I felt trapped and occasionally, for a few days, I would stop reading. But a vague hunger would come over me for books, books that opened up new avenues of feeling and seeing."[2]

In 1927, after years of carefully saving his money, Wright had enough to buy a train ticket to Chicago. "The white South said that it knew 'niggers,' and I was what the white South called a 'nigger.' Well, the white South had never known me—never known what I thought, what I felt. The white South said that I had a 'place' in life. Well, I had never felt my 'place'; or, rather, my deepest instincts had always made me reject the 'place' to which the white South had assigned me. It had never occurred to me that I was in any way an inferior being. And no word that I had ever heard fall from the lips of southern white men had ever made me really doubt the worth of my own humanity."[2]

In Chicago, Wright worked at a variety of jobs, marshalling his best energies for writing. "Working nights, I spent my days in experimental writing, filling endless pages with stream-of-consciousness Negro dialect, trying to depict the dwellers of the Black Belt as I felt and saw them. My reading in sociology had enabled me to discern many strange types of Negro characters, to identify many modes of Negro behavior; and what moved me above all was the frequency of mental illness, that tragic toll that the urban environment exacted of the black peasant. Perhaps my writing was more an attempt at understanding than self-expression. A need that I did not comprehend made me use words to create religious types, criminal types, the warped, the lost, the baffled; my pages were full of tension, frantic poverty, and death.

"But something was missing in my imaginative efforts; my flights of imagination were too subjective, too lacking in reference to social action. I hungered for a grasp of the framework of contemporary living, for a knowledge of the forms of life about me, for eyes to see the bony structures of personality, for theories to light up the shadows of conduct.

"While sorting mail in the post office, I met a young Irish chap whose sensibilities amazed me. We would take a batch of mail in our fingers and, while talking in low monotones out of the sides of our mouths, toss them correctly into their designated holes and suddenly our hands would be empty and we would have no memory of having worked. Most of the clerks could work in this automatic manner. The Irish chap and I had read a lot in common and we laughed at the same sacred things. He was as cynical as I was regarding uplift and hope, and we were proud of having escaped what we called the 'childhood disease of metaphysical fear.' I was introduced to the Irish chap's friends and we formed a 'gang' of Irish, Jewish, and Negro wits who poked fun at government, the masses, statesmen, and political parties. We assumed that all people were good to the degree to which they amused us, or to the extent to which we could make them objects of laughter. We ridiculed all ideas of protest, of organized rebellion or revolution. We felt that all businessmen were thoroughly stupid and that no other group was capable of rising to challenge them. We sneered at voting, for we felt that the choice between one political crook and another was too small for serious thought. We believed that man should live by hard facts alone, and we had so long ago put God out of our minds that we did not even discuss Him.

"Repeatedly I took stabs at writing but the results were so poor that I would tear up the sheets. I was striving for a level of expression that matched those of the novels I read. But I always somehow failed to get onto the page what I thought and felt. Failing at sustained narrative, I compromised by playing with single sentences and phrases. Under the influence of Stein's *Three Lives*, I spent hours and days pounding out disconnected sentences for the sheer love of words."[3]

Wright began to frequent gatherings of young intellectuals, artists, and activists. The Communist Party also attracted him for a number of years, although he never felt totally at ease and eventually resigned his membership. But his early days in the Party were heady, for he was coming to know people of many ethnicities, professions, and backgrounds. A number of the young people he met went on to become eminent artists, writers and composers. His eventual disenchantment with the Communist Party derived from what he perceived as the party's stance against intellectuals.

When Wright left Chicago for New York in 1937, he carried with him the four novellas that in 1938 would be published in a volume entitled *Uncle Tom's Children.* He came to the attention not only of those in the literary world, but in government and politics as well. Eleanor Roosevelt recommended Wright for a Guggenheim Fellowship, which he received in 1939.

He began work on *Native Son,* one of the most controversial American novels published in this century. Part of his inspiration was drawn from newspaper articles about Robert Nixon, a young black who had confessed to murdering five women and brutally raping others, for which he eventually was executed.

The publication of Wright's novel was a major event, drawing both unprecedented acclaim for a black writer, and provoking furious condemnations of his style, themes and politics. The first edition sold out within three hours, was a Book-of-the-Month Club selection, and led to reviews, interviews, debates and profiles on the writer, his work, and his life by both the national and international press.

Writing in *Opportunity,* Sterling Brown praised Wright as "...the first...to give a psychological probing of the consciousness of the outcast, the disinherited, the generation lost in the slum jungles of American civilization."[1]

Eldridge Cleaver believed that "Bigger Thomas, Wright's greatest creation, was a man in violent, though inept, rebellion against the stifling, murderous, totalitarian white world."[1]

The view in *Crisis,* by James W. Ivy, went on to say "*Native Son* is undoubtedly the greatest novel written by an American Negro. In fact it is one of the best American novels, and Mr. Wright is one of the great novelists of this generation."[1]

Native Son was a hit in a Broadway adaptation co-written by Wright and Paul Green, a Pulitzer-prize-winning white playwright concerned with black culture, folklore, and music. The play was staged by Orson Welles and produced by Welles and John Houseman. Canada Lee, as Bigger Thomas, delivered a brilliant performance.

Wright's next major project was *Twelve Million Black Voices.* Photographer Edwin Rosskam supplied the accompanying pictures, culled from his own work as well as from the Farm Security Administration photo collection. Wright's essay not only provided a proud view of African culture, and a lucid though mournful attack on slavery, but heralded more revolutionary attitudes toward civil rights, black power, and nationalism.

Black Boy, Wright's magisterial evocation of his own coming of age and consciousness, was published in 1945. It has been likened to Gorki's autobiography, a masterpiece of world literature. Again, the book's appearance was an important event, with some vehement negative, as well as positive, critical responses. It had a strong impact in the West Indies and Africa, as well as England and Europe.

Gertrude Stein had long been an important influence for Wright. For her part, she thought Wright the best critic her work ever had. Partly through her influence, Wright was invited by the French government to Paris, for one month, all expenses paid. Unbeknowst to Wright, he was under U.S. government surveillance, and the State Department made it difficult for him to get a passport. Eventually, however, he got his papers, and found himself even more of a celebrity in France than in the U.S. A year later, in 1947, he moved his family to Paris.

Wright travelled widely, not only in Europe, but in Africa, Asia and Latin America, on assignment for numerous publications and as the guest of many conferences and symposia.

The circumstances of Wright's death remain unresolved. The official cause was given as a heart attack, but many of his friends and colleagues expressed the opinion that it was not a natural death. They found his relations with his Russian physician—a man who saw few patients and whose means of livelihood were mysterious—troubling. Not long before he died, Wright had been taking a host of drugs in unorthodox combinations. He died suddenly in the Eugene Gibet Clinic, shortly after having been given an injection, the exact need for which has still not been determined.

In 1967, John A. Williams published *The Man Who Cried I Am,* a *roman a clef* whose premise is that Wright was murdered by the CIA. A most complicated and conflicted man, Wright often felt awkwardly poised between his origins and the rage they engendered in him, his considerable success among whites, and disagreements with some of his fellow black writers and activists. His work remains powerful, troubling, and exhilarating.

Footnote Sources:

[1] Margaret Walker, *Richard Wright: Daemonic Genius,* Warner, 1988.
[2] Richard Wright, *Black Boy,* Harper, 1945.
[3] R. Wright, *American Hunger,* Harper, 1977.

■ For More Information See

Books:

Current Biography 1940, H. W. Wilson, 1941.
Ralph Ellison, *Shadow and Act,* Random House, 1945.
Carl Milton Hughes, *The Negro Novelist 1940-1950,* Citadel, 1953.
James Baldwin, *Notes of a Native Sun,* Beacon Press, 1955.
J. Baldwin, *Nobody Knows My Name,* Dial, 1961.
David Littlejohn, *Black on White: A Critical Survey of Writing by American Negroes,* Viking, 1966.
Thomas Knipp, editor, *Richard Wright: Letters to Joe C. Brown,* Kent State University Libraries, 1968.
Constance Webb, *Richard Wright: A Biography,* Putnam, 1968.
Edward Margolies, *The Art of Richard Wright,* Southern Illinois University Press, 1969.
C. W. E. Bigsby, editor, *The Black American Writer: Fiction, Volume One,* Everett/Edwards, 1969.
Robert Bone, *Richard Wright,* University of Minnesota Press, 1969.
Russell Carl Brignano, *Richard Wright: An Introduction to the Man and His Works,* University of Pittsburgh Press, 1970.
Donald B. Gibson, editor, *Five Black Writers,* New York University Press, 1970.
John A. Williams and Dorothy Sterling, *The Most Native of Sons: A Biography of Richard Wright,* Doubleday, 1970.
Houston A. Baker, Jr., *Black Literature in America,* McGraw, 1971.
David Ray and Robert M. Farnsworth, editors, *Richard Wright: Impressions and Perspectives,* University of Michigan Press, 1973.
Michel Fabre, *The Unfinished Quest of Richard Wright,* Morrow, 1973.
David Bakish, *Richard Wright,* Ungar, 1973.
Contemporary Literary Criticism, Gale, Volume 1, 1973, Volume 3, 1975, Volume 4, 1975, Volume 9, 1978, Volume 14, 1980, Volume 21, 1982, Volume 48, 1988.
Addison Gayle, Jr., *The Way of the New World: The Black Novel in America,* Doubleday, 1975.
Morris Dickstein, *Gates of Eden,* Basic Books, 1977.
Evelyn Gross Avery, *Rebels and Victims: The Fiction of Richard Wright and Bernard Malamud,* Kennikat Press, 1979.
Robert Felgar, *Richard Wright,* Twayne, 1980.
A. Gayle, *Richard Wright—Ordeal of a Native Son,* Doubleday, 1980.
Charles T. Davis and M. Fabre, *Richard Wright: A Primary Bibliography,* G. K. Hall, 1982.

M. Fabre, *The World of Richard Wright*, University Press of Mississippi, 1985.

Joyce A. Joyce, *Richard Wright's Art of Tragedy*, University of Iowa Press, 1986.

Keneth Kinnamon and others, *A Richard Wright Bibliography: Fifty Years of Criticism and Commentary, 1933-1982*, Greenwood, 1988.

Joan F. Urban, *Richard Wright*, Chelsea House, 1989.

Periodicals:

New Republic, April 6, 1938, April 7, 1941, March 12, 1945, February 18, 1957, November 24, 1958, February 13, 1961.

Saturday Review, March 2, 1940, June 1, 1940, March 3, 1945, March 28, 1953, October 23, 1954, October 18, 1958, March 30, 1963 (p. 37ff), January 21, 1978 (p. 45ff).

New York Times Book Review, March 2, 1940 (p. 3ff), March 4, 1945 (p. 3), March 22, 1953 (p. 1ff), September 26, 1954, March 18, 1956, February 24, 1957, October 26, 1958, June 26, 1977 (p. 1ff) March 5, 1978 (p. 11ff).

Time, March 4, 1940 (p. 72).

Nation, March 16, 1940, April 5, 1941, April 7, 1945, October 16, 1954, October 25, 1958 (p. 297ff).

Atlantic Monthly, May, 1940 (p. 659ff), June, 1940, March, 1945, May, 1953, March, 1970.

New York Times, June 8, 1942, November 23, 1985 (p. 1), December 7, 1986 (p. 68ff).

"Richard Wright Describes the Birth of *Black Boy*—An Autobiography Destined to Disturb White Egotism," *New York Post*, November 30, 1944.

Graduate Comment, 1964.

Critic, June-July, 1968 (p. 66ff).

New Letters, December, 1971 (p. 24ff).

English Journal, May, 1973 (p. 714).

Novel: A Forum on Fiction, spring, 1974.

Village Voice, July 4, 1977 (p. 80ff).

National Review, Febraury 3, 1978.

Obituaries:

New York Times, November 30, 1960.

New York Herald Tribune, November 30, 1960.

Collections:

Richard Wright Archive, Beinecke Rare Book and Manuscript Library, Yale University.

Northwestern University.

Kent State University.

Schomburg Collection, New York Public Library.

American Library, Paris, France.

Harvard University Libraries.

Patricia Wrightson

B orn June 19, 1921, in Lismore, New South Wales, Australia; daughter of Charles Radcliff (a solicitor) and Alice (a housewife; maiden name, Dyer) Furlonger; married, 1943 (divorced 1953); children: Jennifer Mary Wrightson Ireland, Peter Radcliff. *Education:* Attended St. Catherine's College, and State Correspondence School. *Religion:* Church of England. *Residence:* Lohic, P.O. Box 91, Maclean, New South Wales 2463, Australia. *Agent:* Curtis Brown Pty., Ltd., 27 Union St., Paddington, Sydney, NSW 2021, Australia.

■ Career

Bonalbo District Hospital, Bonalbo, New South Wales, secretary and administrator, 1946-60; writer, 1953—; Sydney District Nursing Association, New South Wales, secretary and administrator, 1960-64; Department of Education, New South Wales, assistant editor of *School Magazine*, 1964-70, editor, 1970-75.

■ Awards, Honors

Book of the Year Award from the Australian Children's Book Council, 1956, for *The Crooked Snake*, Commendation, 1958, for *The Bunyip Hole*, High Commendation, 1973 for *An Older Kind of Magic*, and 1982, for *Behind the Wind;* Book of the Year Award Runner-up from the Australian Children's Book Council, and *Book World*'s Spring Book Festival Award, both 1968, and Hans Christian Andersen Honor List of the International Board on Books for Young People (IBBY), 1970, all for *I Own a Racecourse!*

Book of the Year Award from the Australian Children's Book Council, and one of *New York Times* Outstanding Books, both 1974, IBBY's Honor List for Text, 1976, and *Voice of Youth Advocates*' Annual Selection of Best Science Fiction and Fantasy Titles for Young Adults, and Finish Award for Best Translated Children's Book, both 1988, all for *The Nargun and the Stars;* Officer, Order of the British Empire, 1978; Book of the Year Award from Australian Children's Book Council, and *Guardian* Award Commendation, both 1978, and International Board on Books for Young People Honor List, 1979, all for *The Ice Is Coming;* New South Wales Premier's Award for Ethnic Writing, and selected one of Child Study Association of America's Children's Books of the Year, both 1979, both for *The Dark Bright Water.*

Shortlisted for the *Guardian* Award, 1983, and Carnegie Medal Commendation, Book of the Year Award from the Australian Children's Book Council, *Boston Globe-Horn Book* Award for Fiction, and *Observer* Teenage Fiction Prize, all 1984, all for *A Little Fear;* Dromkeen Medal from the Dromkeen Children's Literature Foundation, 1984, for "a significant contribution to the appreciation and

development of children's literature in Australia'';
Hans Christian Andersen Medal runner-up, 1984,
and Author Award, 1986; chosen to deliver the
sixteenth annual Arbuthnot Lecture, 1985; Golden
Cat Award from the Sjoestrands Forlag AB (Swe-
den), 1986, for ''a contribution to children's and
young adult literature''; Lady Cutler Award, 1986;
Austrian Children and Youth Book Prize Honor
List, 1988, for *Night Outside*; Special Occasional
Award from New South Wales Premier's Literature
Awards, 1988.

■ Writings

Fiction For Young People:

The Crooked Snake (illustrated by Margaret
Horder), Angus & Robertson, 1955, reissued,
Hutchinson, 1972.

The Bunyip Hole (illustrated by M. Horder),
Angus & Robertson, 1957, reissued,
Hutchinson, 1973.

The Rocks of Honey (illustrated by M. Horder),
Angus & Robertson, 1960, reissued, Penguin,
1977.

The Feather Star (ALA Notable Book; illustrated
by Noela Young), Harcourt, 1962.

Down to Earth (illustrated by M. Horder),
Harcourt, 1965.

I Own the Racecourse! (illustrated by M.
Horder), Hutchinson, 1968, published in the
United States as *A Racecourse for Andy* (ALA
Notable Book; *Horn Book* honor list),
Harcourt, 1968.

An Older Kind of Magic (illustrated by N.
Young), Harcourt, 1972.

The Nargun and the Stars (fantasy; ALA
Notable Book; *Horn Book* honor list),
Hutchinson, 1973, Atheneum, 1974, reissued,
Macmillan, 1986.

The Ice Is Coming (young adult; first book in
fantasy trilogy), Atheneum, 1977.

The Dark Bright Water (young adult; second
book in fantasy trilogy), Hutchinson, 1978,
Atheneum, 1979.

Night Outside (illustrated by Jean Cooper-
Brown), Rigby, 1979, published in the United
States (illustrated by Beth Peck), Atheneum,
1985.

Behind the Wind (young adult; third book in
fantasy trilogy), Hutchinson, 1981, published
in the United States as *Journey behind the
Wind*, Atheneum, 1981.

A Little Fear (fantasy; ALA Notable Book; *Horn
Book* honor list), Atheneum, 1983.

Moon-Dark (illustrated by N. Young),
McElderry Books, 1988.

Baylet, McElderry Books, 1989.

The Old, Old Ngrang (illustrated by David
Wong), Nelson Australia, 1989.

Editor:

*Beneath the Sun: An Australian Collection for
Children*, Collins (Australia), 1972.

*Emu Stew: An Illustrated Collection of Stories
and Poems for Children*, Kestrel, 1977.

Wrightson's books have been translated into Croa-
tian, Danish, Finish, German, Greek, Italian, Japanese, Spanish, Norwegian, Slovene, and Swedish.

■ Adaptations

''The Nargun and the Stars'' (television series),
ABC-TV, 1977.

''I Own the Racecourse'' (film), Barron Films,
1985.

■ Work in Progress

A novel.

■ Sidelights

One of Australia's foremost authors of books for
children and young adults, Patricia Wrightson has
been writing for over thirty years. She came upon
the literary scene ''by accident,'' at a time when
few Australian children's authors had yet been
recognized. ''I must, I think, be one of the luckiest
writers who ever lived.

''I was lucky as a nervous, fumbling beginner, in
daring only to write for my children; it took me by
accident into the field where the qualities I value
count most. I was lucky in stumbling into this field
at a moment when it was bursting with life: when
the whole small community connected with children's books was concerned and hopeful and
purposeful; when the climate was right and it was
all beginning. I was so very lucky as to win
Australia's ten-year-old Book Council Award with
my very first book.

''I do think I've been lucky to work in Australia, for
there we had no paths to follow. Most other
countries had well-established paths, and could
pack off a new story to its proper address with
facility: the folk-tale or fantasy, the school story,
the family story, the Puritan or Civil War or
Independence story, and so on. In Australia thirty
years ago we were still exploring paths.

"We were not unusual in that, I know; new paths were being explored all over the world. It was part of the climate of encouragement and acceptance, part of our united belief in the honesty and value of our work. We have all seen the field extending as the new paths opened it up, so that now the work of thirty years ago needs to be seen in the context of its time. But Australian writers, with so small a body of work behind them, could feel that the country's literature was immediately in their hands. Every story that anyone could conceive was his own new concept, not shaped or directed or limited by other people's thinking; to be worked out in his own way and for almost the first time.

"We were lucky writers—I was lucky even in my failures. It can't be common, in the twentieth century, for a writer to discover a hole in his nation's literature through the accident of falling into it; and then to find the missing piece through sheer need, and to have it welcomed so warmly.

"I have been lucky and we have all been lucky. We have been wanted and encouraged, given freedom to develop, in a field that is itself a challenge. For

Ballantine's 1977 paperback cover.

Dust jacket from the 1962 hardcover.

this is the field in which to struggle for directness, sharpness and clarity; in which the need for economy taught one to choose words that suggested more than they said; where a story must unfold soundly and logically if you want it to be taken seriously."[1]

Wrightson's memories of childhood are remarkably vivid. "We had a big timber house on my father's farm, and a series of men worked the farm while my father did his own legal work.

"I was born in 1921, and we lived on that farm until I was four. It seems much longer, maybe because I remember so much. Stealing my sisters' mouth organ, which they wouldn't let me play: carrying it off down the hill, to sit on a stone and make interesting noises that brought my mother to the scene. Playing for hours by the stream, stirring the long green weeds with a stick, while my father was building a waterwheel to pump the water up

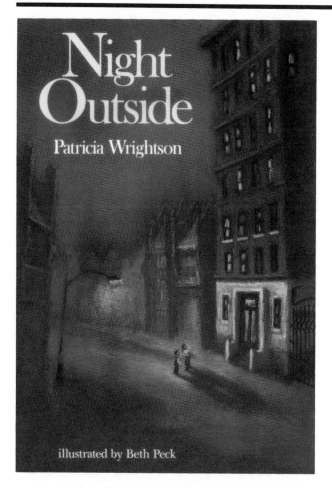

Jacket of the 1985 Atheneum edition.

the hill to the house. Standing with him on a wharf with the sea restless underneath, waiting to meet my mother when she returned from a holiday in the city. She had travelled, as people did then, on the small steamship that bucked and rolled up and down the coast. She had been acutely seasick both ways.

"So many things belong to the farm, and to the year when I was four, that I seem to have been four for years and years. I was still four when my parents decided to try the experiment of living in the city, and there was an auction sale of our furniture. I was deeply and darkly angry with all those people who tramped through the house and took our things away. One or two small and treasured bits I removed and hid—obstinately, over and over, every time my mother put them back.

"We lived for only a year or so in Sydney, for the city experiment was not successful. Two important things happened in that time: we had a baby brother, and my father bought a set of books written by Charles Dickens. Both made a great

difference, but the baby not for some time. By the time he was born I had turned five, and my parents had decided to go back to the northern rivers. My mother went first, taking my sisters and the baby, but I stayed for several months with my father, so that he would not be too lonely. The baby was postponed for me, while my father wound things up in the city.

"The books arrived much earlier. The books of Charles Dickens are crowded with interesting and amusing people, and my father was a great reader. One night, on an impulse, he read a little from *David Copperfield* to my older sisters, and I was allowed to stay and listen. After that, until we were all in our teens, we never allowed him to stop. He read to us every night, going through all those books many times; and much later he read different books to my children. When he began reading to us I was still only four, so I can't imagine a family in which the parents don't share with their children some good books that are too hard for the children to read by themselves.

"My sisters had always been called 'bookworms': by now I was a bookworm too. Our school was a good one, the central school for a large district and one of the biggest in the State; but it had no library. That's how things were in those days. You might perhaps belong to a library in the town, but I don't remember any for children. You had your own books, and lent them to friends and borrowed theirs. We were lucky; we had, between us, a lot of books, and my father bought lots that were 'family' books, mainly for adults but good for children to prowl in.

"We had cut our baby teeth on A. A. Milne and a little of Lear and *Peter Pan and Wendy* and *Alice in Wonderland*. Now we had *Through the Looking Glass* too; I remember being excited because it seemed so much better than *Alice*. Both were about dreams, but *Looking Glass* exactly caught the feeling of a dream. By now, too, we had the Kipling books, a whole series, and Arthur Mee's *Children's Encyclopaedia*; some English school-stories and annuals; a beautiful collection of Greek myths; *Wuthering Heights* and *The Woman in White*; the 'Emily of New Moon' books, the three 'Katy' books, *The Girl of the Lumberlost*, *Little Women*, and a constant flow of minor books that I can't remember.

"Yet, about this time, all these books began to turn me into a muddled sort of person. Without knowing it, I began to feel dissatisfied about something, unsure about something; it was many years before I knew what, or why. Now it seems obvious; but now, since I grew up, I've met many other people of my age who felt the same way, and between us we have come to understand it.

"If you looked at all those books we had as children, and all the others that my friends had when they were children, you would have to notice something strange; they were all fine books that I am glad to have known—but none of them were written by an Australian, or about Australia. A number were American, for American literature is a hundred years older than ours; and, since the country is more like Europe, its early. European writers did not have to struggle with so much that was strange. The rest of our books came from the English literature that our people inherit.

"We did have three Australian books, and borrowed about three more from friends. To children growing up, and reading eagerly all the time, that was very little. We didn't lack Australian books because my parents thought them unimportant but because there were so few.

"We didn't even much like the few we had; there weren't any smugglers' caves, or castles with hidden treasures, or boarding schools, or people who talked in a funny way. There were no snowy Christmases, with Yule logs on the roaring fires and people making punch; no springtime rejoicing, and far too much heat in summer. In fact—very subtly, and without our even knowing it—our books were teaching us that it was not much fun, and not very important, to be Australian; that every other place in the world was more interesting, and books about every other place were better and more exciting.

"I know people of my generation who still feel like that. Some of them are teaching in Australian schools. They are growing fewer, as Australian literature grows. But that would have taken a long time if all Australian writers had grown up thinking their own stories were not worthwhile.

"An Aboriginal child becomes Australian without the need of books—but not without stories and traditions, or without the country itself. I had lived in the country—but I had never met my country face to face, even in books. I didn't do that until we had moved away from the river-plains into the rough hill-country behind.

"I hated it. My sisters, having started high school, were boarding back in civilisation, for of course there were no high schools out here. I thought perhaps I had gone mad, and my parents had

brought me here because this was a place for mad people.

"I'm glad it happened like that: that I came abruptly from city and town into this country and learnt to love it. I'm glad I was still near enough to the ground to discover tiny, strange flowers and examine them, or to stare far up a mighty trunk into the grandeur of some truly ancient gum tree. For I have seen things that are gone now, some of them wonderful things; and if I was too young to know it then, at least I can remember it now.

"I've seen grey, ringbarked trees whose dead trunks bore patterns that were cut into them with stone axes long ago when the trees were still alive; these were the patterns that mark an Aboriginal burial-place, or a sacred meeting-ground. I've climbed steeply up through virgin rain forest by paths of laid stone: paths a single stone in width, laid by brown men along steep hillsides long before Captain Cook saw those hills from the sea. I've been shown great rocks, hidden away in deep forest, about which there are secret stories that only the Aboriginal people know. I've dug up the

Jacket from the 1986 Macmillan edition.

chipped and ground head of a stone axe in my front garden, and have it still.

"I've lived, as people used to do, without electricity: driving to the butter factory to buy a four-foot block of ice for the old ice-chest; making ice cream in a freezer packed with broken ice and coarse salt; ironing with a trio of Potts irons heated on a wood-burning stove. I know how one crystal of salt falling into the custard will ruin the ice cream, and how to tighten the clip of the iron handle with the blade of a knife so that the heavy iron won't crash down on your feet. I know the finicking business of trimming a lamp wick so that it gives the best and steadiest light. I've rolled a forty-gallon drum of water from the dam in the gully to the copper in the back yard, to boil the family wash—and chopped wood for the copper fire.

"I've fought fires for my home without water or the help of a bush brigade. I know how to beat without spreading the fire, and how suddenly it can leap up a tree. I've driven down a steep clay road in the rain, when the car slid all the way side-on with its wheels gripped in the deep ruts, cut by the bullock waggons, and the country tumbled away into dark, wet gorges below. In a drought year when the tanks were low, we have all driven to the swimming hole in the creek for a family bath; by then I had two more brothers, and someone was sure to drop the soap in the deep end of the pool.

"None of it made me Australian, but at least it gave me a clearer view of my country. Meanwhile I had finished primary school, spent a year in boarding school, and been so dreadfully homesick that I was allowed to come home and do high school by correspondence. Perhaps that also widened my view of the country; for the New South Wales Correspondence School is for all those children who live in lonely places, and its magazine helps them to keep in touch.

"I had finished school in 1939, when the Second World War began. Suddenly, all the young men of our district vanished into the forces. A great many girls went too, into the forces or to do war work in the cities. I went to Sydney again, this time with a friend called Doris, to make munitions and help to win the war.

"For a while we stayed with an aunt of mine, but later we took an apartment of our own.

"Having our own apartment was fun, but I don't think we enjoyed the war. We missed the country, and our families. We both had friends and cousins in the forces, country boys who also missed their families. There were generally two or three on leave, and we all looked after each other. Doris and I worked long hours, did a lot of washing and cooking for whoever turned up, saw a good many shows, explored the city and wished for the war to end.

"By the time it did, we were both married. Doris was living not far from the city and I had gone back to my hill-country. I had a year-old daughter and would soon have a son. For the young people of my time, the war that lasted six years had stolen some of our youth. We had finished growing up without Australian books; in a while, some of us began to write them.

"That was when I first began to think how good it would be if my children had more Australian books, along with all the others; books about their own place, and children who lived as they did. The war had made me forget the fun of writing my own stories. I remembered it now, and knew I should write some for my children.

"It took some time to find both the courage and the time, but at last I did. The first two books were called *The Crooked Snake* and *The Bunyip Hole*. They were set in this hill-country where we lived, in the sort of place about which everyone says, 'Where's *that?*' The children in the stories did not find this country boring or unimportant. They rode their bicycles in it, and climbed hills and explored rain forest and grilled sausages on campfires and swam in waterholes, in a way that was real to me. Before I had even finished typing each story, my father was reading to Jenny and Peter the part that was typed so far; and while he read I would sit quietly, watching the children's faces. They were very nice children; they were pretty sure to say that they loved the stories. By watching their faces I knew what they really thought. I could see where something bothered them, and sort it out later.

"When the first, *The Crooked Snake*, was finished and it seemed that the children had really been absorbed in it, I sent it away to a publisher. For a long, long time nothing happened. I wrote to the publishers again, a very short letter with a simple question: 'What page are you up to now?' They answered, at last, that they were indeed going to publish the story.

"It was a surprising time. I had thought of my books as little, local things that hardly anyone would notice; I had never thought how far a book might travel. It was surprising to discover, by winning the [Australian Children's Book Council Book of the Year] award, a whole community of people who were deeply interested in books for children, who noticed every new one, and with whom you could talk seriously and deeply about them.

"When my children were in high school I went to work in Sydney; first to manage a city nursing service and later to help produce *School Magazine.* (This is a magazine that is distributed in all the primary schools of New South Wales.) Work kept me in the city for many years, and *Down to Earth, I Own the Racecourse!* (which in America is called *A Racecourse for Andy*), and *An Older Kind of Magic* have each a city setting. The last one set me on a new course and helped me to discover that elusive quality that is Australian."[2]

Wrightson is known for writing fantasy, drawn from ancient Australian myth. Though she may have discovered this genre inadvertently, she has given much time and energy to its research. "When I first began to talk about Australian fairies, a field worker from the mission stations in the north declared roundly that there was no such thing. Only on second thought did it occur to her that perhaps the material had not been found because it had not been sought.

"The first time I went hunting fairies in the public library, I believed I had found them. They were fairies at least from the fantasy writer's point of view—spirits that anyone might meet at any time and that could therefore enter new stories; spirits not held to be secret or sacred, not involved in creation or preservation but only in the chanciness of daily life. I dug them out of the works of anthropologists and early field workers and of laymen who had lived in sympathetic friendship with Aboriginal Australians—not many, but enough to begin a small collection from which I would select.

"It is not enough to uncover a set of new shapes with new and difficult names and simply to apply these to a set of familiar concepts. If you are searching for an authentic magic with its own powers of conviction and interpretation, you must try to see it truly. Coming to it as a stranger you must turn your back on your own cherished folklore and look at the new one through the eyes of its own country. And if the material has been collected in passing—by collectors chiefly concerned with trade, marriage customs, or sacred beliefs and legends—from a people proud and shy and resentful of misunderstanding, there will be only a few bald words to guide you. You will have to make decisions, not only on the touchy question of sacred-or-available but after that on questions of appearance, personality, turns of speech, and place in the scheme of life. To make those decisions for the living folklore of a hurt and sensitive people is, and should be, terrifying. Perhaps only a writer would be ruthless enough. And even the writer, surely, must also work for a comprehension of folklore and fantasy in general."[3]

Thus were created some of Wrightson's most popular stories, including *The Nargun and the Stars.* "Luckily for me, the Nargun itself caught me and carried me off; and. . .the result was enormously encouraging. When the book appeared, great numbers of people spoke or wrote to me about it. Some were Australians who had been for a long time away from home, and all said the same thing: the Nargun identified something for them, gave them the country as they had known and felt it in an unspoken way. In fact, that indigenous magic did indeed have powers of conviction and interpretation unmatched by the imported kind."[3]

Dust jacket for Wrightson's 1983 novel.

"I had made a rule for myself: never write the same book twice. When your first book has had a surprising success, like *The Crooked Snake*, it is natural to feel that now you know how to do it; you only need to write another book like that one, and it too will succeed. That seemed to me a dangerous idea. You might go on writing for years and never learn anything more. I felt very much a beginner who needed to learn; I had better tackle something different every time. It might be a simple story, easy for other writers, but it should be new and difficult for me."[4]

"I like themes involving some mental exploration and a stretching of understanding. I may be peculiar in my treatment of them. Having discovered such a theme and worked it out fully, I don't like to write a story that demonstrates it with all the flat-footed authority of an adult backed up by print. I may be wrong; and anyway it seems to me a greater and more important achievement to induce a child to think about it for himself and reach his own conclusions. I have confidence in the ability of children's unscarred minds. It seems to me that if my theme provides *me* with a light by which to write my story, the story will reflect this light and will probably set children thinking for themselves, spontaneously."[5]

Wrightson has had a variety of experiences with criticism of her work. "I had a story to write, called *The Rocks of Honey*. It was for the aboriginal and white children of a small outback town, and in working on it I felt like a doctor handling an infected limb: determined not to make any hurt feel worse, nor to avoid any truth merely because it hurt. One of the infections I had to open was the old cry 'Abos stink!' The truth that I wanted to emerge was that, to the aboriginal, whites also stink. But how to make the point without first enlarging on the old, bitter hurt?

"The lancet I chose was laughter. To produce it I used the story of the boiling gum-leaves. I put my two boys, aboriginal and white, in a cubby-house with a can of water and leaves on the boil and allowed that dreadful smell to creep up on them— giving rise to mutual uneasy suspicion, mutual recognition, and finally mutual shouts of relieved laughter. I knew I needn't underline for my chosen readers, and for others the laughter could stand by itself.

"Twenty years later again, an English critic, in a serious critical study, quoted these gum-leaves as evidence of didacticism. He couldn't possibly have understood the unspoken send-up—nor could many Australians without the right background. But surely boiling gum-leaves seems an odd subject for a writer to be didactic about? No doubt he opened the eyes of many students to the insidious nature of this evil. But in doing so he obscured the laughter, which was important.

"Books are not written for critics but for the people who will respond to them, and the writer must depend to some extent on this response. Of course, no story can ever be told as fully as it would happen in life. Not only would it be unbearably slow and boring, but all its points and insights would be lost under the overlay of insignificant detail. No character study can really be full and rounded; if it were, you would see the character only as clearly as you see yourself, which is not very clearly at all. The fullness of life and the roundness of character have to be explored in the writer's mind and then suggested: by the selection of a few details that don't seem selected but suggest many more, by dialogue, by mood and construction, by pauses that emphasize chosen words, by flow and rhythm, and by all the tricks of technique. The less a story has to be told—the less it is loaded with words, explanation, accurate detail—the more spontaneously real it will be.

"It follows, of course, that one of the most delicate balancing feats for the writer is to decide how much to tell and how much only to suggest. The easiest mistake is to tell too little—to omit some clue to character or some minor mechanical detail just because it's so logically clear in the writer's mind. But generally the practiced, consenting reader will assume the right details or quickly adjust if he or she seems to have gone wrong and not even be aware of doing so. Perhaps the critic, being less firmly supported by the story and less intimately in tune with the writer, is more likely to depend on being told.

"Technique is really the writer's instinctive reaching for more story, more brightly illuminated, conveyed in fewer words. It is not meant to put a polish on the story or to be noticed and admired. A technique that is recognized as a technique is one that has failed, at least with that reader. Techniques are not meant to be seen at all; they are meant to work. They are meant to draw the reader, invisibly and unfelt, right into the story. In fact, the way to judge a story is not to take it to pieces like a watch but to read it, to test its power. The critic knows this, too, for he often acts as a reviewer, and his critical study often draws on other reviewers. And reviewers do function as responsive readers. That is their value.

"All my books have taught me something, but perhaps none so startlingly as the one called *The Nargun and the Stars*. It taught me several things: that one light touch of real experience is worth a ton of careful thought; that a device, properly used, becomes an integral part of the story and can't be separated out; and that a consenting reader can come more deeply into the heart of a story, more intimately into the mind of its writer, than the critic ever could."[6]

"The writer with the secret vision, and the lonely need to turn it into a story, will not go away. He has withstood the belief that his craft was sinful, that it was a teaching-aid, that it was outworn, that it had nothing to say; he will not blench at learning that it should be assembled by a committee from prefabricated plastic parts. He will find some crazy, off-beat listener, in the mental homes if necessary, and go on telling stories in his own old way. Perhaps, in some dusty attic, he will even come across an old-steam-driven typewriter, and bring out a copy or two."[1]

"Each book at least from the second on was a move towards...fantasy. Not the escape from life that some people see as fantasy, nor the symbolism of life that is some fantasy, but that strangeness and fullness of life that spills out of the bucket of reality—the human experience of fantasy. I found my footprints damp with it."[7]

Footnote Sources:

[1] Patricia Wrightson, "Hans Christian Andersen Award Acceptance Speech," *Bookbird*, March/April, 1986.

[2] Adele Sarkissian, editor, *Something about the Author Autobiography Series*, Volume 4, Gale, 1987.

[3] P. Wrightson, "Ever Since My Accident: Aboriginal Folklore and Australian Fantasy," *Horn Book*, December, 1980.

[4] P. Wrightson, "Stones into Pools," *Top of the News*, spring, 1985.

[5] John Rowe Townsend, *A Sense of Story*, Lippincott, 1971.

[6] P. Wrightson, "The Geranium Leaf," *Horn Book*, March/April, 1986.

[7] J. R. Townsend, *A Sounding of Storytellers*, Lippincott, 1971.

■ For More Information See

Horn Book, June, 1963 (p. 290), June 1965 (p. 277ff), October, 1972, August, 1974 (p. 382ff), February, 1978 (p. 57ff), April, 1980 (p. 196ff), August, 1981, August, 1982 (p. 478ff), January/February, 1985 (p. 38ff), January/February, 1986 (p. 64ff), September/October, 1986 (p. 572ff), March/April, 1988 (p. 180ff).

Book World, May 5, 1968.

Books and Bookmen, July, 1968.

Cover art by Ronald Himler for the 1989 novel.

National Observer, July 1, 1968.

Young Readers Review, September, 1968.

School Librarian, March, 1969, December, 1973 (p. 359).

Bookbird, number 2, 1970, April, 1984, February, 1986 (p. 4ff), June 15, 1986 (p. 4ff).

H. M. Saxby, *A History of Australian Children's Literature,* Volume 2, Wentworth Books, 1971.

Martha E. Ward and Dorothy A. Marquardt, *Authors of Books for Young People,* Scarecrow, 1971.

Washington Post Book World, November 5, 1972.

Author's Choice/2, Crowell, 1974.

Children's Literature in Education, September, 1974 (p. 12ff), spring, 1978 (p. 43ff).

Signal, January, 1976 (p. 31ff).

Times Literary Supplement, March 25, 1977.

Growing Point, October, 1977 (p. 3182ff), December, 1977 (p. 3217ff), September, 1979 (p. 3563ff).

Doris de Montreville and Elizabeth D. Crawford, *Fourth Book of Junior Authors and Illustrators,* H. W. Wilson, 1978.

Bulletin of the Center for Children's Books, February, 1978, July/August, 1979, November, 1983, October, 1985, May, 1988.

Junior Bookshelf, February, 1978 (p. 52ff), August, 1979 (p. 229ff), December, 1981 (p. 235ff), October, 1983 (p. 215).

D. L. Kirkpatrick, *Twentieth-Century Children's Writers,* St. Martin's, 1978, 2nd edition, 1983.

Starship: The Magazine about Science Fiction, winter/spring, 1982-83.

New York Times Book Review, November 13, 1983 (p. 41), January 29, 1989.

John Rowe Townsend, *Written for Children: An Outline of English-Language Children's Literature,* second revised edition, Lippincott, 1983.

School Library Journal, May, 1984 (p. 14), December, 1985 (p. 96).

New York Public Library News Release, April, 1985.

Publishers Weekly, August 30, 1985 (p. 423), October 31, 1986, October 30, 1987, March 21, 1989.

Zena Sutherland and May Hill Arbuthnot, *Children and Books,* seventh edition, Scott, Foresman, 1986.

Children's Book World, July/August, 1987.

Voice of Youth Advocates, April, 1988.

Collections:

Lu Rees Archives, Canberra College of Advanced Education Library, Australia.

Kerlan Collection at the University of Minnesota.

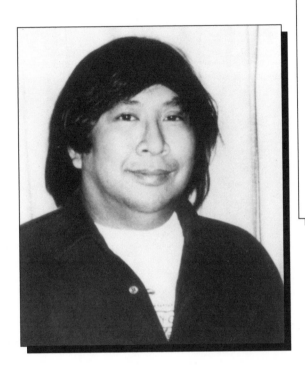

Laurence Yep

Born June 14, 1948, in San Francisco, Calif.; son of Thomas Gim (a postal clerk) and Franche (a housewife; maiden name, Lee) Yep. *Education:* Attended Marquette University, 1966-68; University of California, Santa Cruz, B.A., 1970; State University of New York at Buffalo, Ph.D., 1975. *Home:* 921 Populus Place, Sunnyvale, Calif. 94086. *Agent:* Maureen Walters, Curtis Brown Agency, 10 Astor Place, New York, N.Y. 10003.

■ Career

Writer, 1968—; San Jose City College, San Jose, Calif., teacher, 1975-76; University of California, Berkeley, visiting lecturer in Asian-American studies, 1987-89, writer-in-residence, 1990. *Member:* Science Fiction Writers of America, Society of Children's Book Writer's.

■ Awards, Honors

Book-of-the-Month Club Writing Fellowship, 1970; one of *New York Times* Outstanding Books of the Year, 1975, Newbery Medal Honor Book from the American Library Association, Children's Book Award from the International Reading Association, Jane Addams Children's Book Award Honor Book from the Jane Addams Peace Association, and Carter G. Woodson Book Award from the National Council for Social Studies, all 1976, *Boston Globe-Horn Book* Award Honor Book, 1977, Lewis Carroll Shelf Award, 1979, selected one of New York Public Library's Books for the Teen Age, 1980, 1981, and 1982, and Friends of Children and Literature Award, 1984, all for *Dragonwings; Boston Globe-Horn Book* Award for Fiction, one of *School Library Journal*'s Best Books for Spring, and one of *New York Times* Outstanding Books of the Year, all 1977, and Jane Addams Children's Book Award, 1978, all for *Child of the Owl; Dragon Steel* was selected one of Child Study Association of America's Children's Books of the Year, 1986.

■ Writings

Sweetwater (illustrated by Julia Noonan), Harper, 1973.
Dragonwings (ALA Notable Book), Harper, 1975.
Child of the Owl (*Horn Book* honor list), Harper, 1977.
Seademons: A Novel, Harper, 1977.
Sea Glass, Harper, 1979.
Kind Hearts and Gentle Monsters, Harper, 1982.
The Mark Twain Murders, Four Winds, 1982.
Dragon of the Lost Sea (ALA Notable Book), Harper, 1982.
Liar, Liar, Morrow, 1983.
The Serpent's Children, Harper, 1984.
The Tom Sawyer Fires, Morrow, 1984.

Dragon Steel, Harper, 1985.
Shadow Lord, Pocket Book, 1985.
Mountain Light (sequel to *The Serpent's Children*), Harper, 1985.
Monster Makers, Inc., Arbor House, 1986.
The Curse of the Squirrel (illustrated by Dirk Zimmer), Random House, 1987.
"Age of Wonders" (play), performed by Asian American Theater Company, October, 1987.
(Reteller) *The Rainbow People* (ALA Notable Book; illustrated by David Wiesner), Harper, 1989.
Dragon Cauldron, Harper, 1990.

Contributor:

Donald A. Wollheim and Terry Carr, editors, *World's Best Science Fiction of 1969*, Ace Books, 1969.
Samuel Delaney and Marilyn Hacker, editors, *Quark #2*, Paperback Library, 1971.
David Gerrold, editor, *Protostars*, Ballantine, 1971.
The Demon Children, Avon, 1973.

Hardcover edition of Yep's third novel.

Thomas N. Scortia, editor, *Strange Bedfellows: Sex and Science Fiction*, Random House, 1973.
Harlan Ellison, editor, *Last Dangerous Visions*, Harper, 1975.
Misha Berson, editor, *Between Worlds*, Theater Communication Group, 1990.

Contributor of stories to periodicals, including *Worlds of If* and *Galaxy*.

■ Adaptations

"Dragonwings" (record; cassette; filmstrip with cassette), Miller-Brody, 1979.
"The Curse of the Squirrel" (cassette), Random House, 1989.

Sweetwater is available in Braille and as a "Talking Book."

■ Work in Progress

Butterfly Boy for Farrar, Straus; *Dragon War* for Harper; *Star Fisher* for Morrow; *The Lost Garden* for Silver Burdett; *The Ghostly Rhyme*, a folktale retold, for Harper; *American Dragons* for Harper; editing an Asian-American anthology for young adults.

■ Sidelights

Born June 14, 1948 in San Francisco, California. "In our family's own personal story West Virginia is as much a mythical homeland as China, for my mother was born in Ohio and then raised in West Virginia, where my paternal grandfather started a Chinese laundry in Clarksburg. Subsequently, my mother's family moved to the nearby town of Bridgeport, where they spent most of their childhood....My mother, my uncle, and my aunts had left West Virginia for California when they were all children.

"Both my parents faced problems of acculturation. But my father, who lived in a white neighborhood of San Francisco, was always within walking—and sometimes of necessity—running distance of Chinatown. However, my mother and her family were the only Chinese in the area until another Chinese laundry opened up in competition.

"Of course, my mother's family would not have been the first group of immigrants to face the burden of having two cultures. But most would have solved the problem by clinging only to their old ways and language and pretending that they were on a little island that was supposed to be a part of China. Or, as so many other American families have done, they could have thrown off their ancestral heritage and severed their roots to the past–a simple enough thing for my mother and her brother and sisters since the white children of the town quickly came to accept the laundryman's children on an equal basis.

"However, my mother's family solution was to juggle elements of both cultures. Though they stayed Chinese in some central core, they also developed a curiosity and open-mindedness about the larger white culture around them."[1]

"[I,] having been raised in a Black ghetto and having commuted to a bilingual school in Chinatown,. . .did not confront White American culture until high school. Approaching as something of a stranger, I have been fascinated by all its aspects— from its great novels to its children's literature, comic art, and science fiction, specifically pursuing the figure of the 'stranger' both in my studies and my writing."[2]

After graduating from the University of California, Santa Cruz, Yep received his Ph.D. from the State University of New York at Buffalo. "I have been writing science fiction since I was eighteen (that's when I sold my first story)—getting rejection slips a lot of times. Then a friend of mine who had gone to work at Harper's asked me to think about writing a science fiction book for children, and *Sweetwater* was the result."[3]

In *Sweetwater,* Tyree and his family attempt to make a living in a half submerged city on planet Harmony by scavenging. People who are half of the land and half of the sea are known as Silkies, based, according to Yep, on an old Scottish ballad about Merman. "The thing about science fiction is not so much finding a new machine or a new invention, it's actually seeing human beings in a different situation, in a strange situation. . . .Sometimes I think. . .American science fiction gets lost in gadgetry, and it can be fun, but, the best science fiction writers. . .have solid characters, as well as good, solid scientific background. . . .The thing about science fiction is being able to meet and confront aliens. They used to call them BEMs, or Bug Eyed Monsters—all the monster would do was try to devour you. But I wanted some friendly aliens, aliens that could help you, and not necessarily be completely superior in wisdom, but living their own kind of life."[3]

"It only occurred to me after [*Sweetwater*] was published that the aliens of the novel, the Argans, are similar in some ways to the Chinese in America.

Dust jacket of Yep's multi-award-winning book.

Out of *Sweetwater* grew *Dragonwings*, in which I finally confronted my own Chinese-American identity."[2]

"Once some anthropologists found a primitive tribe whose artists carved statues of powerful simplicity. When the scientists questioned the artists about their art, the artists would not say that they had sculpted the statues; rather they claimed that the statue already lived within each block of wood and told the artist how to free it.

"Something similar happened to me when I tried to write my novel *Dragonwings*. The story of the early Chinese-American aviator seemed to tell itself to me, but it was possible largely because I kept children in mind as the main reading audience.

"But before I can begin to talk about the story of *Dragonwings*, I have to explain my general situation six years before when I first began my general research. Trying to research Chinese-American history—that is, the history of men and women of Chinese ancestry who had been influenced by their experience of America—can be difficult.

The 1982 ALA Notable Book.

"Let us suppose a far distant future in which America has become poor and outdated and its men and women forced to migrate to other countries to find work. Further, let's suppose that many of these emigrants leave Mississippi to work in Iran. A very few of them settle there and raise children, and their children raise children. And then one of their descendants decides to write about his ancestors. It is from this scanty material that he must construct a picture of life in Mississippi three generations ago.

"I tried to understand the background that shaped me. It took some six years of research in the libraries of different cities to find the bits and pieces that could be fitted into Chinese-American history.

"Most of the Chinese who emigrated to America were from Southern China. . . .Because of immense troubles at home, these Southern Chinese came to America since they could send large amounts of money to their families and clans back home. And for a variety of reasons, including prejudice and

fear, it was mostly men who came over. . . .From the 1850s to the 1930s, it was largely a society of bachelors, for when the original men grew old, they sent for their sons, brothers, cousins, and nephews to take their place.

"But a small number of men were able to meet certain special conditions under American law and brought their wives over to join them and start families in America. They created a family society within the shell of the older, larger bachelor society. And this family society, with its determination to sink its roots in America, survived psychologically by selectively forgetting the past history of the bachelor society and the often violent record of confrontations between Chinese and Americans. Ignoring acts of discrimination that happened in their own time, the Chinese-Americans still maintained a discreet distance between themselves and white Americans, choosing to imitate their white counterparts within the confines of Chinatown rather than trying to join the white Americans outside.

"The third generation, my generation, grew up in households in which little or no Chinese was spoken and Chinese myths and legends were looked upon largely as a source of embarrassment. . . .I found that I was truly like Ralph Ellison's Invisible Man—without form, without shape. It was as if all the features on my face had been erased and I was simply a blank mirror reflecting other people's hopes and fears.

"When I did find material on [my ancestors,] I found that the Chinese-Americans had been a faceless crowd for most writers, providing statistical fodder for historians or abstractions for sociologists. I could give the Chinese population in each of California's counties for a fifty year period; but I could not have told you what any of those Chinese hoped for or feared.

"One of the few early Chinese-Americans in my notes to have a name was Fung Joe Guey who flew a biplane of his own construction over in Oakland in 1909. The scene of his flight seemed so vivid to me that it was easy to put it on paper, but trying to explain how he got to that field with his biplane was difficult because I could only find two newspaper articles, the September 23, 1909 issues of the San Francisco *Call* and the San Francisco *Examiner.*

"Since I wanted to respect his historical integrity, I used his flight as the basis for my novel, *Dragonwings;* and to make my own fictional aviator,

Windrider, seem real, I had to recreate the bachelor society itself.

"But I have no...guidelines for creating the Chinatown of seventy years ago, which is the time in which *Dragonwings* is set.

"So in trying to recreate the world of the past, I was like a child myself who must have the most basic things explained to it.

"I had grown up as a child in the 1950s so that my sense of reality was an American one. Now I had to grow up again, but this time in the 1900s, developing a Chinese sense of reality. Milk and cheese had to become exotic to me. An American chessboard would have to seem odd because it would have the river line missing from its middle. The turning point in writing *Dragonwings* came when the checkered tablecloth on a table suddenly seemed strange to me, as if it were too cold and abstract a design because I was used to designs that usually filled up space. So when I chose to describe things from the viewpoint of an eight-year-old Chinese boy, it was more than simply choosing a narrative device; it was close to the process of discovery I myself was experiencing in writing the story.

"But at the same time...I would also have to discover what relationships would be like within that bachelor society–that lonely group of men who spent most of their adult years apart from family and home. So again, it was natural to write about this experience with children as the audience. What were personal relationships like among men who would work for five to ten years or longer before they could visit their families back in China?...I would have to project myself back into the past and see how I myself would react to others in that same situation.

"And the relationship with which I would most easily empathize would be the most elemental relationship, the relationship between parent and child. And since most Chinese-Americans were men at this time, it would be easiest to describe the relationship between father and son—with the mother present only in the emotions and memories of the man and boy. It was within the strong emotional context of this evolving father-son relationship that the boy's relationships to others would unfold.

"Then, too, it would be easier for me to describe the relationship between the boy and his father if I could use the most honest and direct terms.

"To be able to write about the relationship...requires a thorough grounding in the basic ways a culture expresses love and affection; but I was unsure of even that much for the early Chinese-Americans.

"If I kept children in mind as the reading audience, I would keep myself from wandering off into conceptual tangents such as the existential alienation of Chinese-Americans. The important thing, after all, was to give emotional form to the people of that world and not to play intellectual games....When I speak of selecting children as the audience for *Dragonwings*, much of that was intuitive, occurring at a preconscious rather than a conscious level. But I had another reason in writing *Dragonwings* for children. Because children are inexperienced and new to the world in general, their vocabulary and their ability to handle complex grammatical structures are both as limited as their ability to handle abstract concepts, yet this same inexperience is also a source of special strength for children's stories. To write for children, one must try to see things as they do; and trying to look at the world with the fresh, inexperi-

Jacket from the 1985 novel.

enced eyes of a child enables the writer to approach the world with a sense of wonder. (I think I can say this without necessarily sentimentalizing childhood if I add that the sense of wonder produces as many terrors for a child as it does beauties.) Adopting the child's sense of wonder is the reason why—at least for me—the texts of so many picture books approach the lyricism that eludes so many modern poets today with their jaded, world-weary tastes.

"I wanted to utilize this sense of wonder when I wrote *Dragonwings* since I wanted to base a large part of the father's motives upon Chinese dragon myths. I could have given the father more ordinary motives. I could have said he was compensating for feelings of inadequacy by proving he could do anything that white Americans could do. Or I could have left the novel simply as a story...of a far-sighted person among shortsighted people. But the invention with which I was dealing...was a flying machine, a machine that most people were convinced was impossible to build even several years after the Wright Brothers' original flight. When I wrote of the aeroplane, called *Dragonwings*, I was actually dealing with the reach of our imagination.

"In *Dragonwings*, Windrider's former life as a dragon symbolizes [the] same imaginative power in all of us. And so Windrider and his son, Moon Shadow, are engaged not only in the process of discovering America and each other, but also in a pilgrimage, or even a quest for a special moment when they can reaffirm the power of the imagination; that power in each of us to grasp with the mind and heart what we cannot immediately grasp with the hand."[4]

Yep set *Child of the Owl* in a more contemporary Chinatown, where a young Chinese-American girl, discovers her heritage through Chinese folklore and history. "You should always write about what you know: the things you have seen and the things you have thought and, above all, the things you have felt, so that I set my novel in the smaller, quieter Chinatown in which I grew up, before the immigration laws were made fairer in October 1965 so more Asians could enter. The Chinatown of the present day is much larger both in terms of geography and of population. Then, too, since 1965, the upgrading of housing standards (and unfortunately of rents) as well as the advent of Medicare and other social-welfare programs has changed life in Chinatown in many respects—though much remains to be done.

"However, Chinatown is not so much a place as a state of mind—or to be more accurate, a state of heart—and it is this state of mind and of heart that I have tried to explain as much to myself as to others. But the heart is a difficult place to enter, let alone describe, unless one wears some sort of disguise. For this reason, although I have never seen an owl charm or heard a story about owls, I've presented the owl story in Chapter Two, which is based upon stories of filial devotion once popular among the Chinese and upon Chinese folklore concerning owls and other animals.

"I think in the end an owl mask is one many of us could wear."[5]

The early 1980s proved to be prolific for Yep, publishing three mysteries, along with *Kind Hearts and Gentle Monsters*, the story of a high school boy who develops a unique romance with a difficult girl, and *Dragon of the Lost Sea*, a return to fantasy utilizing Chinese myths. *Dragon Steel* is its sequel. "Fantasy and reality both play vital parts in our lives, for we may grasp with the mind and heart what we may not always grasp with the hand. It would be a tragic mistake to insist upon a realistic viewpoint to the exclusion of fantasy. Like the poet, we too have rainbow wings of which we must be aware."[6]

The historical novel *The Serpent's Children* uses the nineteenth-century Chinese Taiping Rebellion as a backdrop. "When I first began to research this story, my original intention was to discover my identity as a Chinese. However, like someone examining a family portrait, the closer I got, the more the faces seemed to dissolve into a collection of discrete dots. As a people, the Chinese were not the homogeneous whole that I had expected. The more I read, the more they seemed to divide into groups and subgroups. Moreover, the people from Kwangtung province, where this story takes place, did not fit at all into passive, self-effacing stereotypes.

"I found the story of dreams and shadows during my high school days, and it has stayed with me to this time. It is actually a Greek tale, but I have heard a Chinese version. At any rate, the spirit of the tale has an Asian flavor and so I've used it. I have lost the notation on the original source, but I remember quite well reading the story in a book of the Loeb classical series."[7]

Yep continued the tale of his characters in *Mountain Light*, where they immigrate to America. "There are two sources of history for anyone who writes historical fiction for children. The first source is the adult version of history with facts and dates and statistics; the second source is a child's version of history.

"Had I only read the first type, I probably would never have written *Dragonwings, Serpent's Children,* or *Mountain Light.* But I grew up with stories about China. However, it was not the China of the travelogues; it was not the China of vast, ancient monuments. It was the China my father knew before he came to America at the age of eight. So it was China as perceived by a child and colored by memory over the years.

"My father has never seen the Great Wall or the Forbidden City. His China was small villages; each village had its own distinctive architecture, depending on which country its men had found employment in. After working in that country, the men would return to their villages in China, and there they would build a home that imitated the houses of the prosperous in the country they had left—though in some places, these transplanted houses might also have gun ports to defend against bandits.

"But the difference between my father's China and the China of the travelogues is the difference between a child's version of history and an adult's. Adult history thunders on a grand scale like a movie in cinemascope; but for all of its size, it is still flat, and its actors are like ants except for a few close-ups of the stars. But a child's history is like a hologram that can be held in the palm, quiet and small but three-dimensional. It treats its subjects with an immediateness that makes them seem to live and breathe.

"Adult history is full of dry discussions of abstractions, such as runaway inflation. But that was just a concept to me until I heard about how my paternal grandmother in China would have to pack a small suitcase full of paper currency just to buy a box of matches. When one hears such anecdotes, the theoretical becomes all too real.

"The drawback in using a child's history is that it is based on a child's egocentric perceptions, which are limited by the very nature of the observer. However, what these perceptions may lose in scope, they gain in concreteness and intimacy with which other people can identify. If this is true of a child's history, it is even truer of historical fiction written for children. While the facts of adult history are necessary for background material, they have as much to do with the creation of a novel as a backdrop has to do with the creation of a play.

The 1984 Harper hardcover edition.

"*Dragonwings* could not discuss the rise of the labor movement in California, but it could show a child's view when a group of angry white workers, who blamed the Chinese labor for their troubles, riot in Chinatown. Nor was there room to discuss psychological traits of the obsessive-compulsive; but I could write about a man intent upon building an airplane.

"Far too often, adult history reads like an autopsy report. Writers spew out statistics like a coroner examining a corpse. Or they array the facts and dates like bones upon a table and consider their job done. But a person is not just a skeleton, and history is not just statistics. So writers of historical fiction must be like necromancers summoning up the spirits of the past. Their stories must be inspired in the original sense of the word, for these writers must breathe their own spirits into their tales before their books can come to life. For these acts of magic they have children's history.

"A child's history, like magic, never quite goes away. It is there, only hidden, like the laughter of unseen children in a garden. Magic and children's history can be cemented over but never buried. Adults can put up steel and lay asphalt, but their buildings and streets can never outlast magic and memory. Memory pays no rent and is assessed no taxes, yet its value is infinite."[1]

In 1987 Yep turned to a new genre. "I've always been a fan of classic horror movies—though I would be scared for days after seeing one. In *The Curse of the Squirrel* I finally achieved an old ambition to write a horror story of my own. But instead of being frightened, I got to laugh a lot."[8]

There are advantanges for Yep in his chosen career as writer. "In a sense I have no one culture to call my own since I exist peripherally in several. However, in my writing I can create my own."[9]

Footnote Sources:

[1] Laurence Yep, "The Green Cord," *Horn Book*, May/June, 1989.

[2] Publicity, Harper.

[3] "The World of Children's Literature" (cassette; hosted by Barbara Rollock), WNYC Radio, November 1, 1976.

[4] L. Yep, "Writing Dragonwings," *Reading Teacher*, January, 1977.

[5] L. Yep, "Afterword," *Child of the Owl*, Harper, 1977.

[6] L. Yep, "Fantasy and Reality," *Horn Book*, April, 1978.

[7] L. Yep, *The Serpent's Children*, Harper, 1984.

[8] L. Yep, *The Curse of the Squirrel*, Random House, 1987.

[9] Anne Commire, editor, *Something about the Author*, Volume 7, Gale, 1975.

■ For More Information See

Francelia Butler, editor, *Children's Literature: Annual of the Modern Language Association Seminar on Children's Literature and the Children's Literature Association*, Temple University Press, 1975.

New York Times Book Review, November 16, 1975 (p. 30), May 22, 1977 (p. 29), January 20, 1980 (p. 30), May 23, 1982 (p. 37), November 6, 1983 (p. 44).

Top of the News, April, 1976 (p. 220ff), fall, 1982 (p. 92ff).

Vector 78, November-December, 1976 (p. 30).

Washington Post Book World, May 1, 1977 (p. E1ff), January 9, 1983 (p. 11ff), November 6, 1983 (p. 17ff).

Jim Roginski, compiler, *Newbery and Caldecott Medalists and Honor Book Winners*, Libraries Unlimited, 1982.

Gerard J. Senick, editor, *Children's Literature Review*, Gale, Volume 3, 1984, Volume 17, 1989.

Daniel C. Marowski, editor, *Contemporary Literary Criticism*, Volume 35, Gale, 1985.

Alleen Pace Nilsen and Kenneth L. Donelson, *Literature for Today's Young Adults*, Scott, Foresman, 1985.

Glenn E. Estes, editor, *Dictionary of Literary Biography*, Volume 52, Gale, 1986.

"Meet the Newbery Author: Laurence Yep" (filmstrip with cassette), Random House, 1986.

Collections:

Galaxy Publishing Company Collection.
Arents Research Library, Syracuse University, New York.

Cumulative Index

Author/Artist Index

The following index gives the number of the volume
in which an author/artist's biographical sketch appears.